MODERN
CULTURE
AND
THE
ARTS

MODERN CULTURE AND THE ARTS

James B. Hall
University of California, Irvine

Barry Ulanov
Barnard College

McGraw-Hill Book Company
New York   St. Louis   San Francisco   Toronto

MODERN CULTURE AND THE ARTS

Library of Congress Catalog Number: 67–19148

The cover is a detail of a photograph taken by Martha Swope during a performance of the New York production of The Blacks *by Jean Genet, which was directed by Gene Frankel.*

W. H. Auden, extract of pp. 5–13, *Making, Knowing and Judging* (Inaugural Lecture 1956), Clarendon Press, 1956. Reprinted by permission of the Clarendon Press, Oxford.

Jacques Barzun, "Myths for Materialists." Originally published in *Chimera,* Vol. IV, No. 3 (Spring 1946).

Bertolt Brecht, "Theatre for Pleasure or Theatre for Learning?", trans. by Edith Anderson, *Mainstream,* XI (June, 1958), pp. 1–9.

John Cage, "Experimental Music," copyright © 1958 by John Cage. "Experimental Music: Doctrine," copyright © 1955 by John Cage. Both reprinted from *Silence* by John Cage by permission of Wesleyan University Press.

Joyce Cary, "The Artist and the World" from *Art and Reality* by Joyce Cary. Copyright © 1958 by Arthur Lucius Michael Cary and David Alexander Ogilvie, Executors, Estate of Joyce Cary. Reprinted by permission of Harper & Row, Publishers, and Curtis Brown Ltd.

Henry Steele Commager, "Television: The Medium in Search of Its Character," *TV Guide,* June 25, 1966.

Aaron Copland, "How We Listen," Chapter 2 from *What to Listen for in Music* by Aaron Copland, rev. ed., 1957. Copyright © 1939 and 1957 by McGraw-Hill Book Co. Used by permission of McGraw-Hill Book Company.

Merce Cunningham, "Space, Time and the Dance," *Transformation,* 1:3, Wittenborn & Co., 1952, pp. 150–151. Also by permission of the author.

Martin Esslin, "The Theatre of the Absurd" from *Theatre in the Twentieth Century,* ed. by Robert Corrigan, Grove Press, 1963.

Leslie A. Fiedler, "The Comics: The Middle Against Both Ends" (originally published under the title "Comic Books: Middle Against Both Ends") from *No! In Thunder* by Leslie Fiedler, Beacon Press. Revised and reprinted with permission of the author.

E. M. Forster, "Art for Art's Sake" from *Two Cheers for Democracy,* copyright 1949 by E. M. Forster. Reprinted by permission of Harcourt, Brace & World, Inc., and Edward Arnold (Publishers) Ltd.

Jean Giraudoux, "Eternal Law of the Dramatist" from *Visitations,* published by Bernard Grasset, Paris, 1952, pp. 115–122. Trans. by Haskell M. Block and reprinted in *The Creative Vision,* copyright Grove Press, Inc., 1960.

E. H. Gombrich, "Meditations on a Hobby Horse or the Roots of Artistic Form," pp. 1–11 from *Meditations on a Hobby Horse and Other Essays on the Theory of Art* by E. H. Gombrich, published by Phaidon Press London and distributed in the U.S.A. by New York Graphic Society, Greenwich, Conn.

Clement Greenberg, "Avant-Garde and Kitsch" from *Art and Culture* by Clement Greenberg. Reprinted by permission of the Beacon Press, copyright © 1961 by Clement Greenberg.

Tyrone Guthrie, "An Audience of One" from *Directors on Directing,* copyright © 1953, 1963 by Toby Cole and Helen Krich Chinoy, reprinted by permission of the publishers, The Bobbs-Merrill Company, Inc.

Stuart Hall and Paddy Whannel, "The Young Audience," © copyright 1964 by Stuart Hall and Paddy Whannel. Revised and reprinted from *The Popular Arts* by Stuart Hall and Paddy Whannel, by permission of Random House, Inc.

Arnold Hauser, "Can Movies Be 'Profound'?", trans. by Ralph Manheim, *The New Partisan Reader, 1945–1953,* ed. by William Phillips and Philip Rahv, Harcourt, Brace & World, Inc., 1953, pp. 276–280. © 1960 by *Partisan Review.*

Andrew Hook, "Commitment and Reality" from *The Novel Today,* Programme and Notes of the International Writers Conference, Edinburgh International Festival, 1962.

Jane Jacobs, "Landmarks, from *Death and Life of Great American Cities* by Jane Jacobs, pp. 384–388. © copyright 1961 by Jane Jacobs. Reprinted by permission of Random House, Inc.

Randall Jarrell, "A Sad Heart at the Supermarket," *Daedalus* (Spring 1960). Copyright 1959 by the American Academy of Arts and Sciences.

Wassily Kandinsky, extract of pp. 23–26, *Concerning the Spiritual in Art,* Documents of Modern Art, A Series, George Wittenborn, Inc. Copyright 1947 by Nina Kandinsky.

Abraham Kaplan, "The Aesthetics of the Popular Arts," *Journal of Aesthetics* (Spring 1966). Based on a paper read for the American Philosophical Association, Milwaukee, May, 1964. Edited and shortened with permission.

Felix Klee, extract of pp. 151–155, *Paul Klee,* George Braziller, Inc. 1962. Reprinted with permission of the publisher.

John A. Kouwenhoven, "What Is 'American' in Architecture and Design?" from *The Beer Can by the High-way* by John A. Kouwenhoven. Copyright © 1961 by John A. Kouwenhoven. Reprinted by permission of Doubleday & Company, Inc.

Constant Lambert, "The Appalling Popularity of Music" from *Music Ho!* by Constant Lambert, Faber & Faber Ltd., publisher.

John Lardner, "Thoughts on Radio-Televese," *The New Yorker,* June 6, 1959. Reprinted by permission; © 1959 The New Yorker Magazine, Inc.

Richard Lippold, "Illusion as Structure" from *Structure in Art and Science,* ed. by Gyorgy Kepes, George Braziller, Inc., 1965. © 1965 George Braziller, Inc. Reprinted with permission of the publisher.

Marshall McLuhan, "The Medium Is the Message," Chapter 1 from *Understanding Media: The Extensions of Man* by Marshall McLuhan. Copyright © 1964 by Marshall McLuhan. Used by permission of McGraw-Hill Book Company.

André Malraux, "Art, Popular Art and the Illusion of the Folk," trans. by William Barrett, *The New Partisan Reader, 1945–1953,* ed. by William Phillips and Philip Rahv, Harcourt, Brace & World, Inc., 1953, pp. 438–446.

Piet Mondrian, extract of pp. 50–53, *Plastic Art and Pure Plastic Art and Other Essays,* Wittenborn & Co., 1945. Copyright 1945 by Harry Holtzman.

Henry Moore, "Notes on Sculpture" from *Sculpture and Drawing,* Vol. I, 4th ed., ed. by David Sylvester, Percy Lund, Humphries & Co., Ltd., Publisher.

Edgar Morin, "The Case of James Dean" from *The Stars* by Edgar Morin, Grove Press, 1960. Reprinted by permission of Georges Borchardt, agent for Editions du Seuil, Paris.

George Nelson, "The Designer in the Modern World" and "The Dead-End Room" reproduced from *Problems of Design* by George Nelson. Copyright 1957. Published by the Whitney Library of Design, New York.

Sean O'Casey, "The Arts Among the Multitude" from *The Green Crow* by Sean O'Casey, George Braziller, Inc., 1956, pp. 163–169. Reprinted by permission of George Braziller, Inc.

José Ortega y Gasset, extracts from "First Installment on the Dehumanization of Art," pp. 19–23; "Art a Thing of No Consequence," pp. 49–52; and "Decline of the Novel," pp. 53–56, *Dehumanization of Art and Notes on the Novel* by José Ortega y Gasset, Princeton University Press, 1948. Reprinted by permission of Princeton University Press.

George Orwell, "Raffles and Miss Blandish" from *Dickens, Dali and Others,* copyright 1946 by George Orwell. Reprinted by permission of Harcourt, Brace & World, Inc., Miss Sonia Brownell and Martin Secker & Warburg Ltd.

I. M. Pei, "The Nature of Urban Spaces," reprinted from
The People's Architects, ed. by Harry S. Ransom, pub-
lished by The University of Chicago Press for Rice
University, 1964, by permission of The University of
Chicago Press.

I. A. Richards, "Poetry and Beliefs" from *Principles of
Literary Criticism* by I. A. Richards, Harcourt, Brace
& World, Inc., 1947. Reprinted by permission of Har-
court, Brace & World, Inc., and Routledge & Kegan
Paul, Ltd.

Alain Robbe-Grillet, "A Future for the Novel" from *For
a New Novel* by Alain Robbe-Grillet, trans. by Richard Howard, pp. 15–24. Reprinted by permission of
Grove Press, Inc. Copyright © 1963 by Les Editions
de Minuit and 1965 by Grove Press, Inc.

Roger Sessions, "The Listener" from *The Musical Experience of Composer, Performer, Listener* by Roger
Sessions, Princeton University, 1950, pp. 87–106. Copyright 1950 by the Princeton University Press. Abridged
and reprinted by permission of Princeton University
Press and the author.

Wallace Stevens, "The Relations Between Poetry and
Painting," copyright 1951 by Wallace Stevens. Reprinted from *The Necessary Angel* by Wallace Stevens
by permission of Alfred A. Knopf, Inc.

Igor Stravinsky, "The Performance of Music." Reprinted
by permission of the publishers from Igor Stravinsky,
Poetics of Music. Cambridge, Mass.: Harvard University Press, copyright 1947 by the President and Fellows
of Harvard College.

John Szarkowski, Introduction from *The Photographer's
Eye* by John Szarkowski, copyright 1966 by The Museum of Modern Art, New York, and reprinted with
its permission.

Dylan Thomas, "Notes on the Art of Poetry," *The Texas
Quarterly,* 1961. Reprinted by permission of Harold
Ober Associates Incorporated. Copyright © 1961 by
Trustees of the Copyrights of Dylan Thomas.

Sybil Thorndike, "I Look at the Audience" from *Theatre
Arts Anthology: A Record and a Prophecy,* ed. by
Gilder et al., pp. 300–303. Copyright 1946 by Theatre
Arts, Inc. Copyright 1950 by Theatre Arts Books. Re-
printed by permission of Theatre Arts Books, New
York, N.Y.

Barry Ulanov, "What Is Jazz?", Chapter 1 from *A History of Jazz in America* by Barry Ulanov. Copyright
1952 by Barry Ulanov. Reprinted by permission of
The Viking Press, Inc.

Paul Valéry, "Pure Poetry: Notes for a Lecture," trans.
by Haskell M. Block and originally published in *The
Creative Vision,* copyright The Grove Press, Inc., 1960.
The authorized English translations of the works of
Paul Valéry vest exclusively in Bollingen Foundation,
New York. Their permission to publish Mr. Block's
translations is gratefully acknowledged.

Mark Van Doren, "What Is a Poet?" from *The Private Reader*, Henry Holt & Company, 1942. Copyright © 1942 by Mark Van Doren. Reprinted by permission of Nannine Joseph, agent for Mark Van Doren.

Robert Warshow, "The Gangster as Tragic Hero" from *The Immediate Experience* by Robert Warshow, Doubleday & Company, Inc., 1962. Copyright by Joseph Goldberg, Trustee of the Estate of Robert Warshow.

Mary Wigman, "Composition in Pure Movement," *Modern Music* (Jan.–Feb. 1931). Copyright by The League of Composers, Inc., and reprinted by permission of the International Society of Composers and Musicians-The League of Composers, Inc.

PREFACE

Coming to terms with modern culture can be an uneasy confrontation, both for the novice and for the initiate. Through a series of noble encounters between the artist and the work of art on the one hand, and the viewer, reader, or listener on the other, enlightenment comes slowly. In matters of art and understanding, yesterday's excitement may become tomorrow's tedium. Traditionally, even the brightest student proceeds by indirection, by picking up what he can when he can, by crises of misunderstanding, or by some kind of contemplative exercise—say, the long stare, which has, if nothing else, the august sanction of the ancient Chinese sage Lao-tze. In the end, however, the student becomes a different—and hopefully a better—person for his encounter with the arts, whatever its nature.

And yet, each day, study in the areas of the arts and humanities becomes more difficult. Materials pile up. Where classical certainty once existed, doubt now prevails, both as to what constitutes the proper material for art and what ways of handling those materials are acceptable. In an increasingly complex world, no matter how handsome to the eye and satisfying to the other senses, there are also increasing occasions for despair. Can one ever understand what the world is about, what art is about, and what man's place is in relation to both?

In the face of these admitted difficulties, this book does not presume to answer such spacious questions. It intends only to make the reader's confrontation with his heritage and his immediate environment more stimulating and enlightening. No book can provide a substitute for the experience of art, but these essays may suggest useful directions and help to minimize misunderstandings and to deepen the student's perception while educating his taste. This, obviously, is no modest undertaking.

Beyond these generalities, the text also attempts to raise issues central to the arts in our time. The major questions seem to us to be asked—and a great many minor ones as well. We suggest no doctrinaire answers and neither do our authors, save by implication. It is, as it always has been, more valuable to examine many ways of thinking and feeling and performing in the arts and the humanities than it is to suggest any single way as the only correct one.

By careful design, then, this volume brings together an uncommonly wide variety of comment on the arts and related issues. The essays represent American and British thought in about equal proportions, along with distinguished contributions from the Continent. The book begins with speculation concerning art and its audiences, the ways that artists approach their viewers and listeners and readers—and the various modes of response. What follows are specific considerations of music, painting and sculpture, the novel and poetry, the theater and the dance, films, television, and photography, and the arts of design—that is, architecture and city planning, industrial design, advertising, and the comic strip. Another kind of essay in this volume comes by bits and pieces—an informal essay by example on the great modern art of photography. These photographs attempt to illuminate some general aspect of the essays they accompany, but, more significantly, they illustrate the photographer's craft, his wit, and upon occasion, his wisdom.

The arrangement of material within each section follows a general plan. Where appropriate, the initial essay represents a somewhat traditional point of view, sometimes from the late nineteenth century, couched in an appropriate literary style. Subsequent pieces are arranged in a rough order of ascending complexity or of fuller development of details. In each section, the essays support an extensive amount of comparison and contrast—whether for formal discussion, assignment, or simple enjoyment. Each essay represents a particular point of view, and each one is interesting for itself, with its own provocative qualities of theory or practice and its own style. Understandably, these styles vary widely from the belletristic to the closely argued statement to the occasional near-banality of journalism. Doubtless, some of the essays are controversial, but so is the present state of the arts which this book seeks not only to explore but to comprehend.

Above all, this book presents the single most important proposition in the arts today, especially in America: the split between the high, or private, arts and the popular arts—the divorce of high-quality art designed for the delectation of the few from the art designed for mass production and mass consumption. A recognition of this duality, in intention and in fact, is of vital importance to all students, to all teachers, to all people, and this collection addresses itself squarely to this timely issue. It may be that our nation's legacy to future generations will be, for better or worse, its contribution to the popular arts. If so, then attention paid to jazz, the movies, television, advertising, pop–rock, and comic books is not energy wasted. Indeed, a central theme of this text is suggested by the title of one of the essays, "Can Movies Be 'Profound'?"

The resourceful reader will find neither the contents nor the structure of the book easily exhausted. Wide variety allows the teacher to focus on the sections which best reflect his own interests and strengths. Common to all uses should be assignments from the first and the final sections; what is assigned from the middle sections depends upon the tenor, the subject matter, and the inclinations of a particular class. In any event, this text is calculated to make the use of resource materials both possible and valuable. The essays can be supported by almost any number of records, slides, films, comic books, advertising art, reproductions of painting and sculpture, or documents on the dance and the theatre. The chief limitation in this matter of supplemental aids is that of local resources. And there is always the television set.

In order not to preempt the teacher's place in the classroom, we have omitted pedagogical apparatus except for headnotes of an introductory nature. To make possible the inclusion of more essays, some pieces have been specially edited; in these essays, cuts are indicated by ellipses. All of the essays, of whatever length, whether written in a classical manner or a style and language close to the present-day vernacular, are intended to quicken the reader's interest in the arts and to illuminate the vital issues that they both pose and reflect.

James B. Hall
University of California, Irvine

Barry Ulanov
Barnard College

TABLE OF CONTENTS

Preface   ix

SECTION 1   ART AND AUDIENCE

Oscar Wilde   The Decay of Lying   3
Sean O'Casey   The Arts Among the Multitude   15
E. M. Forster   Art for Art's Sake   22
André Malraux   Art, Popular Art, and the
Illusion of the Folk   29
José Ortega y Gasset   The Dehumanization of Art   39
Randall Jarrell   A Sad Heart at the Supermarket   47
Abraham Kaplan   The Aesthetics of the
Popular Arts   62

SECTION 2   THE WAY OF MUSIC

Constant Lambert   The Appalling Popularity
of Music   83
John Cage   Experimental Music: Doctrine   88
Aaron Copland   How We Listen   94
Igor Stravinsky   The Performance of Music   103
Barry Ulanov   What Is Jazz?   114
Roger Sessions   The Listener   122
Stuart Hall and   The Young Audience   131
Paddy Whannel

SECTION 3   THE EYE OF A MAN:
PAINTING AND
SCULPTURE

E. H. Gombrich   Meditations on a Hobby Horse
or the Roots of Artistic Form   151
Wassily Kandinsky   Concerning the Spiritual in Art   168
Clement Greenberg   Avant-Garde and Kitsch   175
Henry Moore   Notes on Sculpture   192
Piet Mondrian   Plastic Art and Pure Plastic Art   201
Paul Klee   The Shaping Forces of the Artist   208
Richard Lippold   Illusion as Structure   214

SECTION 4   THE WORD ARTS:
             THE NOVEL

Henry James   The Future of the Novel   231
Joyce Cary   The Artist and the World   243
José Ortega y Gasset Decline of the Novel   248
George Orwell   Raffles and Miss Blandish   251
Andrew Hook   Commitment and Reality   266
Alain Robbe-Grillet A Future for the Novel   272

SECTION 5   THE WORD ARTS:
             POETRY

Mark Van Doren   What Is a Poet?   281
Paul Valéry   Pure Poetry: Notes for a
                     Lecture   288
I. A. Richards   Poetry and Beliefs   296
W. H. Auden   Making, Knowing, and Judging   308
Dylan Thomas   Notes on the Art of Poetry   316
Wallace Stevens   The Relations Between Poetry
                     and Painting   330

SECTION 6   THEATRE AND DANCE

George Bernard Shaw The Problem Play—
                     A Symposium   345
Bertolt Brecht   Theatre for Learning or Theatre
                     for Pleasure   353
Jean Giraudoux   The Eternal Law of the
                     Dramatist   365
Tyrone Guthrie   An Audience of One   368
Dame Sybil Thorndike I Look at the Audience   380
Martin Esslin   The Theatre of the Absurd   384
Merce Cunningham   Space, Time, and Dance   401
Mary Wigman   Composition in Pure Movement   406

SECTION 7   TELEVISION, MOTION
             PICTURES, AND
             PHOTOGRAPHY

Marshall McLuhan   The Medium Is the Message   415
John Lardner   Thoughts on Radio-Televese   430
Henry Steele Commager Television: The Medium in
                       Search of Its Character   434

Arnold Hauser	Can Movies Be "Profound"?	443
Robert Warshow	The Gangster as Tragic Hero	450
Edgar Morin	The Case of James Dean	456
John Szarkowski	The Photographer's Eye	465

SECTION 8   THE DESIGN ARTS:
ADVERTISING TO
ARCHITECTURE

William Morris	A Factory as It Might Be	477
George Nelson	The Designer in the Modern World	486
	The Dead-End Room	492
Jane Jacobs	Landmarks	500
I. M. Pei	The Nature of Urban Spaces	506
Jacques Barzun	Myths for Materialists	514
Leslie A. Fiedler	The Comics: Middle Against Both Ends	526
John A. Kouwenhoven	What Is "American" in Architecture and Design?	539

ART
AND
AUDIENCE

THE
DECAY
OF
LYING

Because he was a wit of renown in an age and in a city where that quality of mind was highly regarded, Oscar Wilde (1854–1905) sometimes caused attention to be diverted from his own best talents and his accomplishments in poetry, the short story, the novel (The Picture of Dorian Gray), *and the drama* (Salome, Lady Windermere's Fan, The Importance of Being Earnest). *If his essays seem racy in tone, his ideas are nearly always worth serious consideration; indeed, Wilde's mind is far more disciplined than one at first suspects. After all, he came to imaginative writing from intensive work in classical studies, both as a scholar and as a translator. Wilde lectured in America in 1882, but to audiences that were probably not up to his sophistication. Back in London, the young Irishman became a celebrated literary lion, but his career collapsed in scandal and a public trial in 1895 for alleged homosexuality and, after two years in prison, lived out his life in self-imposed exile in Paris. The following dialogue, edited especially for this text, expounds a position concerning art and man and nature which may appear startling, but it is not entirely easy to refute.*

Oscar
Wilde

A dialogue. Persons: Cyril and Vivian. Scene: The library of a country house in Nottinghamshire.

Cyril (*coming in through the open window from the terrace*). My dear Vivian, don't coop yourself up all day in the library. It is a perfectly lovely afternoon. . . . Let us go and lie on the grass, and smoke cigarettes, and enjoy Nature.

Vivian. Enjoy Nature! I am glad to say that I have entirely lost that faculty. . . . My own experience is that the more we study Art, the less we care for Nature. What Art really reveals to us is Nature's lack of design, her curious crudities, her extraordinary monotony, her absolutely unfinished condition. Nature has good

3

intentions, of course, but, as Aristotle once said, she cannot carry
them out. Fortunate for us, however, that Nature is so imperfect,
as otherwise we should have had no art at all. As for the infinite
variety of Nature, that is a pure myth. It is not to be found in
Nature herself. It resides in the imagination, or fancy, or cultivated blindness of the man who looks at her.

Cyril. Well, you need not look at the landscape. You can lie
on the grass and smoke and talk.

Vivian. But Nature is so uncomfortable. . . . If Nature had
been comfortable, mankind would never have invented architecture, and I prefer houses to the open air. . . . Egotism itself,
which is so necessary to a proper sense of human dignity, is entirely the result of indoor life. Out of doors one becomes abstract
and impersonal. . . . Nothing is more evident than that Nature
hates Mind. Thinking is the most unhealthy thing in the world,
and people die of it just as they die of any other disease. Fortunately, in England at any rate, thought is not catching. . . .
Shall I read you what I have written? It might do you a great
deal of good.

Cyril. Certainly, if you give me a cigarette. . . .

Vivian (reading in a very clear, musical voice). "THE DECAY
OF LYING: A PROTEST.—One of the chief causes that can be assigned for the curiously commonplace character of most of the
literature of our age is undoubtedly the decay of Lying as an art,
a science, and a social pleasure. The ancient historians gave us
delightful fiction in the form of fact; the modern novelist presents us with dull facts under the guise of fiction. . . . He has not
even the courage of other people's ideas, but insists on going
directly to life for everything, and ultimately, between ency-
clopædias and personal experience, he comes to the ground,
having drawn his types from the family circle or from the
weekly washerwoman, and having acquired an amount of useful
information from which never, even in his most meditative moments, can he thoroughly free himself.

"The loss that results to literature in general from this false
ideal of our time can hardly be overestimated. People have a
careless way of talking about a 'born liar,' just as they talk about
a 'born poet.' But in both cases they are wrong. Lying and poetry
are arts—arts, as Plato saw, not unconnected with each other—
and they require the most careful study, the most disinterested
devotion. Indeed, they have their technique, just as the more

material arts of painting and sculpture have, their subtle secrets
of form and colour, their craft-mysteries, their deliberate artistic
methods. As one knows the poet by his fine music, so one can
recognize the liar by his rich rhythmic utterance, and in neither
case will the casual inspiration of the moment suffice. Here, as
elsewhere, practice must precede perfection. But in modern
days while the fashion of writing poetry has become far too common, and should, if possible, be discouraged, the fashion of lying
has almost fallen into disrepute. Many a young man starts in life
with a natural gift for exaggeration which, if nurtured in congenial and sympathetic surroundings, or by the imitation of the
best models, might grow into something really great and wonderful. But, as a rule, he comes to nothing. He either falls into careless habits of accuracy——"

Cyril. My dear fellow!

Vivian. Please don't interrupt in the middle of a sentence.
"He either falls into careless habits of accuracy, or takes to fre-
quenting the society of the aged and the well-informed. Both
things are equally fatal to his imagination, as indeed they would
be fatal to the imagination of anybody, and in a short time he
develops a morbid and unhealthy faculty of truth-telling, begins
to verify all statements made in his presence, has no hesitation in
contradicting people who are much younger than himself, and
often ends by writing novels which are so like life that no one
can possibly believe in their probability. This is no isolated instance that we are giving. It is simply one example out of many;
and if something cannot be done to check, or at least to modify,
our monstrous worship of facts, Art will become sterile and
Beauty will pass away from the land. . . . Mr. Henry James writes
fiction as if it were a painful duty, and wastes upon mean motives and imperceptible 'points of view' his neat literary style, his
felicitous phrases, his swift and caustic satire. . . . Mrs. Oliphant
prattles pleasantly about curates, lawn-tennis parties, domesticity,
and other wearisome things. Mr. Marion Crawford has im-
molated himself upon the altar of local colour. . . .

Nothing in the whole history of literature is sadder than the
artistic career of Charles Reade. He wrote one beautiful book,
The Cloister and the Hearth, and wasted the rest of his life in a
foolish attempt to be modern, to draw public attention to the
state of our convict prisons, and the management of our private
lunatic asylums. Charles Dickens was depressing enough in all

conscience when he tried to arouse our sympathy for the victims
of the poor-law administration; but Charles Reade, an artist, a
scholar, a man with a true sense of beauty, raging and roaring
over the abuses of contemporary life like a common pamphleteer
or a sensational journalist, is really a sight for the angels to weep
over. Believe me, my dear Cyril, modernity of form and modernity of subject-matter are entirely and absolutely wrong. We
have mistaken the common livery of the age for the vesture of
the Muses, and spend our days in the sordid streets and hideous
suburbs of our vile cities when we should be out on the hillside
with Apollo. Certainly we are a degraded race, and have sold our
birthright for a mess of facts.

Cyril. There is something in what you say, and there is no
doubt that whatever amusement we may find in reading a purely
modern novel, we have rarely any artistic pleasure in re-reading
it. . . . If one cannot enjoy reading a book over and over again,
there is no use reading it at all. But what do you say about the
return to Life and Nature? This is the panacea that is always
being recommended to us.

Vivian. I will read you what I say on that subject. The passage comes later on in the article, but I may as well give it to you
now:—

"The popular cry of our time is 'Let us return to Life and
Nature; they will recreate Art for us, and send the red blood
coursing through her veins; they will shoe her feet with swiftness
and make her hand strong.' But, alas! Nature is always behind the
age. And as for Life, she is the solvent that breaks up Art, the
enemy that lays waste her house."

Cyril. What do you mean by saying that Nature is always
behind the age?

Vivian. Well, perhaps that is rather cryptic. What I mean is
this. If we take Nature to mean natural simple instinct as opposed to self-conscious culture, the work produced under this
influence is always old-fashioned, antiquated, and out of date. . . .
If we regard Nature as the collection of phenomena external
to man, people only discover in her what they bring to her. She
has no suggestions of her own. Wordsworth went to the lakes,
but he was never a lake poet. He found in stones the sermons he
had already hidden there. He went moralizing about the district,
but his good work was produced when he returned, not to

Nature but to poetry. Poetry gave him *Laodamia*, and the fine
sonnets, and the great Ode, such as it is. Nature gave him *Peter
Bell*, and the address to Mr. Wilkinson's spade.

Cyril. I think that view might be questioned. I am rather inclined to believe in the "impulse from a vernal wood," though of
course the artistic value of such an impulse depends entirely on
the kind of temperament that receives it, so that the return to
Nature would come to mean simply the advance to a great personality. You would agree with that, I fancy. However, proceed
with your article.

Vivian (reading). "Art begins with abstract decoration with
purely imaginative and pleasurable work dealing with what is
unreal and non-existent. This is the first stage. Then Life becomes
fascinated with this new wonder, and asks to be admitted into
the charmed circle. Art takes life as part of her rough material,
recreates it, and refashions it in fresh forms, is absolutely indifferent to fact, invents, imagines, dreams, and keeps between herself and reality the impenetrable barrier of beautiful style, of
decorative or ideal treatment. The third stage is when Life gets
the upper hand, and drives Art out into the wilderness. This is
the true decadence, and it is from this that we are now suffering. . . .

Facts are not merely finding a footing-place in history, but
they are usurping the domain of Fancy, and have invaded the
kingdom of Romance. Their chilling touch is over everything.
They are vulgarising mankind. The crude commercialism of
America, its materialising spirit, its indifference to the poetical
side of things, and its lack of imagination and of high unattainable
ideals, are entirely due to that country having adopted for its
national hero a man, who according to his own confession, was
incapable of telling a lie. . . .

Cyril. My dear boy!

Vivian. I assure you: . . .

"Art finds her own perfection within, and not outside of, herself. She is not to be judged by any external standard of resemblance. She is a veil, rather than a mirror. She has flowers that no
forests know of, birds that no woodland possesses. She makes
and unmakes many worlds, and can draw the moon from heaven
with a scarlet thread. Hers are the 'forms more real than living
man,' and hers the great archetypes of which things that have

Oscar Wilde, 1882.
Photograph by Napoleon Sarony. The George Eastman House Collection.

David Mlinaric, 1966.
Photograph by Colin Jones. Life Magazine © Time Inc.

existence are but unfinished copies. Nature has, in her eyes, no laws, no uniformity. . . . She can bid the almond tree blossom in winter, and send the snow upon the ripe cornfield. . . .

Cyril. I should like to ask you a question. What do you mean by saying that life, "poor, probable, uninteresting human life," will try to reproduce the marvels of art? . . . You don't mean to say that you seriously believe that Life imitates Art, that Life in fact is the mirror, and Art the reality?

Vivian. Certainly I do. Paradox though it may seem—and paradoxes are always dangerous things—it is none the less true that Life imitates art far more than Art imitates life. . . . And it has always been so. A great artist invents a type, and Life tries to copy it, to reproduce it in a popular form, like an enterprising publisher. Neither Holbein nor Vandyck found in England what they have given us. They brought their types with them, and Life, with her keen imitative faculty, set herself to supply the master with models. The Greeks, with their quick artistic instinct, understood this, and set in the bride's chamber the statue of Hermes or of Apollo, that she might bear children as lovely as the works of art that she looked at in her rapture or her pain. They knew that Life gains from Art not merely spirituality, depth of thought and feeling, soul-turmoil or soul-peace, but that she can form herself on the very lines and colours of art and can reproduce the dignity of Pheidias as well as the grace of Praxiteles. Hence came their objection to realism. They disliked it on purely social grounds. They felt that it inevitably makes people ugly, and they were perfectly right. We try to improve the conditions of the race by means of good air, free sunlight, wholesome water, and hideous bare buildings for the better housing of the lower orders. But these things merely produce health; they do not produce beauty. For this, Art is required, and the true disciples of the great artist are not his studio-imitators, but those who become like his works of art, be they plastic as in Greek days, or pictorial as in modern times; in a word, Life is Art's best, Art's only pupil.

As it is with the visible arts, so it is with literature. The most obvious and the vulgarest form in which this is shown is in the case of the silly boys who, after reading the adventures of Jack Sheppard or Dick Turpin, pillage the stalls of unfortunate apple-women, break into sweet-shops at night, and alarm old gentlemen who are returning home from the city by leaping out on them in suburban lanes, with black masks and unloaded revolvers. . . . The boy-burglar is simply the inevitable result of life's imitative instinct. He is Fact, occupied as Fact usually is with trying to reproduce Fiction, and what we see in him is repeated on an extended scale throughout the whole of life. Schopenhauer has analysed the pessimism that characterises modern thought, but Hamlet invented it. . . . Think of what we owe to the imitation of Christ, of what we owe to the imitation of Caesar.

Cyril. The theory is certainly a very curious one, but to make it complete you must show that Nature, no less than Life, is an imitation of Art. Are you prepared to prove that?

Vivian. My dear fellow, I am prepared to prove anything.

Cyril. Nature follows the landscape painter then, and takes her effects from him?

Vivian. Certainly. Where, if not from the Impressionists, do we get those wonderful brown fogs that come creeping down our streets, blurring the gas-lamps and changing the houses into monstrous shadows? To whom, if not to them and their master, do we owe the lovely silver mists that brood over our river, and turn to faint forms of fading grace curved bridge and swaying barge? The extraordinary change that has taken place in the climate of London during the last ten years is entirely due to this particular school of Art. . . . Things are because we see them, and what we see, and how we see it, depends on the Arts that have influenced us. To look at a thing is very different from seeing a thing. One does not see anything until one sees its beauty. Then, and then only, does it come into existence. At present, people see fogs, not because there are fogs, but because poets and painters have taught them the mysterious loveliness of such effects. There may have been fogs for centuries in London. I dare say there were. But no one saw them, and so we do not know anything about them. They did not exist till Art had invented them. . . . However, I don't want to be too hard on Nature. I wish the Channel, especially at Hastings, did not look quite so often like a Henry Moore [an English painter of seascapes, 1831–1896], grey pearl with yellow lights, but then, when Art is more varied, Nature will, no doubt, be more varied also. That she imitates Art, I don't think even her worst enemy would deny now. It is the one thing that keeps her in touch with civilized man. But have I proved my theory to your satisfaction?

Cyril. You have proved it to my dissatisfaction, which is

better. But even admitting this strange imitative instinct in Life and Nature, surely you would acknowledge that Art expresses the temper of its age, the spirit of its time, the moral and social conditions that surround it, and under whose influence it is produced.

Vivian. Certainly not! Art never expresses anything but itself. This is the principle of my new aesthetics; and it is this, more than that vital connection between form and substance, on which Mr. Pater dwells, that makes music the type of all the arts. . . . Remote from reality, and with her eyes turned away from the shadows of the cave, Art reveals her own perfection, and the wondering crowd that watches the opening of the marvellous, many-petalled rose fancies that it is its own history that is being told to it, its own spirit that is finding expression in a new form. But it is not so. The highest art rejects the burden of the human spirit, and gains more from a new medium or a fresh material than she does from any enthusiasm for art, or from any lofty passion, or from any great awakening of the human consciousness. She develops purely on her own lines. She is not symbolic of any age. It is the ages that are her symbols.

Cyril. But modern portraits by English painters, what of them? Surely they are like the people they pretend to represent?

Vivian. Quite so. They are so like them that a hundred years from now no one will believe in them. The only portraits in which one believes are portraits where there is very little of the sitter and a very great deal of the artist. Holbein's drawings of the men and women of his time impress us with a sense of their absolute reality. But this is simply because Holbein compelled life to accept his conditions, to restrain itself within his limitations, to reproduce his type, and to appear as he wished it to appear. It is style that makes us believe in a thing—nothing but style. Most of our modern portrait painters are doomed to absolute oblivion. They never paint what they see. They paint what the public sees, and the public never sees anything.

Cyril. Well, after that I think I should like to hear the end of your article.

Vivian. With pleasure. . . .

"What we have to do, what at any rate it is our duty to do, is to revive this old art of Lying. Much of course may be done, in the way of educating the public, by amateurs in the domestic circle, at literary lunches, and at afternoon teas. But this is merely

the light and graceful side of lying, such as was probably heard
at Cretan dinner parties. There are many other forms. Lying for
the sake of gaining some immediate personal advantage, for
instance—lying with a moral purpose, as it is usually called—
though of late it has been rather looked down upon, was extremely popular with the antique world. . . .

Lying for the sake of the improvement of the young, which
is the basis of home education, still lingers amongst us, and its
advantages are so admirably set forth in the early books of Plato's
Republic that it is unnecessary to dwell upon them here. It is a
mode of lying for which all good mothers have peculiar capabili-
ties, but it is capable of still further development, and has been
sadly overlooked by the School Board. Lying for the sake of a
monthly salary is of course well known in Fleet Street, and the
profession of a political leader-writer is not without its advantages. But it is said to be a somewhat dull occupation, and it
certainly does not lead to much beyond a kind of ostentatious
obscurity. The only form of lying that is absolutely beyond
reproach is Lying for its own sake, and the highest development
of this is, as we have already pointed out, Lying in Art. . . . We
must cultivate the lost art of Lying."

Cyril. We must certainly cultivate it at once. But in order to
avoid making any error I want you to tell me briefly the doctrines of the new aesthetics.

Vivian. Briefly, then, they are these. Art never expresses anything but itself. It has an independent life, just as Thought has,
and develops purely on its own lines. It is not necessarily realistic
in an age of realism, nor spiritual in an age of faith. So far from
being the creation of its time, it is usually in direct opposition to
it, and the only history that it preserves for us is the history of its
own progress. Sometimes it returns upon its footsteps, and
revives some antique form, as happened in the archaistic movement of late Greek Art, and in the pre-Raphaelite movement of
our own day. At other times it entirely anticipates its age, and
produces in one century work that it takes another century to
understand, to appreciate, and to enjoy. In no case does it reproduce its age. To pass from the art of a time to the time itself is
the great mistake that all historians commit.

The second doctrine is this. All bad art comes from returning
to Life and Nature, and elevating them into ideals. Life and
Nature may sometimes be used as part of Art's rough material,

but before they are of any real service to art they must be translated into artistic conventions. The moment Art surrenders its
imaginative medium it surrenders everything. As a method
Realism is a complete failure, and the two things that every artist
should avoid are modernity of form and modernity of subject-
matter. To us, who live in the nineteenth century, any century
is a suitable subject for art except our own. The only beautiful
things are the things that do not concern us. It is, to have the
pleasure of quoting myself, exactly because Hecuba is nothing
to us that her sorrows are so suitable a motive for a tragedy. . . .
Life goes faster than Realism, but Romanticism is always in front
of Life.

The third doctrine is that Life imitates Art far more than Art
imitates Life. This results not merely from Life's imitative instinct, but from the fact that the self-conscious aim of Life is to
find expression, and that Art offers it certain beautiful forms
through which it may realize that energy. It is a theory that has
never been put forward before, but it is extremely fruitful, and
throws an entirely new light upon the history of Art.

It follows, as a corollary from this, that external Nature also
imitates Art. The only effects that she can show us are effects
that we have already seen through poetry, or in paintings. This
is the secret of Nature's charm, as well as the explanation of
Nature's weakness.

The final revelation is that Lying, the telling of beautiful
untrue things, is the proper aim of Art. But of this I think I have
spoken at sufficient length. And now let us go out on the terrace,
where "droops the milk-white peacock like a ghost," while the
evening star "washes the dusk with silver." At twilight nature
becomes a wonderfully suggestive effect, and is not without
loveliness, though perhaps its chief use is to illustrate quotations
from the poets. Come! We have talked long enough.

*One of Ireland's foremost playwrights (*Juno and the Paycock, The Plough and the Stars), *Sean O'Casey (1884–1964) displays an understandable concern for the audience for art, and most especially about an audience once termed the "common man," or, more currently, the "proletariat." In the following essay, O'Casey shows a typical awareness of class distinctions and—from this point of view—the power exercised by the dominant social classes in any society. Although he notes the dangers of conformity where art is concerned, O'Casey offers few concrete suggestions to correct the admittedly weak situation of the artist. In any event, for O'Casey's own works to "become . . . common in the home" nothing less would be required than a far-reaching revolution not only in taste but in the nature of society as we presently know it. The difficulties of art and a mass audience make up the subject matter of many of the essays that follow. Among other things, however, O'Casey's writing consistently presents a sinewy and virile language which has considerable appeal to the ear. It is, after all, the performance of a man of the theater.*

THE ARTS AMONG THE MULTITUDE

Sean O'Casey

Talent exists in each human being, for art is an expression natural to all, says Saul Baizerman, the sculptor. So it does and so it is, though you wouldn't think so looking around; great talent in some, talents of many kinds dispersed among all only waiting for the word Go. There are many more than seven arts, including the way of talking—the orator—and the way of walking—the mannequin—to mention only two. They are most manifest in us when we are kids, when we have courage and little shame, for all can hum an air, draw a line or two to make a comic face, dance a childish measure in a game, and walk like a king or queen going to, or coming from, a coronation, or carve a comely boat from a block

of wood; equally possessed of him born rich or of her born poor.
Born in us, but doesn't stay long. Expression of art, or even an
interest in its manifestation by others, dies young among the
multitude of men. Why? Homes and schools first of all, then the
church says a prayer over the dead: a prayer of thanksgiving.
Any interest in art is slowly and politely pressed out of the consciousness of the young rich attending the superior schools, and
roughly driven from the consciousness of those crammed tight
into the inferior ones; youngsters, who, later on, have to labor to
let life provide a leisured class to whom the setting of a horse at
a hedge, the downing of a pheasant, or the shooting of a snipe
gives a more decided thrill than a Beethoven symphony, a painting by Rembrandt, or a play by Shakespeare (though there's an
active beauty in a horse taking a hedge, a pathetic beauty in a
falling snipe, or a pheasant fluttering into death; but little in the
smoke from the guns, and little feeling for beauty in the thought
of him who fires the gun, or in the mind of the fellow or female
riding the horse).

With the bird shooters and horse leapers we have little to do;
they won't matter much later—let them down their pheasants,
jump their horses, and shoot their snipe. We have to do with the
multitude of men and women who swing away with a cackling
grunt of derision from anything in art or literature that doesn't
at once flash a message or a sentimental thrill into their restricted
understanding; the vital ones who have been made dense by rule,
environment, and hard labor. How then are the seven arts to become the companions of the working multitude, for it is these
alone who can give the encouragement the arts desire, and it is
these who need their civilizing influence; it is the multitude that
make life, decide how life shall go, and determine how life shall
look. It is useless to say that the artist can sit safely in his ivory
tower, looking scornfully down from a lancet window at the
people below. He can't, for sooner or later sturdy shoulders
pressing against it will send the ivory tower toppling. The artist
may live on for a while, hearsed in honor from a few; but when
the few go, the end of the artist comes.

How often is Art, in all its forms and fancies, going to make
friends with the multitude? National galleries sheltering the best,
or municipal ones sheltering the worst, aren't much good to the
common man passing through the common hours. For the first,
he rarely goes near them; or, if he does, he has to stiffen himself

into another toilet, be a toff, which unmakes him into another being without flexibility or ease of mind; so that an other than himself goes tiptoe through the elegant halls to see the wonders. He sees little, feels nothing, and goes away tired. The things shown look stately and aloof, guarded by dumb attendants, and seem to shrink within themselves when he comes near, forcing him to imagine that he has no kin with them, and they have no kin with him. Indeed, the pictures on the walls and the bronze or marble figures on their stands seem to be cocking a snook at him. Intimidated, if he mutters a word to a wife or a companion, he mutters a whisper, as if the place were holy ground and there were gods in corners who would hear and be displeased at the sound of a human voice. I don't see much in that, or, I like that a little better, are all the whispers come to: the wolf that should suckle Romulus and Remus is beginning to growl.

This soul adventuring among masterpieces has had no introduction to them through print or book at home; caught ne'er a glance at them during school hours where he went to learn; nor did he see anything like them at church where he went to pray: in these places there were only the cheap illustrated papers, the dusty maps, the tawdry, misshapen images, and the gaudy prints of holy men and holy women.

The multitude will get no savvy from the philosophical, esthetic, analytical, and psychological articles crammed into magazine and journal, or from the treatises on art crowding the shelves of the world's libraries; for none can agree. Every phase of art has its warring judges; every artist has his applauding clique deafening the ears of them who pause to listen. Picasso himself had many phases, and each is living only as concerning himself, for Picasso happens to be a very great painter. Judgments! What damn good are they, bar the judgment of time? Yet we are told by Gino Severini that when Gide went to Russia, he afterwards "refused to express a judgment on Russian literature, and that, to me, seems significant." How significant? Isn't it time for us to leave the Soviet literature aside for a moment, and have a quiet, sensible gawk at our own? Is it any better? In a hundred years, will Gide himself be significant or insignificant? Has what he has written power to alter the shape of things to come? On the whole (though there be no sign of a Tolstoy or even of a Gorky), from my reading of it, I'd say that the Soviet literature with all its many faults, its spasmodic propaganda propagating tediousness, is very much nearer to life living than the best of our own, than the writing of Sartre, Faulkner, Mauriac, Graham Greene, and the rest of them: it is life with its head in the stars compared with life with its head among the maggots. However feeble some of the Soviet novels may be, and many of them are so, in each there is a welcome touch of kindliness, a wave of energy; of the writers we know here, all, or mostly all, plunge their readers into an inhumanity worse, far worse, than man's common inhumanity to man.

Again the same writer says "Mayakovsky and Essenin could for a while live and work by dint of a 'conformity' which with the passage of time became impossible. In fact both ended by committing suicide." There is no evidence whatever to show that either committed suicide because he found the "conformity" impossible. In fact, I can mention names of artists who committed suicide, artists who not only didn't live in the Soviet Union, but never even paid a flying visit there: two painters and one composer here in England, and a painter (Irish) and a dramatist in America. Van Gogh, as far as I know, wasn't pressed towards suicide by any storm of "conformity" blowing from the U.S.S.R. There is a "conformity" here as bitter, silent, and more sinister than the conformity we so often talk about, parade before pitying eyes; while all the time we forget, or ignore, the conforming pressure that tries to stifle the artist in his own country. And here it isn't the "proletarian" who imposes the pressure; it is imposed by those, who, because of a superior education and the use of a better life, should know better. There was, for instance, a roar that was near to a riot when Picasso's pictures were given an exhibition in the Tate Gallery. Stanley Baldwin, then Prime Minister of England, couldn't stand Epstein's *Rima*, to be followed in his opinion by most of those holding any kind of a post in the Government, the Civil Service, the Army and Navy, the Young Men's Christian Association, and the Yeomen of the Guard.

Of course, the Soviet Union makes mistakes, silly ones at times. For instance, the demand for the withdrawal of Picasso's simple portrait of Stalin was a silly order; and the editor of the French journal which published the portrait should have told whatever Soviet emissary who sent the order to go to hell. The same kind of boycott is carried on here (in England), but quietly, with ne'er a shout during the transaction. For instance, a writer holding views displeasing to privilege and power may venture to comment on a review of his work; the editor of the paper in which the review appeared will politely acknowledge receipt of the comments, but they will never be published. A first-class national journal has said of myself that the people who count have decided to ignore O'Casey because of his lamentable judgments. What have lamentable judgments to do with plays, or any kind of literature? One would think that such enlightened folk would show an example to the lesser ones without the law, or those behind the Iron Curtain.

Of course, as Thomas Mann says, a brilliant and clever intellect may be inclined savagely, and maybe sagely, from the brilliant intellect's point of view, to the right, soaring over with style and wit the lesser intellects of the left; but surely the facts are, by and large, that almost all the brilliant and lofty intellects appearing among man have been, directly or indirectly, on the side of humanity. Marching humanity is surrounded with a great cloud of witnesses. As for Ezra Pound's prize—surely he deserved the Bollingen Award for his great contribution to literature, just as he deserved prison for support given to Hitler and Mussolini; just as the seaman who, at the risk of his life, in the novel *Ninety-three*, captured the gun that was rushing round the deck of his ship, threatening disaster, was rewarded with a star for his courage and devotion, and then hanged at the yardarm for his carelessness in not seeing that the gun had been securely lashed to its rings.

"The Christian should be everywhere, and be free everywhere," Maritain is quoted as saying. Let us have a decent laugh here. The poor fellow is free only where the big mass of people care little or nothing for Christianity. And this freedom should belong to the artist too, says Gino Severini. Why to the Christian and to the artist? Why not to all men? Artists and Christians seem to be forever claiming rights they deny to others. In a letter before me, sent by a poet from Argentina, with a play in verse for me to judge, I read: Modern society is complicated. A poet has to live, but he would rather take pen and paper and roam the woods, to pick bluebells and admire the yellow of a cornfield. So would many who make no claim to being poets—though one shouldn't pick the bluebells, but leave them where they grow to show their own beauty to themselves, if no one else be there to see it.

The Arts are for all, like the bluebells, and not for the few. They should become, in some form or another, common in an uncommon way, in the home, in the school, in the church, in the street, and in the parks where man sits to think or look around. They must be brought among the people so that man may become familiar with them, for familiarity breeds, not contempt, but a liking. England began this task well during the Festival of Britain, when artists of all kinds brought before the people many new forms, startling designs—like the Skylon—and many new ways with color and line. Herbert Morrison, then a Cabinet Minister, initiated the event and took responsibility for it. In spite of the heavy and insistent opposition of conservative minds, the Festival was a tremendous success; and Morrison did, not only a good deed, but, possibly, the best deed of his life. Its influence is now being shown in the present Coronation decorations: designs never seen before; graceful and, at times, enchanting; doing away with the vulgar and commonplace bourgeois bunkum art of past ceremonial. Only the parading peers and the minor nobility cling to their old habits, looking ridiculous under the graceful and novel decorations of a new mind with a new outlook.

No one can bind the Muses. Nor Sainte-Beuve, nor Gide, Proust, Zhdanov [Andrei Zhdanov (1896–1948), a powerful Kremlin figure and Stalin's arbiter of the arts], nor anyone else can change to please himself what the Muses decide to say or sing.

*The title of this essay borrows a celebrated phrase
from Walter Pater and the fin de siècle inheritors
of the Aesthetic Movement; the phrase, indeed, had
become something of a benchmark for the
aestheticians—and the aesthetes—of the day. Here,
however, in finely honed and elegant prose, Forster
re-evaluates the implications of "art for art's sake"
in the light of the social and political realities of
1927. The result is an excellent example of the
informed but sceptical mind coming to a generally
pessimistic conclusion about art and the artist in the
twentieth century. E. M. Forster (1879–   ) is
held in great esteem as a novelist—his best known
works are* Howard's End *and* A Passage to India—
*although he inexplicably stopped writing
novels in his early middle age. His* Aspects of
the Novel *is a classic of fiction criticism and
his later collections of essays,* Abinger Harvest
and Two Cheers for Democracy, *offer models of
clean, clear, logical prose.*

ART
FOR
ART'S
SAKE

*E. M.
Forster*

I believe in art for art's sake. It is an unfashion-
able belief, and some of my statements must be
of the nature of an apology. Sixty years ago I
should have faced you with more confidence. A
writer or a speaker who chose "Art for Art's
Sake" for his theme sixty years ago could be
sure of being in the swim, and could feel so con-
fident of success that he sometimes dressed himself in aesthetic costumes suitable to the occasion
—in an embroidered dressing-gown, perhaps, or
a blue velvet suit with a Lord Fauntleroy collar;
or a toga, or a kimono, and carried a poppy or a
lily or a long peacock's feather in his mediaeval
hand. Times have changed. Not thus can I present either myself or my theme to-day. My aim
rather is to ask you quietly to reconsider for a
few minutes a phrase which has been much misused and much abused, but which has, I believe,
great importance for us—has, indeed, eternal importance.

Now we can easily dismiss those peacock's feathers and other affectations—they are but trifles—but I want also to dismiss a more dangerous heresy, namely the silly idea that only art matters, an idea which has somehow got mixed up with the idea of art for art's sake, and has helped to discredit it. Many things, besides art, matter. It is merely one of the things that matter, and high though the claims are that I make for it, I want to keep them in proportion. No one can spend his or her life entirely in the creation or the appreciation of masterpieces. Man lives, and ought to live, in a complex world, full of conflicting claims, and if we simplified them down into the aesthetic he would be sterilised. Art for art's sake does not mean that only art matters and I would also like to rule out such phrases as, "The Life of Art," "Living for Art," and "Art's High Mission." They confuse and mislead.

What does the phrase mean? Instead of generalising, let us take a specific instance—Shakespeare's *Macbeth*, for example, and pronounce the words, *"Macbeth for Macbeth's sake."* What does that mean? Well, the play has several aspects—it is educational, it teaches us something about legendary Scotland, something about Jacobean England, and a good deal about human nature and its perils. We can study its origins, and study and enjoy its dramatic technique and the music of its diction. All that is true. But *Macbeth* is furthermore a world of its own, created by Shakespeare and existing in virtue of its own poetry. It is in this aspect *Macbeth* for *Macbeth's* sake, and that is what I intend by the phrase "art for art's sake." A work of art—whatever else it may be—is a self-contained entity, with a life of its own imposed on it by its creator. It has internal order. It may have external form. That is how we recognise it.

Take for another example that picture of Seurat's which I saw two years ago in Chicago—*"La Grande Jatte."* Here again there is much to study and to enjoy: the pointillism, the charming face of the seated girl, the nineteenth-century Parisian Sunday sunlight, the sense of motion in immobility. But here again there is something more; *"La Grande Jatte"* forms a world of its own, created by Seurat and existing by virtue of its own poetry: *"La Grande Jatte" pour "Le Grande Jatte": l'art pour l'art.* Like *Macbeth* it has internal order and internal life.

It is to the conception of order that I would now turn. This is important to my argument, and I want to make a digression, and glance at order in daily life, before I come to order in art.

In the world of daily life, the world which we perforce inhabit, there is much talk about order, particularly from statesmen and politicians. They tend, however, to confuse order with orders, just as they confuse creation with regulations. Order, I suggest, is something evolved from within, not something imposed from without; it is an internal stability, a vital harmony, and in the social and political category it has never existed except for the convenience of historians. Viewed realistically, the past is really a series of *dis*orders, succeeding one another by discoverable laws, no doubt, and certainly marked by an increasing growth of human interference, but disorders all the same. So that, speaking as a writer, what I hope for to-day is a disorder which will be more favourable to artists than is the present one, and which will provide them with fuller inspirations and better material conditions. It will not last—nothing lasts—but there have been some advantageous disorders in the past—for instance, in ancient Athens, in Renaissance Italy, eighteenth-century France, periods in China and Persia—and we may do something to accelerate the next one. But let us not again fix our hearts where true joys are not to be found. We were promised a new order after the first world war through the League of Nations. It did not come, nor have I faith in present promises, by whomsoever endorsed. The implacable offensive of Science forbids. We cannot reach social and political stability for the reason that we continue to make scientific discoveries and to apply them, and thus to destroy the arrangements which were based on more elementary discoveries. If Science would discover rather than apply—if, in other words, men were more interested in knowledge than in power—mankind would be in a far safer position, the stability statesmen talk about would be a possibility, there could be a new order based on vital harmony, and the earthly millennium might approach. But Science shows no signs of doing this: she gave us the internal combustion engine, and before we had digested and assimilated it with terrible pains into our social system, she harnessed the atom, and destroyed any new order that seemed to be evolving. How can man get into harmony with his surroundings when he is constantly altering them? The future of our race is, in this direction, more unpleasant than we care to admit, and it has sometimes seemed to me that its best chance lies through apathy, uninventiveness, and inertia. Universal exhaustion might promote that Change of Heart which is at present so briskly recommended from a thousand pulpits. Universal exhaustion would certainly be a new experience. The human race has never undergone it, and is still too perky to admit that it may be coming and might result in a sprouting of new growth through the decay.

I must not pursue these speculations any further—they lead me too far from my terms of reference and maybe from yours. But I do want to emphasize that order in daily life and in history, order in the social and political category, is unattainable under our present psychology.

Where is it attainable? Not in the astronomical category, where it was for many years enthroned. The heavens and the earth have become terribly alike since Einstein. No longer can we find a reassuring contrast to chaos in the night sky and look up with George Meredith to the stars, the army of unalterable law, or listen for the music of the spheres. Order is not there. In the entire universe there seem to be only two possibilities for it. The first of them—which again lies outside my terms of reference—is the divine order, the mystic harmony, which according to all religions is available for those who can contemplate it. We must admit its possibility, on the evidence of the adepts, and we must believe them when they say that it is attained, if attainable, by prayer. "O thou who changest not, abide with me," said one of its poets. "*Ordina questo amor, o tu che m'ami,*" said another: "Set love in order thou who lovest me." The existence of a divine order, though it cannot be tested, has never been disproved.

The second possibility for order lies in the aesthetic category, which is my subject here: the order which an artist can create in his own work, and to that we must now return. A work of art, we are all agreed, is a unique product. But why? It is unique not because it is clever or noble or beautiful or enlightened or original or sincere or idealistic or useful or educational—it may embody any of those qualities—but because it is the only material object in the universe which may possess internal harmony. All the others have been pressed into shape from outside, and when their mould is removed they collapse. The work of art stands up by itself, and nothing else does. It achieves something which has often been promised by society, but always delusively. Ancient Athens made a mess—but the *Antigone* stands up. Renaissance

Rome made a mess—but the ceiling of the Sistine got painted. James I made a mess—but there was *Macbeth*. Louis XIV—but there was *Phèdre*. Art for art's sake? I should just think so, and more so than ever at the present time. It is the one orderly product which our muddling race has produced. It is the cry of a thousand sentinels, the echo from a thousand labyrinths; it is the lighthouse which cannot be hidden: *c'est le meilleur témoignage que nous puissions donner de notre dignité* [it is the best witness that we can give of our worth]. *Antigone* for *Antigone's* sake, *Macbeth* for *Macbeth's*, *"La Grande Jatte" pour "La Grande Jatte."*

If this line of argument is correct, it follows that the artist will tend to be an outsider in the society to which he has been born, and that the nineteenth century conception of him as a Bohemian was not inaccurate. The conception erred in three particulars: it postulated an economic system where art could be a full-time job, it introduced the fallacy that only art matters, and it overstressed idiosyncracy and waywardness—the peacock-feather aspect— rather than order. But it is a truer conception than the one which prevails in official circles on my side of the Atlantic—I don't know about yours: the conception which treats the artist as if he were a particularly bright government advertiser and encourages him to be friendly and matey with his fellow citizens, and not to give himself airs.

Estimable is mateyness, and the man who achieves it gives many a pleasant little drink to himself and to others. But it has no traceable connection with the creative impulse, and probably acts as an inhibition on it. The artist who is seduced by mateyness may stop himself from doing the one thing which he, and he alone, can do—the making of something out of words or sounds or paint or clay or marble or steel or film which has internal harmony and presents order to a permanently disarranged planet. This seems worth doing, even at the risk of being called uppish by journalists. I have in mind an article which was published some years ago in the London *Times*, an article called "The Eclipse of the Highbrow," in which the "Average Man" was exalted, and all contemporary literature was censured if it did not toe the line, the precise position of the line being naturally known to the writer of the article. Sir Kenneth Clark, who was at that time director of our National Gallery, commented on this pernicious doctrine in a letter which cannot be too often quoted. "The poet and the artist," wrote Clark, "are important precisely because they are not average men; because in sensibility, intelligence, and power of invention they far exceed the average." These memorable words, and particularly the words "power of invention," are the Bohemian's passport. Furnished with it, he slinks about society, saluted now by a brickbat and now by a penny, and accepting either of them with equanimity. He does not consider too anxiously what his relations with society may be, for he is aware of something more important than that—namely the invitation to invent, to create order, and he believes he will be better placed for doing this if he attempts detachment. So round and round he slouches, with his hat pulled over his eyes, and maybe with a louse in his beard, and—if he really wants one—with a peacock's feather in his hand.

If our present society should disintegrate—and who dare prophesy that it won't?—this old-fashioned and démodé figure will become clearer: the Bohemian, the outsider, the parasite, the rat—one of those figures which have at present no function either in a warring or a peaceful world. It may not be dignified to be a rat, but many of the ships are sinking, which is not dignified either—the officials did not build them properly. Myself, I would sooner be a swimming rat than a sinking ship—at all events I can look around me for a little longer—and I remember how one of us, a rat with particularly bright eyes called Shelley, squeaked out, "Poets are the unacknowledged legislators of the world," before he vanished into the waters of the Mediterranean.

What laws did Shelley propose to pass? None. The legislation of the artist is never formulated at the time, though it is sometimes discerned by future generations. He legislates through creating. And he creates through his sensitiveness and his power to impose form. Without form the sensitiveness vanishes. And form is as important to-day, when the human race is trying to ride the whirlwind, as it ever was in those less agitating days of the past, when the earth seemed solid and the stars fixed, and the discoveries of science were made slowly, slowly. Form is not tradition. It alters from generation to generation. Artists always seek a new technique, and will continue to do so as long as their work excites them. But form of some kind is imperative. It is the surface crust of the internal harmony, it is the outward evidence of order.

My remarks about society may have seemed too pessimistic, but

I believe that society can only represent a fragment of the human spirit, and that another fragment can only get expressed through art. And I wanted to take this opportunity, this vantage ground, to assert not only the existence of art, but its pertinacity. Looking back into the past, it seems to me that that is all there has ever been: vantage grounds for discussion and creation, little vantage grounds in the changing chaos, where bubbles have been blown and webs spun, and the desire to create order has found temporary gratification, and the sentinels have managed to utter their challenges, and the huntsmen, though lost individually, have heard each other's calls, through the impenetrable wood, and the lighthouses have never ceased sweeping the thankless seas. In this pertinacity, there seems to me, as I grow older, something more and more profound, something which does in fact concern people who do not care about art at all.

In conclusion, let me summarise the various categories that have laid claim to the possession of Order.

1. The social and political category. Claim disallowed on the evidence of history and of our own experience. If man altered psychologically, order here might be attainable: not otherwise.

2. The astronomical category. Claim allowed up to the present century, but now disallowed on the evidence of the physicists.

3. The religious category. Claim allowed on the evidence of the mystics.

4. The aesthetic category. Claim allowed on the evidence of various works of art, and on the evidence of our own creative impulses, however weak these may be, or however imperfectly they may function. Works of art, in my opinion, are the only objects in the material universe to possess internal order, and that is why, though I don't believe that only art matters, I do believe in Art for Art's Sake.

André Malraux (1898–   ) enjoys an international reputation as a novelist and as an art historian and art critic. He came to his present post as Minister of Cultural Affairs in the French government of President deGaulle after a career as l'homme engagé, as an often-captured hero of the French Resistance during World War II, and in virtually every war since the 1920s. His most compelling novel, Man's Fate, *came out of his experience in the Chinese Revolution;* Man's Hope *reflects the unrest during and following the Spanish Civil War in which he also fought against Fascism. A comprehensive historian of art (*The Voices of Silence, The Metamorphosis of the Gods*), Malraux is said to have seen more art than any person now living. Having sought out what he believed to be the realities of both war and politics, Malraux is singularly well qualified to speak out not only on the aesthetic qualities of popular art, but on its possible effects on the masses—indeed, on human destiny—as well. In a typical phrase, he names the popular arts "the appeasing arts."*

ART, POPULAR ART, AND THE ILLUSION OF THE FOLK

André Malraux

Folk art no longer exists because the "folk" no longer exists. The modern masses, bound even in rural places to urban civilization, are as different from the craftsmen and the peasants of the great monarchies as from the people of the Middle Ages. The word "people," when Cardinal de Retz applied it to the Parisians, already sounded false; if the Cardinal had not limited himself to Paris, he would have said bourgeoisie or populace. The people that bought religious images and sang popular songs was born of the oldest civilizations of the earth, would have been partly at home in them, and could scarcely read.

When the radio took the place of the yarn,

magazine photography of woodcuts, the detective novel the place of the novel of chivalry, we began to speak of mass art; that is, we confused the art and the media of fiction. There is a novel of the masses, but no Stendhal of the masses; a music for the masses, but no Bach nor Beethoven, whatever people say; a painting for the masses, no Piero della Francesca nor Michelangelo.

It is generally admitted that fiction achieves its effect upon the collective imagination by its compensatory action, and because each of us identifies himself with one hero. The films in which the millionaire marries the seamstress do not, however, dominate the cinema any more than the tales in which the prince marries the milkmaid dominate legend, or than Hercules dominates Greek or Roman mythology. The legend of Saturn [the story of a great Golden Age of dream-like plenty] is not a source of compensation. Nor is the world of fiction the same as that of fairy tales. The latter hint at this world, but they are drawn back toward it. Cloud-cuckoo-land is without adventures, it is marvelous in itself. The Marvelous, like the Sacred (of which it is a kind of minor domain), belongs to the Altogether-Different, a world sometimes consoling and sometimes terrifying, but (to begin with) different from the real world. Although servants dream of marrying princes, preferably charming ones, *Cinderella* is not a pulp novel, for the rats changed into footmen, the pumpkin into a carriage, are as essential to the story as is the marriage. The tale is the story of Cinderella, also of an enchantment; the protagonist of all fairy tales is the fairy. The immense success of *Fantomas* [central character in the enormously popular thrillers of Marcel Alain] did not lie only in Fantomas; in our crime novels, the heroic gangster took the place of the inspired detective, then the ignoble gangster (by orders from above) supplanted the heroic gangster; the audience has remained the same, as has the world of these fictions.

The Marvelous, home of a liberated humanity, has given asylum to different peoples and then annexed them all. But the history of these successive invasions is revealing. If the eternal tragedy that dwells there, from Saturn to Yseult's[1] love philter, has never driven out the old fairy folk, nevertheless the fairy tales became Christianized, the Golden Legend [thirteenth-century compendium of saints' lives] spread abroad, and the novels

---

[1] Variously spelled; the heroine of the medieval romance of Tristan and Iseut, Wagner's Isolde.

of chivalry were born. Rustling with angels, saints, brave knights, demons, and the strange inhabitants of the eternal realm of the exotic, the forest of the Imaginary became the immense echo of medieval man, as Fable had been that of ancient man. Collective dreaming was for a long time the great general human choir.

But one day, the hero ceased to exist: more precisely, he lost his soul.

Beginning with the eighteenth century, the outlaw settles—and more so each century—in the country of the imaginary. The birth of the gentleman thief, a personage as real as Puss-in-Boots, is not at all of the same order as the later idealization of the *condottiere* [professional soldier, leader of gangs of mercenaries in renaissance Italy]. If fiction disappears from painting in the middle of the nineteenth century, it may be because painters no longer believe in the old legendary characters, nor in those of the new fiction. Delacroix paints legend as seen through poetry, not through the novel. Nobody paints the heroes of Eugène Sue's *Mysteries of Paris*, although these invade the imagination of all Europe; beginning with Balzac, contemporary fiction is interpreted by illustrators. Flaubert is born. Art will seek the marvelous in exoticism and history, whose exploration destroys bit by bit the legendary tone. The last French "positive hero" is Napoleon: Meissonier [a genre painter, 1815–1891], a prudent man, represents him as already beaten; and one can scarcely imagine his portrait by Cézanne. No figure took his place. Don Quixote was crazy, but he wanted to be a true hero: a broken inner world is matched by an imaginary world deserted by its saints and its heroes.

It is unwise to think that the emotions modern crowds expect from the arts are necessarily profound. On the contrary, they are often superficial and puerile, and scarcely go beyond the amorous and Christian sentimentalities, the taste for violence, a little cruelty, collective vanity and sensuality. Men and women who were united by the Resistance into a kind of fraternal group expect from the cinema a romantic novel rather than the expression of their fraternity; and the pleasures of romance do not unite, but isolate men. Thousands of human beings can be united by faith or by hope in the revolution, but (except in the language of the propagandists) they are not then masses, but peers: united often by action, always by what, in their own eyes, counts more than themselves. *All collective virtue is born of communion.* In civilizations united by a Truth, usually a transcendent one, art has nourished the highest fiction, the highest part of man. But if the collective belief is broken, fiction is liberated and discovers its own efficaciousness. Fiction has need of an imaginary world, not of an ideal one. Art strives to submit fiction to the demands of quality; but fiction can dispense with them—and the commercial cinema can take the place of the cathedrals. It is then that the real fairy element takes refuge in the comic, and the appeasing arts proliferate upon the broken inner world, the discordant imaginary world.

It is odd that no word, except arts, designates the common character of what we call, separately, bad painting, bad architecture, bad music, etc. The word "painting" not only defines a domain in which art is *possible;* the Sistine ceiling and the cheapest chromo both belong to it. Now, what makes painting an art for us is not an arrangement of colors on a surface, but the quality of this arrangement. Perhaps we have only one word because bad painting has not existed for very long. There is no bad Gothic painting. Not that all Gothic painting is good: but the difference that separates Giotto from the most mediocre of his imitators is not of the same kind as that which separates Renoir from the caricaturists of the *Vie Parisienne* [somewhat bawdy Paris weekly, founded 1863] on the one hand, and from the academicians on the other. The works of a civilization possessing a faith all express the same artistic attitude, imply a single "function" for painting. Giotto and the Gaddi are separated by talent, Degas and his disciple Bonnat by a schism, Renoir and "suggestive" painting by what? By the fact that this last, totally subjected to the spectator, is a form of advertising which aims at selling itself. If there exists only one word to desginate what makes of lines, sounds, words the expression of the greatest human language, and also what assures their almost physical action (for "music" is Bach, but also the most syrupy tango, and even the sound of instruments), it is because there was a time when the distinction between these things had no point; instruments only played real music then, for there was no other. The conflict between the arts and their means is in no way eternal: in painting, it begins with the school of Bologna, i.e., with eclecticism. It would have been inconceivable in the Romanesque period. The symbol of art *understood* by the folk of a coherent (but nontotalitarian) civilization is the Dark Virgin: up to the beginning of this century, many Virgins of the great pilgrimages were dark, because being thus less human, they were more sacred. The cover of *Fantomas*, magazine illustrations, the portraits of Hitler and Stalin are not Dark Virgins. The only plastic art that has spoken to the masses without lying to them was based, not on realism, but on a dream hierarchy ordered by the superhuman: from Sumer to the cathedrals, this developed before the idea of art was conceived.

The success of the appeasing arts is less due to a technique than is commonly held. No doubt, the triumph of a tune throughout the Western world is closer to the success of Bébé Cadum's [soap and powder] advertising or a propaganda slogan than to the glory of J. S. Bach; song, publicity, and propaganda turn an elementary and powerful feeling to the benefit of their author (a bomber above [the figure of] Bébé Cadum in the talcum powder ad would make a better peace poster than Picasso's dove). But their effectiveness comes from a discovery that their technique invokes but does not supply. This discovery is a crystallization of the collective sensibility, made by a man subject to this sensibility —sometimes for the benefit of another person who is not.

Now, the sensibility is vulnerable to those means (sounds, rhymes, words, forms, colors) which were and are still those of the arts. It is all a question of the end these means are to serve. That an artist can express with genius the feelings of a people, even a sect, to which he belongs, Goya and Rembrandt and many others have shown; and it is rare that the artist is only himself. He does not set himself up against the masses in the manner of an aristocrat: in the ages of faith, his genius was inseparable from the dialogue he maintained with the masses. He sets himself up against the modern masses with regard to what they expect of him; like Christopher Columbus against those who wanted to forbid his expedition. And these collective groups are so far from being identical with the people or the proletariat (although both may belong to them) that they were aristocratic and ecclesiastical in the eighteenth century; and the appeasing art, when it became official, owed its unprecedented triumph to the bourgeoisie of the nineteenth century.

But the victory of the independent artists dazzles us so that we

believe the official artists to be as dead as Jesuit painting. Thus
we only see the enveloping atmosphere when its depth makes it
blue. For the official aesthetic, driven out of painting, reigns
everywhere else; in 1950, the spirit of Rochegrosse and Bou-
guereau [decorative painters, 1859–1938 and 1825–1905] is more
influential than the reproductions of Picasso. There may be less
hypocrisy than formerly (some of the prudishness has been left
out), but it is more powerful. The catalogue of the Salon for
1905 does not resemble that of the 1950 Independents, but look
at our illustrated weeklies, whatever the political regime: the
West prefers Cabanel [portraitist, 1823–1889] to Horace Vernet
[battle painter, 1789–1863], and Russia prefers Rochegrosse,
whom it imitates, to Cabanel, whom it forbids. Like bourgeois
painting of which they are the direct heirs, the "arts" desired by
the masses who have lost their myth are arts *in submission.* These
arts aim to act on those to whom they are addressed for the exclusive benefit of those who foster these arts. Taken together,
and apart from some contemporary successes in humor—Charlie
Chaplin's work is a true fairy tale, but a sentimental one—these
are arts of lobotomy. Quality, when they care to have it, is not
their *raison d'être,* but one of their means. We like some poster
artists of great talent. We know that they are not Michelangelo,
not even Klee. Still they are appreciated in the countries of an old
artistic culture more for the charm of their talent than for the
effectiveness of their illustrations: for the most effective advertising is the American, which plays upon conditioned reflexes and
creates for its confections the Imaginary Museum of consumers'
goods. Moreover, the masses are less sensitive to the advertisement, which they do not take seriously, than to the art photo of
the magazines and to the cinema. Both the film and the detective
story aim at "getting bought"; therefore they act physically on
their readers or spectators by their narrative technique, their re-
course to sexuality and violence. The Soviet film aims to set up
an imaginary world, and does so by substituting for the revolutionary epic, or for a threatened Russia, a pious legend and all that
this implies; just as Soviet propaganda conjures up a similar world
in distorting Marxism into the most elementary Manicheanism.
Did the popular songs of old aim to sell themselves? There were
sellers indeed for religious images and the novels of chivalry, but
the intoxication which every author of detective novels hopes to
induce in his reader is not the same as that provided by so many

adventures of Don Quixote. Tales and paintings of martyrs, even
when they are baroque, do not provide "blood in chapter one."
The characteristic of these appeasing arts is not, however, their
violence: in many great works we find the "attack" upon the
reader or the spectator, and we admire Grünewald [Matthias
Grünewald, c.1480–1530, master religious painter famous for the
Isenheim Altarpiece] and the painters of the *Pietà*, Shakespeare,
Balzac, and Dostoevsky—and Beethoven. Nor is this characteristic found only in the employment of physical stimuli: the stimuli of sentimentalism and sensuality are the same as those of
violence (weeping, fainting, suffering . . .) and the great artists
are not always without them. The characteristic of these arts lies,
rather, in the orientation of these means: the violence of Shakespeare is in the service of Prospero, that of Grünewald or Dostoevsky in the service of Christ.

For every true art puts its means, even the most brutal of them,
in the service of a part of man obscurely or vehemently chosen.
There is no more blood in the most violent gangster novel than in
the *Oresteia* or *Oedipus Rex:* but blood does not have the same
significance in both. "Life is a tale told by an idiot, full of sound
and fury, signifying nothing," says Macbeth; but, the witches, by
showing the orchestration of destiny behind all the noise of killing, make *Macbeth* mean something. Grünewald and Goya mean
something. Let us not confuse the pin-up photos with the nudes
of Greece and India, whose very different sensuality bound man
to the cosmos. There is no art without style, and every style implies that man has a meaning, is oriented by some supreme value
—proclaimed or secret—which was called art or painting, as still
happens in modern art. The appeasing media, on the contrary, no
longer bind man to values, but to sensations; he struggles against
nothingness through a succession of moments, whereas every art
and every civilization have bound man to duration if not to
eternity.

That is why it is necessary to distinguish, in every artistic field,
the art itself from its means of achievement and from its power
of diffusion. It is useless to ask whether the means of expression
of the cinema permit it to become an art: for a long time these
means have been superior to those of the theater. But the convincing force with which the cinema incarnates fiction, the
breadth of its audience, do not alter the fact that it can, like the

novel, either meet or conquer the masses, not be passive before them. The novel is born by a process of refinement from the popular tale, but it has become the privileged expression of the tragic and of human experience: *Crime and Punishment* is not an excellent detective story, it is an excellent novel whose plot deals with crime. The novel and cinema for the masses require a single talent, that for narration which assures the effect of the novelist upon his reader, just as sentimental sensuality assures that of dance music, and just as the talent for representation—in the service of a changeable convention—assures that of painting. No genius can make a great work out of a catering fiction: Victor Hugo did not succeed in transforming his conventional *Misérables* into a mythology. Writing can be a decoration stuck on a wall, but art is the digging below the surface: it will not stick on the wall.

The "appeasing arts" are, then, in no sense inferior arts; they act in an opposite direction from the arts; they are, so to speak, anti-arts. And they show us at what point the grip of determinisms, conditionings, and sociologies, so powerful over artistic means, is distinct from the grip which they aim to exercise over the very nature of art. Our civilization—although it often sees in its own art only a superior, sharpened and refined taste—selects among all the forms of the past those in which the artist transmits now his divine side and now his demoniacal side. It matters little to our amateurs that they do not know the gods of the caves, or that the idea of art was unknown to the Magdalenians. You try in vain to work up any passion in them for the lesser Dutch who were not Vermeer. They feel that in Greece and in the Renaissance men were in agreement with the gods, and were not reduced to self-gratification. They affirm that the art of pathos found in the Master of the *Pietà* of Villeneuve and the specialized art of Braque, different as they are, have the same enemy. The arts of the religions in which we do not believe act on us more powerfully than the profane arts, or those of religions that have been reduced to custom. For China there are the Shang [early B.C.] vases, the Wei [386–534] sculpture, Sung [960–1279] painting; for India the Brahmanism and Buddhism of the high periods; the greatness of Greece dies with Phidias. We suspect why our furiously profane art resurrects so many religious arts, and we begin to see an order among these apparently confused resurrections;

they welcome whatever is opposed to appeasement, or what gives
us the illusion of it—and they reject everything that serves it.

On different levels, the naive, the insane, children, primitives, bar-
barians and savages are one with the sculptors of the high periods
in that they seem to neglect the spectator. The arts of the coherent civilizations of the past had the sound of a monologue—
sometimes an imperious monologue—because every dialogue with
the spectator was subordinated to the dialogue which they carried on with their gods or with the part of man they had focused
upon. We cannot be mistaken about it. If we hardly know the
feelings of the Egyptian sculptors of the Old Empire, we do
sense that they were not the feelings that moved Greuze [senti-
mental portrait and genre painter, 1725–1805]. As soon as the art
of mere appeasement is born, we begin to be repelled. Hence our
admiration for the great baroque creators, from Michelangelo to
El Greco, and our disdain for the established baroque; our admiration for certain paintings of Rubens, our irritation before others.
Hence our equivocal relationship with Raphael and our indifference toward his disciples. Stendhal admired Leonardo as the
master of the Lombard school, but we admire in Leonardo the
pictorial intelligence that separates *Mona Lisa* from all the
Herodiads [paintings of Salomé and her mother Herodias with
the decapitated head of John the Baptist]. The school of Bologna
has sunk in our judgment. In the great English portrait painters
a concern with rank makes their portraits seem emptier than their
landscapes—even to themselves, occasionally. We respond to the
second-rate primitives, but not to the mediocre art of the eighteenth century. The reason is that this art is made to order not
only because the painter is paid: it caters to the sentimentality
or the licentiousness of the patron, and to his alone. Boucher
[1703–1770] is neither Titian nor Rubens; Greuze knew so well
what he was doing that certain sketches of his resemble the paintings of Fragonard, not his own. With Fragonard [1732–1806],
with Chardin [1699–1779], art passes into the service of painting
itself, and everything changes. But had not painters been held in
greater submission by the Church? We accept, however, only
those who believed sincerely that the Church united them to
God: the Gothic and not the Jesuit painters. Suger chose the
foreground figures of St. Denis; the sculptors thought he chose
them well—and they were right. To pray in common is not the

common pleasure of going to mass on Sunday; like the art of Boucher and his pupils, every ambitious art of appeasement lives on complicity, not on communion.

Despite our desire to annex everything, the world in which Christ was the perfect man, the world of Nicholas of Cusa [German bishop and philosopher, c.1400–1464] and Raphael, becomes more and more strange to us. But its art was a great conquest, the last of a Christian world as it was the first of a new world. Beginning with the seventeenth century, the art of appeasement will take over all the positions that Christianity abandons, until it proclaims its final triumph in the spicy engraving, the sentimental declamation and the pious painting. Appeasement is very different from the feeling on which civilizations base their relation with the cosmos and with death: men gratify their tastes, but are *dedicated* to values. . . . Their true values are those for which they would accept poverty, derision, and death. That is why in the eighteenth century justice and reason are real values, but not sentimentality and licentiousness. That is why painting, as conceived by the modern painters, is a real value. And whatever is born of the desire for gratification—like sentimentality and [third century B.C.] Alexandrian sensuality, like everything that rejects at once our art and our living culture—*is born of the death of values* and does not replace them.

(*Translated from the French by William Barrett.*)

There are few more accessible approaches to the thought of the Spanish philosopher José Ortega y Gasset (1883–1955) than his little book on The Dehumanization of Art, *from which the following pages come. There are also few more lucid meditations on the meaning of the abstract textures of the modern arts. Reality, Ortega shows, has become something quite special for the painter—and all others who follow his example, in words or movements or sounds. There has been a great flight from vicariousness in the modern arts. The mere reproduction of the world around him no longer absorbs the serious artist. He is also, Ortega suggests, less than awed by the work of art itself. He has renounced pretentiousness. He snaps his fingers at his own procedures with the carefree manner of the young. These few pages assert all this and more, and remarkably enough, when one considers that they were first published in 1925, they do so with a confidence that the subsequent history of the arts more than justifies.*

THE DEHUMANIZATION OF ART

José Ortega y Gasset

With amazing swiftness modern art has split up into a multitude of divergent directions. Nothing is easier than to stress the differences. But such an emphasis on the distinguishing and specific features would be pointless without a previous account of the common fund that in a varying and sometimes contradictory manner asserts itself throughout modern art. Did not Aristotle already observe that things differ in what they have in common? Because all bodies are colored we notice that they are differently colored. Species are nothing if not modifications of a genus, and we cannot understand them unless we realize that they draw, in their several ways, upon a common patrimony.

I am little interested in special directions of modern art and, but for a few exceptions, even less in special works. Nor do I, for that matter, expect anybody to be particularly interested in my valuation of the new artistic produce. Writers who have nothing to convey but their praise or dispraise of works of art had better abstain from writing. They are unfit for this arduous task.

The important thing is that there unquestionably exists in the world a new artistic sensibility.[1] Over against the multiplicity of special directions and individual works, the new sensibility represents the generic fact and the source, as it were, from which the former spring. This sensibility it is worth while to define. And when we seek to ascertain the most general and most characteristic feature of modern artistic production we come upon the tendency to dehumanize art. After what we have said above, this formula now acquires a tolerably precise meaning.

Let us compare a painting in the new [abstract] style with one of, say, 1860. The simplest procedure will be to begin by setting against one another the objects they represent: a man perhaps, a house, or a mountain. It then appears that the artist of 1860 wanted nothing so much as to give to the objects in his picture the same looks and airs they possess outside it when they occur as parts of the "lived" or "human" reality. Apart from this he may have been animated by other more intricate aesthetic ambitions, but what interests us is that his first concern was with securing this likeness. Man, house, mountain are at once recognized, they are our good old friends; whereas on a modern painting we are at a loss to recognize them. It might be supposed that the modern painter has failed to achieve resemblance. But then some pictures of the 1860's are "poorly" painted, too, and the objects in them differ considerably from the corresponding objects outside them. And yet, whatever the differences, the very blunders of the traditional artist point toward the "human" object; they are downfalls on the way toward it and somehow equivalent to the orienting words "This is a cock" with which Cervantes lets the painter Orbanejo enlighten his public [in fact, not enlightening his public at all; the incident in *Don Quixote* is of a bungling painter who needs a title to identify his shoddy work]. In modern paintings the opposite happens. It is not that

---

[1] This new sensibility is a gift not only of the artist proper but also of his audience. When I said above that the new art is an art for artists I understood by "artists" not only those who produce this art but also those who are capable of perceiving purely artistic values.

the painter is bungling and fails to render the natural (natural = human) thing because he deviates from it, but that these deviations point in a direction opposite to that which would lead to reality.

Far from going more or less clumsily toward reality, the artist is seen going against it. He is brazenly set on deforming reality, shattering its human aspect, dehumanizing it. With the things represented on traditional paintings we could have imaginary intercourse. Many a young Englishman has fallen in love with Gioconda. With the objects of modern pictures no intercourse is possible. By divesting them of their aspect of "lived" reality the artist has blown up the bridges and burned the ships that could have taken us back to our daily world. He leaves us locked up in an abstruse universe, surrounded by objects with which human dealings are inconceivable, and thus compels us to improvise other forms of intercourse completely distinct from our ordinary ways with things. We must invent unheard-of-gestures to fit those singular figures. This new way of life which presupposes the annulment of spontaneous life is precisely what we call understanding and enjoyment of art. Not that this life lacks sentiments and passions, but those sentiments and passions evidently belong to a flora other than that which covers the hills and dales of primary and human life. What those ultra-objects[2] evoke in our inner artist are secondary passions, specifically aesthetic sentiments.

It may be said that, to achieve this result, it would be simpler to dismiss human forms—man, house, mountain—altogether and to construct entirely original figures. But, in the first place, this is not feasible.[3] Even in the most abstract ornamental line a stubborn reminiscence lurks of certain "natural" forms. Secondly—and this is the crucial point—the art of which we speak is inhuman not only because it contains no things human, but also because it is an explicit act of dehumanization. In his escape from the human world the young artist cares less for the "*terminus ad quem* [the purpose or goal of an argument]," the startling fauna at which he arrives, than for the "*terminus a quo* [the starting-point of an argument]," the human aspect which he destroys. The question

2 "Ultraism" is one of the most appropriate names that have been coined to denote the new sensibility.
3 An attempt has been made in this extreme sense—in certain works by Picasso—but it has failed signally.

is not to paint something altogether different from a man, a house, a mountain, but to paint a man who resembles a man as little as possible; a house that preserves of a house exactly what is needed to reveal the metamorphosis; a cone miraculously emerging—as the snake from his slough—from what used to be a mountain. For the modern artist, aesthetic pleasure derives from such a triumph over human matter. That is why he has to drive home the victory by presenting in each case the strangled victim.

It may be thought a simple affair to fight shy of reality, but it is by no means easy. There is no difficulty in painting or saying things which make no sense whatever, which are unintelligible and therefore nothing. One only needs to assemble unconnected words or to draw random lines.[4] But to construct something that is not a copy of "nature" and yet possesses substance of its own is a feat which presupposes nothing less than genius.

"Reality" constantly waylays the artist to prevent his flight. Much cunning is needed to effect the sublime escape. A reversed Odysseus, he must free himself from his daily Penelope and sail through reefs and rocks to Circe's Faery. When, for a moment, he succeeds in escaping the perpetual ambush, let us not grudge him a gesture of arrogant triumph, a St. George gesture with the dragon prostrate at his feet.

ART A THING
OF NO CONSEQUENCE

To the young generation art is a thing of no consequence.—The sentence is no sooner written than it frightens me since I am well aware of all the different connotations it implies. It is not that to any random person of our day art seems less important than it seemed to previous generations, but that the artist himself regards his art as a thing of no consequence. But then again this does not accurately describe the situation. I do not mean to say that the artist makes light of his work and his profession; but they interest him precisely because they are of no transcendent importance. For a real understanding of what is happening let us compare

[4] This was done by the Dadaistic hoax. It is interesting to note again (see the above footnote) that the very vagaries and abortive experiments of the new art derive with a certain cogency from its organic principle, thereby giving ample proof that modern art is a unified and meaningful movement.

Woman.
Photograph by Ryszard Horowitz.

Snake in Interior
Photograph by André Kertész

the role art is playing today with the role it used to play thirty years ago and in general throughout the last century. Poetry and music then were activities of an enormous caliber. In view of the downfall of religion and the inevitable relativism of science, art was expected to take upon itself nothing less than the salvation of mankind. Art was important for two reasons: on account of its subjects which dealt with the profoundest problems of humanity, and on account of its own significance as a human pursuit from which the species derived its justification and dignity. It was a remarkable sight, the solemn air with which the great poet or the musical genius appeared before the masses—the air of a prophet and founder of religion, the majestic pose of a statesman responsible for the state of the world.

A present-day artist would be thunderstruck, I suspect, if he were trusted with so enormous a mission and, in consequence, compelled to deal in his work with matters of such scope. To his mind, the kingdom of art commences where the air feels lighter and things, free from formal fetters, begin to cut whimsical capers. In this universal pirouetting he recognizes the best warrant for the existence of the Muses. Were art to redeem man, it could do so only by saving him from the seriousness of life and restoring him to an unexpected boyishness. The symbol of art is seen again in the magic flute of the Great God Pan which makes the young goats frisk at the edge of the grove.

All modern art begins to appear comprehensible and in a way great when it is interpreted as an attempt to instill youthfulness into an ancient world. Other styles must be interpreted in connection with dramatic social or political movements, or with profound religious and philosophical currents. The new style only asks to be linked to the triumph of sports and games. It is of the same kind and origin with them.

In these last few years we have seen almost all caravels of seriousness founder in the tidal wave of sports that floods the newspaper pages. Editorials threaten to be sucked into the abyss of their headlines, and across the surface victoriously sail the yachts of the regattas. Cult of the body is an infallible symptom of a leaning toward youth, for only the young body is lithe and beautiful. Whereas cult of the mind betrays the resolve to accept old age, for the mind reaches plenitude only when the body begins to decline. The triumph of sport marks the victory of the values of youth over the values of age. Note in this context the success of the motion picture, a preeminently corporeal art.

In my generation the manners of old age still enjoyed great prestige. So anxious were boys to cease being boys that they imitated the stoop of their elders. Today children want to prolong their childhood, and boys and girls their youth. No doubt, Europe is entering upon an era of youthfulness.

Nor need this fact surprise us. History moves in long biological rhythms whose chief phases necessarily are brought about not by secondary causes relating to details but by fundamental factors and primary forces of a cosmic nature. It is inconceivable that the major and, as it were, polar differences inherent in the living organism—sex and age—should not decisively mold the profile of the times. Indeed, it can be easily observed that history is rhythmically swinging back and forth between these two poles, stressing the masculine qualities in some epochs and the feminine in others, or exalting now a youthful deportment and then again maturity and old age.

The aspect European existence is taking on in all orders of life points to a time of masculinity and youthfulness. For a while women and old people will have to cede the rule over life to boys; no wonder that the world grows increasingly informal.

All peculiarities of modern art can be summed up in this one feature of its renouncing its importance—a feature which, in its turn, signifies nothing less than that art has changed its position in the hierarchy of human activities and interests. These activities and interests may be represented by a series of concentric circles whose radii measure the dynamic distances from the axis of life where the supreme desires are operating. All human matters— vital and cultural—revolve in their several orbits about the throbbing heart of the system. Art which—like science and politics— used to be very near the axis of enthusiasm, that backbone of our person, has moved toward the outer rings. It has lost none of its attributes, but it has become a minor issue.

The trend toward pure art betrays not arrogance, as is often thought, but modesty. Art that has rid itself of human pathos is a thing without consequence—just art with no other pretenses.

A SAD HEART AT THE SUPERMARKET

This essay's title suggests a contradiction that resides very deep within contemporary American society which is based largely on finance capitalism and is therefore necessarily concerned with commercial values. The implied contradiction between the "sad heart" in the midst of a variety of quasi-necessary "things" can strike the artist—in this instance a poet—as disturbingly sterile. Precisely this notion of sterility is a major theme in the most influential long poem of the twentieth century, T. S. Eliot's, "The Waste Land." The poetic and academic communities of America were greatly saddened in 1965 when Jarrell, out for his customary evening stroll on a quiet street, in Greensboro, North Carolina, was struck and killed instantly by an automobile. Jarrell was a Southerner whose poems frequently dealt with the subject of war; his other works include Pictures from an Institution, *a satirical novel about a women's college, and two well-known essay volumes,* Poetry and the Age *and the collection which takes its title from the essay presented here.*

Randall Jarrell

The Emperor Augustus would sometimes say to his Senate: "Words fail me, my Lords; nothing I can say could possibly indicate the depth of my feelings in this matter." But I am speaking about this matter of mass culture, the mass media, not as an Emperor but as a fool, as a suffering, complaining, helplessly nonconforming poet-or-artist-of-a-sort, far off at the obsolescent rear of things: what I say will indicate the depth of my feelings and the shallowness and one-sidedness of my thoughts. If those English lyric poets who went mad during the eighteenth century had told you why the Age of Enlightenment was driving them crazy, it would have had a kind of documentary interest: what I say may have a kind of documentary interest.

The toad beneath the harrow knows
Exactly where each tooth-point goes;

if you tell me that the field is being harrowed to grow grain for
bread, and to create a world in which there will be no more
famines, or toads either, I will say, "I know"—but let me tell you
where the toothpoints go, and what the harrow looks like from
below.

Advertising men, businessmen, speak continually of "media"
or "the media" or "the mass media"—one of their trade journals
is named, simply, *Media*. It is an impressive word: one imagines
Mephistopheles offering Faust media that no man has ever
known; one feels, while the word is in one's ear, that abstract,
overmastering powers, of a scale and intensity unimagined yesterday, are being offered one by the technicians who discovered
and control them—offered, and at a price. The word, like others,
has the clear fatal ring of that new world whose space we occupy
so luxuriously and precariously; the world that produces mink
stoles, rockabilly records, and tactical nuclear weapons by the
million; the world that Attila, Galileo, Hansel and Gretel never
knew.

And yet, it's only the plural of "medium." "Medium," says the
dictionary, "that which lies in the middle; hence, middle condition or degree. . . . A substance through which a force acts or
an effect is transmitted. . . . That through or by which anything
is accomplished; as, an advertising *medium*. . . . *Biol*. A nutritive
mixture or substance, as broth, gelatin, agar, for cultivating bac-
teria, fungi, etc." Let us name *our* trade journal *The Medium*.
For all these media (television, radio, movies, popular magazines,
and the rest) are a single medium, in whose depths we are all
being cultivated. This medium is of middle condition or degree,
mediocre; it lies in the middle of everything, between a man and
his neighbor, his wife, his child, his self; it, more than anything
else, is the substance through which the forces of our society act
upon us, make us into what our society needs.

And what does it need? For us to need . . . Oh, it needs for us
to do or be many things—to be workers, technicians, executives,
soldiers, housewives. But first of all, last of all, it needs for us to
be buyers; consumers; beings who want much and will want
more—who want consistently and insatiably. Find some spell to
make us no longer want the stoles, the records, and the weapons,
and our world will change into something to us unimaginable.
Find some spell to make us realize that the product or service
which seemed yesterday an unthinkable luxury is today an in-

exorable necessity, and our world will go on. It is the Medium
which casts this spell—which is this spell. As we look at the
television set, listen to the radio, read the magazines, the frontier
of necessity is always being pushed forward. The Medium shows
us what our new needs are—how often, without it, we should
not have known!—and it shows us how they can be satisfied: they
can be satisfied by buying something. The act of buying something is at the root of our world: if anyone wishes to paint the
beginning of things in our society, he will paint a picture of God
holding out to Adam a checkbook or credit card or Charge-
A-Plate.

But how quickly our poor naked Adam is turned into a consumer, is linked to others by the great chain of buying!

> No outcast he, bewildered and depressed:
> Along his infant veins are interfused
> The gravitation and the filial bond
> Of nature that connect him with the world.

Children of three or four can ask for a brand of cereal, sing some
soap's commercial; by the time that they are twelve they are not
children but teen-age consumers, interviewed, graphed, analyzed.
They are on their way to becoming that ideal figure of our culture,
the knowledgeable consumer. I'll define him: the knowledgeable
consumer is someone who, when he goes to Weimar, knows how
to buy a Weimaraner. He has learned to understand life as a series
of choices among the things and services of this world; because of
being an executive, or executive's wife, or performer, or celebrity, or someone who has inherited money, he is able to afford
the choices that he makes, with knowing familiarity, among
restaurants, resorts, clothes, cars, liners, hits or best-sellers of
every kind. We may still go to Methodist or Baptist or Pres-
byterian churches on Sunday, but the Protestant ethic of frugal
industry, of production for its own sake, is gone. Production has
come to seem to our society not much more than a condition
prior to consumption: "The challenge of today," writes a great
advertising agency, "is to make the consumer raise his level of
demand." This challenge has been met: the Medium has found it
easy to make its people feel the continually increasing lacks, the
many specialized dissatisfactions (merging into one great dissatisfaction, temporarily assuaged by new purchases) that it

needs for them to feel. When, in some magazine, we see the
Medium at its most nearly perfect, we hardly know which half is
entertaining and distracting us, which half making us buy: some
advertisement may be more ingeniously entertaining than the
text beside it, but it is the text which has made us long for a
product more passionately. When one finishes *Holiday* or *Harper's Bazaar* or *House and Garden* or *The New Yorker* or *High
Fidelity* or *Road and Track* or—but make your own list—buying something, going somewhere seems a necessary completion
to the act of reading the magazine. Reader, isn't buying or
fantasy-buying an important part of your and my emotional life?
(If you reply, *No,* I'll think of you with bitter envy as more
than merely human; as deeply un-American.) It is a standard
joke of our culture that when a woman is bored or sad she buys
something to make herself feel better; but in this respect we are
all women together, and can hear complacently the reminder of
how feminine this consumer-world of ours is. One imagines as a
characteristic dialogue of our time an interview in which someone is asking of a vague gracious figure, a kind of Mrs. America:
"But while you waited for the Intercontinental Ballistic Missiles
what did you *do?*" She answers: "I bought things."

She reminds one of the sentinel at Pompeii—a space among
ashes, now, but at his post: she too did what she was supposed to
do. . . . Our society has delivered us—most of us—from the bonds
of necessity, so that we no longer need worry about having food
enough to keep from starving, clothing and shelter enough to
keep from freezing; yet if the ends for which we work, of which
we dream, are restaurants and clothes and houses, consumption,
possessions, how have we escaped? We have merely exchanged
man's old bondage for a new voluntary one. But *voluntary* is
wrong: the consumer is trained for his job of consuming as the
factory worker is trained for his job of producing; and the first
is a longer, more complicated training, since it is easier to teach
a man to handle a tool, to read a dial, than it is to teach him to
ask, always, for a name-brand aspirin—to want, someday, a
stand-by generator. What is that? You don't know? I used not to
know, but the readers of *House Beautiful* all know, and now I
know: it is the electrical generator that stands in the basement
of the suburban houseowner, shining, silent, until at last one night
the lights go out, the freezer's food begins to—

Ah, but it's frozen for good, the lights are on forever; the
owner has switched on the stand-by generator.

But you don't see that he really needs the generator, you'd rather have seen him buy a second car? He has two. A second bathroom? He has four. He long ago doubled everything, when the People of the Medium doubled everything; and now that he's gone twice round he will have to wait three years, or four, till both are obsolescent—but while he waits there are so many new needs that he can satisfy, so many things a man can buy.

> Man wants but little here below
> Nor wants that little long,

said the poet; what a lie! Man wants almost unlimited quantities of almost everything, and he wants it till the day he dies.

We sometimes see in *Life* or *Look* a double-page photograph of some family standing on the lawn among its possessions: station wagon, swimming pool, power cruiser, sports car, tape recorder, television sets, radios, cameras, power lawn mower, garden tractor, lathe, barbecue set, sporting equipment, domestic appliances—all the gleaming, grotesquely imaginative paraphernalia of its existence. It was hard to get them on two pages, soon they will need four. It is like a dream, a child's dream before Christmas; yet if the members of the family doubt that they are awake, they have only to reach out and pinch something. The family seems pale and small, a negligible appendage, beside its possessions; only a human being would need to ask, "Which owns which?" We are fond of saying that something-or-other is not just something-or-other but "a way of life"; this too is a way of life—our way, the way.

Emerson, in his spare stony New England, a few miles from Walden, could write:

> Things are in the saddle
> And ride mankind.

He could say more now: that they are in the theater and studio, and entertain mankind; are in the pulpit and preach to mankind. The values of business, in an overwhelmingly successful business society like our own, are reflected in every sphere: values which agree with them are reinforced, values which disagree are cancelled out or have lip-service paid to them. In business what sells is good, and that's the end of it—that is what *good* means; if the world doesn't beat a path to your door, your mousetrap wasn't better. The values of the Medium (which is both a popular business itself and the cause of popularity in other businesses) are business values: money, success, celebrity. If we are representative members of our society, the Medium's values are ours; even when we are unrepresentative, nonconforming, our hands are (too often) subdued to the element they work in, and our unconscious expectations are all that we consciously reject. (Darwin said that he always immediately wrote down evidence against a theory because otherwise, he'd noticed, he would forget it; in the same way we keep forgetting the existence of those poor and unknown failures whom we might rebelliously love and admire.) *If you're so smart why aren't you rich?* is the ground-base of our society, a grumbling and quite unanswerable criticism, since the society's nonmonetary values *are* directly convertible into money. (Celebrity turns into testimonials, lectures, directorships, presidencies, the capital gains of an autobiography *Told To* some professional ghost who photographs the man's life as Bachrach photographs his body.) When Liberace said that his critics' unfavorable reviews hurt him so much that he cried all the way to the bank, one had to admire the correctness and penetration of his press-agent's wit: in another age, what mightn't such a man have become!

Our culture is essentially periodical: we believe that all that is deserves to perish and to have something else put in its place. We speak of "planned obsolescence," but it is more than planned, it is felt—is an assumption about the nature of the world. The present is better and more interesting, more real, than the past; the future will be better and more interesting, more real, than the present. (But, consciously, we do not hold against the present its prospective obsolescence.) Our standards have become, to an astonishing degree, those of what is called "the world of fashion," where mere timeliness—being orange in orange's year, violet in violet's —is the value to which all other values are reducible. In our society "old-fashioned" is so final a condemnation that a man like Norman Vincent Peale can say about atheism or agnosticism simply that it is old-fashioned; the homely recommendation of "Give me that good old-time religion" has become after a few decades the conclusive rejection of "old-fashioned" atheism.

All this is, at bottom, the opposite of the world of the arts, where commercial and scientific progress do not exist; where the bone of Homer and Mozart and Donatello is there, always, under the mere blush of fashion; where the past—the remote past, even

—is responsible for the way that we understand, value, and act in, the present. (When one reads an abstract expressionist's remark that Washington studios are "eighteen months behind" those of his colleagues in New York, one realizes something of the terrible power of business and fashion over those most overtly hostile to them.) An artist's work and life presuppose continuing standards, values stretched out over centuries or millennia, a future that is the continuation and modification of the past, not its contradiction or irrelevant replacement. He is working for the time that wants the best that he can do: the present, he hopes—but if not that, the future. If he sees that fewer and fewer people are any real audience for the serious artists of the past, he will feel that still fewer are going to be an audience for the serious artists of the present, for those who, willingly or unwillingly, sacrifice extrinsic values to intrinsic ones, immediate effectiveness to that steady attraction which, the artist hopes, true excellence will always exert. The past's relation to the artist or man of culture is almost the opposite of its relation to the rest of our society. To him the present is no more than the last ring on the trunk, understandable and valuable only in terms of all the earlier rings. The rest of our society sees only that great last ring, the enveloping surface of the trunk; what's underneath is a disregarded, almost hypothetical foundation. When Northrop Frye writes that "the preoccupation of the humanities with the past is sometimes made a reproach against them by those who forget that we face the past: it may be shadowy, but it is all that is there," he is saying what for the artist or man of culture is self-evidently true; yet for the Medium and the People of the Medium it is as self-evidently false—for them the present (or a past so recent, so quick-changing, so soon-disappearing, that it might be called the specious present) is all that is there.

In the past our culture's frame of reference, its body of common knowledge (its possibility of comprehensible allusion) changed slowly and superficially; the amount added to it or taken away from it in any ten years was a small proportion of the whole. Now in any ten years a surprisingly large proportion of the whole is replaced. Most of the information people have in common is something that four or five years from now they will not even remember having known. A newspaper story remarks in astonishment that television quiz programs have "proved that ordinary citizens can be conversant with such esoterica as jazz, opera, the Bible, Shakespeare, poetry and fisticuffs." You may exclaim, "Esoterica! If the Bible and Shakespeare are esoterica, what is there that's common knowledge?" The answer, I suppose, is that Elfrida von Nardoff and Teddy Nadler [two of television's big-money winners] (the ordinary citizens on the quiz programs) are common knowledge; though not for long. Songs disappear in two or three months, celebrities in two or three years; most of the Medium is lightly felt and soon forgotten. What is as dead as day-before-yesterday's newspaper, the next-to-the-last number on the roulette wheel? and most of the knowledge we have in common is knowledge of such newspapers, such numbers. But the novelist or poet or dramatist, when he moves a great audience, depends upon the deep feelings, the live unforgotten knowledge, that the people of his culture share; if these have become contingent, superficial, ephemeral, it is disastrous for him.

New products and fashions replace the old, and the fact that they replace them is proof enough of their superiority. Similarly, the Medium does not need to show that the subjects that fill it are timely or interesting or important—the fact that they are its subjects makes them so. If *Time, Life,* and the television shows are full of Tom Fool this month, he's no fool. And when he has been gone from them a while, we do not think him a fool—we do not think of him at all. He no longer exists, in the fullest sense of the word "exist": to be is to be perceived, to be a part of the Medium of our perception. Our celebrities are not kings, romantic in exile, but Representatives who, defeated, are forgotten; they had always only the qualities that we delegated to them.

After driving for four or five minutes along the road outside my door, I come to a long row of one-room shacks about the size of kitchens, made out of used boards, metal signs, old tin roofs. To the people who live in them an electric dishwasher of one's own is as much a fantasy as an ocean liner of one's own. But since the Medium (and those whose thought is molded by it) does not perceive them, these people are themselves a fantasy: no matter how many millions of such exceptions to the general rule there are, they do not really exist, but have a kind of anomalous, statistical subsistence; our moral and imaginative view of the world is no more affected by them than by the occupants of some home for the mentally deficient a little farther along the road. If, some night, one of these outmoded, economically deficient ghosts should scratch at my window, I could say only,

"Come back twenty years ago." And if I, as an old-fashioned, one-room poet, a friend of "quiet culture," a "meek lover of the good," should go out some night to scratch at another window, shouldn't I hear someone's indifferent or regretful, "Come back a century or two ago?"

When those whose existence the Medium recognizes ring the chimes of the winter's doorbell, fall through his letter slot, float out onto his television screen, what is he to say to them? A man's unsuccessful struggle to get his family food is material for a work of art—for tragedy, almost; his unsuccessful struggle to get his family a stand-by generator is material for what? Comedy? Farce? Comedy on such a scale, at such a level, that our society and its standards seem, almost, farce? And yet it is the People of the Medium, those who long for and get, or long for and don't get, the generator, whom our culture find representative, who are there to be treated first of all. And the Medium itself— one of the ends of life, something essential to people's under- standing and valuing of their existence, something many of their waking hours are spent listening to or looking at—how is *it* to be treated as subject matter for art? The writer cannot just repro- duce it; should he satirize or parody it? But often parody or satire is impossible, since it is already its own parody; and by the time the writer's work is published, the part of the Medium which is satirized will already have been forgotten. Yet isn't the Medium by now an essential part of its watchers? Those whom Mohammedans speak of as the People of the Book are inex- plicable, surely, in any terms that omit it; we are people of the magazine, the television set, the radio, and are inexplicable in any terms that omit them.

Oscar Wilde's wittily paradoxical statement about Nature's imitation of Art is literally true when the Nature is human nature and the Art that of television, radio, motion pictures, popular magazines. Life is so, people are so, the Medium shows its audi- ence, and most of the audience believe it, expect people to be so, try to be so themselves. For them the People of the Medium are reality, what human beings normally, primarily are: and mere local or personal variations are not real in the same sense. The Medium mediates between us and raw reality, and the media- tion more and more replaces reality for us. In many homes either the television set or the radio is turned on most of the time the family is awake. (Many radio stations have a news broadcast every half hour, and many people like and need to hear it.) It is as if the people longed to be established in reality, to be reminded continually of the "real," the "objective" world—the created world of the Medium—rather than be left at the mercy of actuality, of the helpless contingency of the world in which the radio receiver or television set is sitting. (And surely we can sympathize: which of us hasn't found a similar refuge in the "real," created world of Cézanne or Goethe or Verdi? Yet Dostoievsky's world is too different from Wordsworth's, Piero della Francesca's from Goya's, Bach's from Hugo Wolf's, for us to be able to substitute one homogeneous mediated reality for everyday reality in the belief that it *is* everyday reality.) The world of events and celebrities and performers, the Great World, has become for many listeners, lookers, readers, the world of primary reality: how many times they have sighed at the colorless unreality of their own lives and families, sighed for the bright reality of, say, Lucille Ball's—of some shadow dyed, gowned, directed, produced, and agented into a being as equivocal as that of the square root of minus one. The watchers call the celebrities by their first names, approve or disapprove of "who they're dating," handle them with a mixture of love, identification, envy, and contempt—for the Medium has given its people so terrible a familiarity with everyone that it takes great magnanimity of spirit not to be affected by it. These celebrities are not heroes to us, their valets.

Better to have these real ones play themselves, and not sacrifice too much of their reality to art; better to have the watcher play himself, and not lost too much of himself in art. Usually the watcher is halfway between two worlds, paying full attention to neither: half distracted from, half distracted by, this distraction —and able for the moment not to be affected too greatly, have too great demands made upon him, by either world. For in the Medium, which we escape to from work, nothing is ever *work*, nothing ever makes intellectual or emotional or imaginative demands which we might find it difficult to satisfy. Here in the half-world everything is homogeneous—is, as much as possible, the same as everything else: each familiar novelty, novel familiarity, has the same texture on top and the same attitude and conclusion at bottom; only the middle, the particular subject of the particular program or article, is different. (If it *is* different: everyone is given the same automatic "human interest" treatment, so that it is hard for us to remember, unnecessary for us to remember, which particular celebrity we're reading about this time—often it's the same one, we've just moved to a different magazine.) Heine said that the English had a hundred religions and one sauce; so do we; and we are so accustomed to this sauce or dye or style, the aesthetic equivalent of Standard Brands, that a very simple thing can seem perverse, obscure, without it. And, too, we find it hard to have to shift from one art form to another, to vary our attitudes and expectations, to use our unexercised imaginations. Poetry disappeared long ago, even for most intellectuals; each year fiction is a little less important. Our age is an age of nonfiction; of gossip columns, interviews, photographic essays, documentaries; of articles, condensed or book length, spoken or written; of real facts about real people. Art lies to us to tell us the (sometimes disquieting) truth; the Medium tells us truths, facts, in order to make us believe some reassuring or entertaining lie or half truth. These actually existing celebrities, of universally admitted importance, about whom we are told directly authoritative facts—how can fictional characters compete with them? These *are* our fictional characters, our Lears and Clytemnestras. (This is ironically appropriate, since many of their doings and sayings are fictional, made up by public relations officers, columnists, agents, or other affable familiar ghosts.) And the Medium gives us such facts, such photographs, such tape recordings, such clinical reports not only about the great, but also about (representative samples of) the small; when we have been shown so much about so many—*can* be shown, we feel, anything about anybody—does fiction seem so essential as it once seemed? Shakespeare or Tolstoy can show us all about someone, but so can *Life;* and when *Life* does, it's someone real.

The Medium is half life and half art, and competes with both life and art. It spoils its audience for both; spoils both for its audience. For the People of the Medium life isn't sufficiently a matter of success and glamor and celebrity, isn't entertaining enough, distracting enough, *mediated* enough; and art is too difficult or individual or novel, too restrained or indirect, too much a matter of tradition and the past, of special attitudes and aptitudes: its mediation sometimes is queer or excessive, and sometimes is not even recognizable as mediation. The Medium's mixture of rhetoric and reality, which gives people what we know they want in the form we know they like, is something more efficient and irresistible, more habit-forming, than any art. If a man all his life has been fed a sort of combination of marzipan and ethyl

alcohol—if eating, to him, is a matter of being knocked unconscious by an ice cream soda—can he, by taking thought, come to
prefer a diet of bread and wine, apples and well-water? Will a
man who has spent his life watching gladiatorial games come to
prefer listening to chamber music? And those who produce the
bread and wine and quartets for him—won't they be tempted
either to give up producing them, or else to produce a bread
that's half sugar, half alcohol, a quartet that ends with the cellist
at the violist's bleeding throat?

The Medium represents to the artist all that he has learned not
to do: its sure-fire stereotypes seem to him what any true art,
true spirit, has had to struggle past on its way to the truth. The
artist sees the values and textures of this art substitute replacing
those of his art with most of society, conditioning the expectations of what audience he has kept. Any outsider who has
worked for the Medium will have noticed that the one thing
which seems to its managers most unnatural is for someone to do
something naturally, to speak or write as an individual speaking or
writing to other individuals, and not as a subcontractor supplying
a standardized product to the Medium. It is as if producers, editors, supervisors were particles forming a screen between maker
and public, one that will let through only particles of their own
size and weight (or, as they say, the public's); as you look into
their bland faces, their big horn-rimmed eyes, you despair of
Creation itself, which seems for the instant made in their own
owl-eyed image. There are so many extrinsic considerations
about everything in the work, the maker finds, that by the time
it is finished all intrinsic considerations have come to seem
secondary. It is no wonder that the professional who writes the
ordinary commercial success, the ordinary script, scenario, or
article, resembles imaginative writers less than he resembles
advertising agents, columnists, editors, and producers. He is a
technician who can supply a standard product, a rhetorician who
can furnish a regular stimulus for a regular response, what has
always made the dog salivate in this situation. He is the opposite
of the imaginative artist: instead of stubbornly or helplessly stick-
ing to what he sees and feels, to what seems right for him, true to
reality, regardless of what the others think and want, he gives the
others what they think and want, regardless of what he himself
sees and feels.

Mass culture either corrupts or isolates the writer. His old feeling of oneness, of speaking naturally to an audience with essentially similar standards, is gone; and writers do not any longer have much of the consolatory feeling that took its place, the feeling of writing for the happy few, the kindred spirits whose standards are those of the future. (Today they feel: the future, should there be one, will be worse.) True works of art are more and more produced away from, in opposition to, society. And yet the artist needs society as much as society needs him: as our cultural enclaves get smaller and drier, more hysterical or academic, one mourns for the artists inside them and the public outside. An incomparable historian of mass culture, Ernest van den Haag, has expressed this with laconic force: "The artist who, by refusing to work for the mass market, becomes marginal, cannot create what he might have created had there been no mass market. One may prefer a monologue to addressing a mass meeting. But it is still not a conversation."

Even if the rebellious artist's rebellion is whole-hearted, it can never be whole-stomached, whole-Unconscious'd. Part of him wants to be like his kind, is like his kind; longs to be loved and admired and successful. Our society (and the artist, in so far as he is truly a part of it) has no place set aside for the different and poor and obscure, the fools for Christ's sake: they all go willy-nilly into Limbo. The artist is tempted, consciously, to give his society what it wants, or if he won't or can't, to give it nothing at all; is tempted, unconsciously, to give it superficially independent or contradictory works which are at heart works of the Medium. (Tennessee Williams' *Sweet Bird of Youth* is far less like Chekhov than it is like Mickey Spillane.) It is hard to go on serving both God and Mammon when God is so really ill-, Mammon so really well-organized. Shakespeare wrote for the Medium of his day; if Shakespeare were alive now he'd be writing *My Fair Lady;* isn't *My Fair Lady*, then, our *Hamlet?* shouldn't you be writing *Hamlet* instead of sitting there worrying about your superego? I need my *Hamlet!* So society speaks to the artist; but after he has written it its *Hamlet*, it tries to make sure that he will never do it again. There are more urgent needs that it wants him to satisfy: to lecture to it; to make public appearances, to be interviewed; to be on television shows; to give testimonials; to make trips abroad for the State Department; to judge books for contests or Book Clubs; to read for publishers, judge for publishers, be a publisher for publishers; to be an editor; to teach writing at colleges or writers' conferences; to write scenarios or scripts or articles, articles about his home town for *Holiday,* about cats or clothes or Christmas for *Vogue,* about "How I wrote *Hamlet* " for anything; to . . .

But why go on? I once heard a composer, lecturing, say to a poet, lecturing: "They'll pay us to do *anything,* so long as it isn't writing music or writing poems." I knew the reply that, as a member of my society, I should have made: "So long as they pay you, what do you care?" But I didn't make it—it was plain that they cared. . . . But how many more learn not to care, love what they once endured! It is a whole so comprehensive that any alternative seems impossible, any opposition irrelevant; in the end a man says in a small voice, "I accept the Medium." The Enemy of the People winds up as the People—but where there is no Enemy, the people perish.

The climate of our culture is changing. Under these new rains, new suns, small things grow great, and what was great grows small; whole species disappear and are replaced. The American present is very different from the American past: so different that our awareness of the extent of the changes has been repressed, and we regard as ordinary what is extraordinary (ominous perhaps) both for us and the rest of the world. For the American present is many other peoples' future: our cultural and economic example, is, to much of the world, mesmeric, and it is only its weakness and poverty that prevent it from hurrying with us into the Roman future. Yet at this moment of our greatest power and success, our thought and art are full of troubled gloom, of the conviction of our own decline. When the President of Yale University writes that "the ideal of the good life has faded from the educational process, leaving only miscellaneous prospects of jobs and joyless hedonism," are we likely to find it unfaded among our entertainers and executives? Is the influence of what I have called the Medium likely to make us lead any good life? to make us love and try to attain any real excellence, beauty, magnanimity? or to make us understand these as obligatory but transparent rationalizations, behind which the realities of money and power are waiting?

Matthew Arnold once spoke about our green culture in terms that have an altered relevance (but are not yet irrelevant) to our ripe one. He said: "What really dissatisfies in American civilization is the want of the *interesting,* a want due chiefly to the want

of those two great elements of the interesting, which are elevation and beauty." This use of *interesting* (and, perhaps, this tone
of a curator pointing out what is plain and culpable) shows how
far along in the decline of the West Arnold came; it is only in the
latter days that we ask to be interested. He had found the word in
Carlyle. Carlyle is writing to a friend to persuade him not to
emigrate to the United States; he asks, "Could you banish yourself from all that is interesting to your mind, forget the history,
the glorious institutions, the noble principles of old Scotland—
that you might eat a better dinner, perhaps?" We smile, and feel
like reminding Carlyle of the history, the glorious institutions, the
noble principles of new America, that New World which is,
after all, the heir of the Old. And yet . . . Can we smile as comfortably, today, as we could have smiled yesterday? listen as un-
concernedly, if one taking leave of us some tourist should say,
with the penetration and obtuseness of his kind:

I remember reading somewhere: that which you inherit from
your fathers you must earn in order to possess. I have been so
much impressed with your power and possessions that I have
neglected, perhaps, your principles. The elevation or beauty of
your spirit did not equal, always, that of your mountains and
skyscrapers: it seems to me that your society provides you with
"all that is interesting to your mind" only exceptionally, at odd
hours, in little reservations like those of your Indians. But as for
your dinners, I've never seen anything like them: your daily
bread comes *flambé*. And yet—wouldn't you say?—the more
dinners a man eats, the more comfort he possesses, the hungrier
and more uncomfortable some part of him becomes: inside every
fat man there is a man who is starving. Part of you is being
starved to death, and the rest of you is being stuffed to death. . . .
But this will change: no one goes on being stuffed to death or
starved to death forever.

This is a gloomy, an equivocal conclusion? Oh yes, I come
from an older culture, where things are accustomed to coming
to such conclusions; where there is no last-paragraph fairy to
bring one, always, a happy ending—or that happiest of all endings, no ending at all. And have I no advice to give you, as I go?
None. You are too successful to need advice, or to be able to
take it if it were offered; but if ever you should fail, it is there
waiting for you, the advice or consolation of all the other
failures.

At the present time it should be clear to every responsible observer that the popular arts are very much an integral part of the American scene; furthermore, in America, the acceptance or the rejection of these arts at either the level of production or consumption will not soon be a matter of enforceable legislation. It follows, therefore, that an understanding of the nature of the popular arts can be a valuable part of every student's education. It is appropriate that a professional philosopher—and Professor Kaplan is a specialist in the methodology for behavioral science at the University of Michigan—should suggest certain larger issues of the popular arts. First delivered as a paper before the American Philosophical Association in 1964, this essay has been especially edited for inclusion here. The essay is not so much a departure for Abraham Kaplan as it might seem to those who know him best as co-author of Power and Society *and writer of numerous pieces in that area. The pages devoted to art in his* New World of Philosophy *are, like this piece, sympathetic, informed, and clearly based on a wide experience of the arts.*

THE AESTHETICS OF THE POPULAR ARTS

Abraham Kaplan

Aesthetics is so largely occupied with the good in art that it has little to say about what is merely better or worse, and especially about what is worse. Unremitting talk about the good, however, is not only boring but usually inconsequential as well. The study of *dis*-values may have much to offer both aesthetics and criticism for the same reasons that the physiologist looks to disease and the priest becomes learned in sin. Artistic taste and understanding might better be served by a museum of horribilia, presented as such. It is from this standpoint that I invite attention to the aesthetics of the popular arts.

I

By the popular arts I do not mean what has recently come to be known as pop art. This, like junk art and some of the theater of the absurd, is the present generation's version of dada. In some measure, no doubt, it serves as a device for enlarging the range of artistic possibilities, exploring the beauty in what is conventionally dismissed as meaningless and ugly, as well as the ugliness in what is conventionally extolled as beautiful. Basically, it is a revolt against the artistic establishment, a reaction against the oppressiveness of the academic and familiar. As such, it is derivative as though to say, "You call *this* junk?" If it is lacking in artistic virtue, its vice is like that of watching a voyeur—the sins of another are presupposed. It is what pop art presupposes that I am calling *popular art*.

Second, I do not mean simply *bad art*, neither the downright failures nor those that fall just short of some set of critical requirements. It is a question of *how* they fail and, even more, to what sort of success they aspire. Popular art may be bad art, but the converse is not necessarily true. It is a particular species of the unaesthetic that I want to isolate.

Similarly, I set aside what may be deprecated as merely minor art. Its products are likely to be more popular, in the straightforward sense, than those which have greatness. The *Rubaiyat* may be more widely read than *De rerum natura*, and *The Hound of the Baskervilles* more than *Crime and Punishment*, but each is excellent after its own kind. A work of minor art is not necessarily a minor work. Greatness, that is to say, is a distinctive aesthetic attribute—a matter of scope or depth and so forth; the word is not just a designation for the highest degree of artistic value. The lack of greatness may be a necessary condition for popular art, but most surely it is not a sufficient condition.

The *kind* of taste that the popular arts satisfy, and not how widespread that taste is, is what distinguishes them. On this basis, I provisionally identify my subject as *midbrow art*, to be contrasted with what appeals to either highbrow or lowbrow tastes. Popular art is what is found neither in the literary reviews nor in the pulp magazines, but in the slicks; neither in gallery paintings nor on calendars, but on Christmas cards and billboards; neither

in serious music nor in jazz, but in Tin Pan Alley. The popular arts may very well appeal to a mass audience, but they have characteristics that distinguish them from other varieties of mass art, and distinctive contexts and patterns of presentation. A work of popular art may be a best seller, but it is not assigned in freshman English nor reprinted as a comic. It may win an Academy Award, but it will be shown neither at the local Art Cinema nor on the late, late show.

Many social scientists think that these symptoms—for they are no more than that—provide an etiology of the disease. Midbrow art, they say, is more properly designated *middle-class art*. It is a product of the characteristic features of modern society: capitalism, democracy, and technology. Capitalism has made art a commodity, and provided the means to satisfy the ever widening demands for the refinements of life that earlier periods reserved to a small elite. Democracy, with its apotheosis of majorities and of public opinion, has inevitably reduced the level of taste to that of the lowest common denominator. The technology of the mass media precludes the care and craftsmanship that alone can create works of art. For a time it was fashionable to lay these charges particularly at American doors, to view the popular arts as the distinctive feature of American culture; but by now, I think, most of those who take this line see popular art more generally, if not more generously, as only "the sickness of the age."

My thesis is this: that popular art is not the degradation of taste but its immaturity, not the product of external social forces but produced by a dynamic intrinsic to the aesthetic experience itself. Modern society, like all others, has its own style, and leaves its imprint on all it embraces. But this is only to say that our popular art is *ours*, not that it is our sole possession. Popular art is usually said to stem from about the beginning of the eighteenth century, but in its essence it is not, I think, a particularity of our time and place. It is as universal as art itself.

II

We might characterize popular art first, as is most often done, with respect to its *form*. Popular art is said to be simple and unsophisticated, aesthetically deficient because of its artlessness. It lacks quality because it makes no qualifications to its flat state-

ment. Everything is straightforward, with no place for complications. And it is standardized as well as simplified: one product
is much like another. But it is just the deadly routine that is so
popular. Confronted with that, we know just where we are,
know what we are being offered, and what is expected of us in
return. We can respond with mechanical routines ourselves, and
what could be simpler and more reliably satisfying?

Yet this account of the matter is itself too simple to be satisfactory. For why should simplicity be unaesthetic? Art always
strips away what is unessential, and purity has always been
recognized as a virtue. Put the adjective *classic* before it and
simplicity becomes a term of high regard. What is simple is not
therefore simple-minded. Art always concentrates, indeed it owes
its force to the power of interests that have been secured against
distraction and dissipation. Art, we may say, does away with
unnecessary complications. We can condemn popular art for
treating as expendable the *necessary* complications, but nothing
has been added to our aesthetic understanding till we have been
given some specification of what complexity is necessary and
what is not.

There is a similar lack in the condemnation of popular art as
being standardized. One Egyptian statue is much like another,
after all, just as there are marked resemblances among Elizabethan
tragedies or among Italian operas. Such works are not for that
reason assigned the status of popular art. The standardization of
popular art does not mean that forms are stylized but that they
are *stereotyped*. The failing does not lie in the recurrence of the
forms but in deficiencies even in the first occurrence. The characters and situations of the usual movie, words and music of
popular songs, the scenes and sentiments of magazine illustrations are all very much of a piece, each after its own kind. What
makes them stereotypes is not that each instance of the type so
closely resembles all the others, but that the type as a whole so
little resembles anything outside it.

The stereotype presents us with the blueprint of a form, rather
than the form itself. Where the simplifications of great art show
us human nature in its nakedness, the stereotypes of popular
art strip away even the flesh, and the still, sad music of humanity
is reduced to the rattle of dry bones. It is not simplification but
schematization that is achieved; what is put before us is not the
substance of the text but a reader's digest. All art selects what is

significant and suppresses the trivial. But for popular art the criteria of significance are fixed by the needs of the standardization, by the editor of the digest and not by the author of the reality to be grasped. Popular art is never a discovery, only a reaffirmation. Both producer and consumer of popular art confine themselves to what fits into their own schemes, rather than omitting only what is unnecessary to the grasp of the scheme of things. The world of popular art is bounded by the limited horizons of what we think we know already; it is two-dimensional because we are determined to view it without budging a step from where we stand.

The simplification characteristic of popular art amounts to this, that we restrict ourselves to what *already* comes within our grasp. Every stereotype is the crystallization of a prejudice—that is, a prejudgment. Even the inanimate materials of its medium have been type-cast.

Popular art is dominated throughout by the star system, not only in its actors but in all its elements, whatever the medium. Every work of art, to be sure, has its dominant elements, to which the rest are subordinate. But in popular art it is the dominant ones alone that are the objects of interest, the ground of its satisfaction. By contrast, great art is in this sense pointless; everything in it is significant, everything makes its own contribution to the aesthetic substance. The domain of popular art is, paradoxically, an aristocracy, as it were: some few elements are singled out as the carriers of whatever meaning the work has while the rest are merged into an anonymous mass. The life of the country is reduced to the mannered gestures of its king. It is this that gives the effect of simplification and standardization. The elements of the schema, of course, need not be characters in the strict sense; action, color, texture, melody, or rhythm may all be simplified and standardized in just this way.

What popular art schematizes it also abstracts from a fully aesthetic context. Such an abstraction is what we call a *formula;* in formula art the schema is called upon to do the work of the full-bodied original, as though a newspaper consisted entirely of headlines. The abstraction can always be made, as is implied in the very concept of style, and of specific stylistic traits. We can always apply formulas to art; the point is that popular art gives us the formula but nothing to apply it to. Popular art uses formulas, not for analysis but for the experience itself. Such substance as it has is only the disordered residue of other more or less aesthetic experiences, themselves well on the way towards schematization. Popular art is thus doubly derivative: art first becomes academic and then it becomes popular; as art achieves style it provides the seeds of its own destruction.

Thus popular art may be marked by a great emphasis on its newness—it is first-run, the latest thing. Prior exposure diminishes whatever satisfactions it can provide. Alternatively, it may be endlessly repeated: familiarity gives the illusion of intimacy. Most often, popular art is characterized by a combination of novelty and repetition: the same beloved star appears in what can be described as a new role. The novelty whips up a flagging interest. At the same time the repetition minimizes the demands made on us: we can see at a glance what is going on, and we know already how it will all turn out. Curiosity is easily satisfied, but suspense may be intolerable if we must join in the work of its resolution. We are really safe on the old, familiar ground. Popular art tosses baby in the air a very little way, and quickly catches him again.

In sum, what is unaesthetic about popular art is its formlessness. It does not invite or even permit the sustained effort necessary to the creation of an artistic form. But it provides us with an illusion of achievement while in fact we remain passive.

More specifically, there is work undone on both perceptual and psychodynamic levels.

As to the first, aesthetic *perception* is replaced by mere *recognition*. Perceptual discrimination is cut off, as in most nonaesthetic contexts, at the point where we have seen enough to know what we are looking at. Moreover, the perception is faithful, not to the perceptual materials actually presented, but to the stereotyped expectations that are operative. We perceive popular art only so as to recognize it for what it is, and the object of perception consists of no more than its marks of recognition. This is what is conveyed by the designation *kitch:* an object is kitch when it bears the label *Art* (with a capital "A"), so disposed that we see and respond only to the label.

On the psychodynamic level, the aesthetic *response* is replaced by a mere *reaction*. The difference between them is this: a reaction, in the sense I intend it, is almost wholly determined by the initial stimulus, antecedently and externally fixed, while a response follows a course that is not laid out beforehand but is significantly shaped by a process of self-stimulation occurring then and there. Spontaneity and imagination come into play; in the aesthetic experience we do not simply react to signals but engage in a creative interpretation of symbols. The response to an art object shares in the work of its creation, and only thereby is a work of art produced. But in popular art everything has already been done. Thus the background music for the popular movie signalizes the birth of love with melodious strings and the approach of death by chords on the organ; contrast these signals with the demanding substance of, say, Prokofieff's music for Eisenstein's *Alexander Nevsky*. To vary the metaphor, popular art is a dictatorship forever organizing spontaneous demonstrations and forever congratulating itself on its freedoms.

In the taste for popular art there is a marked intolerance of ambiguity. It is not just that we shrink from doing that much work—the work, that is, of creative interpretation. At bottom, aesthetic ambiguity is frightening. Popular art is a device for remaining in the same old world and assuring ourselves that we like it, because we are afraid to change it.

At best, popular art replaces ambiguity by some degree of complexity. This is most clearly demonstrated by the so-called *adult Western*, which has moved beyond the infantilism of "good guys" and "bad guys," by assigning virtues and vices to both heroes and villains. But the moral qualities themselves remain unambiguous in both sign and substance. The genre, for the most part, is still far from the insight into the nature of good and evil invited, say, by Melville's Captain Ahab or, even more, by his Billy Budd. Yet, *High Noon* is undeniably a far cry from *The Lone Ranger*.

In short, popular art is simple basically in the sense of easy. It contrasts with art in the markedly lesser demands that it makes for creative endeavor on the part of its audience. An artistic form, like a life form, is a creation, and like the living thing again, one which demands a cooperative effort, in this case between artist and audience. We cannot look to popular art for a fresh vision, turn to it for new direction out of the constraints of convention. Unexplored meanings call for their own language, which must be fashioned by a community with the courage and energy of pioneers. But for a new language there must be something new to say; what the pioneer can never do without is—a frontier.

III

Quite another approach to the analysis of popular art is by way of feeling rather than form. Popular art may be characterized by the kinds of emotions involved in it, or by its means of evoking or expressing them.

Thus there is a common view that popular art is merely *entertainment*, in a pejorative sense. It does not instruct, does not answer to any interests other than those aroused then and there; it is just interesting in itself. Popular art offers us something with which to fill our empty lives; we turn to it always in quiet desperation. It is a specific against boredom, and is thus an inevitable concomitant of the industrial civilization that simultaneously gives us leisure and alienates us from anything that might make our leisure meaningful.

Whatever merits this view may have as sociology, as aesthetics I do not find it very helpful. That the interests satisfied by popular art are self-contained is hardly distinctive of the type. All art has inherent value, independent of its direct contributions to extra-aesthetic concerns. And all art has a certain intrinsic value, affording delight in the form and color of the aesthetic surface, independent of depth meaning. That something is entertaining, that it gives joy to the beholder without regard to more serious interests, so-called, is scarcely a reason therefore, for refusing it artistic status. It is surely no more than snobbery or a perverted puritanism to disparage entertainment value, or to deny it to art.

The question still remains, What makes popular art entertaining? To invoke a contrast with boredom is not of much help, for that is a descriptive category, not an explanatory one; as well say that work is an antidote to laziness. Indeed, I think the claim might be more defensible that popular art, far from countering boredom, perpetuates and intensifies it. It does not arouse new interests but reinforces old ones. Such satisfaction as it affords stems from the evocation in memory of past satisfactions, or even from remembered fantasies of fulfillment. What we enjoy is not the work of popular art but what it brings to mind. There is a nostalgia characteristic of the experience of popular art, not because the work as a form is familiar but because its very substance is familiarity.

The skill of the artist is not in providing an experience but in providing occasions for reliving one. In the experience of popular art we lose ourselves, not in a work of art but in the pools of memory stirred up. Poetry becomes a congeries of poetic symbols which now only signalize feeling, as in the lyrics of popular songs; drama presents dramatic materials but does not dramatize them—brain surgery, or landing the crippled airliner; painting becomes illustration or didactic narrative from Jean Greuze to Norman Rockwell.

Conventions are, to be sure, at work; the associations aroused are not wholly adventitious and idiosyncratic. But *convention* is one thing and *style* is another. One is extrinsic to the materials, giving them shape; the other is the very substance of their form. The difference is like that between a railroad track and a satellite's orbit: convention is laid down beforehand, guiding reactions along a fixed path, while style has no existence antecedent to and independent of the ongoing response itself. For this reason popular art so easily becomes dated, as society changes its conventional associations; see today, [the melodramatic play] *A Father's Curse* surely evokes laughter rather than pity or fear. On the other hand, a work of art may become popular as its expressive substance is replaced by associations—Whistler's *"Mother"* is a case in point.

Popular art wallows in emotion while art transcends it, giving us understanding and thereby mastery of our feelings. For popular art, feelings themselves are the ultimate subject matter; they are not present as a quality of the experience of something objectified, but are only stimulated by the object. The addiction to such stimuli is like the frenzied and forever frustrated pursuit of happiness by those lost souls who have never learned that happiness accrues only when the object of pursuit has its own substance. Popular art ministers to this misery, panders to it, we may say. What popular art has in common with prostitution is not that it is commercialized; art also claims its price, and the price is often a high one. The point is that here we are being offered consummations without fulfillment, invited to perform the gestures of love on condition that they remain without meaning. We are not drawn out of ourselves but are driven deeper into loneliness. Emotion is not a monopoly of popular art, as Dickens, Tschaikovsky, or Turner might testify; but these artists do not traffic in emotion. Popular art, on the contrary, deals in nothing else. That is why it is so commonly judged by its impact. To say truly that it is sensational would be high praise; what we usually get is an anaesthetic.

IV

There is yet another reason for questioning whether popular art provides relief from boredom, bringing color into grey lives. The popular audience may be chronically bored, but this is not to say that it is without feeling. On the contrary, it is feeling above all that the audience contributes to the aesthetic situation and that the popular artist then exploits. Popular art does not supply a missing ingredient in our lives, but cooks up a savory mess from the ingredients at hand. In a word, feelings are usually lacking in *depth*, whatever their intensity. Popular art is correspondingly shallow.

Superficial, affected, spurious—this is the dictionary meaning of *sentimental*. So far as feeling goes, it is sentimentality that is most distinctive of popular art. There is a sense, I suppose, in which we could say that all feeling starts as sentiment: however deep down you go you must begin at the surface. The point is that popular art leaves our feelings as it finds them, formless and immature. The objects of sentiment are of genuine worth— cynicism has its own immaturity. But the feelings called forth spring up too quickly and easily to acquire substance and depth. They are so lightly triggered that there is no chance to build up a significant emotional discharge. Sentimentality is a mark always of a certain deficiency of feeling; it is always just words, a promise that scarcely begins to move toward fulfillment.

Yet it is only an excess of a special kind that is in question here. We must distinguish sentimentality from sensibility, that is, a ready responsiveness to demands on our feelings. Art has no purchase at all on insensibility. Unless a man is capable of being moved, and moved deeply, in circumstances where his antecedent interests are not engaged, art has nothing for him. Sensibility becomes sentimental when there is some disproportion between the response and its object, when the response is indiscriminate and uncontrolled. Emotion, Beethoven once said, is for women, and I think we all understand him; but we are to keep in mind the difference between such women as Elizabeth Bennett and her mother.

It is this difference that we want to get at. Dewey comes very near the mark, I believe, in characterizing sentimentality as "excess of receptivity without perception of meaning." It is this lack of meaning, and not intensity of feeling, that makes the receptivity excessive. Popular art is not sentimental because it evokes so much feeling, but because it calls for so much more feeling than either its artist or audience can handle. The trouble is not too much feeling but too little understanding; there is too little to be understood.

Sentimentality, then, moves in a closed circle around the self. The emotions released by a stimulus to sentiment satisfy a proprietary interest, and one which is directed inward. The important thing is that they are *my* feelings, and what is more, feelings about *me*. The prototype of sentimentality is self-pity. Popular art provides subjects and situations that make it easy to see ourselves in its materials. Narcissus, W. H. Auden conjectured, was probably a hydrocephalic idiot, who stared into the pool and concluded, "On me it looks good!" The self-centeredness of popular art is the measure of our own diminishing.

v

Perhaps the most common characterization of popular art is that it is *escapist*. There is no doubt that it can produce a kind of narcosis, a state of insensibility arresting thought and feeling as well as action—in a word, a trance. We do not look at popular art, we stare into it, as we would into flames or moving waters. I think it not accidental that the most popular media, movies and television, are viewed in the dark. The medium is such stuff as dreams are made on.

Popular art seeks to escape ugliness, not to transform it. There is nothing like a pretty face to help you forget your troubles, and popular art can prettify everything, even—and perhaps especially—the face of death. It provides an escape first, therefore, by shutting out the reality, glossing over it.

But popular art is said to do more; it seems to provide an escape not only *from* something but also *to* something else, shuts out the real world by opening the door to another. We do not just forget our troubles but are reminded of them to enjoy the fantasy of overcoming them. Popular art is as likely to relieve anxiety as boredom.

The world of popular art is unreal not just in the sense that it consists of symbols rather than realities—"it's only a movie." Science, too, replaces things by abstract representations of them, but it is not for that reason derogated as an escape from reality. But what makes it science, after all, is that it is capable of bringing us back to the realities, however far from them it detours in its abstractions. Whether symbols are essentially an escape depends at bottom on what they symbolize. Popular art is unreal, not as being sign rather than substance, but because what it signifies is unreal. All art is illusion, inducing us as we experience it to take art for life. But some of it is true to life, illusory without being deceptive. Popular art is a tissue of falsehoods.

Popular art depicts the world, not as it is, nor even as it might be, but as we would have it. Everything in it is selected and placed in our interest. It is a world exhausted in a single perspective—our own—and it is peopled by cardboard figures that disappear when viewed edgewise. We are not to ask whether the rescued maiden can cook, nor do we see the gallant knight through the eyes of the dragon, who is after all only wondering where his next meal will come from. In real drama, said [the nineteenth-century German dramatist] Friedrich Hebbel, all the characters must be in the right. That is how God sees them, which is to say, how they are. Art, like science, raises us up to divine objectivity; popular art is all too human.

It must be admitted that popular art is more sophisticated today than it was a generation or so ago. But often its realism is only another romantic pose. In popular art, it is a matter of taking over the shapes of realism but not the forms. The modern hero of popular art is given a generous admixture of human failings; but no one is really fooled—he is only superman in disguise. Indeed, the disguise is so transparent that it can be discarded: we have come full circle from Nick Carter through Sam Spade to James Bond.

Yet, is not all art fantasy, not the symbolic replication of reality but the fulfillment of a wish? To be sure! But what is wish-fulfilling is the art itself, and not the world it depicts.

For this reason popular art could as well be said to suffer from too little fantasy as too much: it does not do enough with its materials. Its imagination is reproductive rather than creative. When it comes to breaking out of the constraints of reality, what better examples are there than *Midsummer Night's Dream* and

The Tempest, the paintings of Hieronymous Bosch, or the sculpture of the Hindu pantheon? But popular art is so bound to reality it gives us nowhere to escape *to*, save deeper within a self that is already painfully constricted. The eighteenth century usefully distinguished between fancy and imagination, according to whether fantasy has worked far enough to confer reality on its own products. Popular art is all fancy. If it sees the world as a prison, it contents itself with painting on the walls an open door.

Though all art is fantasy, there is a mature as well as an infantile process. Art may be produced for children—Lewis Carroll and Robert Louis Stevenson—or with a childlike quality—Paul Klee and Joan Miro—but it is not therefore childish. It is this childishness, however, that characterizes popular art: the fairy tale is retold for adult consumption, but stripped of just those qualities of creative imagination in which lies the artistry of the original.

In mature fantasy both the reality principle and the pleasure principle are at work. Popular art is concerned only with the pleasure, and for just this reason it can provide only immature satisfactions. In responding to popular art we do not escape from reality—we have not yet attained to the reality. Beneath the pleasure in popular art is the pathos of the note lying outside the orphanage wall: "Whoever finds this, I love you!"

VI

Now, after all, what makes popular art so popular? The usual reply follows the account that conceives of popular art in terms of distinctive features of modern society. The major premise is the alienation and deracination of modern man; the minor premise is that popular art serves to counter these forces, providing a basis for at least an ersatz community. Popular art reaches out to the lowest common denominator of society; it provides the touch of nature that makes all men kin, or, at least, all men who share the conventions of a common culture.

In so far as the function of popular art today is to be explained in terms of social conditions rather than psychic processes, the situation seems to be the reverse of what the previous account relies on. It is not man who is alienated and uprooted,

Photograph by Laurence Fink.

but art. In our time art has become increasingly dissociated from the cultural concerns with which it has been so intimately involved throughout most of its history—religion, love, war, politics, and the struggle for subsistence. Art today is, in Dewey's brilliant phrase, "the beauty-parlor of civilization." Popular art at least pretends to a social relevance, and is not only willing but eager to find a place for itself outside the museum.

Popular art today is neither worse nor more common than it always has been. There is a wider audience today for art of every kind: the mass of the Athenian population were slaves, and not much more than that in Renaissance Italy or Elizabethan England. There may be more poor stuff produced today because there are more people to consume it, but this is even more true, proportionately, for the superior product. Nor do I sympathize with the view that ours is an age of barbarism to be defined, according to Ortega y Gasset, as "the absence of standards to which appeal can be made." What is absent, to my mind, is only a cultural elite that sets forth and enforces the standards; and I say, so much the better! It is ironic that popular art is taken as a sign of barbarism; every real development in the history of art, and not only the modern movement, was first greeted as a repudiation of aesthetic standards. My objection to popular art is just the contrary, that it is too rigidly bound to the standards of the academy. Kitch is the homage paid by popular art to those standards: Oscar and Emmy are avatars of the muse.

Art is too often talked about with a breathless solemnity, and viewed with a kind of religious awe; if high art needs its high priests, I hope that aesthetics will leave that office to the critics. To put it plainly, there is much snobbery in the aesthetic domain, and especially in the contempt for popular art on no other basis than its popularity. We speak of popular art in terms of its media (paperbacks, movies, television) as though to say, "Can any good come out of Nazareth?"; or else by the popular genres (western, mystery, love story, science fiction) as though they can be condemned wholesale. For audiences, art is more of a status symbol than ever; its appearance in the mass media is marked by a flourish of trumpets, as befits its status; the sponsor may even go so far as to omit his commercials. Even where popular art vulgarizes yesterday's art, it might anticipate tomorrow's—baroque once meant something like kitch. I am willing to prophesy that even television has art in its future.

But if not, what then? Aesthetic judgment is one thing and personal taste another. The values of art, like all else aesthetic, can only be analyzed contextually. There is a time and a place even for popular art. Champagne and Napoleon brandy are admittedly the best of beverages; but on a Sunday afternoon in the ballpark we want a coke, or maybe a glass of beer. "Even if we have all the virtues," Zarathustra reminds us, "there is still one thing needful: to send the virtues themselves to sleep at the right time." If popular art gives us pleasant dreams, we can only be grateful —when we have wakened.

THE
WAY
OF
MUSIC

THE APPALLING POPULARITY OF MUSIC

Few writers are so entertaining on the subject of music as Constant Lambert (1905–1951). He was himself a very able composer and conductor, specializing in the ballet. An enthusiast in all branches of his art, his enthusiasm nevertheless knew quite precise limitations. He could not easily stomach pretentiousness or indifference, either in musicians or their audiences, and these vices he regularly attacked in his literate and highly readable critical pieces. The piece that follows comes from Lambert's immensely entertaining collection, Music Ho! *(1934). In spite of references to the famous founding father of the British Broadcasting Corporation, Sir John Reith, and a popular vocalist of the Thirties, Christopher Stone, the piece is not in the least dated. It speaks directly—the only way Lambert ever tried to speak—of the fortunes of music in a day of mass media, surely as much our day as Lambert's.*

Constant Lambert

Music has an odd way of reflecting not only the emotional background of an age but also its physical conditions. The present age is one of overproduction. Never has there been so much food and so much starvation, and (as I pointed out before) never has there been so much music-making and so little musical experience of a vital order.

Since the advent of the gramophone, and more particularly the wireless, music of a sort is everywhere and at every time; in the heavens, the lower parts of the earth, the mountains, the forest and every tree therein. It is a Psalmist's nightmare. At one time a cautious glance round the room assured one, through the absence of a piano, that there would at least be no music after dinner. But today the chances are that one's host is a gramophone bore, intent on exhibiting his fifty-seven varieties of soundbox, or a wireless fiend intent on obtaining the obscurest stations irrespective of programme. It is to be noticed that the more people use the wireless the less they listen to it. Some business men actually leave the wireless on all day so that the noise will be heard as they come up the garden path, and they will be spared the ghastly hiatus of silence that elapses between the slam of the front door and the first atmospheric.

The people, and they are legion, who play bridge to the accompaniment of a loud speaker, cannot be put off their game even by *The Amazing Mandarin* of Béla Bartók. Were The Last Trump to be suddenly broadcast from Daventry by special permission of Sir John Reith—and I can think of no event more gratifying to the stern-minded Governors of the B.B.C.—it is doubtful whether it would interfere with the cry of 'No Trumps' from the card table.

What people do in their own homes is fortunately still their own concern, but what takes place in public streets and public houses concerns us all. The loud speaker is little short of a public menace.

In the neighbourhood where I live, for example, there is a loud speaker every hundred yards or so, and it is only rarely that they are tuned in to different stations. If they are playing the foxtrot I most detest at one corner of the street, I need not think that I can avoid it by walking to the other end. At times there is a certain piquancy in following a tune in two dimensions at once, so to speak—to buy one's cigarettes to the first subject of a symphony, to get scraps of the development as one goes to the newsagent, and to return home to the recapitulation—but the idea of the town as one vast analytical programme, with every pavingstone a barline, soon palls. It would not matter so much were the music bad music but, as the B.B.C. can boast with some satisfaction, most of it is good. We board buses to the strains of Beethoven and drink our beer to the accompaniment of Bach. And yet we pride ourselves on the popular appreciations of these masters.

Here is yet another example of the gradual fusion of highbrow and lowbrow to which I drew attention before. Instead of the admirable old distinction between classical and popular which used to hold good—classics for the concert hall or home, popular for the street and café—classical music is vulgarized and diffused through every highway and byway, and both highbrow and lowbrow are the losers.

The principal objections to music provided by the now almost universal loud speaker are its monotony and unsuitability. Whereas you can escape from a mechanical piano by going to the next café, you can rarely escape from a B.B.C. gramophone hour by going to the next public house because they are almost bound to be presenting the same entertainment to their clients. The whole of London, whatever it is doing, and whatever its moods, is made to listen to the choice of a privileged few or even a privileged one.

To take the example of Mr. Christopher Stone whose well-modulated voice has doubtless given pleasure to millions. At certain hours of the day, it is impossible for anyone to escape from his breezy diffidence. That he is a benevolent autocrat I am sure is true, just as I am sure that his choice of records is reasonably intelligent and eclectic. But the fact remains that he enjoys a position of dictatorship as fantastic as anything in Aldous Huxley's *Brave New World*. At one time G. K. Chesterton propounded the amiable and consoling theory that people would cheat the prophets by refusing to do what was laid down in the pseudo-scientific and so-called 'Utopian' books. It would appear, though, that the most jaundiced of imaginative writers can hardly keep pace with the blessings of mechanical progress, that pass in a year or two from a vicious and improbable fancy to a grimly ineluctable fact.

Even worse than the lack of individual choice in loudspeaker music is the almost invariable unsuitability of its style and timbre. Music in the streets, in cafés, and at fairs is an admirable scheme, but a certain gaiety of outline and pungency of timbre is essential. The Catalan coblas are the ideal example of outdoor music, but anything, from a military band playing Sousa to a man playing Carmen on the ocarina, is preferable to having the strains of the Air on the G String, reduced in quality but amplified in quantity, floating out over the noise of traffic. Even the dance music which on stylistic grounds is to be preferred, in the circumstances, to Beethoven or Bach, has a quality of sickening and genteel refinement not to be found in the exhilarating tintinnabulation of the fast-disappearing mechanical piano. It has actually been suggested that the 'inartistic' confusion of fair music, the dizzy and arbitrary counterpoint of round-abouts, with their whistling organs, should be supplanted by the uniform of blaring synchronized loud speakers.

It is clear that we are fast losing even the minor stimulus of genuine healthy vulgarity. In the present age it is impossible to escape from Culture, and the wholesale and wholetime diffusion of musical culture will eventually produce in us, when we hear a Bach concerto, the faint nausea felt towards a piece of toffee by a worker in a sweet factory.

The same phenomenal indifference towards what they listen to can be seen as clearly in those who have loud speakers thrust upon them as in those who deliberately foster their use. One might have thought that the sturdy British working man entering a public house and being greeted with a talk on the Reclamation of the Zuyder Zee, or a string quartet by Alban Berg, would have requested the proprietor, and not entirely without reason, to 'put a sock in it'; but actually he just sits stolidly there, drinking his synthetic bitter to sounds of synthetic sweetness, not caring whether the loud speaker is tuned in to a jazz band, a talk on wildflowers, a Schönberg opera or a reading from 'The Land' by the authoress. So long as certain waves are set up in the ether to produce a certain reaction on his tympanum he is content. The most severe complaints about the wireless are indeed from people who indignantly discover that for five minutes during the day the machine is not functioning at all.

Far be it from anyone interested in contemporary music to complain that the B.B.C. have the enterprise to put on such works as the operas of Berg and Schönberg. One's complaint is not with the programmes themselves, which, through an independence of advertising interests are of an admirably eclectic nature, but with their intolerably wholesale diffusion through portable sets and loud speakers.

In previous ages, listening to music was a matter of personal choice usually involving either individual skill in joining with other people in singing a madrigal, or at least the concentration, and sacrifice of time and money, required by a cycle of *The Ring*. But now no one can avoid listening to music, whether in town or country, in a motor car, train or restaurant, perched on a hilltop, or immersed in the river. It is even more trying for the musical than for the non-musical; it is impossible for them to escape from their profession or relaxation, as the case may be.

Another symbol of the present age is thus curiously provided. Those who in the eighteenth century felt like killing their fellow creatures were able to exercise their natural faculties with others of the same bent in a comparatively restricted space. The unbellicose were, save in exceptional circumstances, not affected. But today everyone is a potential combatant and will no longer be able to escape mechanized death in the next war than at the present moment he can escape mechanized music.

We have at present no idea of what havoc may be wrought in a few years' time by the combined effect of the noise of city life and the noise of city music—an actual atrophy of the aural nerves would seem to be indicated. Already it is to be observed that people are no longer thrilled or even aggravated by the most powerful of modern tuttis. The explanation is simple. The noise provided by such adjuncts of modern life as the pneumatic drill, the movietone news reel and the war film, leaves the most sadistic and orgiastic of composers at the starting post. When Berlioz wrote the *Symphonie Fantastique* he was providing probably the greatest sonority that anyone, including even those military men present, had ever heard. When George Antheil adds to his score sixteen pianos, an electric buzzer or two, an aeroplane propeller, and a pneumatic drill he is, after all, providing little more than the average background to a telephone conversation.

Although excessive sonority has lost its thrill, we still demand it as an ever-increasing factor in our lives. It is noticeable, indeed, that those whose business lives are the most surrounded by extraneous noises are those who most insist on the continuous support of gramophone and loud speaker during their leisure hours. We live in an age of tonal debauch where the blunting of the finer edge of pleasure leads only to a more hysterical and frenetic attempt to recapture it. It is obvious that second-rate mechanical music is the most suitable fare for those to whom musical experience is no more than a mere aural tickling, just as the prostitute provides the most suitable outlet for those to whom sexual experience is no more than the periodic removal of a recurring itch. The loud speaker is the street walker of music.

The ironies of John Cage (1912–   ) often distract his listeners and his readers from his seriousness as a composer. That he can mean what he says, as well as something more or something less, is quite clear in the amusing monologue for two voices that follows. Cage is the daring composer of exactly timed silences, designed as musical pieces to illustrate the sounds of a concert-hall: chairs creaking, lungs wheezing, programs crackling, rumps twisting and turning. He has invented a whole repertoire of hardware with which to augment and diminish the sounds of the "prepared" piano, as he calls his rearranged instrument, and he has written a score for radios, with each twirling of the dials marked out for the performers. He is also a thoughtful spokesman for experimentation in contemporary music who regards his contemporaries highly—Christian Wolff, Earle Brown, and especially Morton Feldman who graphs directions to his players rather than using conventional notation. This piece requires close reading as it moves through its witty examination of the nature of experimental music in a technological era to make its points about music and sound in general.

EXPERIMENTAL MUSIC: DOCTRINE

John Cage

Joseph Schillinger (referred to by his last name) is the author of an ambitious attempt to reduce music to its mathematical components, a composer, and a teacher. The I Ching, or Book of Changes, by Confucius, is a book of divination by mathematical pattern and precept.

Objections are sometimes made by composers to the use of the term *experimental* as descriptive of their works, for it is claimed that any experiments that are made precede the steps that are finally taken with determination, and that this determination is knowing, having, in fact, a particular, if unconventional, ordering of the elements used in view. These objections are clearly justifiable, but only where, as among contemporary evidences in serial music, it remains a question of making a thing upon the boundaries, structure, and expression on which attention is focused. Where, on the other hand, attention moves towards the observation and audition of many things at once, including those that are environmental—becomes, that is, inclusive rather than exclusive—no question of making, in the sense of forming understandable structures, can arise (one is a tourist), and here the word "experimental" is apt, providing it is understood not as descriptive of an act to be later judged in terms of success and failure, but simply as of an act the outcome of which is unknown. What has been determined?

For, when, after convincing oneself ignorantly that sound has, as its clearly defined opposite, silence, that since duration is the only characteristic of sound that is measurable in terms of silence, therefore any valid structure involving sounds and silences should be based, not as occidentally traditional, on frequency, but rightly on duration, one enters an anechoic chamber, as silent as technologically possible in 1951, to discover that one hears two sounds of one's own unintentional making (nerve's systematic operation, blood's circulation), the situation one is clearly in is not objective (sound-silence), but rather subjective (sounds only), those intended and those others (so-called silence) not intended. If, at this point, one says, "Yes! I do not discriminate between intention and non-intention," the splits, subject-object, art-life, etc., disappear, an identification has been made with the material, and actions are then those relevant to its nature, i.e.:

A sound does not view itself as thought, as ought, as needing another sound for its elucidation, as etc.; it has no time for any consideration—it is occupied with the performance of its characteristics: before it has died away it must have made perfectly exact its frequency, its loudness, its length, its overtone structure, the precise morphology of these and of itself.

Urgent, unique, uninformed about history and theory, beyond the imagination, central to a sphere without surface, its becoming is unimpeded, energetically broadcast. There is no escape from its action. It does not exist as one of a series of discrete steps, but as transmission in all directions from the field's center. It is inextricably synchronous with all other, sounds, non-sounds, which latter, received by other sets than the ear, operate in the same manner.

A sound accomplishes nothing; without it life would not last out the instant.

Relevant action is theatrical (music [imaginary separation of hearing from the other senses] does not exist), inclusive and intentionally purposeless. Theatre is continually becoming that it is becoming; each human being is at the best point for reception. Relevant response (getting up in the morning and discovering onself a musician) (action, art) can be made with any number (including none [none and number, like silence and music, are unreal]) of sounds. The automatic minimum (see above) is two.

Are you deaf (by nature, choice, desire) or can you hear (externals, tympani, labyrinths in whack)?

Beyond them (ears) is the power of discrimination which, among other confused actions, weakly pulls apart (abstraction), ineffectually establishes as not to suffer alteration (the "work"), and unskillfully protects from interruption (museum, concert hall) what springs, elastic, spontaneous, back together again with a beyond that power which is fluent (it moves in or out), pregnant (it can appear when- where- as what-ever [rose, nail, constellation, 485.73482 cycles per second, piece of string]), related (it is you yourself in the form you have that instant taken), obscure (you will never be able to give a satisfactory report even to yourself of just what happened).

In view, then, of a totality of possibilities, no knowing action is commensurate, since the character of the knowledge acted upon prohibits all but some eventualities. From a realist position, such action, though cautious, hopeful, and generally entered into, is unsuitable. An *experimental* action, generated by a mind as empty as it was before it became one, thus in accord with the possibility of no matter what, is, on the other hand, practical. It does not move in terms of approximations and errors, as "informed" action by its nature must, for no mental images of what would happen were set up beforehand; it sees things directly as they are: impermanently involved in an infinite play of interpenetrations. Experimental music—

Question: —in the U.S.A., if you please. Be more specific. What do you have to say about rhythm? Let us agree it is no longer a question of pattern, repetition, and variation.

Answer: There is no need for such agreement. Patterns,

repetitions, and variations will arise and disappear. However, rhythm is durations of any length coexisting in any states of succession and synchronicity. The latter is liveliest, most unpredictably changing, when the parts are not fixed by a score but left independent of one another, no two performances yielding the same resultant durations. The former, succession, liveliest when (as in Morton Feldman's *Intersections*) it is not fixed but presented in situation-form, entrances being at any point within a given period of time.—Notation of durations is in space, read as corresponding to time, needing no reading in the case of magnetic tape.

Question: What about several players at once, an orchestra?

Answer: You insist upon their being together? Then use, as Earle Brown suggests, a moving picture of the score, visible to all, a static vertical line as coordinator, past which the notations move. If you have no particular togetherness in mind, there are chronometers. Use them.

Question: I have noticed that you write durations that are beyond the possibility of performance.

Answer: Composing's one thing, performing's another, listening's a third. What can they have to do with one another?

Question: And about pitches?

Answer: It is true. Music is continually going up and down, but no longer only on those stepping stones, five, seven, twelve in number, or the quarter tones. Pitches are not a matter of likes and dislikes (I have told you about the diagram Schillinger had stretched across his wall near the ceiling: all the scales, Oriental and Occidental, that had been in general use, each in its own color plotted against, no one of them identical with, a black one, the latter the scale as it would have been had it been physically based on the overtone series) except for musicians in ruts; in the face of habits, what to do? Magnetic tape opens the door providing one doesn't immediately shut it by inventing a *phonogène*, or otherwise use it to recall or extend known musical possibilities. It introduces the unknown with such sharp clarity that anyone has the opportunity of having his habits blown away like dust.— For this purpose the prepared piano is also useful, especially in its recent forms where, by alterations during a performance, an otherwise static gamut situation becomes changing. Stringed instruments (not string-players) are very instructive, voices too; and sitting still anywhere (the stereophonic, multiple-loud-speaker manner of operation in the everyday production of sounds and noises) listening. . . .

Question: I understand Feldman divides all pitches into high, middle, and low, and simply indicates how many in a given range are to be played, leaving the choice up to the performer.

Answer: Correct. That is to say, he used sometimes to do so; I haven't seen him lately. It is also essential to remember his notation of super- and subsonic vibrations (*Marginal Intersection No. 1*).

Question: That is, there are neither divisions of the "canvas" nor "frame" to be observed?

Answer: On the contrary, you must give the closest attention to everything.

Question: And timbre?

Answer: No wondering what's next. Going lively on "through many a perilous situation." Did you ever listen to a symphony orchestra?

Question: Dynamics?

Answer: These result from what actively happens (physically, mechanically, electronically) in producing a sound. You won't find it in the books. Notate that. As far as too loud goes: "follow the general outlines of the Christian life."

Question: I have asked you about the various characteristics of a sound; how, now, can you make a continuity, as I take it your intention is, without intention? Do not memory, psychology—

Answer: "—never again."

Question: How?

Answer: Christian Wolff introduced space actions in his compositional process at variance with the subsequently performed time actions. Earle Brown devised a composing procedure in which events, following tables of random numbers, are written out of sequence, possibly anywhere in a total time now and possibly anywhere else in the same total time next. I myself use chance operations, some derived from the *I-Ching*, others from the observation of imperfections in the paper upon which I happen to be writing. Your answer: by not giving it a thought.

Question: Is this athematic?

Answer: Who said anything about themes? It is not a question of having something to say.

Question: Then what is the purpose of this "experimental" music?

Answer: No purposes. Sounds.

Question: Why bother, since, as you have pointed out, sounds are continually happening whether you produce them or not?

Answer: What did you say? I'm still—

Question: I mean—But is this *music?*

Answer: Ah! you like sounds after all when they are made up of vowels and consonants. You are slow-witted, for you have never brought your mind to the location of urgency. Do you need me or someone else to hold you up? Why don't you realize as I do that nothing is accomplished by writing, playing, or listening to music? Otherwise, deaf as a doornail, you will never be able to hear anything, even what's well within earshot.

Question: But, seriously, if this is what music is, I could write it as well as you.

Answer: Have I said anything that would lead you to think I thought you were stupid?

HOW WE LISTEN

Aaron Copland

No career in American music has been more distinguished than that of Aaron Copland (1900–   ), for awards, for the appreciation and attention of audiences, composers, critics. His writing for symphony orchestra, for chamber groups, and for the piano has drawn wide and warm critical reaction. His scores for the ballet, Billy the Kid, Rodeo, *and* Appalachian Spring, *have been particularly successful with audiences, and his compositions for films have also won general approval. He is a particularly lucid explicator of the mysteries of musical process, insisting that much of the notorious obscurity of the art can be dissipated by the development of certain fixed awarenesses on the part of listeners, even untrained ones. Such awarenesses indicate what can and cannot be known about music. Whether or not Copland has satisfactorily defined certainty and uncertainty in listening, he has prepared the way for serious speculation about the nature of the musical experience by all of us, no matter how little or how large our previous instruction in the techniques of music.*

We all listen to music according to our separate capacities. But, for the sake of analysis, the whole listening process may become clearer if we break it up into its component parts, so to speak. In a certain sense we all listen to music on three separate planes. For lack of a better terminology, one might name these: (1) the sensuous plane, (2) the expressive plane, (3) the sheerly musical plane. The only advantage to be gained from mechanically splitting up the listening process into these hypothetical planes is the clearer view to be had of the way in which we listen.

The simplest way of listening to music is to listen for the sheer pleasure of the musical sound itself. That is the sensuous plane. It is the plane on which we hear music without thinking, without considering it in any way. One turns on the radio while doing something else and absentmindedly bathes in the sound. A kind of brainless but attractive state of mind is engendered by the mere sound appeal of the music.

You may be sitting in a room reading this book. Imagine one note struck on the piano. Immediately that one note is enough to change the atmosphere of the room—proving that the sound element in music is a powerful and mysterious agent, which it would be foolish to deride or belittle.

The surprising thing is that many people who consider themselves qualified music lovers abuse that plane in listening. They go to concerts in order to lose themselves. They use music as a consolation or an escape. They enter an ideal world where one doesn't have to think of the realities of everyday life. Of course they aren't thinking about the music either. Music allows them to leave it, and they go off to a place to dream, dreaming because of and apropos of the music yet never quite listening to it.

Yes, the sound appeal of music is a potent and primitive force, but you must not allow it to usurp a disproportionate share of your interest. The sensuous plane is an important one in music, a very important one, but it does not constitute the whole story.

There is no need to digress further on the sensuous plane. Its appeal to every normal human being is self-evident. There is, however, such a thing as becoming more sensitive to the different kinds of sound stuff as used by various composers. For all composers do not use that sound stuff in the same way. Don't get the idea that the value of music is commensurate with its sensuous appeal or that the loveliest sounding music is made by the greatest composer. If that were so, Ravel would be a greater creator than Beethoven. The point is that the sound element varies with each composer, that his usage of sound forms an integral part of his style and must be taken into account when listening. The reader can see, therefore, that a more conscious approach is valuable even on this primary plane of music listening.

The second plane on which music exists is what I have called the expressive one. Here, immediately, we tread on controversial ground. Composers have a way of shying away from any discussion of music's expressive side. Did not Stravinsky himself proclaim that his music was an "object," a "thing," with a life of its own, and with no other meaning than its own purely musical existence? This intransigent attitude of Stravinsky's may be due to the fact that so many people have tried to read different meanings into so many pieces. Heaven knows it is difficult enough to say precisely what it is that a piece of music means, to say it definitely, to say it finally so that everyone is satisfied with your explanation. But that should not lead one to the other extreme of denying to music the right to be "expressive."

My own belief is that all music has an expressive power, some more and some less, but that all music has a certain meaning behind the notes and that that meaning behind the note constitutes, after all, what the piece is saying, what the piece is about. This whole problem can be stated quite simply by asking, "Is there a meaning to music?" My answer to that would be, "Yes." And "Can you state in so many words what the meaning is?" My answer to that would be, "No." Therein lies the difficulty.

Simple-minded souls will never be satisfied with the answer to the second of these questions. They always want music to have a meaning, and the more concrete it is the better they like it. The more the music reminds them of a train, a storm, a funeral, or any other familiar conception the more expressive it appears to be to them. This popular idea of music's meaning—stimulated and abetted by the usual run of musical commentator—should be discouraged wherever and whenever it is met. One timid lady once confessed to me that she suspected something seriously lacking in her appreciation of music because of her inability to connect it with anything definite. That is getting the whole thing backward, of course.

Still, the question remains, How close should the intelligent music lover wish to come to pinning a definite meaning to any particular work? No closer than a general concept, I should say. Music expresses, at different moments, serenity or exuberance, regret or triumph, fury or delight. It expresses each of these moods, and many others, in a numberless variety of subtle shadings and differences. It may even express a state of meaning for which there exists no adequate word in any language. In that case, musicians often like to say that it has only a purely musical meaning. They sometimes go farther and say that *all* music has only a purely musical meaning. What they really mean is that

no appropriate word can be found to express the music's meaning and that, even if it could, they do not feel the need of finding it.

But whatever the professional musician may hold, most musical
novices still search for specific words with which to pin down
their musical reactions. That is why they always find Tchaikovsky easier to "understand" than Beethoven. In the first place, it
is easier to pin a meaning-word on a Tchaikovsky piece than on
a Beethoven one. Much easier. Moreover, with the Russian composer, every time you come back to a piece of his it almost
always says the same thing to you, whereas with Beethoven it is
often quite difficult to put your finger right on what he is saying.
And any musician will tell you that that is why Beethoven is the
greater composer. Because music which always says the same
thing to you will necessarily soon become dull music, but music
whose meaning is slightly different with each hearing has a
greater chance of remaining alive.

Listen, if you can, to the forty-eight fugue themes of Bach's
Well Tempered Clavichord. Listen to each theme, one after
another. You will soon realize that each theme mirrors a different
world of feeling. You will also soon realize that the more beautiful a theme seems to you the harder it is to find any word that
will describe it to your complete satisfaction. Yes, you will certainly know whether it is a gay theme or a sad one. You will be
able, in other words, in your own mind, to draw a frame of
emotional feeling around your theme. Now study the sad one a
little closer. Try to pin down the exact quality of its sadness. Is
it pessimistically sad or resignedly sad; is it fatefully sad or smil-
ingly sad?

Let us suppose that you are fortunate and can describe to your
own satisfaction in so many words the exact meaning of your
chosen theme. There is still no guarantee that anyone else will be
satisfied. Nor need they be. The important thing is that each one
feel for himself the specific expressive quality of a theme or,
similarly, an entire piece of music. And if it is a great work of
art, don't expect it to mean exactly the same thing to you each
time you return to it.

Themes or pieces need not express only one emotion, of
course. Take such a theme as the first main one of the *Ninth
Symphony*, for example. It is clearly made up of different ele-

Pages 98 and 99. Photograph by Dennis Stock. Magnum.

ments. It does not say only one thing. Yet anyone hearing it immediately gets a feeling of strength, a feeling of power. It isn't a power that comes simply because the theme is played loudly. It is a power inherent in the theme itself. The extraordinary strength and vigor of the theme results in the listener's receiving an impression that a forceful statement has been made. But one should never try to boil it down to "the fateful hammer of life," etc. That is where the trouble begins. The musician, in his exasperation, says it means nothing but the notes themselves, whereas the nonprofessional is only too anxious to hang on to any explanation that gives him the illusion of getting closer to the music's meaning.

Now, perhaps, the reader will know better what I mean when I say that music does have an expressive meaning but that we cannot say in so many words what that meaning is.

The third plane on which music exists is the sheerly musical plane. Besides the pleasurable sound of music and the expressive feeling that it gives off, music does exist in terms of the notes themselves and of their manipulation. Most listeners are not sufficiently conscious of this third plane. . . .

Professional musicians, on the other hand, are, if anything, too conscious of the mere notes themselves. They often fall into the error of becoming so engrossed with their arpeggios and staccatos that they forget the deeper aspects of the music they are performing. But from the layman's standpoint, it is not so much a matter of getting over bad habits on the sheerly musical plane as of increasing one's awareness of what is going on, in so far as the notes are concerned.

When the man in the street listens to the "notes themselves" with any degree of concentration, he is most likely to make some mention of the melody. Either he hears a pretty melody or he does not, and he generally lets it go at that. Rhythm is likely to gain his attention next, particularly if it seems exciting. But harmony and tone color are generally taken for granted, if they are thought of consciously at all. As for music's having a definite form of some kind, that idea seems never to have occurred to him.

It is very important for all of us to become more alive to music on its sheerly musical plane. After all, an actual musical material is being used. The intelligent listener must be prepared to increase his awareness of the musical material and what happens to it. He must hear the melodies, the rhythms, the harmonies, the tone colors in a more conscious fashion. But above all he must, in order to follow the line of the composer's thought, know something of the principles of musical form. Listening to all of these elements is listening on the sheerly musical plane.

Let me repeat that I have split up mechanically the three separate planes on which we listen merely for the sake of greater clarity. Actually, we never listen on one or the other of these planes. What we do is to correlate them—listening in all three ways at the same time. It takes no mental effort, for we do it instinctively.

Perhaps an analogy with what happens to us when we visit the theater will make this instinctive correlation clearer. In the theater, you are aware of the actors and actresses, costumes and sets, sounds and movements. All these give one the sense that the theater is a pleasant place to be in. They constitute the sensuous plane in our theatrical reactions.

The expressive plane in the theater would be derived from the feeling that you get from what is happening on the stage. You are moved to pity, excitement, or gayety. It is this general feeling, generated aside from the particular words being spoken, a certain emotional something which exists on the stage, that is analogous to the expressive quality in music.

The plot and plot development is equivalent to our sheerly musical plane. The playwright creates and develops a character in just the same way that a composer creates and develops a theme. According to the degree of your awareness of the way in which the artist in either field handles his material will you become a more intelligent listener.

It is easy enough to see that the theatergoer never is conscious of any of these elements separately. He is aware of them all at the same time. The same is true of music listening. We simultaneously and without thinking listen on all three planes.

In a sense, the ideal listener is both inside and outside the music at the same moment, judging it and enjoying it, wishing it would go one way and watching it go another—almost like the composer at the moment he composes it; because in order to write his music, the composer must also be inside and outside his music, carried away by it and yet coldly critical of it. A subjective and objective attitude is implied in both creating and listening to music.

What the reader should strive for, then, is a more *active* kind of listening. Whether you listen to Mozart or Duke Ellington, you can deepen your understanding of music only by being a more conscious and aware listener—not someone who is just listening, but someone who is listening *for* something.

This crisp piece of writing is a chapter from the
Poetics of Music *by Igor Feodorovich Stravinsky*
(1882–   ). It was written originally in French, and
delivered in that language as one of the Charles Eliot
Norton lectures at Harvard University. In either
language, it has Stravinsky's flair for blunt statement
that challenges and reveals all at once, that uncovers
something about the nature of his art and at least
as much about our own responses to it. "To explain
myself to you is also to explain myself to myself,"
he says elsewhere in the Poetics, *"and to be obliged*
to clear up matters that are distorted or betrayed by
the ignorance and malevolence that one always finds
united by some mysterious bond in most of the
judgments that are passed upon the arts."
Stravinsky's judgments of critics have often been
harsh and much resented, by the critics, anyway.
But their resentment is not easily translated into
harsh judgments of his music. Stravinsky is clearly a
titan of contemporary music, a composer who has
produced work of the highest quality in the modes
of impressionism, neoclassicism, the serial, or

THE
PERFORMANCE
OF
MUSIC

twelve-tone, idiom, to mention a few. A history of
music in the twentieth century could be constructed
simply on the basis of his compositions. Any history
of music in this period
must give great
prominence to such
works of his as The Fire Bird, Le Sacre du
Printemps, L'Histoire du Soldat, *the* Symphony of
Psalms, The Rake's Progress, Orpheus,
Canticum Sacrum, *and* Threni.

Igor
Stravinsky

It is necessary to distinguish two moments, or
rather two states of music: potential music and
actual music. Having been fixed on paper or retained in the memory, music exists already prior
to its actual performance, differing in this respect from all the other arts, just as it differs
from them, . . . in the categories that determine
its perception.

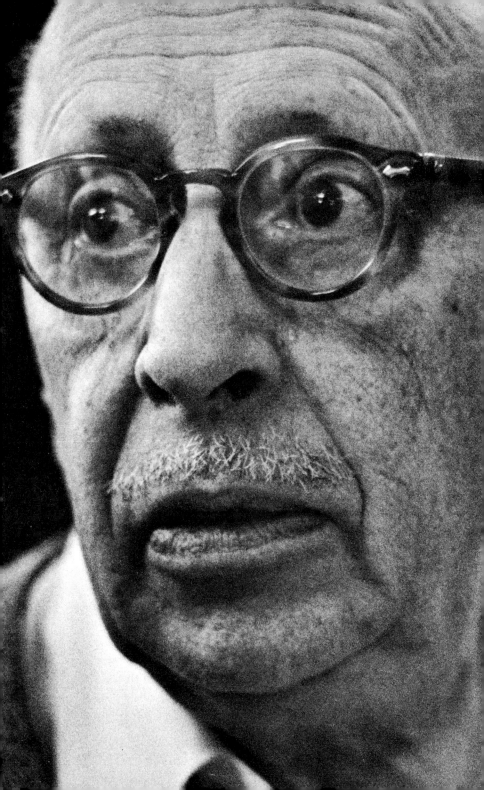

The musical entity thus presents the remarkable singularity of embodying two aspects, of existing successively and distinctly in two forms separated from each other by the hiatus of silence. This peculiar nature of music determines its very life as well as its repercussions in the social world, since it presupposes two kinds of musicians: the creator and the performer.

Let us note in passing that the art of the theater which requires the composition of a text and its translation into oral and visual terms, poses a similar, if not absolutely identical, problem; for there is a distinction that cannot be ignored: the theater appeals to our understanding by addressing itself simultaneously to sight and hearing. Now of all our senses sight is the most closely allied to the intellect, and hearing is appealed to in this case through articulated language, the vehicle for images and concepts. So the reader of a dramatic work can more easily imagine what its actual presentation would be like than the reader of a musical score can imagine how the actual instrumental playing of the score would sound. And it is easy to see why there are far fewer readers of orchestral scores than there are readers of books about music.

In addition, the language of music is strictly limited by its notation. The dramatic actor thus finds he has much more latitude in regard to *chronos* and intonation than does the singer who is tightly bound to *tempo* and *melos*.

This subjection, that is often so trying to the exhibitionism of certain soloists, is at the very heart of the question that we propose to take up now: the question of the executant and the interpreter.

The idea of interpretation implies the limitations imposed upon the performer or those which the performer imposes upon himself in his proper function, which is to transmit music to the listener.

The idea of execution implies the strict putting into effect of an explicit will that contains nothing beyond what it specifically commands.

It is the conflict of these two principles—execution and interpretation—that is at the root of all the errors, all the sins, all the misunderstandings that interpose themselves between the musical work and the listener and prevent a faithful transmission of its message.

Every interpreter is also of necessity an executant. The reverse

Igor Stravinsky.
Photograph by Dennis Stock. Magnum.

is not true. Following the order of succession rather than of precedence, we shall first consider the executant.

It is taken for granted that I place before the performer written music wherein the composer's will is explicit and easily discernible from a correctly established text. But no matter how scrupulously a piece of music may be notated, no matter how carefully it may be insured against every possible ambiguity through the indications of *tempo*, shading, phrasing, accentuation, and so on, it always contains hidden elements that defy definition, because verbal dialectic is powerless to define musical dialectic in its totality. The realization of these elements is thus a matter of experience and intuition, in a word, of the talent of the person who is called upon to present the music.

Thus, in contrast to the craftsman of the plastic arts, whose finished work is presented to the public eye in an always identical form, the composer runs a perilous risk every time his music is played, since the competent presentation of his work each time depends on the unforeseeable and imponderable factors that go to make up the virtues of fidelity and sympathy, without which the work will be unrecognizable on one occasion, inert on another, and in any case betrayed.

Between the executant pure and simple and the interpreter in the strict sense of the word, there exists a difference in make-up that is of an ethical rather than of an aesthetic order, a difference that presents a point of conscience: theoretically, one can only require of the executant the translation into sound of his musical part, which he may do willingly or grudgingly, whereas one has the right to seek from the interpreter, in addition to the perfection of this translation into sound, a loving care—which does not mean, be it surreptitious or openly affirmed, a recomposition.

The sin against the spirit of the work always begins with a sin against its letter and leads to the endless follies which an ever-flourishing literature in the worst taste does its best to sanction. Thus it follows that a *crescendo*, as we all know, is always accompanied by a speeding up of movement, while a slowing down never fails to accompany a *diminuendo*. The superfluous is refined upon; a *piano, piano pianissimo* is delicately sought after; great pride is taken in perfecting useless nuances—a concern that usually goes hand in hand with inaccurate rhythm. . . .

These are just so many practices dear to superficial minds forever avid for, and satisfied with, an immediate and facile success that flatters the vanity of the person who obtains it and perverts the taste of those who applaud it. How many remunerative careers have been launched by such practices! How many times have I been the victim of these misdirected attentions from abstractors of quintessences who waste time splitting hairs over a *pianissimo*, without so much as noticing egregious blunders of rendition! Exceptions, you may say. Bad interpreters should not make us forget the good ones. I agree—noting, however, that the bad ones are in the majority and that the virtuosos who serve music faithfully and loyally are much rarer than those who, in order to get settled in the comfortable berth of a career, make music serve them.

The widespread principles that govern the interpretation of the romantic masters in particular, make these composers the predestined victims of the criminal assaults we are speaking about. The interpretation of their works is governed by extra-musical considerations based on the loves and misfortunes of the victim. The title of a piece becomes an excuse for gratuitous hindthought. If the piece has none, a title is thrust upon it for wildly fanciful reasons. I am thinking of the Beethoven sonata that is never designated otherwise than by the title of "The Moonlight Sonata" without anyone ever knowing why; of the waltz in which it is mandatory to find Frederick Chopin's "Farewell."

Obviously, it is not without a reason that the worst interpreters usually tackle the Romantics. The musically extraneous elements that are strewn throughout their works invite betrayal, whereas a page in which music seeks to express nothing outside of itself better resists attempts at literary deformation. It is not easy to conceive how a pianist could establish his reputation by taking Haydn as his war-horse. That is undoubtedly the reason why that great musician has not won a renown among our interpreters that is in keeping with his true worth.

In regard to interpretation, the last century left us in its ponderous heritage a curious and peculiar species of soloist without precedent in the distant past—a soloist called the orchestra leader.

It was romantic music that unduly inflated the personality of the *Kapellmeister* [concert master] even to the point of conferring upon him—along with the prestige that he today enjoys on his podium, which in itself concentrates attention upon him—the discretionary power that he exerts over the music committed to his care. Perched on his sibylline tripod, he imposes his own movements, his own particular shadings upon the compositions he conducts, and he even reaches the point of talking with a naïve impudence of his specialities, of *his* fifth, of *his* seventh, the way a chef boasts of a dish of his own concoction. Hearing him speak, one thinks of the billboards that recommend eating places to automobilists: "At so-and-so's restaurant, his wines, his special dishes."

There was never anything like it in the past, in times that nevertheless already knew as well as our time go-getting and tyrannical virtuosos, whether instrumentalists or prima donnas. But those times did not yet suffer from the competition and plethora of conductors who almost to a man aspire to set up a dictatorship over music.

Do not think I am exaggerating. A quip that was passed on to me some years ago clearly shows the importance which the conductor has come to take on in the preoccupations of the musical world. One day a person who presides over the fortunes of a big concert agency was being told about the success obtained in Soviet Russia by that famous conductorless orchestra [which Stravinsky describes elsewhere]: "That doesn't make much sense," declared the person in question, "and it doesn't interest me. What I'd really be interested in is not an orchestra without a conductor, but a conductor without an orchestra."

To speak of an interpreter means to speak of a translator. And it is not without reason that a well-known Italian proverb, which takes the form of a play on words, equates translation with betrayal.

Conductors, singers, pianists, all virtuosos should know or recall that the first condition that must be fulfilled by anyone who aspires to the imposing title of interpreter, is that he be first of all a flawless executant. The secret of perfection lies above all in his consciousness of the law imposed upon him by the work he is performing. And here we are back at the great principle of submission that we have so often invoked in the course of our lessons. This submission demands a flexibility that itself requires, along with technical mastery, a sense of tradition and, commanding the whole, an aristocratic culture that is not merely a question of acquired learning.

This submissiveness and culture that we require of the creator, we should quite justly and naturally require of the interpreter as well. Both will find therein freedom in extreme rigor and, in the final analysis, if not in the first instance, success—true success, the legitimate reward of the interpreters who in the expression of their most brilliant virtuosity preserve that modesty of movement and that sobriety of expression that is the mark of thoroughbred artists.

I said somewhere that it was not enough to hear music, but that it must also be seen. What shall we say of the ill-breeding of those grimacers who too often take it upon themselves to deliver the "inner meaning" of music by disfiguring it with their affected airs? For, I repeat, one sees music. An experienced eye follows and judges, sometimes unconsciously, the performer's least gesture. From this point of view one might conceive the process of performance as the creation of new values that call for the solution of problems similar to those which arise in the realm of choreography. In both cases we give special attention to the control of gestures. The dancer is an orator who speaks a mute language. The instrumentalist is an orator who speaks an unarticulated language. Upon one, just as upon the other, music imposes a strict bearing. For music does not move in the abstract. Its translation into plastic terms requires exactitude and beauty: the exhibitionists know this only too well.

The beautiful presentation that makes the harmony of what is seen correspond to the play of sounds demands not only good musical instruction on the part of the performer, but also requires a complete familiarity on his part, whether singer, instrumentalist, or conductor, with the style of the works that are entrusted to him; a very sure taste for expressive values and for their limitations, a secure sense for that which may be taken for granted—in a word, an education not only of the ear, but of the mind.

Such an education cannot be acquired in the schools of music and the conservatories, for the teaching of fine manners is not their object: very rarely does a violin teacher even point out to his pupils that it is ill-becoming, when playing, to spread one's legs too far apart.

It is nonetheless strange that such an educational program is nowhere put into effect. Whereas all social activities are regulated by rules of etiquette and good breeding, performers are still in most cases entirely unaware of the elementary precepts of

musical civility, that is to say of *musical good breeding*—a matter
of common decency that a child may learn. . . .

   The *Saint Matthew's Passion* of Johann Sebastian Bach is written for a chamber-music ensemble. Its first performance in Bach's
lifetime was perfectly realized by a total force of thirty-four
musicians, including soloists and chorus. That is known. And
nevertheless in our day one does not hesitate to present the work,
in complete disregard of the composer's wishes, with hundreds
of performers, sometimes almost a thousand. This lack of understanding of the interpreter's obligations, this arrogant pride in
numbers, this concupiscence of the many, betray a complete lack
of musical education.

   The absurdity of such a practice is in point of fact glaring in
every respect, and above all from the acoustic point of view. For
it is not enough that the sound reach the ear of the public; one
must also consider in what condition, in what state the sound is
received. When the music was not conceived for a huge mass of
performers, when its composer did not want to produce massive
dynamic effects, when the frame is all out of proportion to the
dimensions of the work, multiplication of the number of par-
ticipant performers can produce only disastrous effects.

   Sound, exactly like light, acts differently according to the
distance that separates the point of emission from the point of
reception. A mass of performers situated on a platform occupies
a surface that becomes proportionately larger as the mass becomes more sizeable. By increasing the number of points of
emission one increases the distances that separate these points from
one another and from the hearer. So that the more one multiplies
the points of emission, the more blurred will reception be.

   In every case the doubling of parts weighs down the music
and constitutes a peril that can be avoided only by proceeding
with infinite tact. Such additions call for a subtle and delicate
proportioning that itself presupposes the surest of tastes and a
discriminating culture.

   It is often believed that power can be increased indefinitely by
multiplying the doubling of orchestral parts—a belief that is
completely false: thickening is not strengthening. In a certain
measure and up to a certain point, doubling may give the illusion
of strength by effecting a reaction of a psychological order on
the listener. The sensation of shock stimulates the effect of power
and helps to establish an illusion of balance between the sounding

tonal masses. A good deal might be said in this connection about the balance of forces in the modern orchestra, a balance which is more easily explained by our aural habits than it is justified by exactness of proportions.

It is a positive fact that beyond a certain degree of extension the impression of intensity diminishes instead of increases and succeeds only in dulling the sensation.

Musicians should come to realize that for their art the same holds true as for the art of the billboard: that the blowing-up of sound does not hold the ear's attention—just as the advertising expert knows that letters which are too large do not attract the eye.

A work of art cannot contain itself. Once he has completed his work, the creator necessarily feels the need to share his joy. He quite naturally seeks to establish contact with his fellow man, who in this case becomes his listener. The listener reacts and becomes a partner in the game, initiated by the creator. Nothing less, nothing more. The fact that the partner is free to accept or to refuse participation in the game does not automatically invest him with the authority of a judge.

The judicial function presupposes a code of sanctions which mere opinion does not have at its disposal. And it is quite illicit, to my way of thinking, to set the public up as a jury by entrusting to it the task of rendering a verdict on the value of a work. It is already quite enough that the public is called upon to decide its ultimate fate.

The fate of a work, of course, depends in the final analysis on the public's taste, on the variations of its humor and habits; in a word, on its preferences. But the fate of a work does not depend upon the public's judgment as if it were a sentence without appeal.

I call your attention to this all-important point: consider on the one hand the conscious effort and patient organization that the composing of a work of art requires, and on the other hand the judgment—which is at least hasty and of necessity improvised —that follows the presentation of the work. The disproportion between the duties of the person who composes and the rights of those who judge him is glaring, since the work offered to the public, whatever its value may be, is always the fruit of study, reasoning, and calculation that imply exactly the converse of improvisation.

I have expatiated at some length on this theme in order to make you see more clearly where the true relations between the composer and the public lie, with the performer acting as an intermediary. You will thereby realize more fully the performer's moral responsibility.

For only through the performer is the listener brought in contact with the musical work. In order that the public may know what a work is like and what its value is, the public must first be assured of the merit of the person who presents the work to it and of the conformity of that presentation to the composer's will.

The listener's task becomes especially harrowing where a first hearing is concerned; for the listener in this case has no point of reference and possesses no basis for comparison.

And so it comes about that the first impression, which is so important, the first contact of the newborn work with the public, is completely dependent upon the validity of a presentation that eludes all controls.

Such, then, is our situation before an unpublished work when the quality of the performers before us does not guarantee that the composer will not be betrayed and that we shall not be cheated.

In every period the forming of an elite has given us that advance assurance in matters of social relations which permits us to have full confidence in the unknown performers who appear before us under the aegis of that flawless bearing which education bestows. Lacking a guarantee of this kind, our relations with music would always be unsatisfactory. You will understand, the situation being what it is, why we have stressed at such length the importance of education in musical matters.

We have said previously that the listener was, in a way, called upon to become the composer's partner. This presupposes that the listener's musical instruction and education are sufficiently extensive that he may not only grasp the main features of the work as they emerge, but that he may even follow to some degree the changing aspects of its unfolding.

As a matter of fact, such active participation is an unquestionably rare thing, just as the creator is a rare occurrence in the mass of humanity. This exceptional participation gives the partner such lively pleasure that it unites him in a certain measure with the mind that conceived and realized the work to which he is listening, giving him the illusion of identifying himself with the creator. That is the meaning of Raphael's famous adage: to understand is to equal.

But such understanding is the exception; the ordinary run of listeners, no matter how attentive to the musical process one supposes them to be, enjoy music only in a passive way.

Unfortunately, there exists still another attitude towards music which differs from both that of the listener who gives himself up to the working out of the music—participating in and following it step by step—and from the attitude of the listener who tries docilely to go along with the music: for we must now speak of indifference and apathy. Such is the attitude of snobs, of false enthusiasts who see in a concert or a performance only the opportunity to applaud a great conductor or an acclaimed virtuoso. One has only to look for a moment at those "faces gray with boredom," as Claude Debussy put it, to measure the power music has of inducing a sort of stupidity in those unfortunate persons who listen to it without hearing it. Those of you who have done me the honor of reading the *Chronicles of My Life* perhaps recall that I stress this matter in regard to mechanically reproduced music.

The propagation of music by all possible means is in itself an excellent thing; but by spreading it abroad without taking precautions, by offering it willy-nilly to the general public which is not prepared to hear it, one lays this public open to the most deadly saturation.

The time is no more when Johann Sebastian Bach gladly traveled a long way on foot to hear Buxtehude. Today radio brings music into the home at all hours of the day and night. It relieves the listener of all effort except that of turning a dial. Now the musical sense cannot be acquired or developed without exercise. In music, as in everything else, inactivity leads gradually to the paralysis, to the atrophying of faculties. Understood in this way, music becomes a sort of drug which, far from stimulating the mind, paralyzes and stultifies it. So it comes about that the very undertaking which seeks to make people like music by giving it a wider and wider diffusion, very often only achieves the result of making the very people lose their appetite for music whose interest was to be aroused and whose taste was to be developed.

Few arts have so successfully resisted definition as jazz. In this examination of the various attempts at definition, one of the editors of this volume offers as well some meditations on the history and development of jazz. These pages make up the first chapter of A History of Jazz in America *(1952), one of four volumes by Barry Ulanov (1918–   ) which are devoted to jazz or jazz musicians. In* The Two Worlds of American Art: The Private and the Popular *(1965), he adds another definition of sorts: "Jazz is an art of feeling. Its performers nurture their feelings with the tenderness of a parent, the tension of a frustrated adolescent, and the violence of a dispossessed adult. To find feelings and to hold them, jazz musicians use every means known to art and some new ones that they themselves have invented. Their procedures are alternately controlled and disorderly, anarchical and academic. They have developed virtuoso playing techniques to fit them. They have established a whole new series of traditions. All are in the service of feeling."*

WHAT IS JAZZ?

Barry Ulanov

In *The American Scene*, Henry James said of American cities, "So there it all is; arrange it as you can. Poor dear bad bold beauty; there must indeed be something about her . . . !" The same can be said of American jazz.

On the surface there is disorder and conflict in jazz. No common definition of this music has been reached. It resists dictionary definition, and its musicians splutter nervously and take refuge in the colorful ambiguities of its argot. Nonetheless, its beauty can be probed; its badness can be separated from its boldness. The process is a difficult one, as it is in any art, and in jazz two arts, the composing and the performing arts, are joined together. But if one goes beneath the surface and does not allow the contradictions and the confusions of appearances to put one off, much becomes clear, and the mystery at the center is seen to be the central mystery of all the arts.

The cortex of jazz consists of several layers, alternately hard and soft, complex in structure, and hard to take apart. It is compounded of the history of the music and of the many styles of jazz. At first the history seems disjointed and the styles contradictory. One marks a confounding series of shifts in place and person and style. One finds a music dominated by Negroes in New Orleans, by white musicians in Chicago, by important but apparently unrelated figures in New York. One discovers a disastrous split in jazz inaugurated by the swing era and intensified during the days of bebop and so-called progressive jazz. But then one looks and listens more closely, and order and continuity appear.

Americans have long been wedded to the boom-and-bust cycle, and their culture reflects that dizzying course. Jazz is not like that; it has no cycles; it doesn't spiral. Whether you adopt the approach of the economic historian, the cultural anthropologist, or the aesthetic philosopher, you will not find an easy reflection of a theory in jazz. While much of America—crises and ecstasies and even a moment or two of exaltation—has found its way into jazz, the history of jazz is a curiously even one, chaotic at any instant, but always moving ahead in what is for an art form almost a straight line.

For most of its history, jazz, rejected in its homeland, has had consciously to seek survival, conscientiously to explain and defend its existence. From its early homes, the Ozark hills, the Louisiana bayous, the Carolina cotton fields, the Virginia plantations, through the New Orleans bordellos and barrelhouses to its latter-day efflorescence it has been alternately condemned and misunderstood. Variously banned and bullied and sometimes cheered beyond its merits, jazz has led a lonely life but a full one. It is still with us and looks to be around for quite a while.

No matter what the fortunes of jazz, its nucleus has remained constant, little touched by extravagances of opinion, sympathetic or unsympathetic. The nucleus of jazz—as differentiated from its cortex—contains its nerve center, its source of life, and here are its mystery and meaning. The nucleus of jazz is made up of melody, harmony, and rhythm, the triune qualities of the art of music which, as everybody knows, can be fairly simply defined. In bare definition, melody is any succession of notes, harmony any simultaneity of tones, rhythm the arithmetic measure of notes or tones. In closer examination, melody appears as a vast variety of things, ranging from so simple a tune as "Yankee Doodle" to the complexity of one of Arnold Schönberg's constructions. In more detailed analysis, harmony shows up as a vertical ordering of a Bach fugue, or a tight structuring based entirely on whole tones in the impressionism of Debussy. But bewildering as the complications of melody and harmony can be, they are easier to analyze and verbalize than rhythm or any of its parts, and rhythm is the most important of the three in jazz.

Before attempting a synoptic definition of jazz as a noun (or discussing the misuse of "jazz" as a verb and "jazzy" as an adjective), and of the various corollary terms that explain the meaning of this music, it might be instructive to examine definitions by musicians themselves. The following definitions were made by jazz musicians in 1935, when their music was undergoing a revival as a result of the then current vogue for the jazz that went by the new name of swing. Benny Goodman was a great success, and jam sessions had become public again. Musicians themselves found it difficult to define "swing," by which of course they merely meant the 1935 version of jazz, which wasn't very different from the 1930 or 1925 music. Let us examine the definitions.

Wingy Manone: "Feeling an increase in tempo though you're still playing at the same tempo."

Marshall Stearns and *John Hammond* (jazz authorities) and *Benny Goodman:* "A band swings when its collective improvisation is rhythmically integrated."

Gene Krupa: "Complete and inspired freedom of rhythmic interpretation."

Jess Stacy: "Syncopated syncopation."

Morton Kahn and *Payson Re:* "Feeling a multitude of subdivisions in each beat and playing or implying the accents that you feel; that is, if the tune is played at the proper tempo, so that when you're playing it, you'll feel it inside."

Glenn Miller: "Something that you have to feel; a sensation that can be conveyed to others."

Frankie Froeba: "A steady tempo, causing lightness and relaxation and a feeling of floating."

Louis Armstrong.
Photograph by Dennis Stock. Magnum.

Terry Shand: "A synthetic cooperation of two or more instruments helping along or giving feeling to the soloist performing."

Ozzie Nelson: "A vague something that you seem to feel pulsating from a danceable orchestra. To me it is a solidity and compactness of attack by which the rhythm instruments combine with the others to create within the listeners the desire to dance."

Chick Webb: "It's like lovin' a gal, and havin' a fight, and then seein' her again."

Louis Armstrong: "My idea of how a tune should go."

Ella Fitzgerald: "Why, er—swing is—well, you sort of feel—uh—uh—I don't know—you just swing!"

These musicians were looking for a new set of terms that would catch the beat so basic to jazz; they were stumped for the words to describe the kind of improvisation necessary to jazz.

In the simple, compressed, sometimes too elliptic vocabulary of the jazz musician, one learns a great deal about the music he plays. One learns that "jazz" is a noun, that it is not American popular music (as it has often been thought to be), that the jazz musician is most interested in the rhythmic connotation of the word and in little else. If you tell him that some say the term comes from the phonetic spelling of the abbreviation of a jazz musician named Charles (Charles, Chas., Jass, Jazz), he is not in the least interested. If you tell him that there is a great deal of substance to the claim that the word comes from the French word *jaser*—to pep up, to exhilarate—he may nod his head with a degree of interest but ask you, "What about the beat?" You will learn from the jazz musician that "swing" is no longer a noun, in spite of the fact that it was first so used in the title of a Duke Ellington recording in 1931, "It Don't Mean a Thing if It Ain't Got That Swing," which gives it a kind of ex cathedra endorsement. You will learn that "swing" is a verb, that it is a way of describing the beat, even as Ellington's title for another tune, "Bouncing Buoyancy," is a description of the same beat, even as the term "jump" is, even as "leaps" is, even as the description of jazz as "music that goes" is, even as in the thirties the compliment of "solid" to performer or performance was like "gone," "crazy," "craziest," "the end," and "cool" today. They are descriptions of the beat.

From an examination of jazz musicians' own words, it is possible to glean the subtle, unruly, and almost mystical concept of the jazz spirit, or feeling, or thinking—it is all these things and is so understood by the jazz musician himself. The jazzman has his own way of getting at the center of his music, and thus he formulates his own musical language. Also he converts the musical language into a verbal dialect of his own. In his own set of terms, musical and verbal, he thinks, he feels; he rehearses, he performs; he scores, he improvises; he gets a beat.

To get that elusive beat, a jazzman will do anything. Without it, he cannot do anything. With it, he is playing jazz, and that is a large and satisfying enough accomplishment. When a jazzman picks up a familiar tune, banal or too well-known through much repetition, and alters its rhythmic pattern in favor of a steady if sometimes monotonous beat, and varies its melodies and maybe even changes its chords, he is working freely, easily, and with as much spontaneity as he can bring to his music. That freedom, ease, and spontaneity brought him to jazz; within those determining limits he will find a place for himself or get out, or join one of the bands whose frightening parodies of jazz are so often more popular than the real thing. It is by his formal understanding of certain definite values that the jazz musician has conceived, organized, and developed his art. It has been hot; it has become cool. It has jumped and swung; it has sauntered. It has borrowed; it has originated. It has effected a change, a literal transformation; inherited conventions have gradually been restated, reorganized, and ultimately restructured as a new expression. It may be that jazz musicians have simply rediscovered a controlling factor in music, the improvising performer. Without any awareness of what he has done, the jazzman may have gone back to some of the beginnings of music, tapping once more the creative roots which nourished ancient Greek music, the plain chant, the musical baroque and its immediate successors and predecessors. We know that seventeenth- and eighteenth-century composers were improvisers and that when they brought their scores to other musicians they left the interpretation of parts to the discretion of the performers, even as an arranger for a jazz band does today.

But the jazz musician has brought more than procedures, composing conceptions, and improvisation to his music. Techniques have been developed that have broadened the resources and intensified the disciplines of certain instruments far beyond their use in other music. Colors have been added to solo instruments and to various combinations and numbers of instruments that are utterly unlike any others in music. New textures have emerged from a conception of tonality and of pitch that is not original but is entirely fresh in its application. The improvising jazz musician has a different and more responsible and rewarding position than that of his counterparts in earlier art and folk music. The rhythmic base of music has been reinterpreted, making the central pulse at once more primitive than it has been before in Western music, and more sophisticated in its variety.

This, then, is how one might define jazz: it is a new music of a certain distinct rhythmic and melodic character, one that constantly involves improvisation—of a minor sort in adjusting accents and phrases of the tune at hand, of a major sort in creating music extemporaneously, on the spot. In the course of creating jazz, a melody or its underlying chords may be altered. The rhythmic valuations of notes may be lengthened or shortened according to a regular scheme, syncopated or not, or there may be no consistent pattern of rhythmic variations so long as a steady beat remains implicit or explicit. The beat is usually four quarter-notes to the bar, serving as a solid rhythmic base for the improvisation of soloists or groups playing eight or twelve measures, or some multiple or dividend thereof.

These things are the means. The ends are the ends of all art, the expression of the universal and the particular, the specific and the indirect and the intangible. In its short history, jazz has generally been restricted to short forms and it often been directed toward the ephemeral and the trivial, but so too has it looked toward the lasting perception and the meaningful conclusion. Much of the time jazz musicians have sought and obtained an unashamed aphrodisiac effect; they have also worshiped in their music, variously devout before the one God and the unnamed gods. Like poets and painters, they are of all faiths, their doctrines are many; but they are united in one conviction, that they have found a creative form for themselves, for their time, for their place.

At the opening of the *Gradus ad Parnassum*, the dialogue offered as a study of counterpoint by Johann Josef Fux in 1725, the music master Aloysius warns the student Josef: "You must try to remember whether or not you felt a strong natural inclination to this art even in childhood." The student answers: "Yes, most deeply. Even before I could reason, I was overcome by the force of this strange enthusiasm and I turned all my thoughts and feelings to music. And now the burning desire to understand it possesses me, drives me almost against my will, and day and night lovely melodies seem to sound around me. Therefore I think I no longer have reason to doubt my inclination. Nor do the difficulties of the work discourage me, and I hope that with the help of good health I shall be able to master it." Several jazz musicians have read Fux, even as Haydn and Beethoven did, though perhaps with less immediate application. They have, however, echoed the pupil's "strange enthusiasm"; that, these jazzmen said, was their experience, their "burning desire." Following the "inclination," jazz musicians have not had much of the help of good health; some of them have flaunted their doggedly unreasonable living habits and suffered the personal and public consequences of the habits and of the flaunting. All this their music has reflected, and sometimes it is noisy and grotesque as a result. More often it has a fullness and richness of expression. Slowly, clearly, the music is maturing, and, for it and with it and by it, so are the musicians.

THE LISTENER

Roger Sessions

No one is more concerned with the response of the listener to music than the composer. That concern is meticulously expressed here by the American composer Roger Sessions (1896–   ). Sessions is a distinguished creator in almost all the forms of music—the string quartet, the symphony, the opera, and so on. Very much a man of the twentieth century in style, he is also very much of his own time in his openness to the various ways that listeners approach his art. The mysterious processes of music are made a good deal more understandable in Roger Sessions' detailed and sympathetic examination of the psychology of listening. Fittingly, the language and style are simple and the comparisons to other arts, by which we sometimes are enabled to proceed with greater ease, are frequent.

We are all very much concerned these days, with the listener—the person who neither makes music nor performs it, but simply listens to it. The market is flooded with books of all sorts, fulfilling all sorts of functions for all sorts of listeners, from the child to "the man who enjoys *Hamlet*" and even "the intelligent listener"— analyses to edify him, critical chit-chat to flatter him, and gossip to amuse him. We have grade school, high school, and university courses designed to inform him and, if possible, to educate him in "appreciation," in "intelligent listening," and even "creative listening." On the radio he may find quiz programs, interviews with personalities, broadcast orchestra rehearsals, and spoken program notes, which have been known on occasion to be so long that there is not enough time for the broadcast of the music. Surely we are leaving no stone unturned in the effort to prepare the listener fully for the strenuous task of listening to music.

This is actually a peculiar state of affairs.

Music, and in fact art in general, is not one of the so-called necessities of life, nor does it yield us any of the creature comforts associated with the standard of living of which we are so proud. Why then should we be so concerned about the listener? Is not music available to him, if he wants it? Should we not rather demand simply that the listener be given the best products available? Should we not rather concern ourselves with the quality of our music, and with ways of producing the highest quality, with providing the best possible education for our young musicians, and with creating opportunities for them to function according to their merits? In truth, should we not rather devote ourselves to improving the quality of our music, and to seeing that music of the highest quality is available for all that wish to hear it?

Of course, we have no such choice of alternatives; and the concern that is felt for the listener today is no chance development but the result of the situation in which music finds itself in our contemporary world. . . .

When music or any other product is furnished to millions of individuals, it is bound to become necessary to consider the tastes of those individuals in relation to the product offered them. Those who furnish the product are obliged to produce as efficiently and as cheaply as possible the goods which they can sell to the most people; they are obliged, furthermore, to try to persuade the people to whom they sell that it is preferable to buy the goods that are most cheaply produced; it is furthermore necessary to do everything possible to enhance the value of the goods sold. If they fail to do these things they are taking foolish economic risks. The larger the quantities involved, the greater the potential profits; but while this is true, it is also true that the risks of possible catastrophic loss are greater. These facts are elementary; not only do they apply vitally to the situation of music today, but I believe that an understanding of them is absolutely indispensable if we are to understand any economic, political, or social aspects whatever of the contemporary world.

In brief, the "listener" has become, in relation to these facts, the "consumer," and however unaware we as individuals are of this, it is nevertheless the basic explanation of our interest in him. Though neither he nor we have chosen this role for him, circumstances have made it inevitable. In relation to the same facts (and please note the phrase carefully, for I shall try to show later that these are not the only facts), the status of the artist in our society has undergone a remarkable change. He has become (in relation to the same facts) no longer a cultural citizen, one of the cultural assets of the community with purely cultural responsibilities, but what is sometimes called a cog in the economic machine. He is asked and even in a sense required to justify his existence as a plausible economic risk; to, as we say, "sell" himself as a possible source of economic profit. Then, having done so, he must produce what is required of him in this sense. He, too, has an interest in the listener; it is the listener who buys his wares and therefore justifies his continued existence as an efficient cog. He has to be constantly aware, in fact, of the requirements of the machinery in approximately the terms I have outlined above. For the aims of business are essentially short-range aims, and it is doubtful whether business, as such, can conceivably operate on any other basis. It can allow itself the luxury of the long-range view only to the extent that it builds up enormous surpluses which make risks economically possible, and even then only under circumstances offering reasonable hope of long-range rewards.

Let me say once again that I do not consider this the entire picture of our cultural situation or of our cultural prospects. I shall later try to show why I do not believe it to be so. Furthermore, these remarks are generalizations, and subject to elaboration, with intricate scoring and with many subtleties of nuance. I do not intend to score them for you here. But we cannot understand the listener unless we know who he is in terms of the conditions actually prevalent. We must see him, in other words, not as an abstraction but as an existing and concrete figure in our musical society.

But it is not mainly in his role of consumer that I wish to speak of the listener. The question for us is rather his own experience of music—what hearing and understanding consist in, and, finally, what discrimination involves. What, in other words, is his relationship to music? How can he get the most from it? How can music mean the most to him? In what does his real education consist? Finally, how can he exercise his powers of discrimination in such a way as to promote valid musical experience in others and, so to speak, in the world in general?

I think we can distinguish four stages in the listener's development. First, he must hear; I have already indicated what I mean by this. It is not simply being present when music is performed, nor is it even simply recognizing bits of the music—leit-motifs, or themes, or salient features in a score. It is rather, as it were, opening one's ears to the sounds as they succeed each other, discovering whatever point of contact one can find, and in fact following the music as well as one can in its continuity. We perhaps tend to ignore the fact that listeners are, like composers and performers, variously endowed, and also that they differ very widely in experience. But this initial stage in listening to music is an entirely direct one; the listener brings to the music whatever he can bring, with no other preoccupation than that of hearing. This is of course what is to be desired; it is the condition of his really hearing. He will hear the music only to the extent that he identifies himself with it, establishing a fresh and essentially naïve contact with it, without preconceived ideas and without strained effort.

The second stage is that of enjoyment, or shall we say the primary response. It is perhaps hardly discernible as a "second stage" at all: the listener's reaction is immediate and seems in a sense identical with the act of hearing. Undoubtedly this is what many listeners expect. And yet, on occasion, one may listen to music attentively, without any conscious response to it until afterwards; one's very attention may be so absorbed that a vivid sense of the sound is retained but a sense of communication is experienced only later. It is this sense of communication to which I refer under the term "enjoyment"; obviously, one may not and often does not, in any real sense, "enjoy" what is being communicated. There is certainly some music that we never "enjoy"; experience inevitably fosters discrimination, and there is certainly some truth even in the frequent, seemingly paradoxical, statement that "the more one loves music, the less music one loves." The statement is true in a sense if we understand it as applying to the experience of the individual, and not as a general rule. But if our relation to music is a healthy one—that is to say, a direct and a simple one—our primary and quite spontaneous effort will be to enjoy it. If this effort becomes inhibited it will be by reason of experience and the associations that inevitably follow in its train. We shall in that case have acquired a sense of musical values, and our specific response will be curtailed in deference to the more general response which our musical experience has given us.

The third of the four phases I have spoken of consists in what we call "musical understanding." I must confess that I am not altogether pleased with this term. To speak quite personally if not too seriously, a composer will certainly have every right to feel pleased, but he may not feel entirely flattered, when he is told "I love your music, but of course I have no right to an opinion—I don't really understand it." In what does "musical understanding" consist? The difficulty, I think, comes from the fact that while . . . the instinctive bases of music, the impulses which constitute its raw materials, are essentially of the most primitive sort, yet the organization of these materials, the shaping of them into a means of communication and later into works of art, is, and historically speaking has been, a long and intricate process and one which has few obvious contacts with the world of ordinary experience. The technique of every art has, of course, its esoteric phases; but in the case of visual art even these phases are relatively accessible to the layman, since he can, if he is really interested, grasp them in terms of quite ordinary practical activity. He will have learned early in his life to be aware of the basic facts of size, contour, color, and perspective on very much the same terms as are required for his perception of visual art. He can to a certain extent appreciate the artist's problems in these terms and can define his response, at least on an elementary level, in terms satisfactory to himself. This is even truer in the case of literary art, since he constantly uses words and to a greater or a lesser degree expresses himself by their means. Like Molière's "bourgeois gentleman," he has talked in prose all his life. His feeling for the values of both visual and literary art consists therefore in a high degree of refinement, and an extension, of experiences which are thoroughly familiar to him, through analogies constantly furnished by his ordinary life.

In the case of music there are no such clear analogies. The technical facts which are commonplace to the composer, and even many of those proper to the performer, have no clear analogies in the ordinary experience of the non-musician. The latter finds them quite mysterious and, as I have already pointed out, tends to exaggerate both their uniqueness and their inaccessibility to the layman. And if the latter finds it difficult to conceive of the mere fact of inner hearing and auditory imagination, how much more difficult will he find such a conception as, for instance, tonality, or the musical facts on which the principles of what we call "musical form" are based. He is likely not only to regard music *per se* as a book in principle closed to him, but, through the impressive unfamiliarity of whatever technical jargon he chances to hear, to misunderstand both the nature and the role of musical technique. It is likely to seem to him something of an abstraction, with an existence of its own, to which the sensations and impressions he receives from music are only remotely related, as by-products. How often, for instance, have I been asked whether the study and mastery of music does not involve a knowledge of higher mathematics! The layman is only too likely to react in either one of two ways, or in a combination of both. He is likely, that is, either to regard music as something to which he is essentially a stranger, or else to regard its generally accepted values as arbitrary, pretentious, and academic, and both to give to it and to receive from it far less than his aptitudes warrant.

The surprising thing is that all of these conclusions are based on a mistaken idea as to the real meaning of musical "understanding." Technique is certainly useful, not to say indispensable, to the composer or the performer; a knowledge of musical theory is certainly an advantage to the performer and practically inescapable for the composer. But theory, in the sense of generalization, is not of the least use to the listener; in practice it is a veritable encumbrance if he allows preoccupation with it to interfere with his contact with the music as such. He can certainly derive both interest and help from whatever can be pointed out to him in connection with the specific content of a piece of music; but he will be only misled if he is persuaded to listen in an exploratory rather than a completely receptive spirit. Any effort to help him must be in the direction of liberating, not of conditioning, his ear; and the generalizations of which musical theory consists demonstrably often lead him to strained efforts which are a positive barrier to understanding. The "technique" of a piece of music is essentially the affair of the composer; it is largely even subconscious, and composers frequently are confronted by perfectly real technical facts, present in their music, of which they had no conscious inkling. And do we seriously believe that understanding of Shakespeare, or James Joyce, or William Faulkner has anything to do with the ability to parse the sentences and describe the functions of the various words in *Hamlet* or *Ulysses?*

Of course not. Understanding of music, as relevant for the

listener, means the ability to receive its full message. . . . In the primary sense, the listener's real and ultimate response to music consists not in merely hearing it, but in inwardly reproducing it, and his understanding of music consists in the ability to do this in his imagination. This point cannot be too strongly emphasized. The really "understanding" listener takes the music into his consciousness and remakes it actually or in his imagination, for his own uses. He whistles it on the street, or hums it at his work, or simply "thinks" it to himself. He may even represent it to his consciousness in a more concentrated form—as a condensed memory of sounds heard and felt, reproduced for his memory by a vivid sensation of what I may call character in sound, without specific details but in terms of sensations and impressions remembered.

It is for this reason that I am somewhat skeptical of the helpfulness of the kind of technical tid-bits and quasi-analyses sometimes offered to the listener as aids to understanding. The trouble with them, as so often presented, seems to me that the essential facts of musical technique cannot really be conveyed in this way. To give one instance, musicians talk, for convenience, about what we call the "sonata form." But they know, or should know, that the conception "sonata form" is a rough generalization and that in practice sonatas, at least those written by masters, are individual and that each work has its own form. To speak of "sonata form" without making clear what constitutes "form" in music, as such, is to falsify, not to illuminate. It is to imply that the composer adapts his ideas to a mold into which he then pours the music. It is also to lay far too much emphasis on what are called "themes," to the detriment of the musical flow in its entirety. What the layman needs is not to acquire facts but to cultivate senses: the sense of rhythm, of articulation, of contrast, of accent. He needs to be aware of the progression of the bass as well as the treble line; of a return to the principal or to a subsidiary key, of a far-flung tonal span. He needs to be aware of all these things as events which his ear witnesses and appreciates as a composition unfolds. Whether or not it is a help to have specific instances pointed out to him, it is certain in any case that his main source of understanding will be through hearing music in general, and specific works in particular, repeatedly, and making them his own through familiarity, through memory, and through inner re-elaboration.

I hardly need point out the fact that this is as true in regard to so-called "modern" music as it is to old. Where the music is radically unfamiliar the three processes I have described are slower. It must therefore be heard more often than the older music needs to be heard. At the beginning the impressions will be chaotic—much more chaotic than impressions produced by purely fortuitous sounds. The impression of chaos comes simply from the fact that the sounds and relationships are unfamiliar; their very consistency—since it, too, is based on contexts which are unfamiliar—seems like a denial of logic. As long as this impression prevails the listener has not yet made contact with the music. In connection with contemporary music, I have often observed the first sensations of real contact, while the musical language in question is still essentially unfamiliar but beginning to be intelligible. These first sensations may be acutely pleasurable; the work becomes highly exciting, conveying a kind of superficial excitement which disappears when the stage of real understanding is reached and gives way to an appreciation for the real "message" of the work. Once more, the key to the "understanding" of contemporary music lies in repeated hearing; one must hear it till the sounds are familiar, until one begins to notice false notes if they are played. One can make the effort to retain it in one's head, and one will always find that the accurate memory of sounds heard coincides with the understanding of them. In fact, the power to retain sounds by memory implies that they have been mastered. For the ear by its nature seeks out patterns and relationships, and it is only these patterns that we can remember and that make music significant for us.

The listener's final stage is that of discrimination. It is important that it should be the final stage since real discrimination is possible only with understanding; and both snobbery and immaturity at times foster prejudices which certainly differ from discrimination in any real sense. Actually it is almost impossible not to discriminate if we persist in and deepen our musical experience. We will learn to differentiate between lasting impressions and those which are fleeting, and between the musical experiences which give full satisfaction and those which only partly satisfy us. We will learn to differentiate between our impressions, too, in a qualitative sense. In this way, we cultivate a sense of values to which to refer our later judgment. We will learn that music is unequal in quality; we will possibly learn that instead of speaking of "immortality" in the case of some works and of the ephemeral quality of others, we must conceive of differences in the life span of works—that some works last in our esteem longer than others without necessarily lasting for- ever. We will learn finally to differentiate in the matter of character, to be aware of the differences between works in ways which have no relation to intrinsic worth. In other words, we will become critics. . . .

Let us phrase the question in more general terms: What does the listener demand from music? The answer will inevitably be that a variety of listeners want a variety of things. But on any level it may be taken for granted that the listener wants vital experience, whether of a deeply stirring, brilliantly stimulating, or simply entertaining type. If we understand this we should understand, too, that the composer can effectively furnish it only on his own terms. He can persuade others to love only what he loves himself, and can convince only by means of what fully convinces him. It is for this reason that the artist must be com- pletely free, that such a question as I have stated here can ulti- mately have no importance to him. His obligation is to give the best he can give, wherever it may lead, and to do so without compromise and with complete conviction. This is in fact natural to him; if he is a genuine artist he cannot do otherwise. He can be sure that if he fully achieves his artistic goals, he will find listeners, and that if he has something genuine to say, the number of his listeners will increase, however slowly. This, in any case, will never be for him an artistic preoccupation, however much it may prove to be a practical one.

Composers, like poets, are born, not made; but once born, they have to grow. It is in this sense that a culture will, generally speaking, get the music that it demands. The question, once more, is what we demand of the composer. Do we demand always what is easiest, music that is primarily and invariably entertainment, or do we seriously want from him the best that he has to give? In the latter case, are we willing to come to meet him, to make whatever effort is demanded of us as listeners, in order to get from his music what it has to give us? Once more, it is for the listener and not for the composer, as an individual, that the answer is important. On the answer we ultimately give depends the future of music in the United States.

THE YOUNG AUDIENCE

A great amount of noisy rhetoric has been used up since 1955 in denouncing rock 'n' roll, rock-a-billy, folk-rock, and other teenagers' tastes in music. A certain amount of quiet, if not awed, prose, however, has been devoted to analyzing the fortunes that this music has enabled certain of its practitioners to make. But very little, if any, serious attention has been given to what this music is really like, where it came from, and where it may be going. Two Englishmen, a senior research fellow at the Birmingham University Center for Cultural Studies—Mr. Hall—and an Education Officer at the British Film Institute—Mr. Whannel— have remedied that situation. As part of a long examination of The Popular Arts, *Hall and Whannel deal with the tastes, the tones, and the social psychology of young listeners as these phenomena are reflected in their music and in their ways of response to it. It is, of course, quite proper for Englishmen to sift through these materials: such materials are, after all, as much Anglo as they are American.*

Paddy Whannel
Stuart Hall

Teenage culture is a contradictory mixture of the authentic and the manufactured: it is an area of self-expression for the young and a lush grazing pasture for the commercial providers. One might use the cult figure of the pop singer as an illustration. He is usually a teenager, springing from the familiar adolescent world, and sharing a whole set of common feelings with his audience. But once he is successful, he is transformed into a commercial entertainer by the pop-music business. Yet in style, presentation and the material he performs, he must maintain his close involvement with the teenage world, or he will lose his popularity. The record companies see him as a means of marketing their products—he is a living, animated, commercial image. The audience will buy his records if they like his performances, and thus satisfy the provider's need to keep sales high: but they will also regard the pop singer as a kind of model, an idealized image of success, a glamorized version of themselves.

When commercial providers become involved in creating new fashions and setting styles, they are inevitably caught up in the psychological processes of adolescence, in the crisis of identity which many experience at this age. They provide one set of answers to the search for more meaningful and satisfying adult roles. And the danger is that they will short-circuit this difficult process by offering too limited a range of social models for young people to conform to, a kind of consumer identity, which could be dangerous even when ultimately rejected by them. There seems to be a clear conflict between commercial and cultural considerations here, for which commercial providers take no responsibility.

The commercial images sometimes work in this way because they invoke such powerful elements in the teenage culture. They play upon the self-enclosed, introspective intensity of the teenage world. One aspect of this tribalism which the media exaggerate can be seen lying behind the remarks of a young girl interviewed in a series on adolescents on BBC Schools Television. "You see a woman who is well dressed," she said, "in the latest fashion, made-up and all that. . . . Well, you wouldn't say she's 'modern'—she's 'smart,' but 'modern' is more for young people." This innocent comment catches a feeling which is stressed again in advertising for the teenage market. In a different mode, the song *Teenage Dream,* sung by Terry Dene, carried precisely the same message:

> Mum says we're too young to love
> And Dad agrees it's so
> But the joy and bliss I find in your kiss
> Is a thrill they'll never know

This inward-turning, self-pitying quality of many of the slower teenage ballads, the community of lost-souls feeling invoked in words and rhythms, is both an authentic rendering of an adolescent mood and a stylized exaggeration of it.

This apparent self-sufficiency in teenage culture is not simply a matter of keeping adult experience at arm's length; it is also a by-product of the limited subject-matter and emotions dealt with in commercial entertainments. A study of the lyrics of teenage songs and the situations dramatized in them shows the recurrence of certain set patterns. These all deal with romantic love and sexual feeling. The emotion is intensely depicted, but the set-ups recur with monotonous regularity and the rendered style stereotypes the emotion. They deal exclusively with falling in love, the magic of love fulfilled. Of course, this has been the typical subject matter of popular song throughout the ages. But one has then to compare the actual quality of the statement in pop music with, say, the folk song or the blues or even the pointed Johnny Mercer lyric of the twenties to appreciate the particular flavour, the generalized loneliness and yearning—a yearning of "no-body in particular for anyone-at-all" as Phillip Oakes once wrote.

> Johnny An-gel
> He doesn't even know I exist
> . . . I pray someday he'll love me
> And together we will see
> How lovely Heaven will be.

These songs, and the romantic stories with which they have so much in common, portray what Francis Newton calls "the condition, the anxieties, the bragging and uncertainty of school-age love and increasingly school-age sex." They reflect adolescent difficulties in dealing with a tangle of emotional and sexual problems. They invoke the need to experience life directly and intensely. They express the drive for security in an uncertain and changeable emotional world. The fact that they are produced for a commercial market means that the songs and settings lack a certain authenticity. Yet they also dramatize authentic feelings. They express vividly the adolescent emotional dilemma. And since they are often written on behalf of the adult providers of the entertainment world by teenage stars and songwriters, who share the cultural ethos of their audiences, there is a good deal of interaction and feed-back going on all the time.

These emotions, symbols and situations drawn off from the provided teenage culture contain elements both of emotional realism and of fantasy fulfillment. There is a strong impulse at this age to identify with these collective representations and to use them as guiding fictions. Such symbolic fictions are the folklore by means of which the teenager, in part, shapes and composes his mental picture of the world. It is in this identification that we find an explanation for the behaviour of the teenage "fan," the contrived absurdities of the fan-club, with its sacred relics, ritual strippings of the "hero" and personally autographed images. Fan-club behaviour has now extended to younger teenagers, as can be seen on any public occasion such as the personal appearance of pop groups like The Beatles.

Because of its high emotional content, teenage culture is essentially non-verbal. It is more naturally expressed in music, in dancing, in dress, in certain habits of walking and standing, in certain facial expressions and "looks" or in idiomatic slang. Though there is much to be learned from the lyrics of pop songs, there is more in the *beat* (loud, simple, insistent), the *backing* (strong, guitar-dominated), the *presentation* (larger-than-life, mechanically etherealized), the *inflections* of voice (sometimes the self-pitying, plaintive cry, and later the yeah-saying, affirmative shouting), or the *intonations* (at one stage mid-Atlantic in speech and pronunciation, but more recently rebelliously northern and provincial).[1] One can trace a whole line of development in popular music by listening to intonations—Louis Armstrong's gravelly rasp on the last word in *I Can't Give You Anything But Love, Baby* becomes Elvis Presley's breathy, sensual invocation, "Bab-eh," is then anglicized into Adam Faith's "Boi-by," with a marked Cockney twist (in *What Do You Want If You Don't Want Money?*) and provincialized by groups like The Beatles.

Certain attitudes seem not only to recur with emphasis in the provided culture, but to have found some specially appropriate physical image or presence among teenagers themselves. This teenage "look" can be partly attributed to the designers of mass-produced fashions and off-the-peg clothes and to the cosmetic advice syndicated in girls' and women's magazines. By marketing fashionable styles at reasonable prices, chain stores have played a significant role here. But these styles have a deeper social basis. The very preoccupation with the image of the self is important—pleasing, though often taken to extremes. Dress has become, for the teenager, a kind of minor popular art, and is used to express certain contemporary attitudes. There is, for

[1] See later reference to the extrovert approach of The Beatles.

example, a strong current of social nonconformity and rebelliousness among teenagers. At an early stage these anti-social feelings
were quite active—the rejection of authority in all its forms,
and a hostility towards adult institutions and conventional moral
and social customs. During this period, adult commentators often
misread this generalized nonconformism as a type of juvenile
delinquency, though it had little to do with organized crime and
violence. The "Teddy Boy" style, fashionable some years ago,
with its tumbling waterfall hair-style, fetishistic clothes, long
jackets, velvet collars, thick-soled shoes, and the accoutrements
which went along with them—string ties with silver medallions,
lengthy key-chains, studded ornamental belts—was a perfect
physical expression of this spirit. Contrary to expectations, this
style did not disappear, but persisted in the dress of motorcycle
addicts and "ton-up" kids, but reappeared with the "rockers."
A variant of this non-conformity could be found among "ravers"
or beatniks, with the trend to long hair, heavy sweaters, drain-
piped jeans and boots or black stockings and high heels. The
Teddy Boy look, an historical throw-back, with its recall of
Edwardian times, matched exactly the primitivism of the attitudes
it expressed.

Sometimes this attitude is more inward and internalized, relating to real failures in the relationships between children and
parents, and the sense of being misunderstood. For two teenage
generations at least, James Dean did much to embody and project
this image and to give it a style—his films *Rebel Without A
Cause* and *East of Eden* are classics which, despite their exaggera-
tions (e.g., the chicken-run scene in *Rebel*) and emotional falsity
(the relationship between Dean and his parents in the same film),
have a compulsive and hidden quality, due largely to Dean's true
dramatic gifts. *Rebel Without A Cause*, directed with disturbing
indulgence by Nicholas Ray, who seemed incapable of placing
any distance between his dramatization of the teenage world and
his own point of view, is really a cult film, and its most impressive moments are ritualized scenes from the teenage fantasy
viewed from within the culture itself. In all his films, James Dean
portrayed the ideal of blue-jean innocence, tough and vulnerable
in the same moment, a scowl of disbelief struggling with frankness for mastery in his face and eyes, continual changes of mood
and expression on his features, still, as Edgar Morin describes
him, "hesitating between childhood's melancholy and the mask

of the adult," and with a studied inarticulateness in his gestures and walk. The Dean films have never left the circuit, playing continuously since his death to teenage audiences at the local cinema.

Related to the same set of attitudes, but more recent in origin, is that style of "cool" indifference—a kind of bland knowingness about the ways of the world, even, at times, a disenchantment, an assumed world-weariness. This detachment can be either cynical or sad. It is best described by that evocative word "beat" —but *not* beatnik. It lies behind the mask-like, pasty-faced, heavily mascara'd look which became fashionable among teen-age girls—originally a copy of a Paris style, but when assumed by teenagers suggestive of so much else. There is something of it, too, in the variations of the "continental" or "Italian" style which became required wear for teenage boys when dressed up (elsewhere, jeans are ubiquitous), with its modern, lazy elegance, its smooth, tapered lines, light materials, pointed shoes or boots, and the flat, rather dead "college" haircut which often accompanies it.

The Melody Maker reported (August 1959) that when the jazz critic, Bob Dawbarn, asked Larry Parnes, the pop-music impresario, whether he thought teenage tastes had changed much over the past couple of years, Parnes replied, "They have not so much changed as had their tastes changed for them." One of the main controls which the record and promotion companies exercise over the teenage taste in the pops is the pop singer himself, around whom in recent years there has developed something of a youthful religion of the celebrity. We have seen this search for popular heroes elsewhere—in the careers of the cinema idols. Even in the field of popular music, many will recall the affection with which some of the female singers in war-time were held by radio audiences and the apparently universal appeal of a crooner like Bing Crosby. There was always something domestic and comfortable about Crosby, however, which discouraged wild extravagances among his fans. Something quite new entered this field with Sinatra and Frankie Laine. One can still recall the screaming teenage fans whose cries drowned the final phrases of every Sinatra song on the American programme *Hit Parade* in the forties.

Sinatra, however, provides a useful contrast, where musical ability is concerned, with the younger denizens of the pop-music jungle. Like many of them, his voice is not in itself a powerful or rich musical instrument. Unlike Bessie Smith, who naturally produced a tumultuous sound, Sinatra's is closer to a speaking voice. His material is almost entirely "commercial." Like the teenage stars, he has had to struggle to maintain his place at the top, and this has involved a change in personality and style. Yet his success has depended on two things: a genuine growth in his musical command, and a determination to mature as an artist. Musical command he shows now in several respects: he has developed incomparable jazz phrasing, and his emotional range is quite striking. Compare, for example, the genuine nostalgia of his *Moonlight in Vermont*, the sophisticated edge of *The Lady is a Tramp* and the dramatic performance he gives to *One More For The Road*. His diction is impeccable—clear, hard, articulating the lyrical notes at the ends of lines or in the bridges on songs. The voice is now deeper, rougher, more sophisticated and dry than in the days when he was "momma's little boy" on the *Hit Parade*—but it is also much more interesting. This is because of a depth of personal feeling as well as a certain maturity. He has achieved an effortless ability to swing without the support of elaborate sets on stage, dazzling costumes, echo chambers or physical contortions of the pelvis. Indeed, to judge from his last concert tour, his act is drastically simplified, relaxed and unencumbered. He commands the full stage by his musical intensity— not an "effect," but related to the final product and therefore much more organic. Sometimes he closes his eyes, but the purpose seems to be to "focus" more clearly a difficult note. His throat muscles contract to give the phrase either its soft, off-colour pitch or a particular bite. Both musically and by force of personality—the image of the experienced man who has seen a good deal of life and wants to record it through the medium of popular song—he transforms weak or trite material.

How much of this capacity to grow and deepen as a performer is potentially there among the galaxy of pop singers who have flashed on and off the teenage screen in the last decade? Perhaps it is too early to tell. Yet these groups have achieved in a short spell a degree of popular magic which even seasoned stars like Sinatra might envy. The intensity of rapport between audience and singer cannot be explained wholly in terms of the contrived engineering which makes the singer an idol. As Edgar Morin said, in relation to cinema idols, "In the last analysis it is

neither talent nor lack of talent, neither the cinematic industry
or its advertising, but the need for her which creates the star"
(*The Stars*).

Something in this primitive force depends upon the representative character of the idol's biography. These singers are not
remote stars, like Garbo, but tangible idealizations of the life of
the average teenager—boys next door, of humble beginnings,
almost certainly of working-class family, who have like the
Greek gods done their "labours" as van boy, messenger, truck
driver, film-cutter, or clerk in a routine occupation (that is if
they have not come straight from the "labours" of the classroom). What makes the difference between himself and his
fellows is that he has been touched by success—picked out by a
talent scout from Denmark Street [the center of commercial
music in London] or given a break in some provincial beat club
or created a stir in the columns of a provincial paper. He is
marked out, not so much by his musical talents (which more
than one recording manager has said can be a distinct handicap
in the business) as by his personality.

In what terms is it possible to establish even rough standards
of judgement about this kind of music? There are many forces
at work which inhibit any judgement whatsoever; pop music is
regarded as the exclusive property of the teenager, admission to
outsiders reserved. In these terms, disqualification is by age
limit. But, of course, this is nonsense. Like any other popular
commercial music, teenage pop is light entertainment music,
intended for dancing, singing, leisure and enjoyment. It differs
in character, but not in *kind*, from other sorts of popular music
which have provided a base for commercial entertainment since
the advent of jazz, and before. If we are unable to comment on
its quality and to make meaningful distinctions, it is largely because we lack a vocabulary of criticism for dealing with the
lighter and more transient qualities which are part of a culture of
leisure. We need that vocabulary very much indeed now, since
this is the area in which the new media are at play.

On the other hand, there are counter-forces at work which
dismiss *all* pop music simply because of its teenage connections
and its cult qualities. This reaction is just as dangerous since it is
based on prejudice. It springs in part from the inability of adults
to establish their own points of reference in relation to popular
culture—even though, lying behind the rejection of Elvis Presley,

there is often a secret addiction to Gracie Fields or Vera Lynn [internationally famous British popular singers] or the Charleston or Al Jolson or Nelson Eddy. (One needs to listen carefully to the older Tin Pan Alley tunes which survive in the repertoire of any pub sing-song to detect the connections.) There must also remain the suspicion that pop music provides a sitting target for those who have, for some unaccountable reason, to work off social envy or aggression against the younger generation. From this point of view, contemporary pops could not be better designed, since they are basically loud, raucous, always played at full volume, an obvious affront to good taste. They are frankly sensual in appeal, with persistent themes of youth, love and sex: and these themes are given a physical image in the pop singer himself, whose behaviour on and off stage is a challenge to British modesty and reserve. Worst of all, the music itself is an affirmation of a spirit of adolescent rebelliousness and independence, and therefore, it is supposed, symbolizes some sort of deep undermining of adult authority and tastes.

Pop music may well be all of these things, but that does not help us much at the end of the day. For it is more difficult to judge, keeping one's respect both for the lively qualities embodied and the standards of light entertainment generally, the quality of a music which is so entwined with the cult of its own presentation, so mixed in with the mystic rites of the pop singer and his mythology and so shot through with commercialism. It might be said, then, that the pops cannot be judged at all—but have rather to be seen as part of a whole sub-culture, and handled as one would the chants and ceremonies of a primitive tribe. Are the only standards anthropological?

When an audience can be induced to go crazy for a dance or a particular kind of music, as happened in the history of the twist, what we are observing is not, strictly speaking, the movement of popular taste so much as the creation of artificial wants in the field of commercial culture. Yet, such artificial selection and stimulation of a particular style, fashion or craze operates within a broad field of popular taste or behaviour which makes selective promotion possible. The taste for simple dance music of a popular, inexacting kind certainly exists: the twist campaign was lucky in its timing, and expertly packaged. The connection between the twist craze and the audience is not the simple one which the commercial promoters often seem to claim, but the link is not merely an exploitative one. In some way, the music and the dance do connect wtih the audience. The twist appeals to them through the natural entertainment channels, it offers a pattern of popular activity closely linked with their interests in going out, dancing, parties and social occasions of many kinds. It was personalized through the medium of young singers and entertainers. But it has also been made to connect. The study of the twist is, therefore, interesting, both as an example of the sociology of teenage tastes and as an aspect of the sociology of the entertainment business.

But even this kind of music can still be judged—not so much for its classical stature, its folk roots, its authenticity, but more simply as commercial entertainment music, and according to standards set by the best and most inventive music which has been produced in the past under similar conditions. The similarity between the twist and the Charleston, or between the teenage ballad and the earlier romantic ballad, gives us some rough and ready comparisons, and indicates a useful time-scale. Are the contemporary versions of pop music good even within these limits?

Pop music does have many genuine entertainment qualities. Its beat is simple and repetitive, but it is easily adapted to dancing, especially for audiences who are not particularly sophisticated rhythmically, and therefore find it difficult to adapt physical movement to the subtler rhythms of jazz, especially modern jazz. But it is the pulse which marks off beat from other kinds of commercial dance music, and this is where its primary appeal lies. The beat is strong and insistent. It gives to most pop music more vigour and drive than we find in, say, the big dance-band music, popular until fairly recently. It is crude in its simplicity, but lively and compulsive. And this compulsive quality, pushing the audience into an induced excitement, is the element which connects the music with the culture. The instrumentation has been skilfully adapted to this beat. Thus the guitar holds the highlight; the only other prominent instruments are the "rhythm" or percussion ones—bass, or bass guitar, drums, and piano used as a rhythm, rather than solo instrument. The accompanying guitars, supporting the lead instrument (or more frequently, of course, the singer's voice), can strike one chord on each beat: the drummer, too, taps one stroke for each beat in the bar. In this way, the beat is *reinforced* by several instruments. This gives the music a "rolling-on" rhythm, a "ratchet" effect. In the faster numbers there is no pause at the end of four or eight bars, but the basic pulse drives the rhythm forward to the next bar. All the flowing "line" instruments typical of jazz, such as the trumpet and the saxophone, have been eliminated altogether, or play a subordinate role.

When critics or commentators of pop music are at a loss for words to describe the music they often fall back on the word "swing": "This one really swings." This is a careless use of a word which has some precise meaning in jazz, but which hardly applies at all to pop music. Swing is a difficult element to isolate even in jazz (see, for example, André Hodeir's brave attempt to analyse its meaning in musical terms in his book, *Jazz: Its Evolution and Essence*), but its is certainly the product of rhythmic subtlety, phrasing and accent. These are precisely the qualities which most pop music lacks. The quality which distinguishes the best beat music—in both instrumental and sung versions—is the quality of *drive*. Drive is a combination of heavily accented beat, punch in delivery and sheer physical thrust. It was this thrust which marked out the earlier Elvis Presley records from all his imitators. Presley added to this a crude sensuality of gesture, but also a resonant voice capable of all the notes in both registers, with occasional evocation of the Negro blues and folk country-and-western, both of which are indigenous to the Bible belt around Nashville where he first made his name. Presley sang from the loins (his later work is much more sentimental and *schmaltzy* and lacks any true individuality or excitement). The most memorable notes in an early Elvis record were sensual musical gestures in themselves.

For the most part, American trends and tastes have dominated the pop-music scene ever since the advent of rock-'n-roll. But there has been a continuous and vigorous effort to impose an authentic British style on the music, and thus to give it a more solid foundation in British teenage culture. . . . This trend has now emerged with considerable force with the discovery of very large numbers of pop-music groups, singers and instrumentalists, in the provincial centres of the North. Groups like The Beatles, Gerry and the Pacemakers, Freddie and the Dreamers, etc., have, apparently, continued to produce a kind of native beat music, closer in feel and tempo to skiffle [Britain's rudimentary music, half jazz, half rock, of the Fifties] and early rock-'n-roll than the typical songs familiar in recent years in London; these groups have been singing and playing locally without much impact on the national scene, at weekend dances, beat clubs, local concerts and coffee bars. A city like Liverpool has recently yielded up nearly 400 such groups. The Beatles, for example, sing in aggressively flat Liverpudlian accents, and *The Melody Maker* has recorded the fact that many young groups have travelled north to Liverpool and Manchester in order to pick up an authentic provincial accent. This phenomenon is perhaps simply a sign that the mid-Atlantic affectations adopted by most of the earlier pop singers are beginning to wear off and that the music now has an autonomous life in British teenage culture. But it also seems to mark a return to the older beat style, and suggests that some of the traditions of skiffle groups were maintained, as a kind of local folk music, long after the skiffle craze itself has passed in the south, and, strengthened by its native roots, has now begun to re-emerge within the limits of commercial beat music. The pops are often fed and sustained by infusions of vigour from such sources.

Pop music has a certain vigour, but its lack of variety is staggering. Most of the ballads tend to sound the same even to a sympathetic ear: they are often variations on a basic set of chords and chord sequences. Where old favourites have been reshaped to the beat style, they have lost everything and gained very little in the transposition—except an occasional yodel. Musical formulae have been applied here mercilessly. Variety of tempo, theme, instrumentation or effect are rare. Occasionally, variety is added in the shape of a musical gimmick: castanets or bongoes are introduced for "effect," but which effect is hard to determine, since the music is not a whit more Latin in rhythm. (When in jazz Dizzy Gillespie uses Afro-Cuban rhythmic phrases, or Miles Davis interprets a Latin idiom in his *Sketches of Spain*, the whole cast of the music is changed without the jazz base being abandoned.) The very repetitiveness of the beat in beat music means that special care ought to be taken to compensate for rhythmic monotony. Yet drummers appear, on the whole, content to tap out the same tempo on disc after disc. One can legitimately add a note of distress on the debasement of certain instruments—the saxophone, for example, which, if used at all in beat music, is reduced to honking and snorting as the background to add to the "effects" (in early rock-'n-roll concerts, the saxophonist was often required to perform lying flat on his back).

The conditions of production in pop music so nearly resemble those of the assembly line that it would be unfair to compare this music with folk music or early jazz. A more revealing comparison is with commercial jazz. Certainly, there is nothing even in the most raucous versions of the pops—rock-'n-roll—which equals the insipid formula music produced by so many of the commercial dance bands—the strict metronome-accuracy of Victor Silvester [a well-known bandleader, for many years on the BBC], for example, with its total divorce from swing of any kind. BBC general record programmes provide regular feast-days of music of this sort. In contrast with Silvester, beat music is loud and vulgar, but it is at least music for the living. A good deal of commercial jazz has been produced by groups as keen as the teenage performers to become popular and to make money. (Nat Hentoff reminds us in his book *The Jazz Life*, that much jazz "is a constant battle between raw feeling and what it takes to buy a Cadillac.")

The difference between commercial pops and commercial jazz lies, not in the fact that the music is produced in a commercial environment, since this would be true for both types, but rather in the fact that commercial jazz seems capable of inner growth and change. By inner growth we do not mean changes in the style of the music, for pop music is more subject than perhaps any other to a fashion cycle. But we do mean that commercial jazz has provided for the slow maturing of individual musical talent, and has shown itself as responsive to the demands placed on it by those who play it as it is to those who buy or produce it. It has internal, as well as external, standards by which to measure its success.

We have constantly made comparisons between pop music and jazz. This is because, though there are many individual pop songs worth listening to, in general jazz seems an infinitely richer kind of music, both aesthetically and emotionally. The comparison this way seems much more rewarding than the more typical confrontation which is so frequently made between pop music and classical music. The reference to jazz helps us to make comparisons with another entertainment music, which nevertheless has legitimate uses and discernible standards. The point behind such

comparisons ought not to be simply to wean teenagers away from the juke-box heroes, but to alert them to the severe limitations and the ephemeral quality of music which is so formula-dominated and so directly attuned to the standards set by the commercial market. It is a genuine widening of sensibility and emotional range which we should be working for—an extension of tastes which might lead to an extension of pleasure. The worst thing which we would say of pop music is not that it is vulgar, or morally wicked, but more simply, that much of it is not very good.

Note: The Beatles

In the pop-music field, fashions change so rapidly that it is impossible to keep abreast. Already, when we were writing this [in 1964] we were aware that The Beatles, and groups in their style, were something of a new phenomenon. But it is now clear that they represent a distinctive break with earlier patterns. The pre-eminence of the singer has faded before the "group." The introspective, wistful, romantic mood has given way to a much more affirmative, extrovert, uninhibited style. Love is still the dominant theme, but it is no longer expressed in a "moony" way. There is still a remarkable conformity in the texture of the sounds produced, but they seem less relentlessly "tooled" and manufactured. This stylistic shift is more than a simple trend-change: like each of the previous phases it relates to changes in the audience. The new sound was created, first, in the clubs, and the dances devised on the spot: the movements are, in fact, adaptations of the groups' performance—the jerking on the spot (because the singer cannot move from the microphone?) and the thrust with the shoulders (because the guitarist's left shoulder is free?). In accent, in texture, in inflection, in attack, something of the native quality of life comes through; audiences and performers seem less shielded from one another by the screen of publicity or Big Business. The Beatles belong to Liverpool in a way in which [pop singer] Cliff Richard never belonged anywhere. Their zaniness seems a kind of defense—but it is also a quality of liveliness and energy, without devious complications, frankly indulged. Something of this quality invests the audience and qualifies the disturbing elements of mass hysteria. The fans "play" at being worshippers as The Beatles "play" at being idols. Yet the mass hysteria *is* there and the playfulness is a quality which can be, and has been, marketed.

Many critics are concerned about the "masturbatory quality" of the audiences' response. But the striking thing about The Beatles, and some of their imitators, is that they are essentially childlike, androgynous, pre-pubertal. In their film, *A Hard Day's Night,* they are surrounded by beautiful girls, but they seem unaffected by them. They are much more "themselves" running wild over an empty field. They are not "sex images": they are "dolls," "poppets."

THE
EYE
OF
A
MAN:

Painting and Sculpture

*The language and the point of view of the art
historian have had a very broad influence on critics
and scholars in literature, music, the dance, the film,
television, and all the other arts. The art historian
is a philosopher upon occasion, a psychologist
sometimes, a close inspector of paintings, buildings,
and sculpture always. How much he may bring to
his scrutinies is handsomely indicated here by
Professor Ernst Gombrich (1909–   ), Director
of the Warburg Institute of the University of
London and author of what many believe to be the
clearest and most useful of one-volume art histories,
The Story of Art. In
these meditations, the
subject is the visual arts,
with particular attention to the function of
representation. Some difficult ideas and a few
specialized terms are to be encountered, but the
Vienna-born writer's graceful handling of
English makes these engaging rather than
upsetting encounters. They offer not only
insights into the nature of art but into one's
own nature. That ought to be worth an
occasional foray into the dictionary or a quick
consultation of a footnote at the end.*

MEDITATIONS ON A HOBBY HORSE

OR THE ROOTS OF ARTISTIC FORM

E. H.
Gombrich

The subject of this article is a very ordinary
hobby horse. It is neither metaphorical nor
purely imaginary, at least not more so than the
broomstick on which Swift wrote
his meditations. It is usually content
with its place in the corner of the
nursery and it has no aesthetic ambitions.
Indeed it abhors frills. It is satisfied with its
broomstick body and its crudely carved head
which just marks the upper end and serves as
holder for the reins. How should we address it?
Should we describe it as an 'image of a horse'?
The compilers of the *Pocket Oxford Dictionary*
would hardly have agreed. They defined *image*
as 'imitation of an object's external form' and the
'external form' of a horse is surely not 'imitated'

here. So much the worse, we might say, for the 'external form,'
that elusive remnant of the Greek philosophical tradition which
has dominated our aesthetic language for so long. Luckily there
is another word in the *Dictionary* which might prove more
accommodating: *representation*. To *represent*, we read, can be
used in the sense of 'call up by description or portrayal or imagination, figure, place likeness of before mind or senses, serve or be
meant as likeness of . . . stand for, be specimen of, fill place of,
be substitute for.' A portrayal of a horse? Surely not. A substitute for a horse? Yes. That it is. Perhaps there is more in this
formula than meets the eye.

I

Let us first ride our wooden steed into battle against a number
of ghosts which still haunt the language of art criticism. One of
them we even found entrenched in the *Oxford Dictionary*. The
implication of its definition of an image is that the artist 'imitates'
the 'external form' of the object in front of him, and the beholder, in his turn, recognizes the 'subject' of the work of art by
this 'form.' This is what might be called the traditional view of
representation. Its corollary is that a work of art will either be
a faithful copy, in fact a complete replica, of the object represented, or will involve some degree of 'abstraction.' The artist,
we read, abstracts the 'form' from the object he sees. The
sculptor usually abstracts the three-dimensional form, and abstracts *from* colour; the painter abstracts contours and colours,
and *from* the third dimension. In this context one hears it said
that the draughtsman's line is a 'tremendous feat of abstraction'
because it does not 'occur in nature.' A modern sculptor of
Brancusi's persuasion may be praised or blamed for 'carrying
abstraction to its logical extreme.' Finally the label of 'abstract
art' for the creation of 'pure' forms carries with it a similar implication. Yet we need only look at our hobby horse to see that the
very idea of abstraction as a complicated mental act lands us in
curious absurdities. There is an old music hall joke describing a
drunkard who politely lifts his hat to every lamp-post he passes.
Should we say that the liquor has so increased his power of abstraction that he is now able to isolate the formal quality of
uprightness from both lamp-post and the human figure? Our

mind, of course, works by differentiation rather than by generalization, and the child will for long call all four-footers of a certain size 'gee-gee' before it learns to distinguish breeds and 'forms'![1]

II

Then there is that age-old problem of universals as applied to art. It has received its classical formulation in the Platonizing theories of the Academicians. 'A history-painter,' says Reynolds, 'paints man in general; a portrait-painter a particular man, and therefore a defective model.'[2] This, of course, is the theory of abstraction applied to one specific problem. The implications are that the portrait, being an exact copy of a man's 'external form' with all 'blemishes' and 'accidents,' refers to the individual person exactly as does the proper name. The painter, however, who wants to 'evaluate his style' disregards the particular and 'generalizes the forms.' Such a picture will no longer represent a particular man but rather the class or concept 'man.' There is a deceptive simplicity in this argument, but it makes at least one unwarranted assumption: that every image of this kind necessarily refers to something outside itself—be it individual or class. But nothing of the kind need be implied when we point to an image and say 'this is a man.' Strictly speaking that statement may be interpreted to mean that the image itself is a member of the class 'man.' Nor is that interpretation as farfetched as it may sound. In fact our hobby horse would submit to no other interpretation. By the logic of Reynolds's reasoning it would have to represent the most generalized idea of horseness. But if the child calls a stick a horse it obviously means nothing of the kind. The stick is neither a sign signifying the concept horse nor is it a portrait of an individual horse. By its capacity to serve as a 'substitute' the stick becomes a horse in its own right, it belongs to the class of 'gee-gees' and may even merit a proper name of its own.

When Pygmalion blocked out a figure from his marble he did not at first represent a 'generalized' human form, and then gradually a particular woman. For as he chipped away and made it more lifelike the block was not turned into a portrait—not even in the unlikely case that he used a live model. So when his prayers were heard and the statue came to life she was Galatea and no one else—and that regardless of whether she had been fashioned in an archaic, idealistic, or naturalistic style. The question of reference, in fact, is totally independent of the degree of differentiation. The witch who made a 'generalized' wax dummy of an enemy may have meant it to refer to someone in particular. She would then pronounce the right spell to establish this link— much as we may write a caption under a generalized picture to do the same. But even those proverbial replicas of nature, Madame Tussaud's effigies, need the same treatment. Those in the galleries which are labelled are 'portraits of the great.' The figure on the staircase made to hoax the visitor simply represents 'an' attendant, one member of a class. It stands there as a 'substitute' for the expected guard—but it is not more 'generalized' in Reynolds's sense.

III

The idea that art is 'creation' rather than 'imitation' is sufficiently familiar. It has been proclaimed in various forms from the time of Leonardo, who insisted that the painter is 'Lord of all Things,'[3] to that of Klee, who wanted to create as Nature does.[4] But the more solemn overtones of metaphysical power disappear when we leave art for toys. The child 'makes' a train either of a few blocks or with pencil on paper. Surrounded as we are by posters and newspapers carrying illustrations of commodities or events, we find it difficult to rid ourselves of the prejudice that all images should be 'read' as referring to some imaginary or actual reality. Only the historian knows how hard it is to look at Pygmalion's work without comparing it with nature. But recently we have been made aware how thoroughly we misunderstand primitive or Egyptian art whenever we make the assumption that the artist 'distorts' his motif or that he even wants us to see in his work the record of any specific experience.[5] In many cases these images 'represent' in the sense of being substitutes. The clay horse or servant, buried in the tomb of the mighty, takes the place of the living. The idol takes the place of the god. The question whether it represents the 'external form' of the particular divinity or, for that matter, of a class of demons is quite inappropriate. The idol serves as the substitute of the God in worship and ritual —it is a man-made god in precisely the sense that the hobby horse is a man-made horse; to question it further means to court deception.[6]

There is another misunderstanding to be guarded against. We often try instinctively to save our idea of 'representation' by shifting it to another plane. Where we cannot refer the image to a motif in the outer world we take it to be a portrayal of a motif in the artist's inner world. Much critical (and uncritical) writing on both primitive and modern art betrays this assumption. But to apply the naturalistic idea of portrayal to dreams and visions—let alone to unconscious images—begs a whole number of questions.[7] The hobby horse does not portray our idea of a horse. The fearsome monster or funny face we may doodle on our blotting pad is not projected out of our mind as paint is 'ex-pressed' out of a paint tube. Of course any image will be in some way symptomatic of its maker, but to think of it as of a photograph of a pre-existing reality is to misunderstand the whole process of image-making.

IV

Can our substitute take us further? Perhaps, if we consider how it could become a substitute. The 'first' hobby horse (to use eighteenth-century language) was probably no image at all. Just a stick which qualified as a horse because one could ride on it. The *tertium comparationis,* the common factor, was function rather than form. Or, more precisely, that formal aspect which fulfilled the minimum requirement for the performance of the function—for any 'ridable' object could serve as a horse. If that is true we may be enabled to cross a boundary which is usually regarded as closed and sealed. For in this sense 'substitutes' reach deep into biological functions that are common to man and animal. The cat runs after the ball as if it were a mouse. The baby sucks its thumb as if it were the breast. In a sense the ball 'represents' a mouse to the cat, the thumb a breast to the baby. But here too 'representation' does not depend on formal similarities, beyond the minimum requirements of function. The ball has nothing in common with the mouse except that it is chasable. The thumb nothing with the breast except that it is suckable. As 'substitutes' they fulfill certain demands of the organism. They are keys which happen to fit into biological or psychological locks, or counterfeit coins which make the machine work when dropped into the slot.

In the language of the nursery the psychological function of 'representation' is still recognized. The child will reject a perfectly naturalistic doll in favour of some monstrously 'abstract' dummy which is 'cuddly.' It may even dispose of the element of 'form' altogether and take to a blanket or an eiderdown as its favourite 'comforter'—a substitute on which to bestow its love. Later in life, as the psychoanalysts tell us, it may bestow this same love on a worthy or unworthy living substitute. A teacher may 'take the place' of the mother, a dictator or even an enemy may come to 'represent' the father. Once more the common denominator between the symbol and the thing symbolized is not the 'external form' but the function; the mother symbol would be lovable, the father-imago fearable, or whatever the case may be.

Now this psychological concept of symbolization seems to lead so very far away from the more precise meaning which the word 'representation' has acquired in the figurative arts. Can there be any gain in throwing all these meanings together? Possibly: for anything seems worth trying, to get the function of symbolizing out of its isolation.

The 'origin of art' has ceased to be a popular topic. But the origin of the hobby horse may be a permitted subject for speculation. Let us assume that the owner of the stick on which he proudly rode through the land decided in a playful or magic mood—and who could always distinguish between the two?—to fix 'real' reins and that finally he was even tempted to 'give' it two eyes near the top end. Some grass could have passed for a mane. Thus our inventor 'had a horse.' He had made one. Now there are two things about this fictitious event which have some bearing on the idea of the figurative arts. One is that, contrary to what is sometimes said, communication need not come into this process at all. He may not have wanted to show his horse to anyone. It just served as a focus for his fantasies as he galloped along—though more likely than not it fulfilled this same function for a tribe to which it 'represented' some horse-demon of fertility and power.[8] We may sum up the moral of this 'Just So Story' by saying that substitution may precede portrayal, and creation communication. It remains to be seen how such a general theory can be tested. If it can, it may really throw light on some concrete questions. Even the origin of language, that notorious problem of speculative history,[9] might be investigated from this angle. For what if the 'pow-wow' theory, which sees the root of language in imitation, and the 'pooh-pooh' theory, which sees it in emotive interjection, were to be joined by yet another? We might term it the 'niam-niam' theory postulating the primitive hunter lying awake through hungry winter nights and making the sound of eating, not for communication but as a substitute for eating—being joined, perhaps, by a ritualistic chorus trying to conjure up the phantasm of food.

V

There is one sphere in which the investigation of the 'representational' function of forms has made considerable progress of late, that of animal psychology. Pliny, and innumerable writers after him, have regarded it as the greatest triumph of naturalistic art for a painter to have deceived sparrows or horses. The implication of these anecdotes is that a human beholder easily recognizes a bunch of grapes in a painting because for him recognition is an intellectual act. But for the birds to fly at the painting is a sign of a complete 'objective' illusion. It is a plausible idea, but a wrong one. The merest outline of a cow seems sufficient for a tsetse trap, for somehow it sets the apparatus of attraction in motion and 'deceives' the fly. To the fly, we might say, the crude trap has the 'significant' form—biologically significant, that is. It appears that visual stimuli of this kind play an important part in the animal world. By varying the shapes of 'dummies' to which animals were seen to respond, the 'minimum image' that still sufficed to release a specific reaction has been ascertained.[10] Thus little birds will open their beak when they see the feeding parent approaching the nest, but they will also do so when they are shown two darkish roundels of different size, the silhouette of the head and body of the bird 'represented' in its most 'generalized' form. Certain young fishes can even be deceived by two simple dots arranged horizontally, which they take to be the eyes of the mother fish, in whose mouth they are accustomed to shelter against danger. The fame of Zeuxis will have to rest on other achievements than his deception of birds.

An 'image' in this biological sense is not an imitation of an object's external form but an imitation of certain privileged or relevant aspects. It is here that a wide field of investigation would seem to open. For man is not exempt from this type of reaction.[11] The artist who goes out to represent the visible world is not simply faced with a neutral medley of forms he seeks to 'imitate.' Ours is a structured universe whose main lines of force are still bent and fashioned by our biological and psychological needs, however much they may be overlaid by cultural influences. We know that there are certain privileged motifs in our world to which we respond almost too easily. The human face may be outstanding among them. Whether by instinct or by very early training, we are certainly ever disposed to single out the expressive features of a face from the chaos of sensations that surrounds it, and to respond to its slightest variations with fear or joy. Our whole perceptual apparatus is somehow hypersensitized in this direction of physiognomic vision[12] and the merest hint suffices for us to create an expressive physiognomy that 'looks' at us with surprising intensity. In a heightened state of emotion, in the dark, or in a feverish spell, the looseness of this trigger may assume pathological forms. We may see faces in the pattern of a wallpaper, and three apples arranged on a plate may stare at us like two eyes and a clownish nose. What wonder that it is so easy to 'make' a face with two dots and a stroke even though their geometrical constellation may be greatly at variance with the 'external form' of a real head? The well-known graphic joke of the 'reversible face' might well be taken as a model for experiments which could still be made in this direction. It shows to what extent the group of shapes that can be read as a physiognomy has priority over all other readings. It turns the side which is the right way up into a convincing face and disintegrates the one that is upside down into a mere jumble of forms which is accepted as a strange headgear.[13] In good pictures of this kind it needs a real effort to see both faces at the same time, and perhaps we never quite succeed. Our automatic response is stronger than our intellectual awareness.

Seen in the light of the biological examples discussed above there is nothing surprising in this observation. We may venture the guess that this type of automatic recognition is dependent on the two factors of resemblance and biological relevance, and that the two may stand in some kind of inverse ratio. The greater the biological relevance an object has for us the more will we be attuned to its recognition—and the more tolerant will therefore be our standards of formal correspondence. In an erotically charged atmosphere the merest hint of formal similarity with sexual functions creates the desired response and the same is true of the dream symbols investigated by Freud. The hungry man will be similarly attuned to the discovery of food—he will scan the world for the slightest promise of nourishment. The starving may even project food into all sorts of dissimilar objects—as Chaplin does in *Gold Rush* when his huge companion suddenly appears to him as a chicken. Can it have been some such experience which stimulated our 'niam-niam' chanting hunters to see their longed-for prey in the patches and irregular shapes on the dark cave walls? Could they perhaps gradually have sought this experience in the deep mysterious recesses of the rocks, much as Leonardo sought out crumbling walls to aid his visual fantasies? Could they, finally, have been prompted to fill in such 'readable' outlines with coloured earth—to have at least something 'spearable' at hand which might 'represent' the eatable in some magic fashion? There is no way of testing such a theory, but if it is true that cave artists often 'exploited' the natural formations of the rocks,[14] this, together with the 'eidetic' character of their works,[15] would at least not contradict our fantasy. The great naturalism of cave paintings may after all be a very late flower. It may correspond to our late, derivative, and naturalistic hobby horse.

VI

It needed two conditions, then, to turn a stick into our hobby horse: first, that its form made it just possible to ride on it; secondly—and perhaps decisively—that riding mattered. Fortunately it still needs no great effort of the imagination to understand how the horse could become such a focus of desires and aspirations, for our language still carries the metaphors moulded by a feudal past when to be chival-rous was to be horsy. The same stick that had to represent a horse in such a setting would have become the substitute of something else in another. It might have become a sword, sceptre, or—in the context of ancestor worship—a fetish representing a dead chieftain. Seen from the point of view of 'abstraction,' such a convergence of meanings onto one shape offers considerable difficulties, but from that of psychological 'projection' of meanings it becomes more easily intelligible. After all a whole diagnostic technique has been built up on the assumption that the meanings read into identical forms by different people tell us more about the readers than about the forms. In the sphere of art it has been shown that the same triangular shape which is the favourite pattern of many adjoining American Indian tribes is given different meanings reflecting the main preoccupations of the peoples concerned.[16] To the student of styles this discovery that one basic form can be made to represent a variety of objects may still become significant. For while the idea of realistic pictures being deliberately 'stylized' seems hard to swallow, the opposite idea of a limited vocabulary of simple shapes being used for the building up of different representations would fit much better into what we know of primitive art.

VII

Once we get used to the idea of 'representation' as a two-way affair rooted in psychological dispositions we may be able to refine a concept which has proved quite indispensable to the historian of art and which is nevertheless rather unsatisfactory: that of the 'conceptual image.' By this we mean the mode of representation which is more or less common to children's drawings and to various forms of primitive and primitivist art. The remoteness of this type of imagery from any visual experience has often been described.[17] The explanation of this fact which is most usually advanced is that the child (and the primitive) do not draw what they 'see' but what they 'know.' According to this idea the typical children's drawing of a manikin is really a graphic enumeration of those human features the child remembered.[18] It represents the content of the childish 'concept' of man. But to speak of 'knowledge' or 'intellectual realism' (as the French do[19]) brings us dangerously near to the fallacy of 'abstraction.' So back to our hobby horse. Is it quite correct to say that it consists of features which make up the 'concept' of a horse or that it reflects the memory image of horses seen? No—because this formulation omits one factor: the stick. If we keep in mind that representation is originally the creation of substitutes out of given material we may reach safer ground. The greater the wish to ride, the fewer may be the features that will do for a horse. But at a certain stage it must have eyes—for how else could it see? At the most primitive level, then, the conceptual image might be identified with what we have called the minimum image—that minimum, that is, which will make it fit into a psychological lock. The form of the key depends on the material out of which it is fashioned, and on the lock. It would be a dangerous mistake, however, to equate the 'conceptual image' as we find it used in the historical styles with this psychologically grounded minimum image. On the contrary. One has the impression that the presence of these schemata is always felt but that they are as much avoided as exploited.[20] We must reckon with the possibility of a 'style' being a set of conventions born out of complex tensions. The man-made image must be complete. The servant for the grave must have two hands and two feet. But he must not become a double under the artist's hands. Image-making is beset with dangers. One false stroke and the rigid mask of the face may assume an evil leer. Strict adherence to conventions alone can guard against such dangers. And thus primitive art seems often to keep on that narrow ledge that lies between the lifeless and the uncanny. If the hobby horse became too lifelike it might gallop away on its own.[21]

VIII

The contrast between primitive art and 'naturalistic' or 'illusionist' art can easily be overdrawn.[22] All art is 'image-making' and all image-making is rooted in the creation of substitutes. Even the artist of an 'illusionist' persuasion must make the man-made, the 'conceptual' image of convention his starting point. Strange as it may seem he cannot simply 'imitate an object's external form' without having first learned how to construct such a form. If it were otherwise there would be no need for the innumerable books on 'how to draw the human figure' or 'how to draw ships.' Wölfflin once remarked that all pictures owe more to other pictures than they do to nature.[23] It is a point which is familiar to the student of pictorial traditions but which is still insufficiently understood in its psychological implications. Perhaps the reason is that, contrary to the hopeful belief of many artists, the 'innocent eye' which should see the world afresh would not see it at all. It would smart under the painful impact of a chaotic medley of forms and colours.[24] In this sense the conventional vocabulary of basic forms is still indispensable to the artist as a starting point, as a focus of organization.

How, then, should we interpret the great divide which runs through the history of art and sets off the few islands of illusionist styles, of Greece, of China, and of the Renaissance, from the vast ocean of 'conceptual' art?

One difference, undoubtedly, lies in a change of function. In a way the change is implicit in the emergence of the idea of the image as a 'representation' in our modern sense of the word. As soon as it is generally understood that an image need not exist in its own right, that it may refer to something outside itself and therefore be the record of a visual experience rather than the creation of a substitute, the basic rules of primitive art can be transgressed with impunity. No longer is there any need for that completeness of essentials which belongs to the conceptual style, no longer is there the fear of the casual which dominates the archaic conception of art. The picture of a man on a Greek vase no longer needs a hand or a foot in full view. We know it is meant as a shadow, a mere record of what the artist saw or might see, and we are quite ready to join in the game and to supplement with our imagination what the real motif undoubtedly possessed. Once this idea of the picture suggesting something beyond what is really there is accepted in all its implications—and this certainly did not happen overnight—we are indeed forced to let our imagination play around it. We endow it with 'space' around its forms which is only another way of saying that we understand the reality which it evokes as three-dimensional, that the man could move and that even the aspect momentarily hidden 'was there'.[25] When medieval art broke away from that narrative conceptual symbolism into which the formulas of classical art had been frozen, Giotto made particular use of the figure seen from behind which stimulates our 'spatial' imagination by forcing us to imagine the other side.

Thus the idea of the picture as a representation of a reality outside itself leads to an interesting paradox. On the one hand it compels us to refer every figure and every object shown to that imaginary reality which is 'meant'. This mental operation can only be completed if the picture allows us to infer not only the 'external form' of every object represented but also its relative size and position. It leads us to that 'rationalization of space' we call scientific perspective by which the picture plane becomes a window through which we look into the imaginary world the artist creates there for us. In theory, at least, painting is then conceived in terms of geometrical projection.[26]

The paradox of the situation is that, once the whole picture is regarded as the representation of a slice of reality, a new context is created in which the conceptual image plays a different part. For the first consequence of the 'window' idea is that we cannot conceive of any spot on the panel which is not 'significant', which does not represent something. The empty patch thus easily comes to signify light, air, and atmosphere, and the vague form is interpreted as enveloped by air. It is this confidence in the representational context which is given by the very convention of the frame, which makes the development of impressionist methods possible. The artists who tried to rid themselves of their conceptual knowledge, who conscientiously became beholders of their own work and never ceased matching their created images against their impressions by stepping back and comparing the two—these artists could only achieve their aim by shifting something of the load of creation on to the beholder. For what else does it mean if we are enjoined to step back in turn and watch the coloured patches of an impressionist landscape 'spring to life'? It means that the painter relies on our readiness to take hints, to read contexts, and to call up our conceptual image under his guidance. The blob in the painting by Manet which stands for a horse is no more an imitation of its external form than is our hobby horse. But he has so cleverly contrived it that it evokes the image in us—provided, of course, we collaborate.

Here there may be another field for independent investigation. For those 'privileged' objects which play their part in the earliest layers of image-making recur—as was to be expected—in that of image-reading. The more vital the feature that is indicated by the context and yet omitted, the more intense seems to be the process that is started off. On its lowest level this method of 'suggestive veiling' is familiar to erotic art. Not, of course, to its Pygmalion phase, but to its illusionist applications. What is here a crude exploitation of an obvious biological stimulus may have its parallel, for instance, in the representation of the human face. Leonardo achieved his greatest triumphs of lifelike expression by blurring precisely the features in which the expression resides, thus compelling us to complete the act of creation. Rembrandt could dare to leave the eyes of his moving portraits in the shade because we are thus stimulated to supplement them[27]. The 'evocative' image, like its 'conceptual' counterpart, should be studied against a wider psychological background.

IX

My hobby horse is not art. At best it can claim the attention of iconology, that emerging branch of study which is to art criticism what linguistics is to the criticism of literature. But has not modern art experimented with the primitive image, with the 'creation' of forms, and the exploitation of deep-rooted psychological forces? It has. But whatever the nostalgic wish of their makers, the meaning of these forms can never be the same as that of their primitive models. For that strange precinct we call 'art' is like a hall of mirrors or a whispering gallery. Each form conjures up a thousand memories and after-images. No sooner is an image presented as art than, by this very act, a new frame of reference is created which it cannot escape. It becomes part of an institution as surely as does the toy in the nursery. If—as might be conceivable—a Picasso would turn from pottery to hobby horses and send the products of this whim to an exhibition, we might read them as demonstrations, as satirical symbols, as a declaration of faith in humble things or as self-irony—but one thing would be denied even to the greatest of contemporary artists: he could not make the hobby horse mean to us what it meant to its first creator. That way is barred by the angel with a flaming sword.

NOTES

1. In the sphere of art this process of differentiation rather than abstraction is wittily described by Oliver Wendell Holmes in the essay 'Cacoethes Scribendi', from *Over the Teacups* (London: 1890): 'It's just the same thing as my plan . . . for teaching draw-

ing. . . . A man at a certain distance appears as a dark spot—nothing more. Good. Anybody . . . can make a dot. . . . Lesson No. 1. Make a dot; that is, draw your man, a mile off. . . . Now make him come a little nearer. . . . The dot is an oblong figure now. Good. Let your scholar draw an oblong figure. It is as easy as to make a note of admiration. . . . So by degrees the man who serves as a model approaches. A bright pupil will learn to get the outline of a human figure in ten lessons, the model coming five hundred feet nearer each time.'

2. *Discourses on Art* (Everyman Edition, p. 55). I have discussed the historical setting of this idea in 'Icones Symbolicae', *Journal of the Warburg and Courtauld Institutes*, XI (1948), p. 187, and some of its more technical aspects in a review of Charles Morris, *Signs, Language, and Behavior* (New York: 1946) in *The Art Bulletin*, March, 1949. In Morris's terminology these present meditations are concerned with the status and origin of the 'iconic sign'.

3. Leonardo da Vinci, *Paragone*, edited by I. A. Richter (London: 1949), p. 51.

4. Paul Klee, *On Modern Art* (London, 1948). For the history of the idea of *deus artifex* cf. E. Kris and O. Kurz, *Die Legende vom Künstler* (Vienna: 1934).

5. H. A. Groenewegen-Frankfort, *Arrest and Movement: An Essay on Space and Time in the Representational Art of the Ancient Near East* (London: 1951).

6. Perhaps it is only in a setting of realistic art that the problem I have discussed in 'Icones Symbolicae', loc. cit., becomes urgent. Only then the idea can gain ground that the allegorical image of, say, Justice, must be a portrait of Justice as she dwells in heaven.

7. For the history of this misinterpretation and its consequences cf. my article on 'Art and Imagery in the Romantic Period.' . . .

8. This, at least, would be the opinion of Lewis Spence, *Myth and Ritual in Dance, Game, and Rhyme* (London: 1947). And also of Ben Jonson's Busy, the Puritan: 'Thy Hobby-horse is an Idoll, a feirce and rancke Idoll: And thou, the *Nabuchadnezzar* . . . of the *Faire*, that set'st it up, for children to fall downe to, and worship'. (*Bartholomew Fair*, Act. III, Scene 6).

9. Cf. Géza Révész, *Ursprung und Vorgeschichte der Sprache* (Berne: 1946).

10. Cf. Konrad Lorenz, 'Die angeborenen Formen möglicher Erfahrung', *Zeitschrift für Tierpsychologie* V (1943), and the discussion of these experiments in E. Grassi and Th. von Uexküll, *Vom Ursprung und von den Grenzen der Geisteswissenschaften und Naturwissenschaften* (Bern: 1950).

11. K. Lorenz, loc. cit. The citation of this article does not imply sup-

port of the author's moral conclusions. On these more general issues see K. R. Popper, *The Open Society and Its Enemies*, esp., I, pp. 59 ff. and p. 268.

12. F. Sander, '*Experimentelle Ergebnisse der Gestaltpsychologie*', *Berichte über den* 10. *Kongress für Experimentelle Psychologie* (Jena: 1928), p. 47, notes experiments that show the distance of two dots is much harder to estimate in its variations when these dots are isolated than when they are made to represent eyes in a schematic face and thus attain physiognomic significance.

13. For a large collection of such faces cf. Laurence Whistler, *Oho! The Drawings of Rex Whistler* (London: 1946).

14. G. H. Luquet, *The Art and Religion of Fossil Man* (London: 1930), pp. 141 f.

15. G. A. S. Snijder, *Kretische Kunst* (Berlin: 1936), pp. 68 f.

16. Franz Boas, *Primitive Art* (Oslo: 1927), pp. 118–28.

17. E.g., E. Löwry, *The Rendering of Nature in Early Greek Art* (London: 1907), H. Schaefer, *Von aegyptischer Kunst* (Leipzig: 1930), M. Verworn, *Ideoplastische Kunst* (Jena: 1914).

18. Karl Bühler, *The Mental Development of the Child* (London: 1930), pp. 113–17, where the connection with the linguistic faculty is stressed. A criticism of this idea was advanced by R. Arnheim, 'Perceptual Abstraction and Art', *Psychological Review*, LVI, 1947

19. G. H. Luquet, *L'Art primitif* (Paris: 1930).

20. The idea of avoidance (of sexual symbols) is stressed by A. Ehrenzweig, *Psycho-Analysis of Artistic Vision and Hearing*, (London: 1953), pp. 22–70.

21. E. Kris and O. Kurz, loc. cit., have collected a number of legends reflecting this age-old fear: thus a famous Chinese master was said never to have put the light into the eyes of his painted dragons lest they would fly away.

22. It was the intellectual fashion in German art history to work with contrasting pairs of concepts such as haptic-optic (Riegl), paratactic-hypotactic (Coellen), abstraction-empathy (Worringer), idealism-naturalism (Dvořák), physioplastic-ideoplastic (Verworn), multiplicity-unity (Wölfflin), all of which could probably be expressed in terms of 'conceptual' and 'less conceptual' art. While the heuristic value of this method of antithesis is not in doubt it often tends to introduce a false dichotomy. In my book *The Story of Art* (London: 1950) I have attempted to stress the continuity of tradition and the persistent role of the conceptual image.

23. H. Wölfflin, *Principles of Art History* (New York: 1932).

24. The fallacy of a passive idea of perception is discussed in detail by E. Brunswik, *Wahrnehmung und Gegenstandswelt* (Vienna: 1934). In its application to art the writings of K. Fiedler contain many

valuable hints; cf. also A. Ehrenzweig, loc. cit., for an extreme and challenging presentation of this problem.

25. This may be meant in the rather enigmatic passage on the painter Parrhasius in Pliny's *Natural History*, XXXV, 67, where it is said that 'the highest subtlety attainable in painting is to find an outline . . . which should appear to fold back and to enclose the object so as to give assurance of the parts behind, thus clearly suggesting even what it conceals'.

26. Cf. E. Panofsky, 'The Codex Huygens and Leonardo da Vinci's Art Theory', *Studies of the Warburg Institute*, XIII (London: 1940), pp. 90 f.

27. Cf. J. v. Schlosser, 'Gespräch von der Bildniskunst', *Präludien* (Vienna: 1927), where, incidentally, the hobby horse also makes its appearance.

A few painters in the modern era have been re-
markably articulate about their art in general and
their own aims in particular. One of the most ab-
sorbing to read is Wassily Kandinsky (1866–1944),
perhaps the best known Russian painter in this
century, and the close associate of Paul Klee and
Franz Marc in the founding, in 1912, of the group of
painters called Der Blaue Reiter [*The Blue Rider*]
after one of Kandinsky's paintings. The group was
determined to lead the way back to pure form and
pure color in art. The significance of essentials to
Kandinsky, one of the greatest of abstract painters,
is demonstrated in this opening
section of his famous essay on
the "spiritual" in art. His
reading of the "spiritual" is touched on throughout,
but it is given particular clarity in the illuminating
footnote appended to this excellent translation
from the German, which, in spite
of having been worked on by many
hands, retains the flavor of
Kandinsky's thought and style.

CONCERNING THE SPIRITUAL IN ART

Wassily
Kandinsky

Every work of art is the child of its time; often
it is the mother of our emotions. It follows that
each period of culture produces an art of its
own, which cannot be repeated. Efforts to revive
the art principles of the past at best produce
works of art that resemble a stillborn child. For
example, it is impossible for us to live and feel as
did the ancient Greeks. For this reason those who
follow Greek principles in sculpture reach only
a similarity of form, while the work remains for
all time without a soul. Such an imitation resembles the antics of apes: externally a monkey
resembles a human being; he will sit holding a
book in front of his nose, turning over the pages
with a thoughtful air, but his actions have no
real significance.

But among the forms of art there is another
kind of external similarity, which is founded on a

fundamental necessity. When there is, as sometimes happens, a similarity of inner direction in an entire moral and spiritual milieu, a similarity of ideals, at first closely pursued but later lost to sight, a similarity of "inner mood" between one period and another, the logical consequence will be a revival of the external forms which served to express those insights in the earlier age. This may account partially for our sympathy and affinity with and our comprehension of the work of primitives. Like ourselves, these pure artists sought to express only inner[1] and essential feelings in their works; in this process they ignored as a matter of course the fortuitous.

This great point of inner contact is, in spite of its considerable importance, only one point. Only just now awakening after years of materialism, our soul is infected with the despair born of unbelief, of lack of purpose and aim. The nightmare of materialism, which turned life into an evil, senseless game, is not yet passed;

[1] A work of art consists of two elements, the inner and the outer.

The inner is the emotion in the soul of the artist; this emotion has the capacity to evoke a similar emotion in the observer.

Being connected with the body, the soul is affected through the medium of the senses—the felt. Emotions are aroused and stirred by what is sensed. Thus the sensed is the bridge, i.e., the physical relation, between the immaterial (which is the artist's emotion) and the material, which results in the production of a work of art. And again, what is sensed is the bridge from the material (the artist and his work) to the immaterial (the emotion in the soul of the observer).

The sequence is: emotion (in the artist) → the sensed → the art-work → the sensed → emotion (in the observer).

The two emotions will be like and equivalent to the extent that the work of art is successful. In this respect painting is in no way different from a song: each is a communication. The successful singer arouses in listeners his emotions; the successful painter should do no less.

The inner element, i.e., emotion, must exist; otherwise the work of art is a sham. The inner element determines the form of the work of art.

In order that the inner element, which at first exists only as an emotion, may develop into a work of art, the second element, i.e., the outer, is used as an embodiment. Emotion is always seeking means of expression, a material form, a form that is able to stir the senses. The determining and vital element is the inner one, which controls the outer form, just as an idea in the mind determines the words we use, and not *vice versa*. The determination of the form of a work of art is therefore determined by the irresistible inner force: this is the only unchanging law in art. A beautiful work is the consequence of an harmonious cooperation of the inner and the outer; i.e., a painting is an intellectual organism which, like every other material organism, consists of many parts. (*This explanation by Kandinsky of the relation between internal and external, or inner and outer, is a slightly revised version of a translation by Arthur Jerome Eddy of part of an article by Kandinsky which appeared in Der* Sturm, *Berlin, 1913; cf.* Cubists and Post-Impressionists, *A. C. McClurg, Chicago, 1914, pp. 119–20.*)

Right, Vasily Kandinsky, Sign with Accompaniment, *No. 382, 1927.*
From The Solomon R. Guggenheim Museum, New York City.

Below, Vasily Kandinsky, Arrow, *No. 258, 1923.*
From The Solomon R. Guggenheim Museum, New York City.

it still darkens the awakening soul. Only a feeble light glimmers, a tiny point in an immense circle of darkness. This light is but a presentiment; and the mind, seeing it, trembles in doubt over whether the light is a dream and the surrounding darkness indeed reality. This doubt and the oppression of materialism separate us sharply from primitives. Our soul rings cracked when we sound it, like a precious vase, dug out of the earth, which has a flaw. For this reason, the primitive phase through which we are now passing, in its present derivative form, must be short-lived.

The two kinds of resemblance between the forms of art of today and of the past can be easily recognized as diametrically opposed. The first, since it is external, has no future. The second, being internal, contains the seed of the future. After a period of materialist temptation, to which the soul almost succumbed, and which it was able to shake off, the soul is emerging, refined by struggle and suffering. Cruder emotions, like fear, joy and grief, which belonged to this time of trial, will no longer attract the artist. He will attempt to arouse more refined emotions, as yet unnamed. Just as he will live a complicated and subtle life, so his work will give to those observers capable of feeling them emotions subtle beyond words.

The observer of today is seldom capable of feeling such vibrations. He seeks instead an imitation of nature with a practical function (for example, a portrait in the ordinary sense) or an intuition of nature involving a certain interpretation (e.g., "impressionist" painting) or an inner feeling expressed by nature's forms (as we say, a picture of "mood"[2]). When they are true works of art, such forms fulfil their purposes and nourish the spirit. Though this remark applies to the first case, it applies more strongly to the third, in which the spectator hears an answering chord in himself. Such emotional chords cannot be superficial or without value; the feeling of such a picture can indeed deepen and purify the feeling of the spectator. The spirit at least is preserved from coarseness: such pictures tune it up, as a tuning fork does the strings of a musical instrument. But the subtilization and extension of this chord in time and space remained limited, and the potential power of art is not exhausted by it.

---

[2] Alas, this word, which in the past was used to describe the poetical aspirations of an artist's soul, has been misused and finally ridiculed. Was there ever a great word that the crowd did not try immediately to desecrate?

Imagine a building, large or small, divided into rooms; each room
is covered with canvases of various sizes, perhaps thousands of
them. They represent bits of nature in color—animals in sunlight
or shadow, or drinking, standing in water, or lying on grass; close
by, a "Crucifixion," by a painter who does not believe in Christ;
then flowers, and human figures, sitting, standing, or walking,
and often naked; there are many naked women foreshortened
from behind; apples and silver dishes; a portrait of Mister So-
and-So; sunsets; a lady in pink; a flying duck; a portrait of Lady
X; flying geese; a lady in white; some cattle in shadow, flecked
by brilliant sunlight; a portrait of Ambassador Y; a lady in green.
All this is carefully reproduced in a book with the name of the
artist and the name of the picture. Book in hand, people go from
wall to wall, turning pages, reading names. Then they depart,
neither richer nor poorer, again absorbed by their affairs, which
have nothing to do with art. Why did they come? In every
painting a whole life is mysteriously enclosed, a whole life of
tortures, doubts, of hours of enthusiasm and inspiration.

What is the direction of that life? What is the cry of the
artist's soul, if the soul was involved in the creation? "To send
light into the darkness of men's hearts—such is the obligation of
the artist," said Schumann. "A painter is a man who can draw
and paint everything," said Tolstoi.

Of these two definitions we must choose the second, if we
think of the exhibition just described. With more or less skill,
virtuosity and vigor, objects are created on a canvas, "painted"
either roughly or smoothly. To bring the whole into harmony
on the canvas is what leads to a work of art. With cold eye and
indifferent mind the public regards the work. Connoisseurs admire "technique," as one might admire a tight-rope walker, or
enjoy the "painting quality," as one might enjoy a cake. But
hungry souls go hungry away.

The public ambles through the rooms, saying "nice" or "interesting." Those who could speak have said nothing; those who
could hear have heard nothing. This condition is called "art for
art's sake." This annihilation of internal vibrations that constitute
the life of the colors, this dwindling away of artistic force, is
called "art for art's sake."

The artist seeks material rewards for his facility, inventiveness
and sensitivity. His purpose becomes the satisfaction of ambition
and greediness. In place of an intensive cooperation among artists,

there is a battle for goods. There is excessive competition, over-production. Hatred, partisanship, cliques, jealousy, intrigues are the natural consequences of an aimless, materialist art.[3]

The public turns away from artists who have higher ideals, who find purpose in an art without purpose.

"Comprehension" is educating the spectator to the point of view of the artist. It has been said that art is the child of its time. But such an art can only repeat artistically what is already clearly realized by the contemporary. Since it is not germinative, but only a child of the age, and unable to become a mother of the future, it is a castrated art. It is transitory; it dies morally the moment the atmosphere that nourished it alters.

---

[3] A few exceptions do not affect the truth of this sad and ominous picture; even the exceptions are chiefly believers in the doctrine of art for art's sake. They serve, therefore, a higher ideal, but one which is ultimately a useless waste of their strength. External beauty is one element in a spiritual milieu. But beyond this positive fact (that what is beautiful is good) lies the weakness of a talent not used to the full (*talent* in the biblical sense).

Much of the force of twentieth-century writing about the arts has been sociological in origin and intent. If one follows this approach to the arts, one is directed to economic and social classes, to their various conditions, and to the resultant blunting or (more rarely) sharpening of tastes. Clement Greenberg (1909–   ), in a notable separation of quality from pseudo-quality, defines the aims and achievements of contemporary painting and the values and pretensions of its viewers. The essay, written in 1939 for Partisan Review, *the pre-eminent organ of the sociological esthetic, is a fine example of the work of a tireless spokesman for American abstract painting and painters. It is also a guide, albeit limited, to essential terminology and especially to those two central terms,* avant-garde *and* kitsch.

AVANT-GARDE AND KITSCH

Clement Greenberg

One and the same civilization produces simultaneously two such different things as a poem by T. S. Eliot and a Tin Pan Alley song, or a painting by Braque and a *Saturday Evening Post* cover. All four are on the order of culture, and ostensibly, parts of the same culture and products of the same society. Here, however, their connection seems to end. A poem by Eliot and a poem by Eddie Guest—what perspective of culture is large enough to enable us to situate them in an enlightening relation to each other? Does the fact that a disparity such as this within the frame of a single cultural tradition, is and has been taken for granted—does this fact indicate that the disparity is a part of the natural order of things? Or is it something entirely new, and particular to our age?

The answer involves more than an investigation in aesthetics. It appears to me that it is necessary to examine more closely and with more originality than hitherto the relationship between aesthetic experience as met by the specific—not generalized—individual, and the social and historical contexts in which that experience takes place. What is brought to light will answer, in addition to the question posed above, other and perhaps more important ones.

I

A society, as it becomes less and less able, in the course of its development, to justify the inevitability of its particular forms, breaks up the accepted notions upon which artists and writers must depend in large part for communication with their audiences. It becomes difficult to assume anything. All the verities involved by religion, authority, tradition, style, are thrown into question, and the writer or artist is no longer able to estimate the response of his audience to the symbols and references with which he works. In the past such a state of affairs has usually resolved itself into a motionless Alexandrianism, an academicism in which the really important issues are left untouched because they involve controversy, and in which creative activity dwindles to virtuosity in the small details of form, all larger questions being decided by the precedent of the old masters. The same themes are mechanically varied in a hundred different works, and yet nothing new is produced: Statius, mandarin verse, Roman sculpture, Beaux Arts painting, neo-republican architecture.

It is among the hopeful signs in the midst of the decay of our present society that we—some of us—have been unwilling to accept this last phase for our own culture. In seeking to go beyond Alexandrianism, a part of Western bourgeois society has produced something unheard of heretofore: avant-garde culture. A superior consciousness of history—more precisely, the appearance of a new kind of criticism of society, an historical criticism—made this possible. This criticism has not confronted our present society with timeless utopias, but has soberly examined in the terms of history and of cause and effect the antecedents, justifications, and functions of the forms that lie at the heart of every society. Thus our present bourgeois social order was shown to be, not an eternal, "natural" condition of life, but simply the latest term in a succession of social orders. New perspectives of this kind, becoming a part of the advanced intellectual conscience of the fifth and sixth decades of the nineteenth century, soon were absorbed by artists and poets, even if unconsciously for the most part. It was no accident, therefore, that the birth of the avant-garde coincided chrono-logically—and geographically too—with the first bold develop-ment of scientific revolutionary thought in Europe.

True, the first settlers of bohemia—which was then identical with the avant-garde—turned out soon to be demonstratively uninterested in politics. Nevertheless, without the circulation of revolutionary ideas in the air about them, they would never have been able to isolate their concept of the "bourgeois" in order to define what they were *not*. Nor, without the moral aid of revolu-tionary political attitudes would they have had the courage to assert themselves as aggressively as they did against the prevailing standards of society. Courage indeed was needed for this, because the avant-garde's emigration from bourgeois society to bohemia meant also an emigration from the markets of capitalism, upon which artists and writers had been thrown by the falling away of aristocratic patronage. (Ostensibly, at least, it meant this—meant starving in a garret—although, as will be shown later, the avant-garde remained attached to bourgeois society precisely because it needed its money.)

Yet it is true that once the avant-garde had succeeded in "de-taching" itself from society, it proceeded to turn around and repudiate revolutionary as well as bourgeois politics. The revolu-tion was left inside society, a part of that welter of ideological struggle which art and poetry find so unpropitious as soon as it begins to involve those "precious," axiomatic beliefs upon which culture thus far has had to rest. Hence it was developed that the true and most important function of the avant-garde was not to "experiment," but to find a path along which it would be possible to keep culture *moving* in the midst of ideological confusion and violence. Retiring from the public altogether, the avant-garde poet or artist sought to maintain the high level of his art by both nar-rowing and raising it to the expression of an absolute in which all relativities and contradictions would be either resolved or be-side the point: "Art for art's sake" and "pure poetry" appear, and subject matter or content becomes something to be avoided like a plague.

It has been in search of the absolute that the avant-garde has arrived at "abstract" or "nonobjective" art—and poetry, too. The avant-garde poet or artist tries in effect to imitate God by creating something valid solely on its own terms in the way

nature itself is valid, in the way a landscape—not its picture—
is aesthetically valid; something *given*, increate, independent of
meanings, similars, or originals. Content is to be dissolved so
completely into form that the work of art or literature cannot
be reduced in whole or in part to anything not itself.

But the absolute is absolute, and the poet or artist, being what
he is, cherishes certain relative values more than others. The
very values in the name of which he invokes the absolute are
relative values, the values of aesthetics. And so he turns out to
be imitating, not God—and here I use "imitate" in its Aristotelian
sense—but the disciples and processes of art and literature themselves. This is the genesis of the "abstract."[1] In turning his attention away from subject matter of common experience, the poet
or artist turns it in upon the medium of his own craft. The
nonrepresentational or "abstract," if it is to have aesthetic validity, cannot be arbitrary and accidental, but must stem from
obedience to some worthy constraint or original. This constraint,
once the world of common, extraverted experience has been
renounced, can only be found in the very processes or disciplines
by which art and literature have already imitated the former.
These themselves become the subject matter of art and literature.
If, to continue with Aristotle, all art and literature are imitation,
then what we have here is the imitation of imitat*ing*. To quote
Yeats:

> "Nor is there singing school but studying
> Monuments of its own magnificence."

Picasso, Braque, Mondrian, Miro, Kandinsky, Brancusi, even
Klee, Matisse, and Cézanne, derive their chief inspiration from

---

[1] The example of music, which has long been an abstract art, and which avant-
garde poetry has tried so much to emulate, is interesting. Music, Aristotle said
curiously enough, is the most imitative and vivid of all arts because it imitates its
original—the state of the soul—with the greatest immediacy. Today this strikes
us as the exact opposite of the truth, because no art seems to us to have less reference to something outside itself than music. However, aside from the fact that in a
sense Aristotle may still be right, it must be explained that ancient Greek music
was closely associated with poetry, and depended upon its character as an accessory to verse to make its imitative meaning clear. Plato, speaking of music, says:
"For when there are no words, it is very difficult to recognize the meaning of the
harmony and rhythm, or to see that any worthy object is imitated by them." As
far as we know, all music originally served such an accessory function. Once, however, it was abandoned, music was forced to withdraw into itself to find a constraint
or original. This is found in the various means of its own composition and performance.

the medium they work in.[2] The excitement of their art seems
to lie most of all in its pure preoccupation with the invention
and arrangement of spaces, surfaces, shapes, colors, etc., to the
exclusion of whatever is not necessarily implicated in these
factors. The attention of poets like Rimbaud, Mallarmé, Valéry,
Eluard, Pound, Hart Crane, Stevens, even Rilke and Yeats, appears to be centered on the effort to create poetry and on the
"moments" themselves of poetic conversion rather than on experience to be converted into poetry. Of course, this cannot
exclude other preoccupations in their work, for poetry must deal
with words, and words must communicate. Certain poets, such
as Mallarmé and Valéry,[3] are more radical in this respect than
others—leaving aside those poets who have tried to compose
poetry in pure sound alone. However, if it were easier to define
poetry, modern poetry would be much more "pure" and "abstract." . . . As for the other fields of literature—the definition
of avant-garde aesthetics advanced here is no Procrustean bed.
But aside from the fact that most of our best contemporary
novelists have gone to school with the avant-garde, it is significant that Gide's most ambitious book is a novel about the writing of a novel, and that Joyce's *Ulysses* and *Finnegans Wake*
seem to be above all, as one French critic says, the reduction of
experience to expression for the sake of expression, the expression
mattering more than what is being expressed.

That avant-garde culture is the imitation of imitat*ing*—the fact
itself—calls for neither approval nor disapproval. It is true that
this culture contains within itself some of the very Alexandrianism it seeks to overcome. The lines quoted from Yeats above
referred to Byzantium, which is very close to Alexandria; and in
a sense this imitation of imitat*ing* is a superior sort of Alexandrianism. But there is one most important difference: the avant-
garde moves, while Alexandrianism stands still. And this, precisely, is what justifies the avant-garde's methods and makes them
necessary. The necessity lies in the fact that by no other means
is it possible today to create art and literature of a high order.
To quarrel with necessity by throwing about terms like "for-

---

[2] I owe this formulation to a remark made by Hans Hofmann, the art teacher, in
one of his lectures. From the point of view of this formulation surrealism in plastic
art is a reactionary tendency which is attempting to restore "outside" subject matter.
The chief concern of a painter like Dali is to represent the processes and concepts of
his consciousness, not the processes of his medium.

[3] See Valéry's remarks about his own poetry.

malism," "purism," "ivory tower," and so forth is either dull or
dishonest. This is not to say, however, that it is to the *social*
advantage of the avant-garde that it is what it is. Quite the
opposite.

The avant-garde's specialization of itself, the fact that its best
artists are artists' artists, its best poets, poets' poets, has estranged
a great many of those who were capable formerly of enjoying
and appreciating ambitious art and literature, but who are now unwilling or unable to acquire an initiation into their craft secrets.
The masses have always remained more or less indifferent to
culture in the process of development. But today such culture
is being abandoned by those to whom it actually belongs—our
ruling class. For it is to the latter that the avant-garde belongs.
No culture can develop without a social basis, without a source
of stable income. And in the case of the avant-garde this was
provided by an élite among the ruling class of that society from
which it assumed itself to be cut off, but to which it has always
remained attached by an umbilical cord of gold. The paradox is
real. And now this élite is rapidly shrinking. Since the avant-
garde forms the only living culture we now have, the survival in
the near future of culture in general is thus threatened.

We must not be deceived by superficial phenomena and local
successes. Picasso's shows still draw crowds, and T. S. Eliot is
taught in the universities; the dealers in modernist art are still
in business, and the publishers still publish some "difficult"
poetry. But the avant-garde itself, already sensing the danger, is
becoming more and more timid every day that passes. Academicism and commercialism are appearing in the strangest places.
This can mean only one thing: that the avant-garde is becoming
unsure of the audience it depends on—the rich and the cultivated.

Is it the nature itself of avant-garde culture that is alone responsible for the danger it finds itself in? Or is that only a
dangerous liability? Are there other, and perhaps more important, factors involved?

II

Where there is an avant-garde, generally we also find a rear-
guard. True enough—simultaneously with the entrance of the
avant-garde, a second new cultural phenomenon appeared in the

industrial West: that thing to which the Germans give the wonderful name of *Kitsch:* popular, commercial art and literature
with their chromeotypes, magazine covers, illustrations, ads,
slick and pulp fiction, comics, Tin Pan Alley music, tap dancing,
Hollywood movies, etc., etc. For some reason this gigantic
apparition has always been taken for granted. It is time we
looked into its whys and wherefores.

Kitsch is a product of the industrial revolution which urban-
ized the masses of western Europe and America and established
what is called universal literacy.

Previous to this the only market for formal culture, as dis-
tiguished from folk culture, had been among those who in
addition to being able to read and write could command the
leisure and comfort that always goes hand in hand with cultivation of some sort. This until then had been inextricably associated
with literacy. But with the introduction of universal literacy,
the ability to read and write became almost a minor skill like
driving a car, and it no longer served to distinguish an individual's cultural inclinations, since it was no longer the exclusive
concomitant of refined tastes. The peasants who settled in the
cities as proletariat and petty bourgeois learned to read and
write for the sake of efficiency, but they did not win the leisure
and comfort necessary for the enjoyment of the city's traditional
culture. Losing, nevertheless, their taste for the folk culture whose
background was the countryside, and discovering a new capacity
for boredom at the same time, the new urban masses set up a
pressure on society to provide them with a kind of culture fit
for their own consumption. To fill the demand of the new
market a new commodity was devised: ersatz culture, kitsch,
destined for those who, insensible to the values of genuine culture, are hungry nevertheless for the diversion that only culture
of some sort can provide.

Kitsch, using for raw material the debased and academicized
simulacra of genuine culture, welcomes and cultivates this insensibility. It is the source of its profits. Kitsch is mechanical and
operates by formulas. Kitsch is vicarious experience and faked
sensations. Kitsch changes according to style, but remains always
the same. Kitsch is the epitome of all that is spurious in the life
of our times. Kitsch pretends to demand nothing of its customers
except their money—not even their time.

The precondition for kitsch, a condition without which kitsch would be impossible, is the availability close at hand of a fully matured cultural tradition, whose discoveries, acquisitions, and perfected self-consciousness kitsch can take advantage of for its own ends. It borrows from it devices, tricks, stratagems, rules of thumb, themes, converts them into a system, and discards the rest. It draws its life blood, so to speak, from this reservoir of accumulated experience. This is what is really meant when it is said that the popular art and literature of today were once the daring, esoteric art and literature of yesterday. Of course, no such thing is true. What is meant is that when enough time has elapsed the new is looted for new "twists," which are then watered down and served up as kitsch. Self-evidently, all kitsch is academic, and conversely, all that's academic is kitsch. For what is called the academic as such no longer has an independent existence, but has become the stuffed-shirt "front" for kitsch. The methods of industrialism displace the handicrafts.

Because it can be turned out mechanically, kitsch has become an integral part of our productive system in a way in which true culture could never be except accidentally. It has been capitalized at a tremendous investment which must show commensurate returns; it is compelled to extend as well as to keep its markets. While it is essentially its own salesman, a great sales apparatus has nevertheless been created for it, which brings pressure to bear on every member of society. Traps are laid even in those areas, so to speak, that are the preserves of genuine culture. It is not enough today, in a country like ours, to have an inclination toward the latter; one must have a true passion for it that will give him the power to resist the faked article that surrounds and presses in on him from the moment he is old enough to look at the funny papers. Kitsch is deceptive. It has many different levels, and some of them are high enough to be dangerous to the naïve seeker of true light. A magazine like the *New Yorker*, which is fundamentally high-class kitsch for the luxury trade, converts and waters down a great deal of avant-garde material for its own uses. Nor is every single item of kitsch altogether worthless. Now and then it produces something of merit, something that has an authentic folk flavor; and these accidental and isolated instances have fooled people who should know better.

Kitsch's enormous profits are a source of temptation to the avant-garde itself, and its members have not always resisted this temptation. Ambitious writers and artists will modify their work under the pressure of kitsch, if they do not succumb to it entirely. And then those puzzling borderline cases appear, such as the popular novelist, Simenon, in France, and Steinbeck in this country. The net result is always to the detriment of true culture, in any case.

Kitsch has not been confined to the cities in which it was born, but has flowed out over the countryside, wiping out folk culture. Nor has it shown any regard for geographical and national-cultural boundaries. Another mass product of Western industrial-ism, it has gone on a triumphal tour of the world, crowding out and defacing native cultures in one colonial country after an-other, so that it is now by way of becoming a universal culture, the first universal culture ever beheld. Today the Chinaman, no less than the South American Indian, the Hindu, no less than the Polynesian, have come to prefer to the products of their native art, magazine covers, rotogravure sections, and calendar girls. How is this virulence of kitsch, this irresistible attractiveness, to be explained? Naturally, machine-made kitsch can undersell the native handmade article, and the prestige of the West also helps, but why is kitsch a so much more profitable export article than Rembrandt? One, after all, can be reproduced as cheaply as the other.

In his article on the Soviet cinema in the *Partisan Review*, Dwight Macdonald points out that kitsch has in the last ten years become the dominant culture in Soviet Russia. For this he blames the political regime—not only for the fact that kitsch is the of-ficial culture, but also that it is actually the dominant, most popular culture; and he quotes the following from Kurt Lon-don's *The Seven Soviet Arts:* ". . . the attitude of the masses both to the old and new art styles probably remains essentially de-pendent on the nature of the education afforded them by their respective states." Macdonald goes on to say: "Why after all should ignorant peasants prefer Repin (a leading exponent of Russian academic kitsch in painting) to Picasso, whose abstract technique is at least as relevant to their own primitive folk art as is the former's realistic style? No, if the masses crowd into the Tretyakov (Moscow's museum of contemporary Russian art: kitsch) it is largely because they have been conditioned to shun 'formalism' and to admire 'socialist realism.' "

In the first place it is not a question of a choice between merely the old and merely the new, as London seems to think—but of a

choice between the bad, up-to-date old and the genuinely new.
The alternative to Picasso is not Michelangelo, but kitsch. In the
second place, neither in backward Russia nor in the advanced
West do the masses prefer kitsch simply because their governments condition them toward it. Where state educational systems
take the trouble to mention art, we are told to respect the old
masters, not kitsch; and yet we go and hang Maxfield Parrish
or his equivalent on our walls, instead of Rembrandt and Michelangelo. Moreover, as Macdonald himself points out, around 1925
when the Soviet régime was encouraging avant-garde cinema,
the Russian masses continued to prefer Hollywood movies. No,
"conditioning" does not explain the potency of kitsch. . . .

All values are human values, relative values, in art as well as
elsewhere. Yet there does seem to have been more or less of a
general agreement among the cultivated of mankind over the ages
as to what is good art and what bad. Taste has varied, but not
beyond certain limits: contemporary connoisseurs agree with the
eighteenth-century Japanese that Hokusai was one of the greatest
artists of his time; we even agree with the ancient Egyptians that
Third and Fourth Dynasty art was the most worthy of being
selected as their paragon by those who came after. We may have
come to prefer Giotto to Raphael, but we still do not deny that
Raphael was one of the best painters of his *time*. There has been
an agreement then, and this agreement rests, I believe, on a fairly
constant distinction made between those values only to be found
in art and the values which can be found elsewhere. Kitsch, by
virtue of rationalized technique that draws on science and
industry, has erased this distinction in practice.

Let us see for example what happens when an ignorant Russian
peasant such as Macdonald mentions stands with hypothetical
freedom of choice before two paintings, one by Picasso, the
other by Repin. In the first he sees, let us say, a play of lines,
colors, and spaces that represent a woman. The abstract technique—to accept Macdonald's supposition, which I am inclined
to doubt—reminds him somewhat of the icons he has left behind
him in the village, and he feels the attraction of the familiar. We
will even suppose that he faintly surmises some of the great art
values the cultivated find in Picasso. He turns next to Repin's
picture and sees a battle scene. The technique is not so familiar
—as technique. But that weighs very little with the peasant, for
he suddenly discovers values in Repin's picture which seem far

superior to the values he has been accustomed to finding in icon art; and the unfamiliar technique itself is one of the sources of those values: the values of the vividly recognizable, the miraculous, and the sympathetic. In Repin's picture the peasant recognizes and sees things in the way in which he recognizes and sees things outside of pictures—there is no discontinuity between art and life, no need to accept a convention and say to oneself, that icon represents Jesus because it intends to represent Jesus, even if it does not remind me very much of a man. That Repin can paint so realistically that identifications are self-evident immediately and without any effort on the part of the spectator— that is miraculous. The peasant is also pleased by the wealth of self-evident meanings which he finds in the picture: "it tells a story." Picasso and the icons are so austere and barren in comparison. What is more, Repin heightens reality and makes it dramatic: sunset, exploding shells, running and falling men. There is no longer any question of Picasso or icons. Repin is what the peasant wants, and nothing else but Repin. It is lucky, however, for Repin that the peasant is protected from the products of American capitalism, for he would not stand a chance next to a *Saturday Evening Post* cover by Norman Rockwell.

Ultimately, it can be said that the cultivated spectator derives the same values from Picasso that the peasant gets from Repin, since what the latter enjoys in Repin is somehow art too, on however low a scale, and he is sent to look at pictures by the same instincts that send the cultivated spectator. But the ultimate values which the cultivated spectator derives from Picasso are derived at a second remove, as the result of reflection upon the immediate impression left by the plastic values. It is only then that the recognizable, the miraculous, and the sympathetic enter. They are not immediately or externally present in Picasso's painting, but must be projected into it by the spectator sensitive enough to react sufficiently to plastic qualities. They belong to the "reflected" effect. In Repin, on the other hand, the "reflected" effect has already been included in the picture, ready for the spectator's unreflective enjoyment.[4] Where Picasso paints

---

[4] T. S. Eliot said something to the same effect in accounting for the shortcomings of English Romantic poetry. Indeed the Romantics can be considered the original sinners whose guilt kitsch inherited. They showed kitsch how. What does Keats write about mainly, if not the effect of poetry upon himself?

cause, Repin paints *effect*. Repin pre-digests art for the spectator and spares him effort, provides him with a short cut to the pleasure of art that detours what is necessarily difficult in genuine art. Repin, or kitsch, is synthetic art.

The same point can be made with respect to kitsch literature: it provides vicarious experience for the insensitive with far greater immediacy than serious fiction can hope to do. And Eddie Guest and the *Indian Love Lyrics* are more poetic than T. S. Eliot and Shakespeare.

III

If the avant-garde imitates the processes of art, kitsch, we now see, imitates its effects. The neatness of this antithesis is more than contrived; it corresponds to and defines the tremendous interval that separates from each other two such simultaneous cultural phenomena as the avant-garde and kitsch. This interval, too great to be closed by all the infinite gradations of popularized "modernism" and "modernistic" kitsch, corresponds in turn to a social interval, a social interval that has always existed in formal culture as elsewhere in civilized society, and whose two termini converge and diverge in fixed relation to the increasing or decreasing stability of the given society. There has always been on one side the minority of the powerful—and therefore the cultivated—and on the other the great mass of the exploited and poor —and therefore the ignorant. Formal culture has always belonged to the first, while the last have had to content themselves with folk or rudimentary culture, or kitsch.

In a stable society which functions well enough to hold in solution the contradictions between its classes the cultural dichotomy becomes somewhat blurred. The axioms of the few are shared by the many; the latter believe superstitiously what the former believe soberly. And at such moments in history the masses are able to feel wonder and admiration for the culture, on no matter how high a plane, of its masters. This applies at least to plastic culture, which is accessible to all.

In the Middle Ages the plastic artist paid lip service at least to the lowest common denominators of experience. This even remained true to some extent until the seventeenth century. There was available for imitation a universally valid conceptual reality,

whose order the artist could not tamper with. The subject matter of art was prescribed by those who commissioned works of
art, which were not created, as in bourgeois society, on speculation. Precisely because his content was determined in advance,
the artist was free to concentrate on his medium. He needed not
to be philosopher, or visionary, but simply artificer. As long as
there was general agreement as to what were the worthiest subjects for art, the artist was relieved of the necessity to be original
and inventive in his "matter" and could devote all his energy to
formal problems. For him the medium became, privately, pro-
fessionally, the content of his art, even as today his medium is
the public content of the abstract painter's art—with that difference, however, that the medieval artist had to suppress his professional preoccupation in public—had always to suppress and
subordinate the personal and professional in the finished, official
work of art. If, as an ordinary member of the Christian community, he felt some personal emotion about his subject matter,
this only contributed to the enrichment of the work's public
meaning. Only with the Renaissance do the inflections of the
personal become legitimate, still to be kept, however, within the
limits of the simply and universally recognizable. And only with
Rembrandt do "lonely" artists begin to appear, lonely in their
art.

But even during the Renaissance, and as long as Western art
was endeavoring to perfect its technique, victories in this realm
could only be signalized by success in realistic imitation, since
there was no other objective criterion at hand. Thus the masses
could still find in the art of their masters objects of admiration
and wonder. Even the bird who pecked at the fruit in Zeuxis'
picture could applaud.

It is a platitude that art becomes caviar to the general when the
reality it imitates no longer corresponds even roughly to the
reality recognized by the general. Even then, however, the resentment the common man may feel is silenced by the awe in
which he stands of the patrons of this art. Only when he becomes
dissatisfied with the social order they administer does he begin
to criticize their culture. Then the plebeian finds courage for
the first time to voice his opinions openly. Every man, from the
Tammany alderman to the Austrian house-painter, finds that he
is entitled to his opinion. Most often this resentment toward
culture is to be found where the dissatisfaction with society is a

reactionary dissatisfaction which expresses itself in revivalism and puritanism, and latest of all, in fascism. Here revolvers and torches begin to be mentioned in the same breath as culture. In the name of godliness or the blood's health, in the name of simple ways and solid virtues, the statue-smashing commences.

IV

Returning to our Russian peasant for the moment, let us suppose that after he has chosen Repin in preference to Picasso, the state's educational apparatus comes along and tells him that he is wrong, that he should have chosen Picasso—and shows him why. It is quite possible for the Soviet state to do this. But things being as they are in Russia—and everywhere else—the peasant soon finds that the necessity of working hard all day for his living and the rude, uncomfortable circumstances in which he lives do not allow him enough leisure, energy, and comfort to train for the enjoyment of Picasso. This needs, after all, a considerable amount of "conditioning." Superior culture is one of the most artificial of all human creations, and the peasant finds no "natural" urgency within himself that will drive him toward Picasso in spite of all difficulties. In the end the peasant will go back to kitsch when he feels like looking at pictures, for he can enjoy kitsch without effort. The state is helpless in this matter and remains so as long as the problems of production have not been solved in a socialist sense. The same holds true, of course, for capitalist countries and makes all talk of art for the masses there nothing but demagogy.[5]

---

[5] It will be objected that such art for the masses as folk art was developed under rudimentary conditions of production—and that a good deal of folk art is on a high level. Yes, it is—but folk art is not Athene, and it's Athene whom we want: formal culture with its infinity of aspects, its luxuriance, its large comprehension. Besides, we are now told that most of what we consider good in folk culture is the static survival of dead, formal, artistocratic, cultures. Our old English ballads, for instance, were not created by the "folk," but by the postfeudal squirearchy of the English countryside, to survive in the mouths of the folk long after those for whom the ballads were composed had gone on to other forms of literature. . . . Unfortunately, until the machine-age culture was the exclusive prerogative of a society that lived by the labor of serfs or slaves. They were the real symbols of culture. For one man to spend time and energy creating or listening to poetry meant that another man had to produce enough to keep himself alive and the former in comfort. In Africa today we find that the culture of slave-owning tribes is generally much superior to that of the tribes which possess no slaves.

Where today a political regime establishes an official cultural policy, it is for the sake of demagogy. If kitsch is the official tendency of culture in Germany, Italy, and Russia, it is not because their respective governments are controlled by Philistines, but because kitsch is the culture of the masses in these countries, as it is everywhere else. The encouragement of kitsch is merely another of the inexpensive ways in which totalitarian régimes seek to ingratiate themselves with their subjects. Since these régimes cannot raise the cultural level of the masses—even if they wanted to—by anything short of a surrender to international socialism, they will flatter the masses by bringing all culture down to their level. It is for this reason that the avant-garde is outlawed, and not so much because a superior culture is inherently a more critical culture. (Whether or not the avant-garde could possibly flourish under a totalitarian régime is not pertinent to the question at this point.) As a matter of fact, the main trouble with avant-garde art and literature, from the point of view of fascists and Stalinists, is not that they are too critical, but that they are too "innocent," that it is too difficult to inject effective propaganda into them, that kitsch is more pliable to this end. Kitsch keeps a dictator in closer contact with the "soul" of the people. Should the official culture be one superior to the general mass-level, there would be a danger of isolation.

Nevertheless, if the masses were conceivably to ask for avant-garde art and literature, Hitler, Mussolini and Stalin would not hesitate long in attempting to satisfy such a demand. Hitler is a bitter enemy of the avant-garde, both on doctrinal and personal grounds, yet this did not prevent Goebbels in 1932–1933 from strenuously courting avant-garde artists and writers. When Gottfried Benn, an Expressionist poet, came over to the Nazis he was welcomed with a great fanfare, although at that very moment Hitler was denouncing Expressionism as *Kulturbolschewismus*. This was at a time when the Nazis felt that the prestige which the avant-garde enjoyed among the cultivated German public could be of advantage to them, and practical considerations of this nature, the Nazis being the skillful politicians they are, have always taken precedence over Hitler's personal inclinations. Later the Nazis realized that it was more practical to accede to the wishes of the masses in matters of culture than to those of their paymasters; the latter, when it came to a question of preserving power, were as willing to sacrifice their culture as they were their moral principles, while the former, precisely because power was being withheld from them, had to be cozened in every other way possible. It was necessary to promote in a much more grandiose style than in the democracies the illusion that the masses actually rule. The literature and art they enjoy and understand were to be proclaimed the only true art and literature and any other kind was to be suppressed. Under these circumstances people like Gottfried Benn, no matter how ardently they support Hitler, become a liability; and we hear no more of them in Nazi Germany.

We can see then that although from one point of view the personal Philistinism of Hitler and Stalin is not accidental to the political roles they play, from another point of view it is only an incidentally contributory factor in determining the cultural policies of their respective régimes. Their personal Philistinism simply adds brutality and double-darkness to policies they would be forced to support anyhow by the pressure of all their other policies—even were they, personally, devotees of avant-garde culture. What the acceptance of the isolation of the Russian Revolution forces Stalin to do, Hitler is compelled to do by his acceptance of the contradictions of capitalism and his efforts to freeze them. As for Mussolini—his case is a perfect example of the *disponibilité* of a realist in these matters. For years he bent a benevolent eye on the Futurists and built modernistic railroad stations and government-owned apartment houses. One can still see in the suburbs of Rome more modernistic apartments than almost anywhere else in the world. Perhaps Fascism wanted to show its up-to-dateness, to conceal the fact that it was a retrogression; perhaps it wanted to conform to the tastes of the wealthy élite it served. At any rate Mussolini seems to have realized lately that it would be more useful to him to please the cultural tastes of the Italian masses than those of their masters. The masses must be provided with objects of admiration and wonder; the latter can dispense with them. And so we find Mussolini announcing a "new Imperial style." Marinetti, Chirico, et al. are sent into the outer darkness, and the new railroad station in Rome will not be modernistic. That Mussolini was late in coming to this only illustrates again the relative hesitancy with which Italian Fascism has drawn the necessary implications of its role. . . .

Capitalism in decline finds that whatever of quality it is still capable of producing becomes almost invariably a threat to its own existence. Advances in culture no less than advances in science and industry corrode the very society under whose aegis they are made possible. Here, as in every other question today, it becomes necessary to quote Marx word for word. Today we no longer look towards socialism for a new culture—as inevitably as one will appear, once we do have socialism. Today we look to socialism *simply* for the preservation of whatever living culture we have right now.

Henry Moore (1898–) was for many years a teacher at the Royal College of Art in London and then at the Chelsea School of Art. He organizes his writing like a teacher, systematically; one can almost see the term's work taking shape in these "notes," putting general ideas next to special applications, and setting all in the frame of the history of modern culture. He composes his sculpture with the same systematic precision. Everything is in the service of a full three dimensions. Flatness is out. To make these dimensions clear, he developed a style that is characterized by piercings of his figures and by roundings of their edges that carry the viewer's eye well beyond the surfaces first presented. Moore is a sculptor in depth and a thinker about sculpture in the same dimension.

NOTES ON SCULPTURE

Henry
Moore

It is a mistake for a sculptor or a painter to speak or write very often about his job. It releases tension needed for his work. By trying to express his aims with rounded-off logical exactness, he can easily become a theorist whose actual work is only a caged-in exposition of conceptions evolved in terms of logic and words.

But though the nonlogical, instinctive, sub-conscious part of the mind must play its part in his work, he also has a conscious mind which is not inactive. The artist works with a concentration of his whole personality, and the conscious part of it resolves conflicts, organizes memories, and prevents him from trying to walk in two directions at the same time.

It is likely, then, that a sculptor can give, from his own conscious experience, *clues* which will help others in their approach to sculpture, and this article tries to do this, and no more. It is not a general survey of sculpture, or of my own development, but a few notes on some of the problems that have concerned me from time to time.

THREE DIMENSIONS

Appreciation of sculpture depends upon the ability to respond to form in three dimensions. That is, perhaps, why sculpture has been described as the most difficult of all arts; certainly it is more difficult than the arts which involve appreciation of flat forms, shape in only two dimensions. Many more people are 'form-blind' than colour-blind. The child learning to see first distinguishes only two-dimensional shape; it cannot judge distances, depths. Later, for its personal safety and practical needs, it has to develop (partly by means of touch) the ability to judge roughly three-dimensional distances. But having satisfied the requirements of practical necessity most people go no further. Though they may attain considerable accuracy in the perception of flat form, they do not make the further intellectual and emotional effort needed to comprehend form in its full spatial existence.

This is what the sculptor must do. He must strive continually to think of and use form in its full spatial completeness. He gets the solid shape, as it were, inside his head—he thinks of it, whatever its size, as if he were holding it completely enclosed in the hollow of his hand. He mentally visualizes a complex form *from all round itself:* he knows while he looks at one side what the other side is like; he identifies himself with its centre of gravity, its mass, its weight; he realizes its volume, as the space that the shape displaces in the air.

And the sensitive observer of sculpture must also learn to feel shape simply as shape, not as description or reminiscence. He must, for example, perceive an egg as a simple single solid shape, quite apart from its significance as food, or from the literary idea that it will become a bird. And so with solids such as a shell, a nut, a plum, a pear, a tadpole, a mushroom, a mountain peak, a kidney, a carrot, a tree-trunk, a bird, a bud, a lark, a ladybird, a bullrush, a bone. From these he can go on to appreciate more complex forms or combinations of several forms.

BRANCUSI

Since Gothic, European sculpture had become overgrown with moss, weeds—all sorts of surface excrescences which completely concealed shape. It has been Brancusi's special mission to get rid of this overgrowth, and to make us once more shape-conscious.

To do this he has had to concentrate on very simple direct shapes, to keep his sculpture, as it were, one-cylindered, to refine and polish a single shape to a degree almost too precious. Brancusi's work apart from its individual value has been of great historical importance in the development of contemporary sculpture. But it may now be no longer necessary to close down and restrict sculpture to the single (static) form unit. We can now begin to open out. To relate and combine together several forms of varied sizes, sections and direction, into one organic whole.

SHELLS AND PEBBLES—

BEING CONDITIONED TO RESPOND TO SHAPES

Although it is the human figure which interests me most deeply, I have always paid great attention to natural forms, such as bones, shells, pebbles, etc. Sometimes, for several years running, I have been to the same part of the sea-shore—but each year a new shape of pebble has caught my eye, which the year before, though it was there in hundreds, I never saw. Out of the millions of pebbles passed in walking along the shore, I choose out to see with excitement only those which fit in with my existing form interest at the time. A different thing happens if I sit down and examine a handful one by one. I may then extend my form experience more by giving my mind time to become conditioned to a new shape.

There are universal shapes to which everybody is subconsciously conditioned and to which they can respond if their conscious control does not shut them off.

HOLES IN SCULPTURE

Pebbles show Nature's way of working stone. Some of the pebbles I pick up have holes right through them.

When first working direct in a hard and brittle material like stone, the lack of experience and great respect for the material, the fear of ill-treating it, too often result in relief surface carving, with no sculptural power.

But with more experience the completed work in stone can be

kept within the limitations of its material, that is, not be weakened beyond its natural constructive build, and yet be turned from an inert mass into a composition which has a full form existence, with masses of varied sizes and sections working together in spatial relationship.

A piece of stone can have a hole through it and not be weakened—if the hole is of a studied size, shape and direction. On the principle of the arch it can remain just as strong.

The first hole made through a piece of stone is a revelation.

The hole connects one side to the other, making it immediately more three-dimensional.

A hole can itself have as much shape-meaning as a solid mass.

Sculpture in air is possible, where the stone contains only the hole, which is the intended and considered form.

The mystery of the hole—the mysterious fascination of caves in hillsides and cliffs.

SIZES AND SCALE

There is a right physical size for every idea.

Pieces of good stone have stood about my studio for long periods, because, though I've had ideas which would fit their proportions and materials perfectly, their size was wrong.

There is a side to scale not to do with its actual physical size, its measurement in feet and inches—but connected with vision.

A carving might be several times over life size and yet be petty and small in feeling—and a small carving only a few inches in height can give the feeling of huge size and monumental grandeur, because the vision behind it is big. Example: Michelangelo's drawings or a Masaccio madonna—and the Albert Memorial.

Yet actual physical size has an emotional meaning. We relate everything to our own size, and our emotional response to size is controlled by the fact that men on the average are between five and six feet high.

An exact model to one-tenth scale of Stonehenge, where the stones would be less than us, would lose all its impressiveness.

Sculpture is more affected by actual size considerations than painting. A painting is isolated by a frame from its surroundings (unless it serves just a decorative purpose), and so retains more easily its own imaginary scale.

If practical considerations allowed me (cost of material, of transport, etc.) I should like to work on large carvings more often than I do. The average in-between size does not disconnect an idea enough from prosaic everyday life. The very small or the very large take on an added size emotion.

Recently I have been working in the country, where, carving in the open air, I find sculpture more natural than in a London studio, but it needs bigger dimensions. A large piece of stone or wood placed almost anywhere at random in a field, orchard or garden, immediately looks right and inspiring.

DRAWING AND SCULPTURE

My drawings are done mainly as a help towards making sculpture —as a means of generating ideas for sculpture, tapping oneself for the initial idea; and as a way of sorting out ideas and developing them.

Also, sculpture compared with drawing is a slow means of expression, and I find drawing a useful outlet for ideas which there is not time enough to realize as sculpture. And I use drawing as a method of study and observation of natural form (drawings from life, drawings of bones, shells, etc.)

And I sometimes draw just for its own enjoyment.

Experience, though, has taught me that the difference there is between drawing and sculpture should not be forgotten. A sculptural idea which may be satisfactory as a drawing always needs some alteration when translated into sculpture.

At one time whenever I made drawings for sculpture I tried to give them as much the illusion of real sculpture as I could—that is, I drew by the method of illusion, of light falling on a solid object. But now I find that carrying a drawing so far that it becomes a substitute for the sculpture either weakens the desire to do the sculpture, or is likely to make the sculpture only a dead realization of the drawing.

I now leave a wider latitude in the interpretation of the drawings I make for sculpture, and draw often in line and flat tones without the light and shade illusion of three dimensions; but this does not mean that the vision behind the drawing is only two-dimensional.

ABSTRACTION AND SURREALISM

The violent quarrel between the abstractionists and the surrealists seems to me quite unnecessary. All good art has contained both abstract and surrealist elements, just as it has contained both classical and romantic elements—order and surprise, intellect and imagination, conscious and unconscious. Both sides of the artist's personality must play their part. And I think the first inception of a painting or a sculpture may begin from either end. As far as my own experience is concerned, I sometimes begin a drawing with no preconceived problem to solve, with only the desire to use pencil on paper, and make lines, tones and shapes with no conscious aim; but as my mind takes in what is so produced a point arrives where some idea becomes conscious and crystallizes, and then a control and ordering begins to take place.

Or sometimes I start with a set subject, or to solve, in a block of stone of known dimensions, a sculptural problem I've given myself, and then consciously attempt to build an ordered relationship of forms, which shall express my idea. But if the work is to be more than just a sculptural exercise, unexplainable jumps in the process of thought occur; and the imagination plays its part.

It might seem from what I have said of shape and form that I regard them as ends in themselves. Far from it. I am very much aware that associational, psychological factors play a large part in sculpture. The meaning and significance of form itself probably depends on the countless associations of man's history. For example, rounded forms convey an idea of fruitfulness, maturity, probably because the earth, women's breasts, and most fruits are rounded, and these shapes are important because they have this background in our habits of perception. I think the humanist organic element will always be for me of fundamental importance in sculpture, giving sculpture its vitality. Each particular carving I make takes on in my mind a human, or occasionally animal, character and personality, and this personality controls its design and formal qualities, and makes me satisfied or dissatisfied with the work as it develops.

Above, photograph by George W. Martin.

Right, photograph by Bob Barrett, ASMP.

My own aim and direction seems to be consistent with these beliefs, though it does not depend upon them. My sculpture is becoming less representational, less an outward visual copy, and so what some people would call more abstract; but only because I believe that in this way I can present the human psychological content of my work with the greatest directness and intensity.

In the struggle to bring painting into the modern world as an art altogether alive to that world, all sorts of groups and movements with their special vocabularies have emerged. The Dutch painter Piet Mondrian (1872–1912) was a leader of one of the most influential of these groups which gathered around the magazine De Stijl in 1917. He was also the founder and premier performer of the rituals of Neo-Plasticism. That formidable name intends to convey a reliance on the line and on the mixing of horizontal and vertical units in rigidly controlled proportions. The style has long since become world-famous, not only in Mondrian's paintings, but in countless imitations in advertising art, in building facades, and even in dress design. The overtones of the style are not so well known, though, as this excellent statement by Mondrian demonstrates. They deserve full attention, particularly by those who find Mondrian's paintings beguiling—and who does not? In keeping with his plastic—or neo-plastic—principles, Mondrian writes tersely, assertively, compendiously. He says what he has to say and stops.

PLASTIC ART AND PURE PLASTIC ART

Piet Mondrian

Although art is fundamentally everywhere and always the same, nevertheless two main human inclinations, diametrically opposed to each other, appear in its many and varied expressions. One aims at the *direct creation of universal beauty*, the other at the *aesthetic expression of oneself*, in other words, of that which one thinks and experiences. The first aims at representing reality objectively, the second subjectively. Thus we see in every work of figurative art the desire, objectively, to represent beauty, solely through form and color, in mutually balanced relations, and, at the same time, an attempt to express that which these forms, colors and relations arouse in us. This latter attempt must of necessity result in an individual expression which veils the pure representation of beauty. Nevertheless, both the two opposing elements (universal–individual) are indispensable if the work is to arouse emotion. Art had to find the right solution. In spite of the dual nature of the creative inclinations, figurative art has produced a harmony through a certain coordination between objective and subjective expression. For the spectator, however, who demands a pure representation of beauty, the individual expression is too predominant. For the artist the search for a unified expression through the balance of two opposites has been, and always will be, a continual struggle.

Throughout the history of culture, art has demonstrated that universal beauty does not arise from the particular character of the form, but from the dynamic rhythm of its inherent relationships, or—in a composition—from the mutual relations of forms. Art has shown that it is a question of determining the relations. It has revealed that the forms exist only for the creation of relationships; that forms create relations and that relations create forms. In this duality of forms and their relations neither takes precedence.

The only problem in art is to achieve a balance between the subjective and the objective. But it is of the utmost importance that this problem should be solved, in the realm of plastic art—technically, as it were—and not in the realm of thought. The work of art must be "produced," "constructed." One must create as objective as possible a representation of forms and relations. Such work can never be empty because the opposition of its constructive elements and its execution arouse emotion.

If some have failed to take into account the inherent character of the form and have forgotten that this—untransformed—predominates, others have overlooked the fact than an individual expression does not become a universal expression through figurative representation, which is based on our conception of feeling, be it classical, romantic, religious, surrealist. Art has shown that universal expression can only be created by a *real equation of the universal and the individual*.

Gradually art is purifying its plastic means and thus bringing out the relationships between them. Thus, in our day two main tendencies appear: the one maintains the figuration, the other eliminates it. While the former employs more or less complicated and particular forms, the latter uses simple and neutral forms, or, ultimately, the free line and the pure color. It is evident that the latter (non-figurative art) can more easily and thoroughly free itself from the domination of the subjective than can the figurative tendency; particular forms and colors (figurative art) are more easily exploited than neutral forms. It is, however, necessary to point out that the definitions "figurative" and "non-figurative" are only approximate and relative. For every form, even every line, represents a figure; no form is absolutely neutral. Clearly, everything must be relative, but, since we need words to make our concepts understandable, we must keep to these terms.

Among the different forms we may consider those as being neutral which have neither the complexity nor the particularities possessed by the natural forms or abstract forms in general. We may call those neutral which do not evoke individual feelings or ideas. Geometrical forms being so profound an abstraction of form may be regarded as neutral; and on account of their tension and the purity of their outlines they may even be preferred to other neutral forms.

If, as conception, non-figurative art has been created by the mutual interaction of the human duality, this art has been *realized* by the mutual interaction of *constructive elements and their inherent relations*. This process consists in mutual purification; purified constructive elements set up pure relationships, and these in their turn demand pure constructive elements. Figurative art of today is the outcome of figurative art of the past, and non-figurative art is the outcome of the figurative art of today. Thus the unity of art is maintained.

If non-figurative art is born of figurative art, it is obvious that the two factors of human duality have not only changed, but have also approached one another towards a mutual balance, towards unity. One can rightly speak of an *evolution in plastic art*. It is of the greatest importance to note this fact, for it reveals the true way of art; the only path along which we can advance. Moreover, the evolution of the plastic arts shows that the dualism which has manifested itself in art is only relative and temporal. Both science and art are discovering and making us aware of the fact that *time is a process of intensification*, an evolution from the individual towards the universal, of the subjective towards the objective, towards the essence of things and of ourselves.

A careful observation of art since its origin shows that artistic expression seen from the outside is *not a process of prolongment but of intensifying one and the same thing*, universal beauty; and that seen from the inside *it is a growth*. Extension results in a continual repetition of nature; it is not human and art cannot follow it. So many of these repetitions which parade as "art" clearly cannot arouse emotions.

Through intensification one creates successively on more profound planes; extension remains always on the same plane. Intensification, be it noted, is diametrically opposed to extension; they are at right angles to each other as are length and depth. This fact shows clearly the temporal opposition of non-figurative art.

But if throughout its history art has meant a *continuous and gradual change in the expression of one and the same thing*, the opposition of the two trends—in our time so clear-cut—is actually an unreal one. It is illogical that the two principal tendencies in art, figurative and non-figurative (objective and subjective), should be so hostile. Since art is in essence universal, its expression cannot rest on a subjective view. Our human capacities do not allow of a perfectly objective view, but that does not imply that the plastic expression of art is based on subjective conception. Our subjectivity realizes that it does not create the work.

If the two human inclinations already mentioned are apparent in a work of art, they have both collaborated in its realization, but it is evident that the work will clearly show which of the two has predominated. In general, owing to the complexity of forms and the vague expression of relations, the two creative inclinations will appear in the work in a confused manner. Although in general there remains much confusion, today the two inclinations appear more clearly defined as two tendencies: *figurative and non-figurative art*. So-called non-figurative art often also creates a particular representation; figurative art, on the other hand, often neutralizes its forms to a considerable extent. The fact that art which is really nonfigurative is rare does not detract from its value; evolution is always the work of pioneers, and their followers are always small in number. This following is not a clique; it is the result of all the existing social forces; it is composed of all those who through innate or acquired capacity are ready to represent the existing degree of human evolution. At a time when so much attention is paid to the collective, to the "mass," it is necessary to note that evolution, ultimately, is never the expression of the mass. The mass remains behind yet urges the pioneers to creation. For the pioneers, the social contact is

Mondrian's Doorway, Paris, 1926.
Photograph by André Kertész.

indispensable, but not in order that they may know that what they are doing is necessary and useful, nor in order that "collective approval may help them to persevere and nourish them with living ideas." This contact is necessary only in an indirect way; it acts especially as an obstacle which increases their determination. The pioneers create through their reaction to external stimuli. They are guided not by the mass but by that which they see and feel. They discover consciously or unconsciously the fundamental laws hidden in reality, and aim at realizing them. In this way they further human development. They know that humanity is not served by making art comprehensible to everybody; to try this is to attempt the impossible. One serves mankind by enlightening it. Those who do not see will rebel, they will try to understand and will end up by "seeing." In art the search for a content which is collectively understandable is false; the content will always be individual. Religion, too, has been debased by that search.

Art is not made for anybody and is, at the same time, for everybody. It is a mistake to try to go too fast. The complexity of art is due to the fact that different degrees of its evolution are present at one and the same time. The present carries with it the past and the future. But we need not try to foresee the future; we need only take our place in the development of human culture, a development which has made non-figurative art supreme. It has always been only one struggle, of only one real art: to create universal beauty. This points the way for both present and future. We need only continue and develop what already exists. The essential thing is that *the fixed laws of the plastic arts must be realized.* These have shown themselves clearly in non-figurative art.

Today one is tired of the dogmas of the past, and of truths once accepted but successively jettisoned. One realizes more and more the relativity of everything, and therefore one tends to reject the idea of fixed laws, of a single truth. This is very understandable, but does not lead to profound vision. For there are "made" laws, "discovered" laws, but also laws—a truth for all time. These are more or less hidden in the reality which surrounds us and do not change. Not only science, but art also, shows us that reality, at first incomprehensible, gradually reveals itself, by the mutual relations that are inherent in things. Pure science and pure art, disinterested and free, can lead the advance in the recognition of the laws which are based on these relationships. A great scholar has recently said that pure science achieves practical results for humanity. Similarly, one can say that pure art, even though it appear abstract, can be of direct utility for life.

Art shows us that there are also constant truths concerning forms. Every form, every line has its own expression. This objective expression can be modified by our subjective view but it is no less true for that. Round is always round and square is always square. Simple though these facts are, they often appear to be forgotten in art. Many try to achieve one and the same end by different means. In plastic art this is an impossibility. In plastic art it is necessary to choose constructive means which are of one piece with that which one wants to express.

Art makes us realize that there are *fixed laws which govern and point to the use of the constructive elements, of the composition and of the inherent interrelationships between them.* These laws may be regarded as subsidiary laws to the *fundamental* law of equivalence which creates *dynamic equilibrium and reveals the true content of reality.*

THE SHAPING FORCES OF THE ARTIST

Paul Klee

It is fitting that the last painter in this section should be Paul Klee (1879–1940). One of the great modern artists, Klee was also one of the most broadly experienced, a musician, a master teacher and maker of teaching theory, a fine writer. His art is full of delicate lines, soft ironies, respect for the primitive and the immediate, reverence for the "moment" and all the imaginative resources any instant may contain. This statement, the last portion of a talk given in Germany in 1924, is a reasoned defense of his own art and much of the art of his time. It has almost all the elements of his drawing and painting in it, all except the ironies. He means exactly what he says. And perhaps much of what he says is what modern art "means."

I should now like to consider the question of the object, and attempt to show why the artist so frequently arrives at an apparently arbitrary "deformation" of the natural form of an object. In the first place he does not attribute to this natural form such crucial importance as do the realists who criticize him. For he does not regard these terminal forms as expressing the essence of nature's creative process. He is more concerned with the shaping forces than with the terminal forms. Perhaps we may say that he is an involuntary philosopher. And although he is not such an optimist as to affirm that this is the best of all possible worlds, neither does he say that this world surrounding us is so bad that he wants to have no part in copying its images. What he does say is the following:

The existing shape of the world is by no means the only possible shape! Therefore the artist directs a searching and penetrating look at the existing forms of nature. The more deeply he looks, the easier he finds it to extend his vision from the present to the past. Instead of the present shapes of nature, he more and more sees that the essential image of creation is genesis. He hazards the bold thought that the process of creation can scarcely be over and done with as yet, and so he extends the universal creative process both backward and forward, thus conferring duration upon genesis. He goes still farther. First lingering in this world, he says to himself: This world looked different in the past, and in the future it will also look different. Then, sliding toward otherworldliness, he decides: On other planets it may well have assumed altogether different forms.

To wander about this way along the natural paths of creation is good training for the artist. It can stir him to the depths of his being; and once he has been set in motion he will seek freedom of development along his own creative paths. And when he has had the benefit of such freedom, we cannot blame him for deciding that the present state of the phenomenal world, as he happens to encounter it, is hamstrung, accidentally, temporally and spatially hamstrung, and much too limited in comparison to his deeper visions and far-ranging sensibilities.

And isn't it true that if we only take the relatively small step of glancing into a microscope, we will see images that we would all call fantastic and exaggerated if we happened to see them in a painting without realizing the joke? Mr. X, coming across a reproduction of a microphotograph in a cheap journal, would exclaim indignantly: Are those supposed to be natural forms? Why, the man just doesn't know how to draw!

Then does the artist have to deal with microscopy? History? Palaeontology? Only by way of comparison, only by way of gaining greater scope, not so that he has to be ready to prove his fidelity to nature! The main thing is freedom, a freedom which does not necessarily retrace the course of evolution, or project what forms nature will some day display, or which we may some day discover on other planets; rather, a freedom which insists on its right to be just as inventive as nature in her grandeur is inventive. The artist must proceed from the type to the prototype!

The artist who soon comes to a halt en route is one who has pretensions, but no more. The artists with real vocations nowadays are those who travel to within fair distance of that secret cavern where the primal law is hidden; where the central organ of all temporal and spatial movement—we may call it the brain or

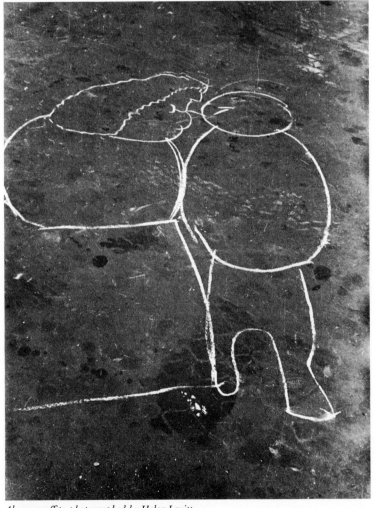

Above, graffito photographed by Helen Levitt.
From A Way of Seeing. Photographs of New York *by Helen Levitt with an essay by James Ag*

Right, Paul Klee, The Notorious One, F. 2, 1929.
From The Solomon R. Guggenheim Museum, New York City.

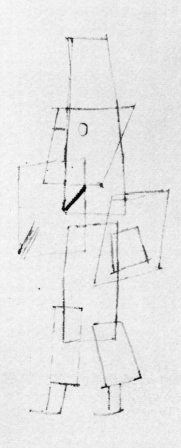

the heart of creation—makes everything happen. What artist would not wish to dwell there—in the bosom of nature, in the primordial source of creation, where the secret key to everything is kept? But not all are meant to reach it. Everyone must go where his own instinct leads him. Thus the impressionists who today are our polar opposites were in their own time absolutely right to stay with the hair-roots, the ground-cover of everyday phenomena. But our own instinct drives us downward, deep down to the primal source. Whatever emerges from this activity, call it what you will, dream, idea, fantasy, should be taken quite seriously if it combines with proper pictorial elements and is given form. Then curiosities become realities, realities of art, which add something more to life than it usually seems to have. For then we no longer have things seen and reproduced with more or less display of temperament, but we have visionary experiences made visible.

"With proper pictorial elements," I have said. For that tells us whether the result is a painting or something else, and what kind of painting it is to be.

Our age has passed through many confusions and vicissitudes, or so it seems to us, for we may be so close that our judgment is faulty. But one general tendency seems to be gradually winning ground among artists, even among the youngest of them: pure cultivation of these pictorial elements and their pure application. The myth about the childishness of my drawing must have started with those linear structures in which I attempted to combine the idea of an object—a man, say—with pure representation of the linear elements. If I wanted to render a man "just as he is," I would need such a bewildering complex of lines that pure presentation of the elements would be impossible; instead, they would be blurred to the point of being unrecognizable. Moreover, I don't at all want to represent a man as he is, but only as he might be.

Only by such procedures can I succeed in combining philosophy with the pure practice of my art.

These principles hold true for the entire procedure. Blurring must be everywhere avoided, in dealing with colors too. This effort to avoid blurring lies behind what people sneer at as the "false" coloration in modern art.

As I have just suggested in my remark on "childishness," I also deal separately with the various elements of painting. That is, I am also a draftsman. I have tried pure drawing; I have tried pure chiaroscuro painting; and I have tried all sorts of experiments with color as these arose out of my meditations on the color wheel. Thus I have worked out the various types of colored chiaroscuro painting, complementary color painting, particolored painting and totally colored painting. And in each case I have combined these experiments with the more subconscious dimensions of painting.

Then I have tried all possible syntheses of the two types, combining and recombining, but always trying to keep hold of the pure elements as far as possible. Sometimes I dream of a work of vast expanse which would encompass the whole realm of elements, objects, contents and styles. Doubtless that will remain a dream, but it is good occasionally to imagine this possibility which at present remains a vague one.

Creation cannot be done with undue haste. A thing must grow, must mature, and if the time ever comes for that vast, all-embracing work, so much the better. We must go on seeking. We have found parts of it, but not yet the whole. Nor do we have the strength for it as yet, for we have no public supporting us. But we are seeking a public; we have made a beginning at the Bauhaus. We have begun with a community to which we are giving everything we have to give. More than that we cannot do.

What dimension is to Henry Moore, illusion is to Richard Lippold (1915–). A master of the delicate art of wire-sculpture, Lippold jumps, skips, and pirouettes through space like a high-wire artist. He does as much again in his teaching and writing, forcing his reader to confront illusion not only in words but in the non-verbal elements that are so much a part of our experience of the modern book or magazine page. We must "read" Lippold's black and white pages and the two with what he calls "a cryptic diagram" as carefully as the text that contains them. For what they promise is a deeper grasp of illusion and thus, in Lippold's terms, of life itself.

ILLUSION AS STRUCTURE

Richard Lippold

Structure is illusion. The greatest wonder of the many wonders of this century is this fact. For the first time in his history, man is able to prove —or at least is on the verge of proving—that all of the means he has ever used to define the nature of nature, and thus his own nature, is the illusion afforded him by his meager senses and sensitivities. His ever-changing definitions, calculations, analyses, measurements, descriptions, propositions, proofs, answers, certainties—even uncertainties and questions: all are illusion. Even the disillusion so produced becomes illusion. A few decades ago such utterances might have come only from an Eastern mystic, surely not from a Western artist, let alone a Western scientist; yet I, as a Western artist, base these remarks not on the currently fashionable mystique of Zen Buddhism, but on the almost identical findings, if different phrasings, of Western science.

It can almost be said that this age of disillusion is in reality an age of dissolution. The rapid succession of theories destroyed by science has left even the scientist with grave doubts as to the meaning of *anything* beyond its own momentary mention. A young Nobel Prize scientist, still in his twenties, speaking recently at a Massachusetts Institute of Technology symposium, said that things were happening so fast in physics these days that he could not understand at all what the "younger" men were talking about.

On what is this dissolution based? Insofar as I, as a layman, can understand it (although as an artist I have long "known" it), what seems to have happened to an understanding of the structure of matter (the same process applies to psychic, social, and philosophical structures as well) is that with every effort to describe it from one point of view, a new point of view manifests itself. Just when the most minute particle, for example, has been described for us, it seems to disappear, or at least to transfer its "true" existence to some other area of "reality"—from physical matter to electrical energy, for instance. Recently even the smallest electrical particle has been assumed to be a tiny bit of whirling space, inexplicably thrown into a dervish-like vortex, emanating energies as by-products whose illusory forms (waves, electrical impulses) we interpret as "matter" through our limited perceptions. We have come, since my childhood, from the "knowledge" that we are chemically ninety-five percent water to the "certainty" that we are physically one hundred percent "empty" space!

However, it may only seem to our impoverished intelligences that the tiny vortexes of our atomic "structure" are whirling, or are even what we call Space. Even if they can be said to be whirling, we know now that movement is relative, and their speed may be such that they are also standing still, as we are told *we* would be if we "traveled" at the speed of light. Or their movement in space, which we now "know" is infinite and endless, would imply that they really are going nowhere, because there is no "where." We can no longer ask "where" or "when." (As I write this, an astronaut has just flown out of February twenty-first into February twentieth and back again, not only once, but several times! If we cannot say "where" he is or "when" he is, can we even ask "what" he is?) On the one hand then, we seem to have come empirically to the same point of view as the religious one which has warned us for a long time that "all is vanity."

On the other hand, no sooner has all matter, all identity of place and time thus vanished into the greater "void" of space, than science suspects, by observing nature's penchant for symmetry, that space cannot be empty. Apparently it seems "empty" only because of our meager access to its "total" properties. Space is now supposedly *stuffed* with conjectured, therefore as yet immeasurable, Matter and Anti-matter. We are, according to recent reports, merely the lucky (or unlucky) debris of a constant warfare between this Matter and Anti-matter, which fills up the interstices of space whose most minimal, detectable particles are merely a kind of dead residue of the battle. We are like the slower lemmings who escape suicide through native lethargy—or at least our atomic particles are, if we still wish, as "whole" men, to remain blameless in this newer situation. Yet it must seem small comfort that we "exist" because our most minute particles are either ashes or pacifists.

Again we are confronted by a new version of a familiar duality: all or nothing. Like previous alternatives, innocence or experience, grace or disgrace, they provide for the return of guilt through doubt.

But are they alternatives? Is perhaps "all" also "nothing" and "nothing" also "all"? To swing for a moment a few degrees on the inflexibly mounted axis of human perception, the seeming alternative can be viewed in another way. The alternative exists because what we call Nature is always posing paradoxes. As has been pointed out, Nature has a penchant for symmetry, but she has as much a penchant against it, by means of the chance effects of the inter-relation of all things. So the "laws" of Nature which seem to cause each member of her family to establish its unique identity (we plant an acorn; we do not get a monkey), are modified by the accidents which befall existence (rains may sweep away the nut, enemies consume, or friends nourish it). The "law" is the ideal form (the potential "void" of static, timeless space), "chance" is the modifier of the ideal (the unseen warfare of Matter and Anti-matter, charging and shaping "space").

Together, the peace *and* the war, the empty *and* the full, are responsible for the existence of form.

Thus has science, at long last, later than art and philosophy, brought us face to face with the necessity to see that we cannot choose between the empty and the full and pretend to be alive, because they are the same thing. I have attempted to express this situation visually by four of the six pages in the center of this article.

The first two pages are white ("empty") and the last two
pages are black ("full"). In graphic terms, these are as opposite
qualities as I am able to produce to make my point. But in
actuality what are they? Of course the white pages are "inex-
perienced," and the black pages are "experienced," full to the
point of literal saturation. No room is left for another event. In
relation to the consideration of matter in science as I referred to
it above, the white pages are like the seemingly pure state of
absolute space, of the "nothing" whose self-movements may gen-
erate energy; and the black pages are the material sediment
of all the apparent energy which fills the void of non-being: a
dense, solid, tangible mass of total "stuff." But are they? Or,
more properly, is it?

The answer is self-evident: the white pages are stuffed to the
full with "emptiness," while the black pages are deliciously void
of "nothing." Thus each is equally empty and equally full. There
is no choice as to condition. Even if we attempt to choose on the
basis of white and black alone, who can say, except from
prejudice, that white is empty, is nothing, and black is full, is
everything? Or vice versa? All we can attempt to say is that
white is the absence of black, and black is the absence of white;
by this very implication the existence of the other is assured.

If, then, both are possible, yet neither is sufficient, it would
seem, as I began by stating, that if only paradox is "real," all other
"reality," or form, is illusion.

We in the West particularly have been prone to accept the
deceits of "calculable" or "definable" structures and to defend
them to the death. As seen in the arts, we have insisted on every
conceivable "truth" about form, from the security of the "mass"
of the pyramids to the security of "pure space" in the empty
walls of an Yves Klein exhibition, with, of course, every imagi-
nable variant and combination to suit our changing concepts. (Yet
a close look at "mass" reveals that even the densest metal is so
full of "space" that all kinds of energies pass through it unimpeded. Cosmic rays and television shows pass through any
mountain—as well as the "mass" of our own bodies—quite freely.
As for "pure space": a cubic centimeter of the space in Mr.
Klein's "emptiness" has enough cosmic energy in it to populate
a universe.)

We have embraced symmetry as an ideal and we have rejected
it as an empty conceit. We have reduced vision to a calculated

formula of constructed elements, and rejected it for an "automatic" compilation of the debris of order. Who of us has been "right"? "Neither, said the moon" (said Emily Dickinson), "That is best which is not. . . ." Not mass, not void; not anything in between. Not symmetry, not law, not disorder, not chaos; not anything in between. Only NOTHING. . . .

But NATURE! we cry. NATURE is not *Nothing!* NATURE has evidence for whatever we wish to believe! NATURE *loves* symmetry; look at the human body, or a snowflake; read this news item: "Sundsvall, Sweden, July 27 (AP)—Two cars of the same make and the same color collided head-on outside Sundsvall. Both drivers were thrown against their cars' windshields and were treated at the local hospital for cuts. One driver was Finn Gagner, aged twenty-five. The other was Dag Gagner, twenty-five. They are identical twins. . . ." What a magnificent, symmetrical, orderly event!—except that it was, of course, an accident.

For those who seek to prove it, Nature can be said to *hate* symmetry. Look *closely* at the right side and left side of a face; no two snowflakes are ever identical; chance events are the only real determiners of character, from the shape and size of a tree to the "choice" of one's love.

But these are the very clues to our contemporary feelings about structure. Symmetry is an accident of disorder, yet accident is the order of non-symmetry—what Hans Arp calls the "Laws of Chance," or the scientist approximates with his "Second Law of Thermodynamics." The wildest of neo-Dada "happenings" can be as carefully calculated and reconstructed as a master plan for the sewers of New York City. In fact, since there is no "time" and "space," *all* events and objects are merely immediate sensations. Order is but an event of the briefest duration, for nothing is identical from moment to moment. The warfare of Matter and Anti-matter is in us all, growth and decay rotate in their orbits as steadily and simultaneously as Venus and Mars about the Sun, pursuing and pursued. What can be left but staticity and the total "mass" of nothingness? Obviously what can be left can just as well be called everythingness. It is true that Nature is not only Nothing; Nature is also Everything.

In the face of this totality, revealed for us now by Science as well as by Philosophy and Religion (in this sense, Science *becomes* our contemporary Philosophy and Religion), how can this be made visible, sensible to our human equipment?

Between the white pages and the black pages in this article are
two pages carrying a cryptic diagram. Into the space of the
white pages have filtered energetic particles of black, or one can
say that the space of the black pages has fissured, and whiteness
has isolated the particles of black, like a gigantic magnification,
revealing the inner "structure" of black. Because of this "space,"
as in the mountain or the metal, the "solid" black has only been
an illusion all along. Referring back to the white pages, we can
say the same. This is a magnification of them also, revealing the
invisible energies inherent in what seems to be pure space, like
Matter and Anti-matter made visible.

It will be noted on close inspection, that there is an "order"
to the little particles, yet it is as deceptive an order, in its relation to "reality," as is the order of the chaotic struggle of Matter
and Anti-matter in relation to the form of shapes in space. Its
deception lies in the fact that this diagram is part of a study for
a piece of sculpture which in its finished state is never seen to
have the symmetry and systematic arrangement of this, its inner
"structure." I have chosen to leave the drawing unidentified,
because the sculpture exists and is experienced on its own terms
beyond this part of its creation, much as we exist and relate to
what we call "life" beyond and in addition to the interstices of
our atomic structures, the vacancies in our psyches, the silences
in our senses, and the various energies which occupy all of these
in part.

This drawing then, is both something *and* nothing; it is black
and white, it is empty *and* full. It is as "abstract" as the principles
behind the operation of all things, and it is as "real" as the operation of those principles. It is a visual set of laws which in the
finished sculpture are broken by the "accidents" of four-dimen-
sional existence, of light, of point of view, and of perspective. It
is also, conversely, the accident of a particular artist's vision in a
particular moment in "history," thus becoming a specific, identifiable entity, a "law"—a formula for these particular chance
occurrences.

In all these respects, this drawing and the kind of sculpture
which it represents, is relevant to the point of view to which
Science is bringing us, and which frees us for the first time from
decision as well as from indecision. Without "time," we have all
of Time; with all of Space, we have no need to choose a particular "space." Like this sculpture, we know the "mass" of space,

and the "movement" of staticity; for, although the sculpture's own movement, or activity between its parts, or human movement in relation to it may or may not exist, its very being in a state of relationship is no more nor less than the great staticity of all universal events at a given instant, and, as I have already pointed out, at the very next instant everything will be (apparently) different again. Another static moment will have appeared, and, together with the first, will be assumed to be movement by our feeble perceptions and the deceptions of memory. Like all assumptions, this is illusion.

It is quite true that our arrival at a point of no decision in the arts and sciences, more or less simultaneously at this "moment," is in itself another illusion. True to human form, the general awareness of this illusion at this juncture has effected another choice: acceptance of the illusion, or rejection of it (which is to say acceptance of disillusion). But it is quite natural that in being free *from* decision, we are at once free *for* it as well. Our "moment" still triumphs!

The proof of this paradox is visible in the world of sculpture, as I have already pointed out. The decision to abandon law and order, as in the selection of debris and automatism, leads at once to the proscribed law of anarchy—a law none-the-less, and inviolable in the direction of any "outer" law. The decision to employ pristine materials and "orderly" procedures, "free" from predetermined forms and processes, exposes it to the hazards of the evolution of its own growth, and the distortions of external efforts, like the "growth" of all living things in Nature. Which is free, and which slave?

Seen in this light, works evolved from interests described above operate either as protest (through disillusion) or as illustration (through dedicatory illusion) of the same current attitudes. The black is contained in the white; the white is possessed by the black. All structure in contemporary sculpture, to be a part of this "static" moment, must be a part of this new illusion, just as sculptural structures of the "past" were a part of the illusions of those moments. "Ultimate Reality" is so far removed still from our awareness that we have only contemporary illusions on which to erect our forms. It is irrelevant whether they come from science or from somewhere else. The delight of science at this point is its surprise with its discovery that it too is only a small illusion in the mind of man.

In this way, the scientist, the artist, and the prophet are one, for it is the general acceptance of a particular illusion which motivates and unifies mankind at any given time. To abandon this illusion to chaos or to embrace previous illusions is to die. Creativity, like life and like love, depends on a man's ability to accept an illusion, to be aware of it, and to sustain it. Only in this way can he find a structure for his life and for his work. Illusion *is* structure.

THE
WORD
ARTS:

The Novel

Henry James (1843–1916) was the most distin-
guished American novelist (The Portrait of a Lady,
The Turn of the Screw, The Ambassadors, *to men-*
tion some of the most famous) of his time, an age
notable for the high development of the novel as an
art form. Possibly above all other American men
of letters, James's life long interest lay in literary
theory, and he was an influential reviewer and

THE

critic of prose fiction. In this essay, James clearly
defines the conflict between the values of mass
distribution and mass readership and those of high

FUTURE

quality work designed for a
discerning taste. In addition to
suggesting the obligations of both

OF

novelist and reader, James also voices his lofty
expectations for the novel. Even a close reading,

THE

however, may not reveal James's final estimate
of the "future" of the novel, an art form to
which so much of his life was devoted.

NOVEL

Henry
James

Beginnings, as we all know, are usually small
things, but continuations are not always strik-
ingly great ones, and the place occupied in the
world by the prolonged prose fable has become,
in our time, among the incidents of literature,
the most surprising example to be named of
swift and extravagant growth, a development
beyond the measure of every early appearance.
It is a form that has had a fortune so little to
have been foretold at its cradle. The germ of
the comprehensive epic was more recognizable
in the first barbaric chant than that of the novel
as we know it today in the first anecdote retailed
to amuse. It arrived, in truth, the novel, late at
self-consciousness; but it has done its utmost ever
since to make up for lost opportunities. The
flood at present swells and swells, threatening
the whole field of letters, as would often seem,
with submersion. It plays, in what may be called
the passive consciousness of many persons, a part
that directly marches with the rapid increase of

the multitude able to possess itself in one way and another of the *book*. The book, in the Anglo-Saxon world, is almost everywhere, and it is in the form of the voluminous prose fable that we see it penetrate easiest and farthest. Penetration appears really to be directly aided by mere mass and bulk. There is an immense public, if public be the name, inarticulate, but abysmally absorbent, for which, at its hours of ease, the printed volume has no other association. This public—the public that subscribes, borrows, lends, that picks up in one way and another, sometimes even by purchase—grows and grows each year, and nothing is thus more apparent than that of all the recruits it brings to the book the most numerous by far are those that it brings to the "story."

This number has gained, in our time, an augmentation from three sources in particular, the first of which, indeed, is perhaps but a comprehensive name for the two others. The diffusion of the rudiments, the multiplication of common schools, has had more and more the effect of making readers of women and of the very young. Nothing is so striking in a survey of this field, and nothing to be so much borne in mind, as that the larger part of the great multitude that sustains the teller and the publisher of tales is constituted by boys and girls; by girls in especial, if we apply the term to the later stages of the life of the innumerable women who, under modern arrangements, increasingly fail to marry—fail, apparently, even, largely, to desire to. It is not too much to say of many of these that they live in a great measure by the immediate aid of the novel—confining the question, for the moment, to the fact of consumption alone. The literature, as it may be called for convenience, of children is an industry that occupies by itself a very considerable quarter of the scene. Great fortunes, if not great reputations, are made, we learn, by writing for schoolboys, and the period during which they consume the compound artfully prepared for them appears—as they begin earlier and continue later—to add to itself at both ends. This helps to account for the fact that public libraries, especially those that are private and money-making enterprises, put into circulation more volumes of "stories" than of all other things together of which volumes can be made. The published statistics are extraordinary, and of a sort to engender many kinds of uneasiness. The sort of taste that used to be called "good" has nothing to do with the matter: we are so demonstrably in the presence of millions for whom taste is but an obscure, confused, immediate instinct. In the flare of railway bookstalls, in the shop-fronts of most booksellers, especially the provincial, in the ad-vertisements of the weekly newspapers, and in fifty places be-sides, this testimony to the general preference triumphs, yielding a good-natured corner at most to a bunch of treatises on athletics or sport, or a patch of theology old and new.

The case is so marked, however, that illustrations easily over-flow, and there is no need of forcing doors that stand wide open. What remains is the interesting oddity or mystery—the anomaly that fairly dignifies the whole circumstance with its strangeness: the wonder, in short, that men, women, and children *should* have so much attention to spare for improvisations mainly so arbitrary and frequently so loose. That, at the first blush, fairly leaves us gaping. This great fortune then, since fortune it seems, has been reserved for mere unsupported and unguaranteed history, the *inexpensive* thing, written in the air, the record of what, in any particular case, has *not* been, the account that remains responsible, at best, to "documents" with which we are practically unable to collate it. This is the side of the whole business of fiction on which it can always be challenged, and to that degree that if the general venture had not become in such a manner the admiration of the world it might but too easily have become the derision. It has in truth, I think, never philosophically met the challenge, never found a formula to inscribe on its shield, never defended its position by any better argument than the frank, straight blow: "Why am I not so unprofitable as to be preposterous? Because I can do *that*. There!" And it throws up from time to time some purely practical masterpiece. There is nevertheless an admirable minority of intelligent persons who care not even for the masterpieces, nor see any pressing point in them, for whom the very form itself has, equally at its best and at its worst, been ever a vanity and a mockery. This class, it should be added, is beginning to be visibly augmented by a different circle al-together, the group of the formerly subject, but now estranged, the deceived and bored, those for whom the whole movement too decidedly fails to live up to its possibilities. There are people who have loved the novel, but who actually find themselves drowned in its verbiage, and for whom, even in some of its ap-proved manifestations, it has become a terror they exert every ingenuity, every hypocrisy, to evade. The indifferent and the

Henry James.
Photograph by E. O. Hoppe, Biblioteque Nationale, Paris. Courtesy of
The New York Public Library.

alienated testify, at any rate, almost as much as the omnivorous, to the reign of the great ambiguity, the enjoyment of which rests, evidently, on a primary need of the mind. The novelist can only fall back on that—on his recognition that man's constant demand for what he has to offer is simply man's general appetite for a *picture*. The novel is of all pictures the most comprehensive and the most elastic. It will stretch anywhere—it will take in absolutely anything. All it needs is a subject and a painter. But for its subject, magnificently, it has the whole human consciousness. And if we are pushed a step farther backward, and asked why the representation should be required when the object represented is itself mostly so accessible, the answer to that appears to be that man combines with his eternal desire for more experience an infinite cunning as to getting his experience as cheaply as possible. He will steal it whenever he can. He likes to live the life of others, yet is well aware of the points at which it may too intolerably resemble his own. The vivid fable, more than anything else, gives him this satisfaction on easy terms, gives him knowledge abundant yet vicarious. It enables him to select, to take and to leave; so that to feel he can afford to neglect it he must have a rare faculty, or great opportunities, for the extension of experience—by thought, by emotion, by energy—at first hand.

Yet it is doubtless not this cause alone that contributes to the contemporary deluge; other circumstances operate, and one of them is probably, in truth, if looked into, something of an abatement of the great fortune we have been called upon to admire. The high prosperity of fiction has marched, very directly, with another "sign of the times," the demoralization, the vulgarization of literature in general, the increasing familiarity of all such methods of communication, the making itself supremely felt, as it were, of the presence of the ladies and children—by whom I mean, in other words, the reader irreflective and uncritical. If the novel, in fine, has found itself, socially speaking, at such a rate, the book *par excellence*, so on the other hand the book has in the same degree found itself a thing of small ceremony. So many ways of producing it easily have been discovered that it is by no means the occasional prodigy, for good or for evil, that it was taken for in simpler days, and has therefore suffered a proportionate discredit. Almost any variety is thrown off and taken up, handled, admired, ignored by too many people, and this, precisely, is the point at which the question of its future becomes one with that of the future of the total swarm. How are the generations to face, at all, the monstrous multiplications? Any speculation on the further development of a particular variety is subject to the reserve that the generations may at no distant day be obliged formally to decree, and to execute, great clearings of the deck, great periodical effacements and destructions. It fills, in fact, at moments the expectant ear, as we watch the progress of the ship of civilization—the huge splash that must mark the response to many an imperative, unanimous "Overboard!" What at least is already very plain is that practically the great majority of volumes printed within a year cease to exist as the hour passes, and give up by that circumstance all claim to a career, to being accounted or provided for. In speaking of the future of the novel we must of course, therefore, be taken as limiting the inquiry to those types that have, for criticism, a present and a past. And it is only superficially that confusion seems here to reign. The fact that in England and in the United States every specimen that sees the light may look for a "review" testifies merely to the point to which, in these countries, literary criticism has sunk. The review is in nine cases out of ten an effort of intelligence as undeveloped as the ineptitude over which it fumbles, and the critical spirit, which knows where it is concerned and where not, is not touched, is still less compromised, by the incident. There are too many reasons why newspapers must live.

So, as regards the tangible type, the end is that in its un-defended, its positively exposed state, we continue to accept it, conscious even of a peculiar beauty in an appeal made from a footing so precarious. It throws itself wholly on our generosity, and very often indeed gives us, by the reception it meets, a use-ful measure of the quality, of the delicacy, of many minds. There is to my sense no work of literary, or of any other, art, that any human being is under the smallest positive obligation to "like." There is no woman—no matter of what loveliness—in the presence of whom it is anything but a man's unchallengeably *own* affair that he is "in love" or out of it. It is not a question of manners; vast is the margin left to individual freedom; and the trap set by the artist occupies no different ground—Robert Louis Stevenson has admirably expressed the analogy—from the offer of her charms by the lady. There only remain infatuations that we envy and emulate. When we do respond to the appeal, when we *are* caught in the trap, we are held and played upon; so that how in the world can there *not* still be a future, however late in the day, for a contrivance possessed of this precious secret? The more we consider it the more we feel that the prose picture can never be at the end of its tether until it loses the sense of what it can do. It can do simply everything, and that is its strength and its life. Its plasticity, its elasticity are infinite; there is no color, no extension it may not take from the nature of its subject or the temper of its craftsman. It has the extraordinary advantage—a piece of luck scarcely credible—that, while capable of giving an impression of the highest perfection and the rarest finish, it moves in a luxurious independence of rules and restrictions. Think as we may, there is nothing we can mention as a consideration outside itself with which it must square, nothing we can name as one of its peculiar obligations or interdictions. It must, of course, hold our attention and reward it, it must not appeal on false pretenses; but these necessities, with which, obviously, disgust and displeasure interfere, are not peculiar to it— all works of art have them in common. For the rest it has so clear a field that if it perishes this will surely be by its fault—by its superficiality, in other words, or its timidity. One almost, for the very love of it, likes to think of its appearing threatened with some such fate, in order to figure the dramatic stroke of its revival under the touch of a life-giving master. The temperament of the artist can do so much for it that our desire for some exemplary felicity fairly demands even the vision of that supreme proof. If we were to linger on this vision long enough, we should doubtless, in fact, be brought to wondering—and still for very loyalty to the form itself—whether our own prospective conditions may not before too long appear to many critics to call for some such happy *coup* on the part of a great artist yet to come.

There would at least be this excuse for such a reverie: that speculation is vain unless we confuse it, and that for ourselves the most convenient branch of the question is the state of the industry that makes its appeal to readers of English. From any attempt to measure the career still open to the novel in France I may be excused, in so narrow a compass, for shrinking. The French, as a result of having ridden their horse much harder than we, are at a different stage of the journey, and we have doubtless many of their stretches and baiting-places yet to traverse. But if the range grows shorter from the moment we drop to inductions drawn only from English and American material, I am not sure that the answer comes sooner. I should have at all events—a formidably large order—to plunge into the particulars of the question of the present. If the day *is* approaching when the respite of execution for almost any book is but a matter of mercy, does the English novel of commerce tend to strike us as a production more and more equipped by its high qualities for braving the danger? It would be impossible, I think, to make one's attempt at an answer to that riddle really interesting without bringing into the field many illustrations drawn from individuals—without pointing the moral with names both conspicuous and obscure. Such a freedom would carry us, here, quite too far, and would moreover only encumber the path. There is nothing to prevent our taking for granted all sorts of happy symptoms and splendid promises—so long, of course, I mean, as we keep before us the general truth that the future of fiction is intimately bound up with the future of the society that produces and consumes it. In a society with a great and diffused literary sense the talent at play can only be a less negligible thing than in a society with a literary sense barely discernible. In a world in which criticism is acute and mature such talent will find itself trained, in order successfully to assert itself, to many more kinds of precautionary expertness than in a society in which the art I have named holds an inferior place or makes a sorry figure. A community addicted to reflection and fond of ideas will try experiments with the "story" that will be left untried in a community mainly devoted to traveling and shooting, to pushing trade and playing football. There are many judges, doubtless, who hold that experiments—queer and uncanny things at best—are not necessary to it, that its face has been, once for all, turned in one way, and that it has only to go straight before it. If that is what it is actually doing in England and America the main thing to say about its future would appear to be that this future will in very truth more and more define itself as negligible. For all the while the immense variety of life will stretch away to right and to left, and all the while there may be, on such lines, perpetuation of its great mistake of failing of intelligence. That mistake will be, ever, for the admirable art, the only one really inexcusable, because of being a mistake about, as we may say, its own soul. The form of novel that is

stupid on the general question of its freedom is the single form
that may, *a priori*, be unhesitatingly pronounced wrong.

The most interesting thing today, therefore, among ourselves
is the degree in which we may count on seeing a sense of that
freedom cultivated and bearing fruit. What else is this, indeed,
but one of the most attaching elements in the great drama of
our wide English-speaking life! As a novel is at any moment the
most immediate and, as it were, admirably *treacherous* picture
of actual manners—indirectly as well as directly, and by what it
does not touch as well as by what it does—so its present situation, where we are most concerned with it, is exactly a reflection
of our social changes and chances, of the signs and portents that
lay most traps for most observers, and make up in general what
is most "amusing" in the spectacle we offer. Nothing, I may say,
for instance, strikes me more as meeting this description than the
predicament finally arrived at, for the fictive energy, in consequence of our long and most respectable tradition of making it
defer supremely, in the treatment, say, of a delicate case, to the
inexperience of the young. The particular knot the coming
novelist who shall prefer not simply to beg the question will
have here to untie may represent assuredly the essence of his
outlook. By what it shall decide to do in respect to the "young"
the great prose fable will, from any serious point of view, practically see itself stand or fall. What is clear is that it has, among us,
veritably never chosen—it has, mainly, always obeyed an un-
reasoning instinct of avoidance in which there has often been
much that was felicitous. While society was frank, was free
about the incidents and accidents of the human constitution, the
novel took the same robust ease as society. The young then were
so very young that they were not table-high. But they began to
grow, and from the moment their little chins rested on the
mahogany, Richardson and Fielding began to go under it. There
came into being a mistrust of any but the most guarded treatment
of the great relation between men and women, the constant
world-renewal, which was the conspicuous sign that whatever
the prose picture of life was prepared to take upon itself, it was
not prepared to take upon itself not to be superficial. Its position
became very much: "There are other things, don't you know?
For heaven's sake let *that* one pass!" And to this wonderful
propriety of letting it pass the business has been for these so many
years—with the consequences we see today—largely devoted.

These consequences are of many sorts, not a few altogether charming. One of them has been that there is an immense omission in our fiction—which, though many critics will always judge that it has vitiated the whole, others will continue to speak of as signifying but a trifle. One can only talk for one's self, and of the English and American novelists of whom I am fond, I am so superlatively fond that I positively prefer to take them as they are. I cannot so much as imagine Dickens and Scott *without* the *"love-making"* left, as the phrase is, out. They were, to my perception, absolutely right—from the moment their attention to it could only be perfunctory—practically not to deal with it. In all their work it is, in spite of the number of pleasant sketches of affection gratified or crossed, the element that matters least. Why not therefore assume, it may accordingly be asked, that discriminations which have served their purpose so well in the past will continue not less successfully to meet the case? What will you have better than Scott and Dickens?

Nothing certainly *can* be, it may at least as promptly be replied, and I can imagine no more comfortable prospect than jogging along perpetually with a renewal of such blessings. The difficulty lies in the fact that two of the great conditions have changed. The novel is older, and so are the young. It would seem that everything the young can possibly do for us in the matter has been successfully done. They have kept out one thing after the other, yet there is still a certain completeness we lack, and the curious thing is that it appears to be they themselves who are making the grave discovery. "You have kindly taken," they seem to say to the fiction-mongers, "our education off the hands of our parents and pastors, and that, doubtless, has been very convenient for *them*, and left them free to amuse themselves. But what, all the while, pray, if it is a question of education, have you done with your own? These are directions in which you seem dreadfully untrained, and in which *can* it be as vain as it appears to apply to you for information?" The point is whether, from the moment it is a question of averting discredit, the novel can afford to take things quite so easily as it has, for a good while now, settled down into the way of doing. There are too many sources of interest neglected—whole categories of manners, whole corpuscular classes and provinces, museums of character and condition, unvisited; while it is on the other hand mistakenly taken for granted that safety lies in all the loose and thin material that keeps reappearing in forms at once ready-made and sadly the worse for wear. The simple themselves may finally turn against our simplifications; so that we need not, after all, be more royalist than the king or more childish than the children. It is certain that there is no real health for any art—I am not speaking, of course, of any mere industry—that does not move a step in advance of its farthest follower. It would be curious—really a great comedy—if the renewal were to spring just from the satiety of the very readers for whom the sacrifices have hitherto been supposed to be made. It bears on this that as nothing is more salient in English life today, to fresh eyes, than the revolution taking place in the position and outlook of women—and taking place much more deeply in the quiet than even the noise on the surface demonstrates—so we may very well yet see the female elbow itself, kept in increasing activity by the play of the pen, smash with final resonance the window all this time most superstitiously closed. The particular draught that has been most deprecated will in that case take care of the question of freshness. It is the opinion of some observers that when women do obtain a free hand they will not repay their long debt to the precautionary attitude of men by unlimited consideration for the natural delicacy of the latter.

To admit, then, that the great anodyne can ever totally fail to work, is to imply, in short, that this will only be for some grave fault in some high quarter. Man rejoices in an incomparable faculty for presently mutilating and disfiguring any plaything that has helped create for him the illusion of leisure; nevertheless, so long as life retains its power of projecting itself upon his imagination, he will find the novel works off the impression better than anything he knows. Anything better for the purpose has assuredly yet to be discovered. He will give it up only when life itself too thoroughly disagrees with him. Even then, indeed, may fiction not find a second wind, or a fiftieth, in the very portrayal of that collapse? Till the world is an unpeopled void there will be an image in the mirror. What need more immediately concern us, therefore, is the care of seeing that the image shall continue various and vivid. There is much, frankly, to be said for those who, in spite of all brave pleas, feel it to be considerably menaced, for very little reflection will help to show us how the prospect strikes them. They see the whole business too divorced on the one side from observation and perception, and on the other from the art and taste. They get too little of the first-hand impression, the effort to penetrate—that effort for which the French have the admirable expression to *fouiller*—and still less, if possible, of any science of composition, any architecture, distribution, proportion. It is not a trifle, though indeed it is the concomitant of an edged force, that "mystery" should, to so many of the sharper eyes, have disappeared from the craft, and a facile flatness be, in place of it, in acclaimed possession. But these are, at the worst, even for such of the disconcerted, signs that the novelist, not that the novel, has dropped. So long as there is a subject to be treated, so long will it depend wholly on the treatment to rekindle the fire. Only the ministrant must really approach the altar; for if the novel *is* the treatment, it is the treatment that is essentially what I have called the anodyne.

THE ARTIST AND THE WORLD

Joyce Cary

A prolific novelist of exceptional range—his best known trilogy consists of Herself Surprised, To Be a Pilgrim, *and* The Horse's Mouth—*Joyce Cary (1888–1957) here suggests the broad relationship which obtains between the artist and the society in which he happens to live. Understandably this relationship is an uneasy one, partaking (at least in Cary's works) of the comic, the absurd, the pathetic. This essay suggests that the world is a very real place and that the artist must do what he can to transcend imperfect conditions not only in the extensional world, but in himself as well.*

This is an attempt to examine the relation of the artist with the world as it seems to him, and to see what he does with it. That is to say, on the one side with what is called the artist's intuition, on the other with his production, or the work of art.

My only title to discuss the matter is some practical knowledge of two arts. I know very little about aesthetic philosophy, so I shall try, as far as possible, to speak from practical experience.

It is quite true that the artist, painter, writer or composer starts always with an experience that is a kind of discovery. He comes upon it with the sense of a discovery; in fact, it is truer to say that it comes upon *him* as a discovery. It surprises him. This is what is usually called an intuition or an inspiration. It carries with it always the feeling of directness. For instance, you go walking in the fields and all at once they strike you in quite a new aspect: you find it extraordinary that they should be like that. This is what happened to Monet as a young man. He suddenly saw the fields, not as solid flat objects covered with grass or useful crops and dotted with trees, but as colour in astonishing variety and subtlety of gradation. And this gave him a delightful and quite new pleasure. It was a most exciting discovery, especially as it was a discovery of something real. I mean, by that, something independent of Monet himself. That, of course, was half the pleasure. Monet has discovered a truth about the actual world.

This delight in discovery of something new in or about the world is a natural and primitive thing. All children have it. And it often continues until the age of twenty or twenty-five, *even* throughout life.

Children's pleasure in exploring the world, long before they can speak, is very obvious. They spend almost all their time at it. We don't speak of their intuition, but it is the same thing as the intuition of the artist. That is to say, it is direct knowledge of the world as it is, direct acquaintance with things, with characters, with appearance, and this is the primary knowledge of the artist and writer. This joy of discovery is his starting point.

Croce, probably the most interesting of the aesthetic philosophers, says that art is simply intuition. But he says, too, that intuition and expression are the same thing. His idea is that we can't know what we have intuited until we have named it, or given it a formal character, and this action is essentially the work of art.

But this is not at all the way it seems to an artist or a writer. To him, the intuition is quite a different thing from the work of art. For the essential thing about the work of art is that it is work, and very hard work too. To go back to the painter. He has had his intuition, he has made his discovery, he is eager to explore it, to reveal it, to fix it down. For, at least in a grown, an educated man, intuitions are highly evanescent. This is what Wordsworth meant when he wrote of their fading into the light of common day.

I said the joy of discovery often dies away after twenty years or so. And this is simply a truth of observation; we know it from our own experience. The magic object that started up before our eyes on a spring day in its own individual shape, is apt, in the same instant, to turn into simply another cherry tree, an ordinary specimen of a common class. We have seen it and named it pretty often already. But Housman, as poet, fixed his vision of the cherry tree before it had changed into just another tree in blossom.

Housman fixed it for himself and us, but not by an immediate act, indistinguishable from the intuition. He had to go to work and find words, images, rhyme, which embodied his feeling about the tree, which fixed down its meaning for him, so that he could have it again when he wanted it, and also give it to us. He made a work of art, but he made it by work.

So for the painter, when he has his new, his magic landscape in front of him; he has to fix it down. And at once he is up against enormous difficulties. He has only his paints and brushes, and a flat piece of canvas with which to convey a sensation, a feeling, about a three-dimensional world. He has somehow to translate an intuition from real objects into a formal and ideal arrangement of colours and shapes, which will still, mysteriously, fix and convey his sense of the unique quality, the magic of these objects in their own private existence. That is to say, he has a job that requires thought, skill, and a lot of experience.

As for the novelist, his case is even worse. He starts also with his intuition, his discovery; as when Conrad, in an Eastern port, saw a young officer come out from a trial in which he had been found guilty of a cowardly desertion of his ship and its passengers after a collision. The young man had lost his honour and Conrad realised all at once what that meant to him, and he wrote *Lord Jim* to fix and communicate that discovery in its full force.

For that he had to invent characters, descriptions, a plot. All these details, as with the painter, had to enforce the impression, the feeling that he wanted to convey. The reader had to *feel*, at the end of the tale, 'That is important, that is true'. It's no good if he says, 'I suppose that is true, but I've heard it before'. In that case Conrad has failed, at least with that reader. For his object was to give the reader the same discovery, to make him feel what it meant to that young man to lose his honour, and how important honour is to men.

And to get this sharp and strong feeling, the reader must not be confused by side issues. All the scenes and characters, all the events in the book, must contribute to the total effect, the total meaning. The book must give the sense of an actual world with real characters. Otherwise they won't engage the reader's sympathy, his feelings will never be concerned at all.

But actual life is not like that, it doesn't have a total meaning, it is simply a wild confusion of events from which we have to select what we think significant for ourselves. Look at any morning paper. It makes no sense at all—it means nothing but chaos. We read only what we think important; that is to say, we provide our own sense to the news. We have to do so because otherwise it wouldn't be there. To do this, we have to have some standard of valuation, we have to know whether the political event is more important than a murder, or a divorce than the stock market, or the stock market than who won the Derby.

The writer, in short, has to find some meaning in life before he gives it to us in a book. And his subject-matter is much more confused than that of a painter. Of course, in this respect, everyone is in the same boat. Everyone, not only the writer, is presented with the same chaos, and is obliged to form his own idea of the world, of what matters and what doesn't matter. He has to do it, from earliest childhood, for his own safety. And if he gets it wrong, if his idea does not accord with reality, he will suffer for it. A friend of mine, as a child, thought he could fly, and jumped off the roof. Luckily he came down in a flower-bed and only broke a leg.

This seems to contradict what I said just now about the chaos which stands before us every morning. For the boy who failed to fly did not suffer only from bad luck. He affronted a law of gravity, a permanent part of a reality objective to him. As we know very well, underneath the chaos of events, there are laws, or if you like consistencies, both of fact and feeling. What science calls matter, that is to say, certain fixed characteristics of being, presents us with a whole framework of reality which we defy at our peril. Wrong ideas about gravity or the wholesomeness of prussic acid are always fatal.

So, too, human nature and its social relations present certain constants. Asylums and gaols are full of people who have forgotten or ignored them. On the other hand, we can still comprehend and enjoy palaeolithic art and Homer. Homer's heroes had the same kind of nature as our own.

These human constants are also a part of reality objective to us, that is, a permanent character of the world as we know it. So we have a reality consisting of permanent and highly obstinate facts, and permanent and highly obstinate human nature. And human nature is always in conflict with material facts, although men are themselves most curious combinations of fact and feeling, and actually require the machinery of their organism to realise their emotions, their desires and ambitions. Though the ghost could not exist without the machine which is at once its material form, its servant, its limitation, its perfection and its traitor, it is always trying to get more power over it, to change it.

Men have in fact obtained more power over matter, but to change it is impossible. It may be said that all works of art, all ideas of life, all philosophies are 'As if', but I am suggesting that they can be checked with an objective reality. They might be called propositions for truth and their truth can be decided by their correspondence with the real. Man can't change the elemental characters. If you could, the world would probably vanish into nothing. But because of their very permanence, you can assemble them into new forms. You can build new houses with the bricks they used for the oldest Rome, because they are still bricks. For bricks that could stop being bricks at will would be no good to the architect. And a heart that stopped beating at its own will would be no good to the artist. The creative soul needs the machine, as the living world needs a fixed character, or it could not exist at all. It would be merely an idea. But by a paradox we have to accept, part of this fixed character is the free mind, the creative imagination, in everlasting conflict with facts, including its own machinery, its own tools.

DECLINE OF THE NOVEL

As a philosopher and aesthetician, José Ortega y Gasset (1883–1955) brings uncommon weight and sensibility to bear on the possible future of the novel. Nevertheless, the author's implied assumptions concerning the nature of the artist's imagination, the possible variety of human emotion, character, and motive, the nature of literary "materials" all demand close inspection. For example, if it were once true that novels did not "sell well" as he says in his opening statement, that is hardly the case today. Does this discrepancy, in itself, either refute or substantiate the argument on that point?

José Ortega y Gasset

Publishers complain that novels do not sell well, and it is true that the reading public buys fewer novels while the demand for books of a theoretical character is relatively increasing. This statistical fact, even if there were no more intrinsic reasons, would suffice to make us suspect that something is amiss with the literary genre of the novel. When I hear a friend, particularly if he is a young writer, calmly announce that he is working on a novel I am appalled, and I feel that in his case I should be trembling in my boots. Perhaps I am wrong, but I cannot help scenting behind such an equanimity an alarming dose of incomprehension. To produce a good novel has always been a difficult thing. But while, before, it was enough to have talent the difficulty has now grown immeasurably, for to be a gifted novelist is no longer a guaranty for producing a good novel.

Unawareness of this fact is one component of the aforementioned incomprehension. Anyone who gives a little thought to the conditions of a work of art must admit that a literary genre may wear out. One cannot dismiss the subject by comfortably assuming that artistic creation depends on nothing but the artist's personal power

called inspiration or talent—in which case decadence of a genre
would be due exclusively to an accidental lack of talents, and the
sudden appearance of a man of genius would at any time automatically turn the tide. Better beware of notions like genius and
inspiration; they are a sort of magic wand and should be used
sparingly by anybody who wants to see things clearly. Imagine
a woodsman, the strongest of woodsmen, in the Sahara desert.
What good are his bulging muscles and his sharp ax? A woodsman without woods is an abstraction. And the same applies to
artists. Talent is but a subjective disposition that is brought to
bear upon a certain material. The material is independent of
individual gifts; and when it is lacking genius and skill are of
no avail.

Just as every animal belongs to a species, every literary work
belongs to a genre. (The theory of Benedetto Croce who denies
the existence of literary forms in this sense has left no trace in
aesthetics.) A literary genre, the same as a zoological species,
means a certain stock of possibilities; and since in art only those
possibilities count, which are different enough not to be considered replicas of one another, the resources of a literary genre
are definitely limited. It is erroneous to think of the novel—and
I refer to the modern novel in particular—as of an endless field
capable of rendering ever new forms. Rather it may be compared
to a vast but finite quarry. There exist a definite number of possible themes for the novel. The workmen of the primal hour had
no trouble finding new blocks—new characters, new themes.
But present-day writers face the fact that only narrow and
concealed veins are left them.

With this stock of objective possibilities, which is the genre,
the artistic talent works, and when the quarry is worked out,
talent, however great, can achieve nothing. Whether a genre is
altogether done for can, of course, never be decided with mathematical rigor; but it can at times be decided with sufficient
practical approximation. At least, that the material is getting
scarce may appear frankly evident.

This, I believe, is now happening to the novel. It has become
practically impossible to find new subjects. Here we come upon
the first cause of the enormous difficulty, an objective not a
personal difficulty, of writing an acceptable novel at this advanced stage.

During a certain period novels could thrive on the mere

novelty of their subjects which gratuitously added an induced current, as it were, to the value proper of the material. Thus many novels seemed readable which we now think a bore. It is not for nothing that the novel is called "novel." The difficulty of finding new subjects is accompanied by another, perhaps more serious, dilemma. As the store of possible subjects is more and more depleted the sensibility of the reading public becomes subtler and more fastidious. Works that yesterday would still have passed, today are deemed insipid. Not only is the difficulty of finding new subjects steadily growing, but ever "newer" and more extraordinary ones are needed to impress the reader. This is the second cause of the difficulty with which the genre as such is faced in our time.

Proof that the present decline is due to more fundamental causes than a possibly inferior quality of contemporary novels is given by the fact that, as it becomes more difficult to write novels, the famous old or classical ones appear less good. Only a very few have escaped drowning in the reader's boredom.

This development is inevitable and need not dishearten the novelists. On the contrary; for they themselves are bringing it about. Little by little they train their public by sharpening the perception, and refining the taste, of their readers. Each work that is better than a previous one is detrimental to this and all others of the same level. Triumph cannot help being cruel. As the victor wins the battle at the cost of smashing the foe, thus the superior work automatically becomes the undoing of scores of other works that used to be highly thought of.

In short, I believe that the genre of the novel, if it is not yet irretrievably exhausted, has certainly entered its last phase, the scarcity of possible subjects being such that writers must make up for it by the exquisite quality of the other elements that compose the body of a novel.

George Orwell's novels (Animal Farm, 1984) *and essays* (Homage to Catalonia, Shooting an Elephant) *generally reflect an intense concern for social problems and a fiercely independent socialism. Born in 1903, after an education at Eton, Orwell became a civil police officer in Burma; increasingly, he became interested in politics and in the late 1930's fought and was wounded in the Spanish Civil War. Orwell died in 1950. The following essay, which is atypically nonpolitical, uses imaginative writing—two novels—as a basis for cultural generalization. This kind of analysis assumes that the hero-types and their implied ethical stances may be a kind of index to the ethical beliefs or to the code of conduct of an era. (Later in this text an essay by Leslie Fiedler makes use of comic books for a similar kind of analysis.)*

RAFFLES AND MISS BLANDISH

George Orwell

Nearly half a century after his first appearance, Raffles, "the amateur cracksman," is still one of the best-known characters in English fiction. Very few people would need telling that he played cricket for England, had bachelor chambers in the Albany and burgled the Mayfair houses which he also entered as a guest. Just for that reason he and his exploits make a suitable background against which to examine a more modern crime story such as *No Orchids for Miss Blandish.* Any such choice is necessarily arbitrary—I might equally well have chosen *Arsene Lupin,* for instance—but at any rate *No Orchids* and the Raffles books[1] have the common quality of being crime stories which play the limelight on the criminal rather than the policeman. For sociological purposes they can be compared. *No*

---

[1] *Raffles, A Thief in the Night* and *Mr. Justice Raffles,* by E. W. Hornung. The third of these is definitely a failure, and only the first has the true Raffles atmosphere. Hornung wrote a number of crime stories, usually with a tendency to take the side of the criminal. A successful book in rather the same vein as *Raffles* is *Stingaree.*

Orchids is the 1939 version of glamorised crime, *Raffles* the 1900 version. What I am concerned with here is the immense difference in moral atmosphere between the two books, and the change in the popular attitude that this probably implies.

At this date, the charm of *Raffles* is partly in the period atmosphere and partly in the technical excellence of the stories. Hornung was a very conscientious and on his level a very able writer. Anyone who cares for sheer efficiency must admire his work. However, the truly dramatic thing about Raffles, the thing that makes him a sort of byword even to this day (only a few weeks ago, in a burglary case, a magistrate referred to the prisoner as "a Raffles in real life"), is the fact that he is a *gentleman*. Raffles is presented to us—and this is rubbed home in countless scraps of dialogue and casual remarks—not as an honest man who has gone astray, but as a public-school man who has gone astray. His remorse, when he feels any, is almost purely social; he has disgraced "the old school," he has lost his right to enter "decent society," he has forfeited his amateur status and become a cad. Neither Raffles nor Bunny appears to feel at all strongly that stealing is wrong in itself, though Raffles does once justify himself by the casual remark that "the distribution of property is all wrong anyway." They think of themselves not as sinners but as renegades, or simply as outcasts. And the moral code of most of us is still so close to Raffles's own that we do feel his situation to be an especially ironical one. A West End club man who is really a burglar! That is almost a story in itself, is it not? But how if it were a plumber or a greengrocer who was really a burglar? Would there be anything inherently dramatic in that? No—although the theme of the "double life," of respectability covering crime, is still there. Even Charles Peace in his clergyman's dog-collar seems somewhat less of a hypocrite than Raffles in his Zingari blazer.

Raffles, of course, is good at all games, but it is peculiarly fitting that his chosen game should be cricket. This allows not only of endless analogies between his cunning as a slow bowler and his cunning as a burglar, but also helps to define the exact nature of his crime. Cricket is not in reality a very popular game in England—it is nowhere near so popular as football, for instance—but it gives expression to a well-marked trait in the English character, the tendency to value "form" or "style" more highly than success. In the eyes of any true cricket-lover it is possible for an inning of ten runs to be "better" (*i.e.* more elegant) than an inning of a hundred runs: cricket is also one of the very few games in which the amateur can excel the professional. It is a game full of forlorn hopes and sudden dramatic changes of fortune, and its rules are so ill-defined that their interpretation is partly an ethical business. When Larwood, for instance, practised body line bowling in Australia he was not actually breaking any rule: he was merely doing something that was "not cricket." Since cricket takes up a lot of time and is rather an expensive game to play, it is predominantly an upper-class game, but for the whole nation it is bound up with such concepts as "good form," "playing the game," etc., and it has declined in popularity just as the tradition of "don't hit a man when he's down" has declined. It is not a twentieth-century game, and nearly all modern-minded people dislike it. The Nazis, for instance, were at pains to discourage cricket, which had gained a certain footing in Germany before and after the last war. In making Raffles a cricketer as well as a burglar, Hornung was not merely providing him with a plausible disguise; he was also drawing the sharpest moral contrast that he was able to imagine.

Raffles, no less than *Great Expectations* or *Le Rouge et le Noir,* is a story of snobbery, and it gains a great deal from the precariousness of Raffles's social position. A cruder writer would have made the "gentleman burglar" a member of the peerage, or at least a baronet. Raffles, however, is of upper-middle-class origin and is only accepted by the aristocracy because of his personal charm. "We were in Society but not of it," he says to Bunny towards the end of the book; and "I was asked about for my cricket." Both he and Bunny accept the values of "Society" unquestionably, and would settle down in it for good if only they could get away with a big enough haul. The ruin that constantly threatens them is all the blacker because they only doubtfully "belong." A duke who has served a prison sentence is still a duke, whereas a mere man about town, if once disgraced, ceases to be "about town" for evermore. The closing chapters of the book, when Raffles has been exposed and is living under an assumed name, have a twilight of the gods feeling, a mental atmosphere rather similar to that of Kipling's poem, "Gentleman Rankers":

> "Yes, a trooper of the forces—
> Who has run his own six horses!" etc.

Raffles now belongs irrevocably to the "cohorts of the damned." He can still commit successful burglaries, but there is no way back into Paradise, which means Piccadilly and the M.C.C. [The Middlesex Cricket Club]. According to the public-school code there is only one means of rehabilitation: death in battle. Raffles dies fighting against the Boers (a practised reader would foresee this from the start), and in the eyes of both Bunny and his creator this cancels his crimes.

Both Raffles and Bunny, of course, are devoid of religious belief, and they have no real ethical code, merely certain rules of behaviour which they observe semi-instinctively. But it is just here that the deep moral difference between *Raffles* and *No Orchids* becomes apparent. Raffles and Bunny, after all, are gentlemen, and such standards as they do have are not to be violated. Certain things are "not done," and the idea of doing them hardly arises. Raffles will not, for example, abuse hospitality. He will commit a burglary in a house where he is staying as a guest, but the victim must be a fellow-guest and not the host. He will not commit murder,[2] and he avoids violence wherever possible and prefers to carry out his robberies unarmed. He regards friendship as sacred, and is chivalrous though not moral in his relations with women. He will take extra risks in the name of "sportsmanship," and sometimes even for æsthetic reasons. And above all, he is intensely patriotic. He celebrates the Diamond Jubilee ("For sixty years, Bunny, we've been ruled over by absolutely the finest sovereign the world has ever seen") by despatching to the Queen, through the post, an antique gold cup which he has stolen from the British Museum. He steals, from partly political motives, a pearl which the German Emperor is sending to one of the enemies of Britain, and when the Boer War begins to go badly his one thought is to find his way into the fighting line. At the front he unmasks a spy at the cost of revealing his own identity, and then dies gloriously by a Boer bullet. In this combination of crime and patriotism he resembles

---

2 1945. Actually Raffles does kill one man and is more or less consciously responsible for the death of two others. But all three of them are foreigners and have behaved in a very reprehensible manner. He also, on one occasion, contemplates murdering a blackmailer. It is, however, a fairly well-established convention in crime stories that murdering a blackmailer "doesn't count."

his near-contemporary Arsene Lupin, who also scores off the German Emperor and wipes out his very dirty past by enlisting in the Foreign Legion.

It is important to note that by modern standards Raffles's crimes are very petty ones. Four hundred pounds' worth of jewellery seems to him an excellent haul. And though the stories are convincing in their physical detail, they contain very little sensationalism—very few corpses, hardly any blood, no sex crimes, no sadism, no perversions of any kind. It seems to be the case that the crime story, at any rate on its higher levels, has greatly increased in blood-thirstiness during the past twenty years. Some of the early detective stories do not even contain a murder. The Sherlock Holmes stories, for instance, are not all murders, and some of them do not even deal with an indictable crime. So also with the John Thorndyke stories, while of the Max Carrados stories only a minority are murders. Since 1918, however, a detective story not containing a murder has been a great rarity, and the most disgusting details of dismemberment and exhumation are commonly exploited. Some of the Peter Wimsey stories, for instance, display an extremely morbid interest in corpses. The Raffles stories, written from the angle of the criminal, are much less anti-social than many modern stories written from the angle of the detective. The main impression that they leave behind is of boyishness. They belong to a time when people had standards, though they happened to be foolish standards. Their key-phrase is "not done." The line that they draw between good and evil is as senseless as a Polynesian taboo, but at least, like the taboo, it has the advantage that everyone accepts it.

So much for *Raffles*. Now for a header into the cesspool. *No Orchids for Miss Blandish*, by James Hadley Chase, was published in 1939, but seems to have enjoyed its greatest popularity in 1940, during the Battle of Britain and the blitz. In its main outlines its story is this:

Miss Blandish, the daughter of a millionaire, is kidnapped by some gangsters who are almost immediately surprised and killed off by a larger and better organised gang. They hold her to ransom and extract half a million dollars from her father. Their original plan had been to kill her as soon as the ransom-money was received, but a chance keeps her alive. One of the gang is a young man named Slim, whose sole pleasure in life consists in driving knives into other people's bellies. In childhood he has graduated by cutting up living animals with a pair of rusty scissors. Slim is sexually impotent, but takes a kind of fancy to Miss Blandish. Slim's mother, who is the real brains of the gang, sees in this the chance of curing Slim's impotence, and decides to keep Miss Blandish in custody till Slim shall have succeeded in raping her. After many efforts and much persuasion, including the flogging of Miss Blandish with a length of rubber hosepipe, the rape is achieved. Meanwhile Miss Blandish's father has hired a private detective, and by means of bribery and torture the detective and the police manage to round up and exterminate the whole gang. Slim escapes with Miss Blandish and is killed after a final rape, and the detective prepares to restore Miss Blandish to her family. By this time, however, she has developed such a taste for Slim's caresses[3] that she feels unable to live without him, and she jumps out of the window of a sky-scraper.

Several other points need noticing before one can grasp the full implications of this book. To begin with, its central story bears a very marked resemblance to William Faulkner's novel, *Sanctuary*. Secondly, it is not, as one might expect, the product of an illiterate hack, but a brilliant piece of writing, with hardly a wasted word or a jarring note anywhere. Thirdly, the whole book, *récit* as well as dialogue, is written in the American language; the author, an Englishman who has (I believe) never been in the United States, seems to have made a complete mental transference to the American underworld. Fourthly, the book sold, according to its publishers, no less than half a million copies.

I have already outlined the plot, but the subject-matter is much more sordid and brutal than this suggests. The book contains eight full-dress murders, an unassessable number of casual killings and woundings, an exhumation (with a careful reminder of the stench), the flogging of Miss Blandish, the torture of another woman with red-hot cigarette-ends, a strip-tease act, a third-degree scene of unheard-of cruelty and much else of the same kind. It assumes great sexual sophistication in its readers (there is a scene, for instance, in which a gangster, presumably of masochistic tendency, has an orgasm in the moment of being knifed), and it takes for granted the most complete corruption

---

[3] 1945. Another reading of the final episode is possible. It may mean merely that Miss Blandish is pregnant. But the interpretation I have given above seems more in keeping with the general brutality of the book.

and self-seeking as the norm of human behaviour. The detective, for instance, is almost as great a rogue as the gangsters, and actuated by nearly the same motives. Like them, he is in pursuit of "five hundred grand." It is necessary to the machinery of the story that Mr. Blandish should be anxious to get his daughter back, but apart from this, such things as affection, friendship, good nature or even ordinary politeness simply do not enter. Nor, to any great extent, does normal sexuality. Ultimately only one motive is at work throughout the whole story: the pursuit of power.

It should be noticed that the book is not in the ordinary sense pornography. Unlike most books that deal in sexual sadism, it lays the emphasis on the cruelty and not on the pleasure. Slim, the ravisher of Miss Blandish, has "wet, slobbering lips": this is disgusting, and it is meant to be disgusting. But the scenes describing cruelty to women are comparatively perfunctory. The real high-spots of the book are cruelties committed by men upon other men: above all, the third-degreeing of the gangster, Eddie Schultz, who is lashed into a chair and flogged on the windpipe with truncheons, his arms broken by fresh blows as he breaks loose. In another of Mr. Chase's books, *He Won't Need It Now*, the hero, who is intended to be a sympathetic and perhaps even noble character, is described as stamping on somebody's face, and then, having crushed the man's mouth in, grinding his heel round and round in it. Even when physical incidents of this kind are not occurring, the mental atmosphere of these books is always the same. Their whole theme is the struggle for power and the triumph of the strong over the weak. The big gangsters wipe out the little ones as mercilessly as a pike gobbling up the little fish in a pond; the police kill off the criminals as cruelly as the angler kills the pike. If ultimately one sides with the police against the gangsters, it is merely because they are better organised and more powerful, because, in fact, the law is a bigger racket than crime. Might is right: *væ victis*.

As I have mentioned already, *No Orchids* enjoyed its greatest vogue in 1940, though it was successfully running as a play till some time later. It was, in fact, one of the things that helped to console people for the boredom of being bombed. Early in the war the *New Yorker* had a picture of a little man approaching a news-stall littered with papers with such headlines as "Great Tank Battles in Northern France," "Big Naval Battle in the

North Sea," "Huge Air Battles over the Channel," etc., etc. The
little man is saying, "*Action Stories*, please." That little man
stood for all the drugged millions to whom the world of the
gangsters and the prize-ring is more "real," more "tough," than
such things as wars, revolutions, earthquakes, famines and pesti-
lences. From the point of view of a reader of *Action Stories*, a
description of the London blitz, or of the struggles of the European underground parties, would be "sissy stuff." On the other
hand, some puny gun-battle in Chicago, resulting in perhaps half
a dozen deaths, would seem genuinely "tough." This habit of
mind is now extremely widespread. A soldier sprawls in a muddy
trench, with the machine-gun bullets crackling a foot or two
overhead, and whiles away his intolerable boredom by reading
an American gangster story. And what is it that makes that
story so exciting? Precisely the fact that people are shooting at
each other with machine-guns! Neither the soldier nor anyone
else sees anything curious in this. It is taken for granted that an
imaginary bullet is more thrilling than a real one.

The obvious explanation is that in real life one is usually a
passive victim, whereas in the adventure story one can think of
oneself as being at the centre of events. But there is more to it
than that. Here it is necessary to refer again to the curious fact of
No Orchids being written—with technical errors, perhaps, but
certainly with considerable skill—in the American language.

There exists in America an enormous literature of more or less
the same stamp as *No Orchids*. Quite apart from books, there is
the huge array of "pulp magazines," graded so as to cater to
different kinds of fantasy, but nearly all having much the same
mental atmosphere. A few of them go in for straight pornography, but the great majority are quite plainly aimed at sadists
and masochists. Sold at threepence a copy under the title of
Yank Mags,[4] these things used to enjoy considerable popularity
in England, but when the supply dried up owing to the war,
no satisfactory substitute was forthcoming. English imitations
of the "pulp magazine" do now exist, but they are poor things
compared with the original. English crook films, again, never
approach the American crook film in brutality. And yet the
career of Mr. Chase shows how deep the American influence

---

[4] They are said to have been imported into this country as ballast, which accounted
for their low price and crumpled appearance. Since the war the ships have been
ballasted with something more useful, probably gravel.

has already gone. Not only is he himself living a continuous fantasy-life in the Chicago underworld, but he can count on hundreds of thousands of readers who know what is meant by a "clipshop" or the "hotsquat," do not have to do mental arithmetic when confronted by "fifty grand," and understand at sight a sentence like "Johnnie was a rummy and only two jumps ahead of the nut-factory." Evidently there are great numbers of English people who are partly Americanised in language and, one ought to add, in moral outlook. For there was no popular protest against *No Orchids*. In the end it was withdrawn, but only retrospectively, when a later work, *Miss Callaghan Comes to Grief*, brought Mr. Chase's books to the attention of the authorities. Judging by casual conversations at the time, ordinary readers got a mild thrill out of the obscenities of *No Orchids*, but saw nothing undesirable in the book as a whole. Many people, incidentally, were under the impression that it was an American book reissued in England.

The thing that the ordinary reader *ought* to have objected to— almost certainly would have objected to, a few decades earlier —was the equivocal attitude towards crime. It is implied throughout *No Orchids* that being a criminal is only reprehensible in the sense that it does not pay. Being a policeman pays better, but there is no moral difference, since the police use essentially criminal methods. In a book like *He Won't Need It Now* the distinction between crime and crime-prevention practically disappears. This is a new departure for English sensational fiction, in which till recently there has always been a sharp distinction between right and wrong and a general agreement that virtue must triumph in the last chapter. English books glorifying crime (modern crime, that is—pirates and highwaymen are different) are very rare. Even a book like *Raffles*, as I have pointed out, is governed by powerful taboos, and it is clearly understood that Raffles's crimes must be expiated sooner or later. In America, both in life and fiction, the tendency to tolerate crime, even to admire the criminal so long as he is successful, is very much more marked. It is, indeed, ultimately this attitude that has made it possible for crime to flourish upon so huge a scale. Books have been written about Al Capone that are hardly different in tone from the books written about Henry Ford, Stalin, Lord Northcliffe and all the rest of the "log cabin to White House" brigade. And switching back eighty years, one finds Mark Twain adopting much the same attitude towards the disgusting bandit Slade, hero of twenty-eight murders, and towards the Western desperadoes generally. They were successful, they "made good," therefore he admired them.

In a book like *No Orchids* one is not, as in the old-style crime story, simply escaping from dull reality into an imaginary world of action. One's escape is essentially into cruelty and sexual perversion. *No Orchids* is aimed at the power-instinct, which *Raffles* or the Sherlock Holmes stories are not. At the same time the English attitude towards crime is not so superior to the American as I may have seemed to imply. It too is mixed up with power-worship, and has become more noticeably so in the last twenty years. A writer who is worth examining is Edgar Wallace, especially in such typical books as *The Orator* and the Mr. J. G. Reeder stories. Wallace was one of the first crime-story writers to break away from the old tradition of the private detective and make his central figure a Scotland Yard official. Sherlock Holmes is an amateur, solving his problems without the help and even, in the earlier stories, against the opposition of the police. Moreover, like Lupin, he is essentially an intellectual, even a scientist. He reasons logically from observed fact, and his intellectuality is constantly contrasted with the routine methods of the police. Wallace objected strongly to this slur, as he considered it, on Scotland Yard, and in several newspaper articles he went out of his way to denounce Holmes by name. His own ideal was the detective inspector who catches criminals not because he is intellectually brilliant but because he is part of an all-powerful organization. Hence the curious fact that in Wallace's most characteristic stories the "clue" and the "deduction" play no part. The criminal is always defeated either by an incredible coincidence, or because in some unexplained manner the police know all about the crime beforehand. The tone of the stories makes it quite clear that Wallace's admiration for the police is pure bully-worship. A Scotland Yard detective is the most powerful kind of being that he can imagine, while the criminal figures in his mind as an outlaw against whom anything is permissible, like the condemned slaves in the Roman arena. His policemen behave much more brutally than British policemen do in real life—they hit people without provocation, fire revolvers past their ears to terrify them and so on—and some of the stories exhibit a fearful intellectual

sadism. (For instance, Wallace likes to arrange things so that
the villain is hanged on the same day as the heroine is married.)
But it is sadism after the English fashion: that is to say, it is
unconscious, there is not overtly any sex in it, and it keeps
within the bounds of the law. The British public tolerates a
harsh criminal law and gets a kick out of monstrously unfair
murder trials: but still this is better, on any count, than tolerating
or admiring crime. If one must worship a bully, it is better
that he should be a policeman than a gangster. Wallace is still
governed to some extent by the concept of "not done." In *No
Orchids* anything is "done" so long as it leads on to power. All
the barriers are down, all the motives are out in the open. Chase
is a worse symptom than Wallace, to the extent that all-in
wrestling is worse than boxing, or Fascism is worse than capitalist
democracy.

In borrowing from William Faulkner's *Sanctuary*, Chase only
took the plot; the mental atmosphere of the two books is not
similar. Chase really derives from other sources, and this particular bit of borrowing is only symbolic. What it symbolises
is the vulgarisation of ideas which is constantly happening, and
which probably happens faster in an age of print. Chase has
been described as "Faulkner for the masses," but it would be
more accurate to describe him as Carlyle for the masses. He is a
popular writer—there are many such in America, but they are
still rarities in England—who has caught up with what it is
now fashionable to call "realism," meaning the doctrine that
might is right. The growth of "realism" has been the great
feature of the intellectual history of our own age. Why this
should be so is a complicated question. The interconnection
between sadism, masochism, success-worship, power-worship,
nationalism and totalitarianism is a huge subject whose edges
have barely been scratched, and even to mention it is considered
somewhat indelicate. To take merely the first example that comes
to mind, I believe no one has ever pointed out the sadistic and
masochistic element in Bernard Shaw's work, still less suggested
that this probably has some connection with Shaw's admiration
for dictators. Fascism is often loosely equated with sadism, but
nearly always by people who see nothing wrong in the most
slavish worship of Stalin. The truth is, of course, that the countless English intellectuals who kiss the arse of Stalin are not
different from the minority who give their allegiance to Hitler

Orwell's world.
Photograph by Ernst Haas. Magnum.

or Mussolini, nor from the efficiency experts who preached "punch," "drive," "personality" and "learn to be a Tiger man" in the nineteen-twenties, nor from that older generation of intellectuals, Carlyle, Creasey and the rest of them, who bowed down before German militarism. All of them are worshipping power and successful cruelty. It is important to notice that the cult of power tends to be mixed up with a love of cruelty and wickedness *for their own sakes*. A tyrant is all the more admired if he happens to be a bloodstained crook as well, and "the end justifies the means" often becomes, in effect, "the means justify themselves provided they are dirty enough." This idea colours the outlook of all sympathisers with totalitarianism, and accounts, for instance, for the positive delight with which many English intellectuals greeted the Nazi-Soviet pact. It was a step only doubtfully useful to the U.S.S.R., but it was entirely unmoral, and for that reason to be admired; the explanations of it, which were numerous and self-contradictory, could come afterwards.

Until recently the characteristic adventure stories of the English-speaking peoples have been stories in which the hero fights *against odds*. This is true all the way from Robin Hood to Pop-eye the Sailor. Perhaps the basic myth of the Western world is Jack the Giant-killer, but to be brought up to date this should be renamed Jack the Dwarf-killer, and there already exists considerable literature which teaches, either overtly or implicitly, that one should side with the big man against the little man. Most of what is now written about foreign policy is simply an embroidery on this theme, and for several decades such phrases as "Play the game," "Don't hit a man when he's down" and "It's not cricket" have never failed to draw a snigger from anyone of intellectual pretensions. What is comparatively new is to find the accepted pattern according to which (*a*) right is right and wrong is wrong, whoever wins, and (*b*) weakness must be respected, disappearing from popular literature as well. When I first read D. H. Lawrence's novels, at the age of about twenty, I was puzzled by the fact that there did not seem to be any classification of the characters into "good" and "bad." Lawrence seemed to sympathise with all of them about equally and this was so unusual as to give me the feeling of having lost my bearings. To-day no one would think of looking for heroes and villains in a serious novel, but in lowbrow fiction one still expects to find a sharp distinction between right and wrong and between legality and illegality. The common people, on the whole, are still living in the world of absolute good and evil from which the intellectuals have long since escaped. But the popularity of *No Orchids* and the American books and magazines to which it is akin shows how rapidly the doctrine of "realism" is gaining ground.

Several people, after reading *No Orchids*, have remarked to me, "It's pure Fascism." This is a correct description, although the book has not the smallest connection with politics and very little with social or economic problems. It has merely the same relation to Fascism as, say, Trollope's novels have to nineteenth-century capitalism. It is a day dream appropriate to a totalitarian age. In his imagined world of gangsters Chase is presenting, as it were, a distilled version of the modern political scene, in which such things as mass bombing of civilians, the use of hostages, torture to obtain confessions, secret prisons, execution without trial, floggings with rubber truncheons, drownings in cesspools, systematic falsification of records and statistics, treachery, bribery and quislingism are normal and morally neutral, even admirable when they are done in a large and bold way. The average man is not directly interested in politics, and when he reads, he wants the current struggles of the world to be translated into a simple story about individuals. He can take an interest in Slim and Fenner as he could not in the G. P. U. and the Gestapo. People worship power in the form in which they are able to understand it. A twelve-year-old boy worships Jack Dempsey. An adolescent in a Glasgow slum worships Al Capone. An aspiring pupil at a business college worships Lord Nuffield. A *New Statesman* reader worships Stalin. There is a difference in intellectual maturity, but none in moral outlook. Thirty years ago the heroes of popular fiction had nothing in common with Mrs. Chase's gangsters and detectives, and the idols of the English liberal intelligentsia were also comparatively sympathetic figures. Between Holmes and Fenner on the one hand, and between Abraham Lincoln and Stalin on the other, there is a similar gulf.

One ought not to infer too much from the success of Mr. Chase's books. It is possible that it is an isolated phenomenon, brought about by the mingled boredom and brutality of war. But if such books should definitely acclimatise themselves in

England, instead of being merely a half-understood import from America, there would be good grounds for dismay. In choosing *Raffles* as a background for *No Orchids* I deliberately chose a book which by the standards of its time was morally equivocal. Raffles, as I have pointed out, has no real moral code, no religion, certainly no social consciousness. All he has is a set of reflexes —the nervous system, as it were, of a gentleman. Give him a sharp tap on this reflex or that (they are called "sport," "pal," "woman," "king and country" and so forth), and you get a predictable reaction. In Mr. Chase's books there are no gentlemen and no taboos. Emancipation is complete, Freud and Machiavelli have reached the outer suburbs. Comparing the schoolboy atmosphere of the one book with the cruelty and corruption of the other, one is driven to feel that snobbishness, like hypocrisy, is a check upon behaviour whose value from a social point of view has been underrated.

This essay by Andrew Hook of the University of Edinburgh explores the generally gray area of a writer's commitment (or lack of it) to society, to politics, to reform, to propaganda—this last, perhaps, in behalf of his own country, Scotland. Many writers have placed their gifts in the service of some "higher" cause; the social concerns of Dos Passos and Steinbeck are peculiarly American examples. In another way, Tolstoy used his literary talent to dramatize his version of a Christian ethic; by contrast, some writers in the U.S.S.R. today see themselves as "engineers of the human mind." In America, the writer's concept of his commitment to society is largely a matter of individual conscience, but most writers understand very well that this delicate issue may affect the acceptance of their work.

COMMITMENT AND REALITY

Andrew
Hook

While his *Crack-Up* articles, which tried to account for an overwhelming sense of personal frustration and failure, were appearing in *Esquire*, Scott Fitzgerald received a letter from his friend Dos Passos of which this is part:

I've been wanting to see you, naturally, to argue about your *Esquire* articles.—Christ man, how do you find time in the middle of the general conflagration to worry about all that stuff? . . . After all not many people write as well as you do. Here you've gone and spent forty years in perfecting an elegant and complicated piece of machinery (tool I was going to say) and the next forty years is the time to use it—or as long as the murderous forces of history will let you.

The date is 1936 and this is the letter of a committed writer to one he regards as uncommitted. Dos Passos cannot understand why at this critical moment of time Fitzgerald should allow himself to be so taken up with personal, individ-

ual problems and concerns. As an artist he should be preoccupied
not with the cracking-up of his own life, but with what Dos
Passos recognises as the imminent dissolution and disintegration
of the society and the world of which he is part. For Dos
Passos the duty of the writer is not to look inward, to the
exploration of the individual consciousness, but outward to society at large, to the broader forces and movements which
mould and control man's destiny. The final confrontation is not
that of man and his deepest, truest, thinking and feeling self,
but that of man and 'the murderous forces of history.' Just such
an argument as this over the necessary priority of either the
inner, psychological reality, or the outer, social reality lies behind every debate on commitment.

Dos Passos' last phrase, however—the murderous forces of
history—provides us with a clue to the origins of commitment
as an ideal for the writer. Commitment, as it is generally understood—the acceptance by the writer of an extra-artistic, usually
political, programme of action and belief which lies behind his
creative endeavours—depends essentially on a Romantic view of
society, of what society stands for. In the eighteenth century in
England, writers such as Pope and Swift were just as much
committed, committed to a dream, a vision of the ideal society,
as any of the English or French or American writers of the nine-
teen-thirties. But their dream was the dream of all of their society; their vision was a vision to which all reasonable men gave
their consent—hence the power with which they assailed the
non-ideal elements in their society. This typical Augustan situation, however, in which individual values reflected social values,
in which the individual found the values in which he believed
endorsed and upheld by the society of which he was part, was
not an enduring one. Whether it had ever in fact been more than
a literary reality may be open to question. But the point is that
the development of Romanticism meant it ceased even to be that.
One of the manifold meanings of Romanticism is precisely a new
interest in the individual as individual rather than as member of
society, a turning away from society to the individual as the focus
of interest, the centre of consciousness. The consequence was that
social and individual values tended to diverge. And for the Romantic artist, as for a great many other artists and writers down
to the present day, society came to be seen not as the institution-
alised defender and protector of humane values, of 'the good life,'

but as a vast, imponderable, unregenerate mass, destructive of everything the good life embodies.

Where the Augustan artist is typically the spokesman for, the defender of, the ideals of his society, the Romantic artist is again and again the defender of ideals to which he feels his society is hostile. Seeing society in this light, as something by definition destructive of individual values, how could the post-Augustan writer respond? How could he preserve and defend those values in which he believed? One method was that of strategic withdrawal. The artist embraced his alienation from society, defined himself as artist precisely by that alienation, and proclaimed the absolute autonomy of art and artistic values. The other was the method of counter-attack, by which the artist provided society with images of its own repressiveness and destructiveness, and by so doing implicitly or explicitly pointed the way to social reformation.

It has already been noted that Romanticism involved a new interest in the individual—in the individual and his personal response to experience; a cultivation then of the feelings, of the individual sensibility. But the question of the relationship between the individual response and the established, impersonal, social realities, between what might be called the private and public visions of reality, is at once problematical. The artist who pursues the first of the methods mentioned above—the method that may produce the doctrine of art for art's sake—unhesitatingly follows his private vision to the total disregard of any kind of public reality. He is committed, in other words, to the cultivation of the self, the individual sensibility. The artist who follows the second way—the prototype of what we understand by the committed writer—also pursues a private vision; only to realise it he becomes preoccupied with the external, social reality. Neither method, that is, successfully overcomes the difficulty of relating the private and public worlds, the inner world of private sensibility and the outer world of social reality.

Jane Austen was probably the last English writer for whom these two worlds could be readily reconciled—and of course Jane Austen looks back to the eighteenth century rather than on to the nineteenth. Certainly the work of her contemporaries and successors manifests no such harmonious reconciliation; rather have private sensibility and public reality remained firmly

opposed to each other. Once the personal response to experience
was allowed superior validity, perhaps such an opposition followed inevitably; certainly once the artistic effort itself came to
be identified wholly with the cultivation of the individual sensibility, once the private vision came to be equated with the life
of the imagination, then reconciliation was problematical indeed.

But for the majority of Victorian writers an unheeding pursuit
of the private vision, at the expense of the surrounding social
reality, was never even a possibility. Most of the Victorians were
all too aware of that social reality with its orthodoxies of conduct
and beliefs, established and sanctioned by custom, tradition, and
even religion. For most of the Victorians society represented
a reality that could not be denied or ignored, towards which the
artist as man, and probably as artist too, owed certain responsibilities, certain duties. It is, in fact, the recognition and acceptance
of these duties and responsibilities which create the 'divided
self' of the typical Victorian artist, drawn by both the public
and private worlds. The Victorian artist comes more and more
to identify the sources of his creative inspiration with something
that is private and individual, something entirely detached from
the normal, social world, something which may even be inimical
to that everyday world of moral choices and responsibilities.
Carried to an extreme, this identification of the sources of creative inspiration with something dangerously private and non-
moral, brings the artist to a basic mistrust of the imagination
itself, to the belief that the palace of art may be a lotos island,
a seduction from the real world of essential moral responsibility.
Wordsworth, Tennyson, Arnold, Charlotte Brontë, George Eliot,
George Meredith—all of them were aware of such a danger.
And surely it is feelings of a similar kind about the status of the
imaginative process which underlie most of the modern argu-
ments in favour of commitment.

But 'duty'—the escape route from the self—which we may
fairly see as the Victorian version of 'commitment', did not
prove itself a powerful, creative stimulus. The careers of, say,
Wordsworth and Tennyson rather suggest the reverse. 'Duty',
seen as something opposed to the cultivation, or indulgence, of
the individual sensibility, seems to have had a deadening effect
upon that sensibility, that is, upon the springs of creative expression. Only when the conflict between the private and public

worlds was raised to the level of a dialogue between 'duty' and the 'self' did any kind of imaginative release follow—as novels such as *Jane Eyre, The Mill on the Floss,* and *The Ordeal of Richard Feverel* suggest.

The doctrine of the essentially private and individual nature of the aesthetic response to experience, and of the autonomy of that response, was one that survived unscathed in the literary revolution that occurred early in this century. Hence the choice for the modern writer between commitment and non-commitment is essentially the same choice as his Victorian predecessor made between duty and the self. No doubt, of course, the choice is often not a fully conscious one, and no doubt, too, most writers would be unwilling to accept either of the extreme positions advocated by its partisans. Certainly few of the great writers of the twentieth century have been prepared to accept the logic of art for art's sake; but few too, it seems to me, have been prepared to accept engagement with the external, social reality as the only kind of engagement that matters. To do so would amount to a denial of the validity of the individual, feeling response —which remains identified with the sources of the creative process itself.

The example of those writers who have accepted the ideal of commitment certainly does not suggest that commitment necessarily produces any kind of creative sterility. But commitment does tend in practice to mean the rejection of whole areas of human experience—areas accessible only through the exercise of the individual sensibility. If over-cultivation of the private sensibility leads to narrowness, limitation, and finally to a self-indulgent turning away from the external world altogether, commitment can lead to undesirable limitations of a different kind —limitations in kinds of subject-matter and in methods of rendering experience. The committed writer tends to over-simplify; to see human experience only in terms of the pattern to which he is committed. This is perhaps the greatest weakness of all committed, social realist writing; the individual is seen as the helpless victim of the murderous forces of history and society, and as such he ceases to be an individual. In *The Grapes of Wrath,* for example, the members of the Joad family are intended to be representative of an underprivileged and exploited section of American society. But their representative nature—the sense in

which they illustrate the pattern—seems in some typical way to
act against their full imaginative realisation.

But the work of John Dos Passos himself provides us with a
perfect symbol of the basic difficulty confronting the writer preoccupied with the nature of the external, social reality. *USA*,
Dos Passos' trilogy about American society, greatly underrated by current fashions, is of course in the main dedicated to
that reality. But Dos Passos is impelled to admit into this public
world, the other private, passional world of the individual sensibility: hence the recurring device of the Camera Eye which
renders the individual response to experience.

Dos Passos' instinct that the private and public visions of the
individual and society must be combined is clearly a sound one.
And one may go on believing that some kind of reconcilation
can be obtained irrespective of whether one begins with Dos
Passos' 'murderous forces of history' or with Fitzgerald's exploration of the individual consciousness.

A FUTURE FOR THE NOVEL

Alain Robbe-Grillet's prose fiction and his literary theory alike are concerned with the nouveau roman *and the new purpose of the novel. A traditional goal of the novelist has been to depict the world as it really exists; for Robbe-Grillet (1922–   ), however, this reality is of a "scientific" kind, the focus being on information not refracted through human perception. Thus the objects "establish themselves" and their presence is the story. Understandably, this narrative technique by comparison with conventional narration has a free-wheeling, often disjointed effect. These effects are seen in his novels, one of which is* The Voyeur, *and in the film for which he wrote the scenario,* Last Year at Marienbad.

Alain Robbe-Grillet It seems hardly reasonable at first glance to suppose that an entirely *new* literature might one day—now, for instance—be possible. The many attempts made these last thirty years to drag fiction out of its ruts have resulted, at best, in no more than isolated works. And—we are often told—none of these works, whatever its interest, has gained the adherence of a public comparable to that of the bourgeois novel. The only conception of the novel to have currency today is, in fact, that of Balzac.

Or that of Mme. de La Fayette. Already sacrosanct in her day, psychological analysis constituted the basis of all prose: it governed the conception of the book, the description of its characters, the development of its plot. A "good" novel, ever since, has remained the study of a passion—or of a conflict of passions, or of an absence of passion—in a given milieu. Most of our contemporary novelists of the traditional sort—those, that is, who manage to gain the approval of their readers—could insert long passages from *The Princess of Clèves* or *Père Goriot* into their own books without awakening

the suspicions of the enormous public which devours whatever
they turn out. They would merely need to change a phrase here
and there, simplify certain constructions, afford an occasional
glimpse of their own "manner" by means of a word, a daring
image, the rhythm of a sentence. . . . But all acknowledge, without seeing anything peculiar about it, that their preoccupations
as writers date back several centuries.

What is so surprising about this, after all? The raw material
—the French language—has undergone only very slight modifications for three hundred years; and if society has been gradually
transformed, if industrial techniques have made considerable
progress, our intellectual civilization has remained much the
same. We live by essentially the same habits and the same pro-
hibitions—moral, alimentary, religious, sexual, hygienic, etc. And
of course there is always the human "heart," which as everyone
knows is eternal. There's nothing new under the sun, it's all been
said before, we've come on the scene too late, etc., etc.

The risk of such rebuffs is merely increased if one dares claim
that this new literature is not only possible in the future, but is
already being written, and that it will represent—in its fulfillment—a revolution more complete than those which in the
past produced such movements as romanticism or naturalism.

There is, of course, something ridiculous about such a promise
as "Now things are going to be different!" How will they be
different? In what direction will they change? And, especially,
why are they going to change now?

The art of the novel, however, has fallen into such a state of
stagnation—a lassitude acknowledged and discussed by the whole
of critical opinion—that it is hard to imagine such an art can
survive for long without some radical change. To many, the
solution seems simple enough: such a change being impossible,
the art of the novel is dying. This is far from certain. History
will reveal, in a few decades, whether the various fits and starts
which have been recorded are signs of a death agony or of a
rebirth.

In any case, we must make no mistake as to the difficulties such
a revolution will encounter. They are considerable. The entire
caste system of our literary life (from publisher to the humblest
reader, including bookseller and critic) has no choice but to
oppose the unknown form which is attempting to establish itself.

The minds best disposed to the idea of a necessary transformation, those most willing to countenance and even to welcome
the values of experiment, remain, nonetheless, the heirs of a tradition. A new form will always seem more or less an absence of
any form at all, since it is unconsciously judged by reference
to the consecrated forms. In one of the most celebrated French
reference works, we may read in the article on Schoenberg:
"Author of audacious works, written without regard for any
rules whatever"! This brief judgment is to be found under the
heading *Music,* evidently written by a specialist.

The stammering newborn work will always be regarded as a
monster, even by those who find experiment fascinating. There
will be some curiosity, of course, some gestures of interest,
always some provision for the future. And some praise; though
what is sincere will always be addressed to the vestiges of
the familiar, to all those bonds from which the new work has
not yet broken free and which desperately seek to imprison it
in the past.

For if the norms of the past serve to measure the present, they
also serve to construct it. The writer himself, despite his desire
for independence, is situated within an intellectual culture and a
literature which can only be those of the past. It is impossible for
him to escape altogether from this tradition of which he is the
product. Sometimes the very elements he has tried hardest to
oppose seem, on the contrary, to flourish more vigorously than
ever in the very work by which he hoped to destroy them; and
he will be congratulated, of course, with relief for having cultivated them so zealously.

Hence it will be the specialists in the novel (novelists or critics;
or overassiduous readers) who have the hardest time dragging
themselves out of its rut.

Even the least conditioned observer is unable to see the world
around him through entirely unprejudiced eyes. Not, of course,
that I have in mind the naive concern for objectivity which the
analysts of the (subjective) soul find it so easy to smile at. Objectivity in the ordinary sense of the word—total impersonality of
observation—is all too obviously an illusion. But *freedom* of
observation should be possible, and yet it is not. At every moment, a continuous fringe of culture (psychology, ethics, metaphysics, etc.) is added to things, giving them a less alien aspect,

one that is more comprehensible, more reassuring. Sometimes the camouflage is complete: a gesture vanishes from our mind, supplanted by the emotions which supposedly produced it, and we remember a landscape as *austere* or *calm* without being able to evoke a single outline, a single determining element. Even if we immediately think, "That's literary," we don't try to react against the thought. We accept the fact that what is *literary* (the word has become pejorative) functions like a grid or screen set with bits of different colored glass that fracture our field of vision into tiny assimilable facets.

And if something resists this systematic appropriation of the visual, if an element of the world breaks the glass, without finding any place in the interpretative screen, we can always make use of our convenient category of "the absurd" in order to absorb this awkward residue.

But the world is neither significant nor absurd. It *is*, quite simply. That, in any case, is the most remarkable thing about it. And suddenly the obviousness of this strikes us with irresistible force. All at once the whole splendid construction collapses; opening our eyes unexpectedly, we have experienced, once too often, the shock of this stubborn reality we were pretending to have mastered. Around us, defying the noisy pack of our animistic or protective adjectives, things *are there*. Their surfaces are distinct and smooth, *intact*, neither suspiciously brilliant nor transparent. All our literature has not yet succeeded in eroding their smallest corner, in flattening their slightest curve.

The countless movie versions of novels that encumber our screens provide an occasion for repeating this curious experiment as often as we like. The cinema, another heir of the psychological and naturalistic tradition, generally has as its sole purpose the transposition of a story into images: it aims exclusively at imposing on the spectator, through the intermediary of some well-chosen scenes, the same meaning the written sentences communicated in their own fashion to the reader. But at any given moment the filmed narrative can drag us out of our interior comfort and into this proffered world with a violence not to be found in the corresponding text, whether novel or scenario.

Anyone can perceive the nature of the change that has occurred. In the initial novel, the objects and gestures forming the very fabric of the plot disappeared completely, leaving behind only their *significations:* the empty chair became only absence or expectation, the hand placed on a shoulder became a sign of friendliness, the bars on the window became only the impossibility of leaving. . . . But in the cinema, one *sees* the chair, the movement of the hand, the shape of the bars. What they signify remains obvious, but instead of monopolizing our attention, it becomes something added, even something in excess, because what affects us, what persists in our memory, what appears as essential and irreducible to vague intellectual concepts are the gestures themselves, the objects, the movements, and the outlines, to which the image has suddenly (and unintentionally) restored their *reality*.

It may seem peculiar that such fragments of crude reality, which the filmed narrative cannot help presenting, strike us so vividly, whereas identical scenes in real life do not suffice to free us of our blindness. As a matter of fact, it is as if the very conventions of the photographic medium (the two dimensions, the black-and-white images, the frame of the screen, the difference of scale between scenes) help free us from our own conventions. The slightly "unaccustomed" aspect of this reproduced world reveals, at the same time, the unaccustomed character of the world that surrounds us: it, too, is unaccustomed insofar as it refuses to conform to our habits of apprehension and to our classification.

Instead of this universe of "signification" (psychological, social, functional), we must try, then, to construct a world both more solid and more immediate. Let it be first of all by their *presence* that objects and gestures establish themselves, and let this presence continue to prevail over whatever explanatory theory that may try to enclose them in a system of references, whether emotional, sociological, Freudian, or metaphysical.

In this future universe of the novel, gestures and objects will be *there* before being *something;* and they will still be there afterwards, hard, unalterable, eternally present, mocking their own "meaning," that meaning which vainly tries to reduce them to the role of precarious tools, of a temporary and shameful fabric woven exclusively—and deliberately—by the superior human truth expressed in it, only to cast out this awkward auxiliary into immediate oblivion and darkness.

Delphine Seyrig in Last Year at Marienbad, *Alain Resnais, Director.*
Photograph courtesy of the Office du Cinema Français, New York City.

Henceforth, on the contrary, objects will gradually lose their instability and their secrets, will renounce their pseudo-mystery, that suspect interiority which Roland Barthes has called "the romantic heart of things." No longer will objects be merely the vague reflection of the hero's vague soul, the image of his torments, the shadow of his desires. Or rather, if objects still afford a momentary prop to human passions, they will do so only provisionally, and will accept the tyranny of significations only in appearance—derisively, one might say—the better to show how alien they remain to man.

As for the novel's characters, they may themselves suggest many possible interpretations; they may, according to the pre-occupations of each reader, accommodate all kinds of comment —psychological, psychiatric, religious, or political—yet their indifference to these "potentialities" will soon be apparent. Whereas the traditional hero is constantly solicited, caught up, destroyed by these interpretations of the author's, ceaselessly projected into an immaterial and unstable *elsewhere*, always more remote and blurred, the future hero will remain, on the contrary, *there*. It is the commentaries that will be left elsewhere; in the face of his irrefutable presence, they will seem useless, superfluous, even improper.

Exhibit X in any detective story gives us, paradoxically, a clear image of this situation. The evidence gathered by the inspectors —an object left at the scene of the crime, a movement captured in a photograph, a sentence overheard by a witness—seem chiefly, at first, to require an explanation, to exist only in relation to their role in a context which overpowers them. And already the theories begin to take shape: the presiding magistrate attempts to establish a logical and necessary link between things; it appears that everything will be resolved in a banal bundle of causes and consequences, intentions and coincidences. . . .

But the story begins to proliferate in a disturbing way: the witnesses contradict one another, the defendant offers several alibis, new evidence appears that had not been taken into account. . . . And we keep going back to the recorded evidence: the exact position of a piece of furniture, the shape and frequency of a fingerprint, the word scribbled in a message. We have the mounting sense that nothing else is *true*. Though they may conceal a mystery, or betray it, these elements which make a mockery of systems have only one serious, obvious quality, which is to *be there*.

The same is true of the world around us. We had thought to control it by assigning it a meaning, and the entire art of the novel, in particular, seemed dedicated to this enterprise. But this was merely an illusory simplification; and far from becoming clearer and closer because of it, the world has only, little by little, lost all its life. Since it is chiefly in its presence that the world's reality resides, our task is now to create a literature which takes that presence into account.

All this might seem very theoretical, very illusory, if something were not actually changing—changing totally, definitively—in our relations with the universe. Which is why we glimpse an answer to the old ironic question, "Why now?" There is today, in fact, a new element that separates us radically this time from Balzac as from Gide or from Mme. de La Fayette: it is the destitution of the old myths of "depth."

We know that the whole literature of the novel was based on these myths, and on them alone. The writer's traditional role consisted in excavating Nature, in burrowing deeper and deeper to reach some ever more intimate strata, in finally unearthing some fragment of a disconcerting secret. Having descended into the abyss of human passions, he would send to the seemingly tranquil world (the world on the surface) triumphant messages describing the mysteries he had actually touched with his own hands. And the sacred vertigo the reader suffered then, far from causing him anguish or nausea, reassured him as to his power of domination over the world. There were chasms, certainly, but thanks to such valiant speleologists, their depths could be sounded.

It is not surprising, given these conditions, that the literary phenomenon par excellence should have resided in the total and unique adjective, which attempted to unite all the inner qualities, the entire hidden soul of things. Thus the word functioned as a trap in which the writer captured the universe in order to hand it over to society.

The revolution which has occurred is in kind: not only do we no longer consider the world as our own, our private property, designed according to our needs and readily domesticated, but we no longer even believe in its "depth." While essentialist conceptions of man met their destruction, the notion of "condition" henceforth replacing that of "nature," the *surface* of things has ceased to be for us the mask of their heart, a sentiment that led to every kind of metaphysical transcendence.

Thus it is the entire literary language that must change, that is changing already. From day to day, we witness the growing repugnance felt by people of greater awareness for words of a visceral, analogical, or incantatory character. On the other hand, the visual or descriptive adjective, the word that contents itself with measuring, locating, limiting, defining, indicates a difficult but most likely direction for a new art of the novel.

THE
WORD
ARTS:

Poetry

WHAT IS A POET?

*Accomplished in virtually every form of letters,
Mark Van Doren (1894–   ) is known as critic and
teacher, novelist and short-story writer, editor, but
he is perhaps most famous as a practicing poet. This
essay, which is intended largely as a corrective to
received notions concerning the nature of the poet,
draws on biographical materials from the lives of the
great poets of the past. Although the poet may be
virtually any physical type and belong to
nearly any profession—from physician to
professional thief—one central thing remains
clear: above all the poet is gifted with language, a
"sayer, not a seer." His artistic constructions with
words, his poems, ensure for the poet a kind of
immortality more or less in spite of the role which
society forces upon him.*

*Mark
Van Doren*

Poetry speaks for itself. But poets, curiously
enough, do not; and so it is time that they be
defended against the silent charge, all the more
damning because it is so silent, that they are a
special race of men and women, different from
all other creatures of their kind and possessed of
faculties which would make them, if we knew
them, only too wonderful to live with, not to
say too embarrassing. I should like to relieve
them from the burden of being queer. Poets are
supposed to be a suffering race, but the only
thing they suffer from is the misapprehension
that they are endowed with a peculiar set of
thoughts and feelings. Particularly feelings. It
consists, to speak for the moment historically, in
the notion that the poet has always and must
always cut the same figure he has cut during the
past hundred and fifty years. It consists in ex-
pecting him to be a Shelley, a Keats, a Byron, a
Poe, a Verlaine, a Swinburne, a Dowson. He
may be another one of those, to be sure; but he
may also be any kind of person under the sun.
My only conception of the poet is that he is a

person who writes poetry. That sounds absurdly simple, but it is arrived at after reflection upon the innumerable kinds of poetry which poets have written, and upon the baffling variety of the temperaments which these poets have revealed.

Here is the figure we have set up. A lost man with long hair. Tapering fingers at the ends of fluttering arms. An air of abstraction in the delicate face, but more often a look of shy pain as some aspect of reality—a man or a woman, a grocer's bill, a train, a load of bricks, a newspaper, a noise from the street—makes itself manifest. He is generally incompetent. He cannot find his way, he forgets where he is going, he has no aptitude for business, he is childishly gullible and so the prey of human sharks, he cares nothing for money, he is probably poor, he will sacrifice his welfare for a whim, he stops to pet homeless cats, he is especially knowing where children are concerned (being a child himself), he sighs, he sleeps, he wakes to sigh again. The one great assumption from which the foregoing portrait is drawn is an assumption which thousands of otherwise intelligent citizens go on. It is the assumption that the poet is more sensitive than any other kind of man, that he feels more than the rest of us and is more definitely the victim of his feeling.

I am tempted to assert that the poet is as a matter of fact less sensitive than other men. I shall make no such assertion for the simple reason that to do so would be to imply that I know what kind of man he necessarily is. The poet is not anything necessarily. He may be sensitive, and he may not; the question has nothing directly to do with his being a poet. Certainly there have been poets with thick hides. We have to account for the fact that Browning looked more like a business man than he did like a poet, whatever a poet is supposed to look like; that Horace was plump, phlegmatic, easy-going, shrewd, and sensible; that Dryden was an excellent trader in literary affairs; that Pope was so insensitive, at least to the sufferings of others, that he poured an emetic into the tea of a publisher with whom he had quarreled; that Li Po and most of the other great Chinese poets were government officials; that Robert Frost is to all outward appearances —and what other appearances are there?—a New England farmer.

There is reason for supposing that no artist is as sensitive in one respect as the man who is not an artist. He is not so likely, that is, to be overwhelmed by his own feelings. Consider what he does with his feelings. He uses them, deliberately, for the purposes of his art. The ordinary man, meaning for the moment the man who is not an artist, may be so affected by the death of a parent, for instance, that he becomes dumb. There was Daudet, however, who at the funeral of his mother could not help composing the room where he stood into a room that would be the setting for a new story. The artist is callous, and must be so in order to keep his mind clear for the work he has before him. So also the poet must be sensitive to words, rhythms, ideas; but in the very act of perceiving them clearly, in realizing them for what they are worth, he distinguishes himself from the race of men who feel and only feel. When we read the poetry of a man like Pope who was extraordinarily, almost abnormally, susceptible to the charms of verbal music we can have no doubt that he was, in that one department of his existence, all sense. We are not justified, however, in going on to grant him a sensitive heart. He seems to have had another kind, and in the ordinary man it would be denounced as ugly.

From the notion that the poet is deeply affected by life we often proceed to the notion that he cannot stand a great deal of it; we say he dies young. To be sure there are the English romantic poets to support our error, and to be sure they are always conspicuously present in spirit when poetry is under discussion, since it was their generation that gave us our conception of poetry and the poet; we still are in their period. But even as we talk this way we seem to forget that one of them was Wordsworth, who lived in perfect peace until he was eighty. We forget that Dryden lived to seventy, Shakespeare to fifty-two, Browning to seventy-seven, Tennyson to eighty-three, Milton to sixty-six, Herrick to eighty-three, Spenser to almost fifty, and Chaucer to an even sixty. We disregard the great age of Homer when he died, at least if the traditions be true. And anyway the ancient traditions about poets have their significance. For one of them was that poets die old; hence the bust of Homer, wrinkled, composed, resigned, with sunken eyes. The three great tragic poets of Greece died old indeed; Aeschylus at sixty-nine, Sophocles at ninety, and Euripides at seventy-five. Virgil and Horace gave up the struggle in their fifties, Lucretius committed suicide, it is said, at forty-three or forty-four, and Catullus, like Shelley, was extinguished at thirty; but Ovid, for all his banishment to a cold, uncomfortable part of the world, and his probable suffering there, lived into his sixtieth year; and Ennius, first of all the known Roman poets, saw seventy. Dante had a hard life, but it lasted fifty-six years. Racine went on to sixty; Goethe expired peacefully, calling for more light, at eighty-three. And what of the greatest English poet in recent times? Thomas Hardy, who did not even begin to consider himself a professional poet until he was more than fifty-five, wrote fourteen hundred pages of verse after that, and when he died at eighty-eight was busy with the preparation of a new volume, which appeared posthumously.

Another burden of which poets should be relieved is the burden of being strangely wise. They have been called prophets and seers, clairvoyants, informers, transformers, and what not. All this, too, in spite of the impracticality attributed to them. Indeed, there seems to be a connection between the two attributes. The poets know nothing of the world, but they may tell us a good deal about life; not life as we live it, but life, shall we say, as we ought to live it. By virtue of their stupidity in ordinary affairs they somehow become conversant with the truth. So runs another legend, and one as limited as the rest. For it has no foundation if the whole history of poetry be taken into account. In a primitive tribe the poet is also the medicine man, the priest, and the foreteller of future events, since it is in verse that these functionaries speak. Among savages, then, the poet is a prophet. But nowhere else. The division of labor has gone on; the prophet is the prophet, in verse or in prose as the occasion may be; the poet is the poet, and always in verse. The poet is a sayer, not a seer. Wordsworth brought on a considerable confusion by insisting that the poet is one who goes to Nature for her secrets, which are substantially the secrets of existence, and then comes back with the dew of knowledge on his lips. The poet, in other words, is equipped with a peculiar mind which enables him to plumb—or fathom, or penetrate, or see through, or pierce; the phrase matters not—the world's appearances. For us the appearances, for him the reality behind. Thus he not only cursed his successors with the responsibility of being prophets; he cursed them also with the duty of being acquainted with Nature, and of pretending to some sort of mastery over her. The truth, I suspect, is that the poet is no more of a magician in this respect than the scientist is. And think of the poets, long ago and since, who have never been the least bit interested in the out-of-doors. Dr. Johnson said that he was unable to tell the difference between one

green field and another. Milton got his flowers and mountains out
of old books; Spenser got his landscapes out of sixteenth-century
woodcuts; Dante read Nature as a work in theology; Horace was
comfortable in the presence of his hills only when a few friends
from Rome were with him to drink wine and make remarks
about life; Virgil in the country was concerned with husbandry
and the diseases of sheep; Ovid would not look at a tree unless it
had once contained a nymph.

The poet may think anything, feel anything, do anything; he
may or may not be a wanderer; he may or may not love his home
better than any other plot of ground; he may love children;
he may hate them; he may be restless under the pressure of a
domestic establishment; he may get his chief joy out of a wife
and kitchen; he may inhabit a palace; he may shiver in a garret;
he may be noble; he may be mean. He is not limited, in other
words, more than other men. Yet we go on limiting him. And to
what? To a simpering, humorless, nervous existence which for all
the world we should be unwilling to share with him. No wonder
we don't like him, and no wonder we don't enjoy reading what
we think he must have written.

PURE POETRY: NOTES FOR A LECTURE

A poet of major stature in France, Paul Valéry (1871–1945) has been a widely influential commentator on the nature of poetry and the implied roles of the poet. The following "notes" formed the basis of a lecture delivered in late 1927; since that time, the phrase "pure poetry" has passed into the vocabulary of criticism and poetic theory. Among other things, this essay is notable for an analytic approach, combined with a rare speculative turn of mind, the whole being a particularly "French" statement on the problem central to all the word arts: the paradox that language which is necessarily used by all men, is equally necessarily the vehicle of artistic expression when it is exploited by the professional poet. Valéry's resolution of this problem and others invites comparison with the statements of I. A. Richards, in the essay that follows this one.

*Paul
Valéry*

Today there is a good deal of excitement in the world (I mean in the world of the most precious and most useless things) over these two words: *pure poetry*. I am somewhat responsible for this excitement. A few years ago, in a preface to a friend's book of poems, I happened to express these words without attaching any extreme importance to them and without foreseeing the conclusions that various persons concerned with poetry would draw from them. I knew quite well what I meant by those words, but I did not know that they would give rise to such reverberations and reactions among lovers of literature. I merely wanted to draw attention to a fact, and certainly not to set forth a theory or, worse yet, establish a doctrine and regard as heretics those who would not share it.

To my mind, every written work, every product of language, contains certain fragments or recognizable elements endowed with proper-

ties that we will examine and which I will provisionally call
poetic. Whenever speech exhibits *a certain deviation* from the
most direct expression—that is, the most *insensible* expression of
thought; whenever these deviations make us aware in some way
of a world of relationships distinct from purely practical reality,
we conceive more or less clearly of the possibility of enlarging
this exceptional area, and we have the sensation of seizing the
fragment of a noble and living substance which is perhaps capable
of development and cultivation; and which, once developed and
used, constitutes poetry in its artistic effect.

Whether it is possible to make a work of art consisting wholly
of these recognizable elements, so fully distinct from those of
the language I have called *insensible*—whether it is possible, consequently, in a work written in verse or otherwise, to give the
impression of a complete system of *reciprocal* relations between
our images and ideas on the one hand and our means of expression on the other, a system which would correspond especially
to the creation of an emotive state of mind—this, on the whole, is
the problem of pure poetry. I mean *pure* in the way in which
the doctor speaks of pure water. I mean that the question is to
know if we can bring about a work which would be *pure* of
elements that are not poetic. I have always held, and still do,
that this is an unattainable object, and that poetry is always an
effort to approach this purely ideal condition. In sum, what we
call a *poem* is made up in practice of fragments of *pure poetry*
inserted into the substance of a discourse. A very beautiful line
is a very pure element of poetry. The banal comparison of a
beautiful line to a diamond makes it clear that the feeling of this
quality of purity is in every mind.

The inconvenience of this phrase, *pure poetry*, is that it makes
one think of a moral purity which is not the issue here, for the
idea of pure poetry is for me, quite the contrary, an essentially
analytic idea. Pure poetry is, in sum, a fiction deduced from observation which should help us make precise our idea of poems
in general and guide us in the difficult and important study of
the diverse and multiform relations of language to the effects it
produces on men. It would, perhaps, be much better instead of
pure poetry to say *absolute poetry*, and we should then have to
understand it as a search for the effects resulting from the relationships of words, or rather of the interrelations of their reso-
nances, which suggests, in sum, *an exploration of the whole*

domain of the sensibility that is governed by language. This exploration might be made gropingly, for such is the way it is generally done. But it is not impossible that it may one day be carried out systematically.

I have tried to construct and I am trying to give a clear idea of the poetic problem or, at least, what I believe to be a *clearer* idea of this problem. It is remarkable that these questions should today arouse a widespread interest. Never, it seems, has so large a public been concerned. We can be present at discussions, we can see experiments that are not restricted, as in times past, to narrow cliques and to a very small number of amateurs and experimenters; but more wonderful yet, in our age we see even in the public at large a kind of interest, sometimes impassioned, attach itself to these almost theological discussions. (What can be more theological than to debate, for example, on inspiration and labor, on the value of intuition and of the artifices of art? Have we not here problems altogether comparable to the famous theological problem of grace and works? Likewise, there are problems in poetry which, opposing the rules that have been determined and fixed by tradition and the immediate data of personal experience or of personal meaning, are absolutely analogous to the problems that are similarly found in the domain of theology, between the personal meaning, the direct knowledge of divine things, and the teachings of various religions, the texts of the Scriptures and dogmatic forms. . . .)

But I come to the subject now with the firm intention of saying nothing that is a matter of sheer assertion or the result of light speculation. Let us go back to this word, "poetry," and let us observe first of all that this beautiful name engenders two distinct orders of concepts. We speak of "poetry" and we speak of "a poem." We say of a scene, a situation, and sometimes of a person, that they are *poetic;* on the other hand, we also speak of *the art of poetry* and we say: "This poem is beautiful." But in the first case we are concerned with the evidence of a certain kind of feeling; everyone is familiar with this peculiar trembling comparable to our condition when we feel ourselves excited, enchanted, by the effect of certain events. This condition is entirely independent of any determinate work of art and results naturally and spontaneously from a certain accord between our inner disposition, physical and psychic, and the circumstances (real or

ideal) which act on us. But on the other hand, when we say
the art of poetry or when we speak of *a poem* we are concerned
clearly with the means of bringing about a condition analogous
to the preceding condition, of artificially producing this kind of
feeling. And this is not all. The means which serve to bring about
this condition must be those which belong to the properties and
the mechanism of articulate language. The feeling which I spoke
of can be brought about by things. It can also be brought about
by means quite different from those of language, such as architecture, music, etc., but poetry properly named has as its essence
the use of the devices of language. As for independent poetic
feeling, let us observe that it is distinguished from other human
feelings by a singular character, an admirable property: that it
tends to give us the sense of an illusion or the illusion of a world
(of a *world* in which events, images, beings, things, if they do
resemble those which inhabit the ordinary world, are, on the
other hand, inexplicably but intimately related to the whole of
our sensibility). Known objects and beings are thus in some way
—forgive the expression—*musicalized;* they have become harmonious and resonant, and as if *in tune* with our sensibility.
Poetic experience defined in this way bears great similarities to
the dream state, or at least to the condition produced in certain
dreams. Dream, when we return to it through memory, makes us
understand that our consciousness can be awakened or filled, and
satisfied, by a whole range of productions that differ noticeably
in their laws from ordinary productions of perception. But this
emotive world that we can know at times through dream can
not be entered or left at will. *It is enclosed in us and we are enclosed in it,* which means that we have no way of acting on it
in order to modify it and that, on the other hand, it can not co-
exist with our great power of action over the external world. It
appears and disappears capriciously, but man has done for it
what he has done or tried to do for everything precious and
perishable: he has sought for and has found the means of recreat-
ing this condition at will, of regaining it when he wishes, and
finally, of artificially developing these natural products of his
sentient being. In some sort of way he has managed to extract
from nature and redeem from the blind movement of time these
formations or constructions that are so uncertain; in this design
he makes use of several devices which I have already mentioned.
Now, among these means of producing a poetic world, of repro-

ducing and enriching it, perhaps the most venerable and also the
most complex and the most difficult to use is language.

At this point I must make you feel or understand to what extent the task of the poet in the modern age is a delicate one, and
how many difficulties (of which, happily, he is not always aware)
the poet encounters in his task. Language is a common and practical element; it is thereby necessarily a coarse instrument, for
everyone handles and appropriates it according to his needs and
tends to deform it according to his personality. Language, no
matter how personal it may be or how close the way of thinking
in words may be to our spirit, is nevertheless *of statistical origin*
and has *purely practical ends.* Now the poet's problem must be
*to derive from this practical instrument the means of creating a
work essentially not practical.* As I have already told you, it is a
matter, for him, of creating a world or an order of things, a system of relations, without any relationship to the practical order.
   To make you understand all the difficulties of this task, I am
going to *compare the poet's gifts with those of the musician.*
How fortunate is the musician! The evolution of his art has
given him an altogether privileged position for centuries. What
does music consist of? The sense of hearing gives us *the universe
of noises.* Our ear admits an infinite number of sensations that it
receives in some kind of order and of which it can single out four
distinct qualities. Now ancient observations and very old experiments have made it possible to deduce, from *the universe of
noises,* the system or *the universe of sounds*—which are particularly simple and recognizable noises, particularly prone to form
combinations, associations, whose structure, sequence, differences
or resemblances are perceived by the ear, or rather by the understanding, as soon as they are produced. These elements are pure
or are composed of pure—that is to say, recognizable—elements.
They are sharply defined and—a very important point—the way
has been found to produce them in a constant and identical manner by means of instruments which are, basically, true instruments of measure. A musical instrument is one that can be gauged
and used in such a way that from given actions a given result can
be uniformly obtained. And here we see the remarkable result
of this organization of the province of hearing: as the world of
sounds is quite separate from that of noises, and as our ear is

also accustomed to distinguishing them clearly, it follows that *if a pure sound*—that is, a relatively exceptional sound—*happens to be heard, at once a particular atmosphere is created, a particular state of expectation is produced in our senses, and this expectation tends,* to some degree, *to give rise to sensations of the same kind, of the same purity, as the sensation produced.* If a pure sound is produced in a concert hall, *everything is changed within us;* we await the production of music. If, on the contrary, the reverse is tried; if during the performance of a composition in a concert hall a noise should be heard (a falling chair, the voice or cough of a listener), at once we feel that something inside us has been broken, there has been a violation of some sort of substance or law of association; *a universe is shattered,* a charm is wiped out.

Thus for the musician, before he has begun his work, all is in readiness so that the operation of his creative spirit may find, right from the start, the appropriate matter and means, without any possibility of error. He will not have to make this matter and means submit to any modification; he need only assemble elements which are clearly defined and ready-made.

But in how different a situation is the poet! Before him is ordinary language, this aggregate of means which are not suited to his purpose, not made for him. There have not been physicians to determine the relationships of these means for him; there have not been constructors of scales; no diapason, no metronome, no certitude of this kind. He has nothing but the coarse instrument of the dictionary and the grammar. Moreover, he must address himself not to a special and unique sense like *hearing,* which the musician bends to his will, and which is, besides, the organ *par excellence* of expectation and attention; but rather to a general and diffused expectation, and he does so through a language which is a very odd mixture of incoherent *stimuli.* Nothing is more complex, more difficult to make out, than the strange combination of qualities that exists in language. Everyone knows quite well how rare indeed are the agreements *of sound and sense;* and moreover, we all know that a discourse can develop qualities altogether different. A discourse can be logical and completely void of harmony; it can be harmonious and insignificant: it can be clear and lacking in any sort of beauty; it can be prose or poetry; and it is enough, to sum up all of these independent modes, to mention the various sciences which have been created to exploit this diversity of language and to study it under different aspects. Language is subject, in turn, to *phonetics*, along with *metrics* and *rhythm;* it has a *logical* aspect and a *semantic* aspect; it includes *rhetoric* and *syntax*. We know that all these diverse disciplines can be brought to bear on the same text in many mutually exclusive ways. . . . Here we have the poet come to grips with this ensemble so diverse and so rich in initial capacities; too rich, in sum, not to be confused. It is from it that he must draw his *art object*, the contrivance to produce poetic emotion—that is, he must force the practical instrument, the coarse instrument created by anyone at all, the instrument of every moment, used for immediate needs and modified at every instant by the living, to become, for the time that his attention gives to the poem, the substance of a selected emotive condition, quite distinct from all of the accidental conditions of indeterminate length which make up ordinary sensory or psychic existence. We can say without exaggeration that the common language is the fruit of the disorder of common life, because men of every sort, subject to an innumerable quantity of conditions and needs, receive it and make use of it as best they can for their desires and their interests so as to make possible relations between them; while the language of the poet, although he necessarily makes use of the elements furnished by this statistical disorder, constitutes, on the contrary, *an effort of man in isolation* to create an artificial and ideal order by means of a substance of vulgar origin.

If this paradoxical problem could be wholly resolved; that is, if the poet could manage to construct works where nothing that partakes of prose would be present—poems where the musical continuity would never be interrupted, where the relationships of meanings would be themselves forever like harmonica relations, *where the transmutation of thoughts from one into the other would be more important than any thought*, where the play of figures would contain the reality of the Subject—then we could talk about *pure poetry* as though it existed. Such is not the case: the practical or pragmatic part of language, the logical habits and forms and, as I have indicated, the disorder, the irrationality that we find in the vocabulary (because of infinitely various derivations from very different ages in which the elements of the language were introduced) make the existence of these creations of absolute poetry impossible; but it is easy to conceive that the notion of such an ideal or imaginary condition is very precious for the appreciation of all observable poetry.

The conception of pure poetry is one of an inaccessible kind, of an ideal limit of the desires, the efforts, and the powers of the poet. . . .

POETRY AND BELIEFS

After World War I, most notably in England, the nature of both poetry and criticism underwent a new kind of scrutiny. In addition to speculations by such poets as Eliot and Pound, many contributions —and indeed attacks—came from other disciplines, from philosophy, semantics, and most cogently from the emergent field of psychology. The most exciting comments, often directed at the fundamentals of imaginative writing, came from the Cambridge professor and poet I. A. Richards (1893–), whose analytical methods essentially begot the whole school of the "New Criticism." The following essay is a chapter from one of his most influential works, Principles of Literary Criticism *(1924).*

*I. A.
Richards*

What I see very well is the wide-spread, infinite harm of putting fancy for knowledge (to speak like Socrates), or rather of living by choice in a twilight of the mind where fancy and knowledge are indiscernible.—*Euripides the Rationalist.*

It is evident that the bulk of poetry consists of statements which only the very foolish would think of attempting to verify. They are not the kind of things which can be verified. If we recall what was said in [an earlier chapter] as to the natural generality or vagueness of reference we shall see another reason why references as they occur in poetry are rarely susceptible of scientific truth or falsity. Only references which are brought into certain highly complex and very special combinations, so as to correspond to the ways in which things actually hang together, can be either true or false, and most references in poetry are not knit together in this way.

But even when they are, on examination, frankly false, this is no defect. Unless, indeed, the obviousness of the falsity forces the reader to reactions which are incongruent or disturbing to the poem. And equally, a point more often misunderstood, their truth, when they are true, is no merit.[1] The people who say 'How True!' at intervals while reading Shakespeare are misusing his work, and, comparatively speaking, wasting their time. For all that matters in either case is acceptance, that is to say, the initiation and development of the further response.

Poetry affords the clearest examples of this subordination of reference to attitude. It is the supreme form of *emotive* language. But there can be no doubt that originally all language was emotive; its scientific use is a later development, and most language is still emotive. Yet the late development has come to seem the natural and the normal use, largely because the only people who have reflected upon language were at the moment of reflection using it scientifically.

The emotions and attitudes resulting from a statement used emotively need not be directed towards anything to which the statement refers. This is clearly evident in dramatic poetry, but much more poetry than is usually supposed is dramatic in structure. As a rule a statement in poetry arouses attitudes much more wide and general in direction than the references of the statement. Neglect of this fact makes most verbal analysis of poetry irrelevant. And the same is true of those critical but emotive utterances about poetry which gave rise to this discussion. No one, it is plain, can read poetry successfully, without, consciously or unconsciously, observing the distinction between the two uses of words. That does not need to be insisted upon. But further no one can understand such utterances about poetry as that quoted from Dr. Mackail in [an earlier] chapter, or Dr. Bradley's cry that "Poetry is a spirit", or Shelley's that "A poem is the very image of life expressed in its eternal truth", or the passages quoted above from Coleridge, without distinguishing the making of a statement from the incitement or expression of an attitude. But too much inferior poetry has been poured out

---

[1] No merit, that is, *in this connection*. There may be some exceptions to this, cases in which the explicit recognition of the truth of a statement as opposed to the simple acceptance of it, is *necessary* to the full development of the further response. But I believe that such cases will on careful examination be found to be very rare which competent readers. Individual differences, corresponding to the different degrees to which individuals have their belief feelings, their references, and their attitudes entangled, are to be expected. There are, of course, an immense number of scientific beliefs present among the conditions of every attitude. But since acceptances would do equally well in their place they are not *necessary* to it.

as criticism, too much sack and too little bread; confusion between the two activities, on the part of writers and readers alike, is what is primarily responsible for the backwardness of critical studies. What other stultifications of human endeavour it is also responsible for we need not linger here to point out. The separation of prose from poetry, if we may so paraphrase the distinction, is no mere academic activity. There is hardly a problem outside mathematics which is not complicated by its neglect, and hardly any emotional response which is not crippled by irrelevant intrusions. No revolution in human affairs would be greater than that which a wide-spread observance of this distinction would bring about.

One perversion in especial needs to be noticed. It is constantly present in critical discussion, and is in fact responsible for Revelation Doctrines. Many attitudes, which arise without dependence upon any reference, merely by the interplay and resolution of impulses otherwise awakened, can be momentarily encouraged by suitable beliefs held as scientific beliefs are held. So far as this encouragement is concerned, the truth or falsity of these beliefs does not matter, the immediate effect is the same in either case. When the attitude is important, the temptation to base it upon some reference which is treated as established scientific truths are treated is very great, and the poet thus easily comes to invite the destruction of his work; Wordsworth puts forward his Pantheism, and other people doctrines of Inspiration, Idealism and Revelation.

The effect is twofold; an appearance of security and stability is given to the attitude, which thus seems to be justified; and at the same time it is no longer so necessary to sustain this attitude by the more difficult means peculiar to the arts, or to pay full attention to form. The reader can be relied upon to do more than his share. That neither effect is desirable is easily seen. The attitude for the sake of which the belief is introduced is thereby made not more but less stable. Remove the belief, once it has affected the attitude; the attitude collapses. It may later be restored by more appropriate means, but that is another matter. And all such beliefs are very likely to be removed; their logical connections with other beliefs scientifically entertained are, to say the least, shaky. In the second place these attitudes, produced not by the appropriate means but, as it were by a short cut, through beliefs, are rarely so healthy, so vigorous and full of life as the others. Unlike attitudes normally produced they usually require an increased stimulus every time that they are reinstated. The belief has to grow more and more fervent, more and more convinced, in order to produce the same attitude. The believer has to pass from one paroxysm of conviction to another, enduring each time a greater strain.

This substitution of an intellectual formula for the poem or work of art is of course most easily observed in the case of religion, where the temptation is greatest. In place of an experience, which is a direct response to a certain selection of the possibilities of stimulation, we have a highly indirect response, made, not to the actual influences of the world upon us, but to a special kind of belief as to some particular state of affairs.[2] There is a suppressed conditional clause implicit in all poetry. If things were such and such then . . . and so the response develops. The amplitude and fineness of the response, its sanction and authority, in other words, depend upon this freedom from actual assertion in all cases in which the belief is questionable on any ground whatsoever. For any such assertion involves suppressions, of indefinite extent, which may be fatal to the wholeness, the *integrity* of the experience. And the assertion is almost always unnecessary; if we look closely we find that the greatest poets, as poets, though frequently not as critics, refrain from assertion. But it is easy, by what seems only a slight change of approach, to make the initial step an act of faith, and to make the whole response dependent upon a belief as to a matter of fact. Even when the belief is true, the damage done to the whole experience may be great, in the case of a person whose reasons for this belief are inadequate, for example, and the increased temporary vivacity which is the cause of perversion is no sufficient compensation. As a convenient example it may be permissible to refer to the Poet Laureate's anthology, *The Spirit of Man*, and I have the less hesitation since the passages there gathered together are chosen with such unerring taste and discrimination. But to turn them into a statement of a philosophy is very noticeably to degrade them and to re-

---

[2] In view of a possible misunderstanding at this point, compare Chapter X, especially the final paragraph. If a belief in Retributive Justice, for example, is fatal to *Prometheus Unbound*, so in another way is the belief that the Millennium is at hand. To steer an unperplexed path between these opposite dangers is extremely difficult. The distinctions required are perhaps better left to the reader's reflection than laboured further in the faulty terminology which alone at present is available.

strict and diminish their value. The use of verse quotations as
chapter headings is open to the same objection. The experiences
which ensue may seem very similar to the experiences of free
reading; they feel similar; but all signs which can be most trusted,
after-effects for example, show them to be different. The vast
differences in the means by which they are brought about is also
good ground for supposing them to be dissimilar, but this difference is obscured through the ambiguities of the term 'belief'.

There are few terms which are more troublesome in psychology than belief, formidable though this charge may seem.
The sense in which we believe a scientific proposition is not the
sense in which we believe emotive utterances, whether they are
political 'We will not sheathe the sword', or critical 'The progress of poetry is immortal', or poetic. Both senses of belief are
complicated and difficult to define. Yet we commonly appear to
assume that they are the same or that they differ only in the
kind and degree of evidence available. Scientific belief we may
perhaps define as readiness to act as though the reference symbolised by the proposition which is believed were true. Readiness
to act in *all* circumstances and in *all* connections into which it
can enter. This rough definition would, of course, need elaborat-
ing to be complete, but for our present purposes it may suffice.
The other element usually included in a definition of belief,
namely a feeling or emotion of acceptance, the 'This is sooth,
accept it!' feeling, is often absent in scientific belief and is not
essential.

Emotive belief is very different. Readiness to act as though
some references were true is often involved, but the connections
and circumstances in which this readiness remains are narrowly
restricted. Similarly the extent of the action is ordinarily limited. Consider the acceptances involved in the understanding of a
play, for example. They form a system any element of which is
believed while the rest are believed and so long as the acceptance
of the whole growing system leads to successful response. Some,
however, are of the form 'Given this then that would follow',
general beliefs, that is to say, of the kind which led Aristotle, in
the passage quoted above, to describe Poetry as a more philosophical thing than history because chiefly conversant of universal truth. But if we look closely into most instances of such
beliefs we see that they are entertained only in the special circumstances of the poetic experience. They are held as condi-

tions for further effects, our attitudes and emotional responses, and not as we hold beliefs in laws of nature, which we expect to find verified on all occasions. If dramatic necessities were actually scientific laws we should know much more psychology than any reasonable person pretends that we do. That these beliefs as to "how any person of a certain character would speak or act, probably or necessarily", upon which so much drama seems to depend, are not scientific, but are held only for the sake of their dramatic effect, is shown clearly by the ease with which we abandon them if the advantage lies the other way. The medical impossibility of Desdemona's last speech is perhaps as good an example as any.

The bulk of the beliefs involved in the arts are of this kind, provisional acceptances, holding only in special circumstances (in the state of mind which is the poem or work of art) acceptances made for the sake of the 'imaginative experience' which they make possible. The difference between these emotive beliefs and scientific beliefs is not one of degree but of kind. As feelings they are very similar, but as attitudes their difference in structure has widespread consequences.

There remains to be discussed another set of emotive effects which may also be called beliefs. Instead of occurring part way in, or at the beginning of a response, they come as a rule at the end, and thus are less likely to be confused with scientific beliefs. Very often the whole state of mind in which we are left by a poem, or by music, or, more rarely perhaps, by other forms of art, is of a kind which it is natural to describe as a belief. When all provisional acceptances have lapsed, when the single references and their connections which may have led up to the final response are forgotten, we may still have an attitude and an emotion which has to introspection all the characters of a belief. This belief, which is a consequence not a cause of the experience, is the chief source of the confusion upon which Revelation Doctrines depend.

If we ask what in such cases it is which is believed, we are likely to receive, and to offer, answers both varied and vague. For strong belief-feelings, as is well known and as is shown by certain doses of alcohol or hashish, and pre-eminently of nitrous oxide, will readily attach themselves to almost any reference, distorting it to suit their purpose. Few people without experience of the nitrous-oxide revelation have any conception of their capacity for believing or of the extent to which belief-feelings and attitudes are parasitic. Thus when, through reading *Adonais,* for example, we are left in a strong emotional attitude which feels like belief, it is only too easy to think that we are believing in immortality or survival, or in something else capable of statement, and fatally easy also to attribute the value of the poem to the alleged effect, or conversely to regret that it should depend upon such a scientifically doubtful conclusion. Scientific beliefs, as opposed to these emotive beliefs, are beliefs '*that* so and so'. They can be stated with greater or less precision, as the case may be, but always in some form. It is for some people difficult to admit beliefs which are objectless, which are not about anything or in anything; beliefs which cannot be stated. Yet most of the beliefs of children and primitive peoples, and of the unscientific generally seems to be of this kind. Their parasitic nature helps to confuse the issue. What we have to distinguish are beliefs which are grounded in fact, i.e., are due to reference, and beliefs which are due to other causes, and merely attach themselves to such references as will support them.

That an objectless belief is a ridiculous or an incomplete thing is a prejudice deriving only from confusion. Such beliefs have, of course, no place in science, but in themselves they are often of the utmost value. Provided always that they do not furnish themselves with illicit objects. It is the objectless belief which is masquerading as a belief in this or that, which is ridiculous; more often than not it is also a serious nuisance. When they are kept from tampering with the development of reference such emotional attitudes may be, as revelation doctrines in such strange forms maintain, among the most important and valuable effects which the arts can produce.

It is often held that recent generations suffer more from nervous strain than some at least of their predecessors, and many reasons for this have been suggested. Certainly the types of nervous disease most prevalent seem to have changed. An explanation not sufficiently noticed perhaps is the break-down of traditional accounts of the universe, and the strain imposed by the vain attempt to orient the mind by belief of the scientific kind alone. In the pre-scientific era, the devout adherent to the Catholic account of the world, for example, found a sufficient basis for nearly all his main attitudes in what he took to be scientific truth. It would be fairer to say that the difference between

ascertained fact and acceptable fiction did not obtrude itself for
him. To-day this is changed, and if he believes such an account,
he does not do so, if intelligent, without considerable difficulty
or without a fairly persistent strain. The complete sceptic, of
course, is a new phenomenon, dissenters in the past having commonly disbelieved only because they held a different belief of the
same kind. These topics have, it is true, been touched upon by
psycho-analysts, but not with a very clear understanding of the
situation. The Vienna School would merely have us [do?] away
with antiquated lumber; the Zurich School would hand us a new
outfit of superstitions. Actually what is needed is a habit of
mind which allows both reference and the development of attitudes their proper independence. This habit of mind is not to be
attained at once, or for most people with ease. We try desperately
to support our attitudes with beliefs as to facts, verified or accepted as scientifically established, and by so doing we weaken
our own emotional backbone. For the justification of any attitude *per se* is its success for the needs of the being. It is not
justified by the soundness of the views which may seem to be,
and in pathological cases are, its ground and causes. The source
of our attitudes should be in experience itself; compare Whitman's praise of the cow which does not worry about its soul.
Opinion as to matters of fact, knowledge, belief, are not necessarily involved in any of our attitudes to the world in general,
or to particular phases of it. If we bring them in, if, by a psychological perversion only too easy to fall into, we make them the
basis of our adjustment, we run extreme risks of later disorgani-
sation elsewhere.

Many people find great difficulty in accepting or even in understanding this position. They are so accustomed to regarding
'recognised facts' as the natural basis of attitudes, that they
cannot conceive how anyone can be otherwise organised. The
hard-headed positivist and the convinced adherent of a religion
from opposite sides encounter the same difficulty. The first at
the best suffers from an insufficient material for the development of his attitudes; the second from intellectual bondage and
unconscious insincerity. The one starves himself; the other is
like the little pig in the fable who chose to have his house built
of cabbages and ate it, and so the grim wolf with privy paw
devoured him. For clear and impartial awareness of the nature
of the world in which we live and the development of attitudes

which will enable us to live in it finely are both necessities, and neither can be subordinated to the other. They are almost independent, such connections as exist in well-organised individuals being adventitious. Those who find this a hard saying may be invited to consider the effect upon them of those works of art which most unmistakably attune them to existence. The central experience of Tragedy and its chief value is an attitude indispensable for a fully developed life. But in the reading of *King Lear* what facts verifiable by science, or accepted and believed in as we accept and believe in ascertained facts, are relevant? None whatever. Still more clearly in the experiences of some music, of some architecture and of some abstract design, attitudes are evoked and developed which are unquestionably independent of all beliefs as to fact, and these are exceptional only in being protected by accident from the most insidious perversion to which the mind is liable. For the intermingling of knowledge and belief is indeed a perversion, through which both activities suffer degradation.

These objectless beliefs, which though merely attitudes seem to be knowledge, are not difficult to explain. Some system of impulses not ordinarily in adjustment within itself or adjusted to the world finds something which orders it or gives it fit exercise. Then follows the peculiar sense of ease, of restfulness, of free, unimpeded activity, and the feeling of acceptance, of something more positive than acquiescence. This feeling is the reason why such states may be called beliefs. They share this feeling with, for example, the state which follows the conclusive answering of a question. Most attitude-adjustments which are successful possess it in some degree, but those which are very regular and familiar, such as sitting down to meat or stretching out in bed, naturally tend to lose it. But when the required attitude has been long needed, where its coming is unforeseen and the manner in which it is brought about complicated and inexplicable, where we know no more than that formerly we were unready and that now we are ready for life in some particular phase, the feeling which results may be intense. Such are the occasions upon which the arts seem to lift away the burden of existence, and we seem ourselves to be looking into the heart of things. To be seeing whatever it is as it really is, to be cleared in vision and to be recipients of a revelation.

We have considered already the details of these states of consciousness and their conjectural impulse basis. We can now take this feeling of a revealed significance, this attitude of readiness, acceptance and understanding, which has led to so many Revelation Doctrines, not as actually implying knowledge, but for what it is—the conscious accompaniment of our successful adjustment to life. But it is, we must admit, no certain sign by itself that our adjustment is adequate or admirable. Even the most firm adherents to Revelation Doctrines admit that there are bogus revelations, and on our account it is equally important to distinguish between 'feelings of significance' which indicate that all is well and those which do not. In a sense all indicate that *something* is going well, otherwise there would be no acceptance, no belief but rejection. The real question is 'What is it?' Thus after the queer reshuffling of inhibitions and releases which follows the taking of a dose of alcohol, for example, the sense of revelation is apt to occur with unusual authority. Doubtless this feeling of significance is a sign that as the organism is for the moment, its affairs are for the moment thriving. But when the momentary special condition of the system has given place to the more usual, more stable and more generally advantageous adjustment, the authority of the vision falls away from it; we find that what we were doing is by no means so wonderful or so desirable as we thought and that our belief was nonsensical. So it is less noticeably with many moments in which the world seems to be showing its real face to us.

The chief difficulty of all Revelation Doctrines has always been to discover what it is which is revealed. If these states of mind are knowledge it should be possible to state what it is that they know. It is often easy enough to find something which we can suppose to be what we know. Belief feelings, we have seen, are *parasitic*, and will attach themselves to all kinds of hosts. In literature it is especially easy to find hosts. But in music, in the non-representative arts of design, in architecture or ceramics, for example, the task of finding something to believe, or to believe in, is not so easy. Yet the 'feeling of significance' is as common[3] in these other arts as in literature. Denial of this is usually proof only of an interest limited to literature.

[3] Cf. Gurney, *The Power of Sound*, p. 126. "A splendid melodic phrase seems continually not like an object of sense, but like an *affirmation;* not so much prompting admiring ejaculation as compelling passionate assent." His explanation, through

This difficulty has usually been met by asserting that the alleged knowledge given in the revelation is non-intellectual. It refuses to be rationalised, it is said. Well and good; but if so why call it knowledge? Either it is capable of corroborating or of conflicting with the other things we usually call knowledge, such as the laws of thermodynamics, capable of being stated and brought into connection with what else we know; or it is not knowledge, not capable of being stated. We cannot have it both ways, and no sneers at the limitations of logic, the commonest of the resources of the confused, amend the dilemma. In fact it resembles knowledge only in being an attitude and a feeling very similar to some attitudes and feelings which may and often do accompany knowledge. But 'Knowledge' is an immensely potent emotive word engendering reverence towards any state of mind to which it is applied. And these 'feelings of significance' are those among our states of mind which most deserve to be revered. That they should be so obstinately described as knowledge even by those who most carefully remove from them all the characteristics of knowledge is not surprising.

Traditionally what is said to be known thus mystically through the arts is Beauty, a remote and divine entity not otherwise to be apprehended, one of the Eternal Absolute Values. And this is doubtless emotively a way of talking which is effective for a while. When its power abates, as the power of such utterances will, there are several developments which may easily be used to revive it. "Beauty is eternal, and we may say that it is already manifest as a heavenly thing—the beauty of Nature is indeed an earnest [proof] to us of the ultimate goodness which lies behind the apparent cruelty and moral confusion of organic life. . . . Yet we feel that these three are ultimately one, and human speech bears constant witness to the universal conviction that Goodness is beautiful, that Beauty is good, that Truth is Beauty. We can hardly avoid the use of the word 'trinity', and if we are theists at all we cannot but say that they are one, because they are the manifestation of one God. If we are not theists there is no explanation."[4]

---

association with speech, seems to me inadequate. He adds that the use of terms such as *"expressiveness* and *significance,* as opposed to meaninglessness and triviality, may be allowed, without the implication of any reference to transcendental views which one may fail to understand, or theories of interpretation which one may entirely repudiate."

[4] Percy Dearmer, *The Necessity of Art*, p. 180.

Human speech is indeed the witness, and to what else does it not witness? It would be strange if in a matter of such moment as this the greatest of all emotive words did not come into play. "In religion we believe that God is Beauty and Life, that God is Truth and Light, that God is Goodness and Love, and that because he is all these they are all one, and the Trinity in Unity and Unity in Trinity is to be worshipped."[5] No one who can interpret emotive language, who can avoid the temptation to illicit belief so constantly presented by it need find such utterances 'meaningless.' But the wrong approach is easy and far too often pressingly invited by the speakers, labouring themselves under misconceptions. To excite a serious and reverent attitude is one thing. To set forth an explanation is another. To confuse the two and mistake the incitement of an attitude for a statement of fact is a practice which should be discouraged. For intellectual dishonesty is an evil which is the more dangerous the more it is hedged about with emotional sanctities. And after all there *is* another explanation, which would long ago have been quietly established to the world's great good had men been less ready to sacrifice the integrity of their thought and feeling for the sake of a local and limited advantage.

The last movement of this machine to think with is now completed. I am too well acquainted with it, and have spent too many hours putting it together to suppose that it can be worked equally well by every reader. Half these hours have in fact been spent in simplifying its structure, in taking out reservations and qualifications, references to other views, controversial matter, and supernumerary distinctions. From one point of view, it would be a better book with these left in, but I wished to make it manageable by those who had not spent a quite disproportionate amount of energy in reflection upon abstract matters. And if to some readers parts of it appear unnecessary—either *irrelevant*, in the one case, or *over-obvious* in the other—I have nothing to add which would make them change their opinion. The first I can only ask to look again, with the hope that a connection which has been missed will be noticed. The second, I would remind that I write in an age when, in the majority of social circles, to be seriously interested in art is to be thought an oddity.

[5] A. W. Pollard, *ibidem*, p. 135.

*W. H. Auden (1907–) came to prominence as
one of a group of new writers at Oxford University
in the early 1930s. Now a widely honored
professional poet, Auden is an American citizen and
a long-time resident of New York City. The essay
which follows is highly personal but, by intention,
also suggests a kind of allegory on the literary and
social processes that help bring a poetic talent to
maturity. In this connection, it is interesting to
speculate on the nature and the function of the
"Censor" which is mentioned several times in the
text. The student who might himself wish to
write will find cogent, witty advice on the
matters of apprenticeship, imitation, and the
kinds of reading best calculated to help the
emerging poet.*

MAKING, KNOWING, AND JUDGING

W. H.
Auden

I began writing poetry myself
because one Sunday afternoon in March 1922, a
friend suggested that I should: the thought had
never occurred to me. I scarcely knew any poems
—*The English Hymnal*, the *Psalms*, *Struwwel-
peter* and the mnemonic rhymes in *Kennedy's
Shorter Latin Primer* are about all I remember—
and I took little interest in what is called Imaginative Literature. Most of my reading had been
related to a private world of Sacred Objects. Aside
from a few stories like George MacDonald's *The
Princess and the Goblin* and Jules Verne's *The
Child of the Cavern*, the subjects of which
touched upon my obsessions, my favourite books
bore such titles as *Underground Life, Machinery
for Metalliferous Mines, Lead and Zinc Ores of
Northumberland and Alston Moor*, and my conscious purpose in reading them had been to gain
information about my sacred objects. At the
time, therefore, the suggestion that I write
poetry seemed like a revelation from heaven for
which nothing in my past could account.

Looking back, however, I now realize that I had read the technological prose of my favourite books in a peculiar way. A word
like *pyrites*, for example, was for me, not simply an indicative
sign; it was the Proper Name of a Sacred Being, so that, when I
heard an aunt pronounce it *pirrits*, I was shocked. Here pronunciation was more than wrong, it was ugly. Ignorance was
impiety.

It was Edward Lear, I believe, who said that the true test of
imagination is the ability to name a cat, and we are told in the
first chapter of *Genesis* that the Lord brought to unfallen Adam
all the creatures that he might name them and whatsoever Adam
called every living creature, that was the name thereof, which
is to say, its Proper Name. Here Adam plays the role of the
Proto-poet, not the Proto-prosewriter. A Proper Name must
not only refer, it must refer aptly and this aptness must be
publicly recognizable. It is curious to observe, for instance, that
when a person has been christened inaptly, he and his friends
instinctively call him by some other name. Like a line of poetry,
a Proper Name is untranslatable. Language is prosaic to the degree that 'It does not matter what particular word is associated
with an idea, provided the association once made is permament.'[1]
Language is poetic to the degree that it does matter.

The power of verse [writes Valéry] is derived from an indefinable
harmony between what it *says* and what it *is*. Indefinable is essential
to the definition. The harmony ought not to be definable, when it can
be defined it is imitative harmony and that is not good. The impossibility of defining the relation, together with the impossibility of
denying it, constitutes the essence of the poetic line.[2]

The poet is someone, says Mallarmé, who 'de plusieurs vocables
refait un mot total'[3] and the most poetical of all scholastic disciplines is, surely, Philology, the study of language in abstraction
from its uses so that words become, as it were, little lyrics about
themselves.

Since Proper Names in the grammatical sense refer to unique
objects, we cannot judge their aptness without personal acquaintance with what they name. To know whether *Old Foss* was an

1 George Boule, *An Investigation of the Laws of Thought.*
2 *Tel Quel,* ii.
3 *Divagations,* Crise de Vers.

apt name for Lear's cat, we should have had to have known
them both. A line of poetry like

A drop of water in the breaking gulf[4]

is a name for an experience we all know so that we can judge
its aptness, and it names, as a Proper Name cannot, relations and
actions as well as things. But Shakespeare and Lear are both
using language in the same way and, I believe, for the same
motive, but into that I shall go later. My present point is that,
if my friend's suggestion met with such an unexpected response,
the reason may have been that, without knowing it, I had been
enjoying the poetic use of language for a long time.

A beginner's efforts cannot be called bad or imitative. They
are imaginary. A bad poem has this or that fault which can be
pointed out; an imitative poem is a recognizable imitation of this
or that poem, this or that poet. But about an imaginary poem
no criticism can be made since it is an imitation of poetry-in-
general. Never again will a poet feel so inspired, so certain of
genius, as he feels in these first days as his pencil flies across the
page. Yet something is being learned even now. As he scribbles
on he is beginning to get the habit of noticing metrical quantities,
to see that any two-syllable word in isolation must be either a
ti-tum, a *tum-ti* or, occasionally, a *tum-tum*, but that when associated with other words it can sometimes become a *ti-ti;* when
he discovers a rhyme he has not thought of before, he stores
it away in his memory, a habit which an Italian poet may not
need to acquire but which an English poet will find useful.

And, though as yet he can only scribble, he has started reading
real poems for pleasure and on purpose. Many things can be said
against anthologies, but for an adolescent to whom even the
names of most of the poets are unknown, a good one can be
an invaluable instructor. I had the extraordinary good fortune to
be presented one Christmas with the De La Mare anthology
Come Hither. This had, for my purposes, two great virtues.
Firstly, its good taste. Reading it today, I find very few poems
which I should have omitted and none which I should think
it bad taste to admire. Secondly, its catholic taste. Given the
youthful audience for which it was designed, there were certain
kinds of poetry which it did not represent, but within those

[4] *Comedy of Errors*, II. 2.

limits the variety was extraordinary. Particularly valuable was
its lack of literary class-consciousness, its juxtaposition on terms
of equality of unofficial poetry, such as counting-out rhymes,
and official poetry such as the odes of Keats. It taught me at the
start that poetry does not have to be great or even serious to be
good, and that one does not have to be ashamed of moods in
which one feels no desire whatsoever to read *The Divine Comedy*
and a great desire to read

> When other ladies to the shades go down,
> Still Flavia, Chloris, Celia stay in town.
> These Ghosts of Beauty ling'ring there abide,
> And haunt the places where their Honour died.[5]

Matthew Arnold's notion of Touchstones by which to measure
all poems has always struck me as a doubtful one, likely to turn
readers into snobs and to ruin talented poets by tempting them
to imitate what is beyond their powers.

A poet who wishes to improve himself should certainly keep
good company, but for his profit as well as for his comfort the
company should not be too far above his station. It is by no
means clear that the poetry which influenced Shakespeare's development most fruitfully was the greatest poetry with which
he was acquainted. Even for readers, when one thinks of the
attention that a great poem demands, there is something frivolous
about the notion of spending every day with one. Masterpieces
should be kept for High Holidays of the Spirit.

I am not trying to defend the aesthetic heresy that one subject
is no more important than any other, or that a poem has no
subject or that there is no difference between a great poem
and a good one—a heresy which seems to me contrary to human
feeling and common sense—but I can understand why it exists.
Nothing is worse than a bad poem which was intended to be
great.

So a would-be poet begins to learn that poetry is more various
than he imagined and that he can like and dislike different poems
for different reasons. His Censor, however, has still not yet been
born. Before he can give birth to him, he has to pretend to be
somebody else; he has to get a literary transference upon some
poet in particular.

---

[5] Alexander Pope, *Epigram.*

If poetry were in great public demand so that there were over-worked professional poets, I can imagine a system under which an established poet would take on a small number of apprentices who would begin by changing his blotting paper, advance to typing his manuscripts and end up by ghost-writing poems for him which he was too busy to start or finish. The apprentices might really learn something for, knowing that he would get the blame as well as the credit for their work, the Master would be extremely choosey about his apprentices and do his best to teach them all he knew.

In fact, of course, a would-be poet serves his apprenticeship in a library. This has its advantages. Though the Master is deaf and dumb and gives neither instruction nor criticism, the apprentice can choose any Master he likes, living or dead, the Master is available at any hour of the day or night, lessons are all for free, and his passionate admiration of his Master will ensure that he work hard to please him.

To please means to imitate and it is impossible to do a recognizable imitation of a poet without attending to every detail of his diction, rhythms and habits of sensibility. In imitating his Master, the apprentice acquires a Censor for he learns that, no matter how he finds it, by inspiration, by potluck or after hours of laborious search, there is only one word or rhythm or form that is the *right* one. The right one is still not yet the *real* one, for the apprentice is ventriloquizing but he has got away from poetry-in-general; he is learning how *a* poem is written. Later in life, incidentally, he will realize how important is the art of imitation, for he will not infrequently be called upon to imitate himself.

My first Master was Thomas Hardy, and I think I was very lucky in my choice. He was a good poet, perhaps a great one, but not *too* good. Much as I loved him, even I could see that his diction was often clumsy and forced and that a lot of his poems were plain bad. This gave me hope where a flawless poet might have made me despair. He was modern without being too modern. His world and sensibility were close enough to mine—curiously enough his face bore a striking resemblance to my father's—so that, in imitating him, I was being led towards not away from myself, but they were not so close as to obliterate my identity. If I looked through his spectacles, at least I was conscious of a certain eye-strain. Lastly, his metrical variety, his fondness for complicated stanza forms, were an invaluable training in the craft of making. I am also thankful that my first Master did not write in free verse or I might then have been tempted to believe that free verse is easier to write than stricter forms, whereas I know it is infinitely more difficult.

Presently the curtain rises on a scene rather like the finale to Act II of *Die Meistersinger*, the setting of which in my own memories is geographically close to this afternoon. Let us call it The Gathering of the Apprentices. The apprentices gather together from all over and discover that they are a new generation; somebody shouts the word 'modern' and the riot is on. The New Iconoclastic Poets and Critics are discovered—when I was an undergraduate a critic could still describe Mr. T. S. Eliot, O.M., as 'a drunken helot'—the poetry which these new authorities recommend becomes the Canon, that on which they frown is thrown out of the window. There are gods whom it is blasphemy to criticize and devils whose names may not be mentioned without execrations. The apprentices have seen a great light while their tutors sit in darkness and the shadow of death.

Really, how do the dons stand it, for I'm sure this scene repeats itself year after year. When I recall the kindness of our tutors, the patience with which they listened, the courtesy with which they hid their boredom, I am overwhelmed by their sheer goodness. I suppose that, having got there, they knew that the road of excess can lead to the palace of Wisdom, though it frequently does not.

An apprentice discovers that there is a significant relation between the statement 'Today I am nineteen' and the statement 'Today is February the twenty-first, 1926'. If the discovery goes to his head, it is, nevertheless, a discovery he must make for, until he realizes that all the poems he has read, however different they may be, have one common characteristic, they have all been written, his own writing will never cease to be imitative. He will never know what he himself *can write* until he has a general sense of what *needs to be written*. And this is the one thing his elders cannot teach him, just because they are his elders; he can only learn it from his fellow apprentices with whom he shares one thing in common, they are contemporaries.

The discovery is not wholly pleasant. If the young speak of

the past as a burden it is a joy to throw off, behind their words may often lie a resentment and fright at realizing that the past will not carry them on its back.

The critical statements of the Censor are always polemical advice to his poet, meant not as objective truths but as pointers, and in youth which is trying to discover its own identity, the exasperation at not having yet succeeded naturally tends to express itself in violence and exaggeration.

If an undergraduate announces to his tutor one morning that Gertrude Stein is the greatest writer who ever lived or that Shakespeare is no good, he is really only saying something like this: 'I don't know what to write yet or how, but yesterday while reading Gertrude Stein, I thought I saw a clue' or 'Reading Shakespeare yesterday, I realized that one of the faults in what I write is a tendency to rhetorical bombast'.

Fashion and snobbery are also valuable as a defence against literary indigestion. Regardless of their quality, it is always better to read a few books carefully than skim through many, and, short of a personal taste which cannot be formed overnight, snobbery is as good a principle of limitation as any other.

I am eternally grateful, for example, to the musical fashion of my youth which prevented me from listening to Italian Opera until I was over thirty, by which age I was capable of really appreciating a world so beautiful and so challenging to my own cultural heritage.

The apprentices do each other a further mutual service which no older and sounder critic could do. They read each other's manuscripts. At this age a fellow apprentice has two great virtues as a critic. When he reads your poem, he may grossly overestimate it, but if he does, he really believes what he is saying; he never flatters or praises merely to encourage. Secondly, he reads your poem with that passionate attention which grown-up critics only give to masterpieces and grown-up poets only to themselves. When he finds fault, his criticisms are intended to help you to improve. He really wants your poem to be better.

It is just this kind of personal criticism which, in later life when the band of apprentices have dispersed, a writer often finds it so hard to get. The verdicts of reviewers, however just, are seldom of any use to him. Why should they be? A critic is dealing with a published work, not a manuscript. His job is to tell the public what that work is, not tell its author what he should and could have written instead. Yet this is the only kind of criticism from which an author can benefit. Those who could do it for him are generally, like himself, too elsewhere, too busy, too married, too selfish.

We must assume that our apprentice does succeed in becoming a poet, that, sooner or later, a day arrives when his Censor is able to say truthfully and for the first time: 'All the words are right, and all are yours.'

His thrill at hearing this does not last long, however, for a moment later comes the thought: 'Will it ever happen again?' Whatever his future life as a wage-earner, a citizen, a family man may be, to the end of his days his life as a poet will be without anticipation. He will never be able to say: 'Tomorrow I will write a poem and, thanks to my training and experience, I already know I shall do a good job.' In the eyes of others a man is a poet if he has written one good poem. In his own he is only a poet at the moment when he is making his last revision to a new poem. The moment before, he was still only a potential poet: the moment after he is a man who has ceased to write poetry, perhaps for ever.

NOTES ON THE ART OF POETRY

Dylan Thomas

At Laugharne, in the summer of 1951, Dylan Thomas (1914–1953) wrote the following replies to questions posed by a student. If the questions are very general, they elicit a response of unusual candor; if the impression is strong that the poet often proceeded largely by indirection—or chance—there is something of this quality in some of his best works. At the same time, however, he enjoys the reputation of an exceedingly conscientious craftsman. In any event, his statement that "the joy and function of poetry is . . . the celebration of man, which is also the celebration of God" suggests a lofty concept of poetry and the poet's function. Thomas's death at the age of thirty-nine was apparently the result of unresolvable inner conflicts—and alcoholism—in about equal proportions.

You want to know why and how I just began to write poetry, and which poets or kinds of poetry I was first moved and influenced by.

To answer the first part of this question, I should say I wanted to write poetry in the beginning because I had fallen in love with words. The first poems I knew were nursery rhymes, and before I could read them for myself I had come to love just the words of them, the words alone. What the words stood for, symbolised, or meant, was of very secondary importance. What mattered was the *sound* of them as I heard them for the first time on the lips of the remote and incomprehensible grown-ups who seemed, for some reason, to be living in my world. And these words were, to me, as the notes of bells, the sounds of musical instruments, the noises of wind, sea, and rain, the rattle of milkcarts, the clopping of hooves on cobbles, the fingering of branches on a window pane, might be to someone, deaf from birth, who has miraculously found his hearing. I did not care what the

words said, overmuch, nor what happened to Jack and Jill and the
Mother Goose rest of them; I cared for the shapes of sound that
their names, and the words describing their actions, made in my
ears; I cared for the colours the words cast on my eyes. I realise
that I may be, as I think back all that way, romanticising my reactions to the simple and beautiful words of those pure poems; but
that is all I can honestly remember, however much time might
have falsified my memory. I fell in love—that is the only expression I can think of—at once, and am still at the mercy of words,
though sometimes now, knowing a little of their behaviour very
well, I think I can influence them slightly and have even learned
to beat them now and then, which they appear to enjoy. I tumbled
for words at once. And, when I began to read the nursery rhymes
for myself, and, later, to read other verses and ballads, I knew
that I had discovered the most important things, to me, that
could be ever. There they were, seemingly lifeless, made only of
black and white, but out of them, out of their own being, came
love and terror and pity and pain and wonder and all the other
vague abstractions that make our ephemeral lives dangerous,
great, and bearable. Out of them came the gusts and grunts and
hiccups and heehaws of the common fun of the earth; and though
what the words meant was, in its own way, often deliciously
funny enough, so much funnier seemed to me, at that almost
forgotten time, the shape and shade and size and noise of the
words as they hummed, strummed, jugged and galloped along.
That was the time of innocence; words burst upon me, unencumbered by trivial or portentous association; words were
their spring-like selves, fresh with Eden's dew, as they flew out
of the air. They made their own original associations as they
sprang and shone. The words, "Ride a cock-horse to Banbury
Cross," were as haunting to me, who did not know then what a
cock-horse was nor cared a damn where Banbury Cross might
be, as, much later, were such lines as John Donne's, "Go and
catch a falling star, Get with child a mandrake root," which
also I could not understand when I first read them. And as I read
more and more, and it was not all verse, by any means, my love
for the real life of words increased until I knew that I must live
with them and *in* them always. I knew, in fact, that I must be
a writer of words, and nothing else. The first thing was to feel
and know their sound and substance; what I was going to do with
those words, what use I was going to make of them, what I was

going to *say* through them, would come later. I knew I had to know them most intimately in all their forms and moods, their ups and downs, their chops and changes, their needs and demands. (Here, I am afraid, I am beginning to talk too vaguely. I do not like writing *about* words, because then I often use bad and wrong and stale and wooly words. What I like to do is to treat words as a craftsman does his wood or stone or what-have-you, to hew, carve, mould, coil, polish and plane them into patterns, sequences, sculptures, fugues of sound expressing some lyrical impulse, some spiritual doubt or conviction, some dimly-realised truth I must try to reach and realise). It was when I was very young, and just at school, that, in my father's study, before homework that was never done, I began to know one kind of writing from an-other, one kind of goodness, one kind of badness. My first, and greatest, liberty was that of being able to read everything and anything I cared to. I read indiscriminately, and with my eyes hanging out. I could never have dreamt that there were such goings-on in the world between the covers of books, such sand-storms and ice-blasts of words, such slashing of humbug, and humbug too, such staggering peace, such enormous laughter, such and so many blinding bright lights breaking across the just-awaking wits and splashing all over the pages in a million bits and pieces all of which were words, words, words, and each of which was alive forever in its own delight and glory and oddity and light (I must try not to make these supposedly helpful notes as confusing as my poems themselves.) I wrote endless imitations, though I never thought them to be imitations but, rather, wonderfully original things, like eggs laid by tigers. They were imitations of anything I happened to be reading at the time: Sir Thomas Browne, de Quincey, Henry Newbolt, the Ballads, Blake, Baroness Orczy, Marlowe, Chums, the Imagists, the Bible, Poe, Keats, Lawrence, Anon., and Shakespeare. A mixed lot, as you see, and randomly remembered. I tried my callow hand at almost every poetical form. How could I learn the tricks of a trade unless I tried to do them myself? I learned that the bad tricks come easily; and the good ones, which help you to say what you think you wish to say in the most meaningful, moving way, I am still learning. (But in earnest company you must call these tricks by other names, such as technical devices, prosodic experiments, etc.)

The writers, then, who influenced my earliest poems and

stories were, quite simply and truthfully, all the writers I was
reading at the time, and, as you see from a specimen list higher
up the page, they ranged from writers of schoolboy adventure
yarns to incomparable and inimitable masters like Blake. That is,
when I began, bad writing had as much influence on my stuff
as good. The bad influences I tried to remove and renounce
bit by bit, shadow by shadow, echo by echo, through trial and
error, through delight and disgust and misgiving, as I came to
love words more and to hate the heavy hands that knocked them
about, the thick tongues that [had] no feel for their multi-
tudinous tastes, the dull and botching hacks who flattened them
out into a colourless and insipid paste, the pedants who made
them moribund and pompous as themselves. Let me say that the
things that first made me love language and want to work *in* it
and *for* it were nursery rhymes and folk tales, the Scottish
Ballads, a few lines of hymns, the most famous Bible stories
and the rhythms of the Bible, Blake's "Songs of Innocence,"
and the quite incomprehensible magical majesty and nonsense
of Shakespeare heard, read, and near-murdered in the first
forms of my school.

You ask me, next, if it is true that three of the dominant influences on my published prose and poetry are Joyce, the Bible,
and Freud. (I purposely say my 'published' prose and poetry, as
in the preceding pages I have been talking about the primary
influences upon my very first and forever unpublishable ju-
venilia.) I cannot say that I have been 'influenced' by Joyce,
whom I enormously admire and whose "Ulysses," and earlier
stories I have read a great deal. I think this Joyce question arose
because somebody once, in print, remarked on the closeness of
the title of my book of short stories, "Portrait of the Artist As
a Young Dog" to Joyce's title, "Portrait of the Artist as a Young
Man." As you know, the name given to innumerable portrait
paintings by their artists is, "Portrait of the Artist as a Young
Man"—a perfectly straightforward title. Joyce used the painting-
title for the first time as the title of a literary work. I myself
made a bit of doggish fun of the *painting*-title and, of course,
intended no possible reference to Joyce. I do not think that
Joyce has had any hand at all in my writing; certainly, his
"Ulysses" has not. On the other hand, I cannot deny that the
shaping of some of my "Portrait" stories might owe something
to Joyce's stories in the volume "Dubliners." But then, "Dub-

liners" was a pioneering work in the world of the short story, and no good storywriter since can have failed, in some way, however little, to have benefited by it.

The Bible, I have referred to in attempting to answer your first question. Its great stories, of Noah, Jonah, Lot, Moses, Jacob, David, Solomon and a thousand more, I had, of course, known from very early youth; the great rhythms had rolled over me from the Welsh pulpits; and I read, for myself, from Job and Ecclesiastes; and the story of the New Testament is part of my life. But I have never sat down and studied the Bible, never consciously echoed its language, and am, in reality, as ignorant of it as most brought-up Christians. All of the Bible that I use in my work is remembered from childhood, and is the common property of all who were brought up in English-speaking communities. Nowhere, indeed, in all my writing, do I use any knowledge which is not commonplace to any literate person. I *have* used a few difficult words in early poems, but they are easily looked-up and were, in any case, thrown into the poems in a kind of adolescent showing-off which I hope I have now discarded.

And that leads me to the third 'dominant influence': Sigmund Freud. My only acquaintance with the theories and discoveries of Dr. Freud has been through the work of novelists who have been excited by his case-book histories, of popular newspaper scientific-potboilers who have, I imagine, vulgarised his work beyond recognition, and of a few modern poets, including Auden, who have attempted to use psychoanalytical phraseology and theory in some of their poems. I have read only one book of Freud's, "The Interpretation of Dreams," and do not recall having been influenced by it in any way. Again, no honest writer today can possibly avoid being influenced by Freud through his pioneering work into the Unconscious and by the influence of those discoveries on the scientific, philosophic, and artistic work of his contemporaries: but not, by any means, necessarily through Freud's own writing.

To your third question—Do I deliberately utilise devices of rhyme, rhythm, and word-formation in my writing—I must, of course, answer with an immediate Yes. I am a painstaking, conscientious, involved, and devious craftsman in words, however unsuccessful the result so often appears, and to whatever wrong uses I may apply my technical paraphernalia. I use everything and anything to make my poems work and move in the direction

I want them to: old tricks, new tricks, puns, portmanteau-words, paradox, allusion, paronomasia, paragram, catachresis, slang, assonantal rhymes, vowel rhymes, sprung rhythm. Every device there is in language is there to be used if you will. Poets have got to enjoy themselves sometimes, and the twisting and convolutions of words, the inventions and contrivances, are all part of the joy that is part of the painful, voluntary work.

Your next question asks whether my use of combinations of words to create something new, "in the Surrealist way," is according to a set formula or is spontaneous.

There is a confusion here, for the Surrealists' set formula *was* to juxtapose the unpremeditated.

Let me make it clearer if I can. The Surrealists—(that is, super-realists, or those who work *above* realism)—were a coterie of painters and writers in Paris, in the nineteen twenties, who did not believe in the conscious selection of images. To put it in another way: They were artists who were dissatisfied with both the realists—(roughly speaking, those who tried to put down in paint and words an actual representation of what they imagined to be the real world in which they lived)—and the impressionists who, roughly speaking again, were those who tried to give an impression of what they imagined to be the real world. The Surrealists wanted to dive into the subconscious mind, the mind below the conscious surface, and dig up their images from there without the aid of logic of reason, and put them down, illogically and unreasonably, in paint and words. The Surrealists affirmed that, as three quarters of the mind was submerged, it was the function of the artist to gather his material from the greatest, submerged mass of the mind rather than from that quarter of the mind which, like the tip of an iceberg, protruded from the subconscious sea. One method the Surrealists used in their poetry was to juxtapose words and images that had no rational relationship; and out of this they hoped to achieve a kind of subconscious, or dream, poetry that would be truer to the real, imaginative world of the mind, mostly submerged, than is the poetry of the conscious mind that relies upon the rational and logical relationship of ideas, objects, and images.

This is, very crudely, the credo of the Surrealists, and one with which I profoundly disagree. I do not mind from where the images of a poem are dragged up; drag them up, if you like, from the nethermost sea of the hidden self; but, before they reach paper, they must go through all the rational processes of the intellect. The Surrealists, on the other hand, put their words down together on paper exactly as they emerge from chaos; they do not shape these words or put them in order; to them, chaos *is* the shape and order. This seems to me to be exceedingly presumptuous; the Surrealists imagine that whatever they dredge from their subconscious selves and put down in paint or in words must essentially be of some interest or value. I deny this. One of the arts of the poet is to make comprehensible and articulate what might emerge from subconscious sources; one of the great main uses of the intellect is to *select*, from the amorphous mass of subconscious images those that will best further his imaginative purpose, which is to write the best poem he can.

And question five is, God help us, what is my definition of Poetry?

I myself, do not read poetry for anything but pleasure. I read only the poems I like. This means, of course, that I have to read a lot of poems I don't like before I find the ones I do, but, when I *do* find the ones I do, then all I can say is "Here they are," and read them to myself for pleasure.

Read the poems you like reading. Don't bother whether they're important, or if they'll live. What does it matter what poetry *is*, after all? If you want a definition of poetry, say: "Poetry's what makes me laugh or cry or yawn, what makes my toenails twinkle, what makes me want to do this or that or nothing," and let it go at that. All that matters about poetry is the enjoyment of it, however tragic it may be. All that matters is the eternal movement behind it, the vast undercurrent of human grief, folly, pretension, exaltation, or ignorance, however unlofty the intention of the poem.

You can tear a poem apart to see what makes it technically tick, and say to yourself, when the works are laid out before you, the vowels, the consonants, the rhymes and rhythms. "Yes, this is *it*. This is why the poem moves me so. It is because of the craftsmanship." But you're back again where you began. You're back with the mystery of having been moved by words. The best craftsmanship always leaves holes and gaps in the works of the poem so that something that is *not* in the poem can creep, crawl, flash, or thunder in.

The joy and function of poetry is, and was, the celebration of man, which is also the celebration of God.

The Feel of Light, 1966.
Photograph by Jerry Uelsmann.

Chambered Nautilus, 1927.
Photograph by Edward Weston. Courtesy of Cole Weston.

Shell and Rock Arrangement, 1931.
Photograph by Edward Weston. Courtesy of Cole Weston.

Three Pears and an Apple, c. 1921.
Photograph by Edward Steichen. From the Collection of The Museum of Modern Art,
New York City.

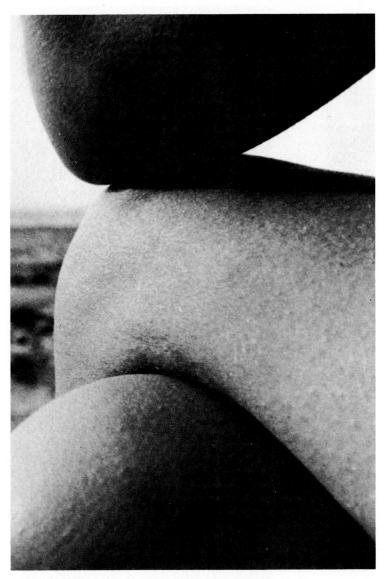

Normandy, 1959.
Photograph by Bill Brandt. Rapho Guillumette Pictures, Inc.

Still-Life, Brooklyn.
Photograph by Harold Feinstein.

A lawyer by training and a successful executive for an insurance company, Wallace Stevens (1879–1955) was one of America's most accomplished poets of the present century. His intense, life-long involvement with French culture, most notably poetry and painting, found expression in prose works which speculate not only on the nature and function of poetry, but on poetry's relationship with the other arts as well. In the present essay, from The Necessary Angel, *Stevens comes to terms with the delicate area where poetry and painting may intersect. It is typical of Stevens's thought that he should see both poetry and painting as functions of the imagination and of the "miraculous reason" as common to the imaginations of all artists. The present essay is rich in referential materials and cogent in its discourse; in addition to being one of the most valuable essays of its kind in this collection, it is doubtless the most difficult. Nevertheless, as with all of Stevens' work, it nobly repays close study.*

THE RELATIONS BETWEEN POETRY AND PAINTING

Wallace
Stevens

I

Roger Fry concluded a note on Claude by saying that "few of us live so strenuously as never to feel a sense of nostalgia for that Saturnian reign to which Virgil and Claude can waft us." He spoke in that same note of Corot and Whistler and Chinese landscape and certainly he might just as well have spoken, in relation to Claude, of many poets, as, for example, Chénier or Wordsworth. This is simply the analogy between two different forms of poetry. It might be better to say that it is the identity of poetry revealed as between poetry in words and poetry in paint.

Poetry, however, is not limited to Virgilian landscape, nor painting to Claude. We find the poetry of mankind in the figures of the old men

of Shakespeare, say, and the old men of Rembrandt; or in the
figures of Biblical women, on the one hand, and of the madonnas
of all Europe, on the other; and it is easy to wonder whether the
poetry of children has not been created by the poetry of the
Child, until one stops to think how much of the poetry of the
whole world is the poetry of children, both as they are and as
they have been written of and painted, as if they were the creatures of a dimension in which life and poetry are one. The poetry
of humanity is, of course, to be found everywhere.

   There is a universal poetry that is reflected in everything. This
remark approaches the idea of Baudelaire that there exists an
unascertained and fundamental aesthetic, or order, of which
poetry and painting are manifestations, but of which, for that
matter, sculpture or music or any other aesthetic realization
would equally be a manifestation. Generalizations as expansive as
these: that there is a universal poetry that is reflected in everything or that there may be a fundamental aesthetic of which
poetry and painting are related but dissimilar manifestations, are
speculative. One is better satisfied by particulars.

   No poet can have failed to recognize how often a detail or
remark, apropos in respect to painting, applies also to poetry.
The truth is that there seems to exist a corpus of remarks in respect to painting, most often the remarks of painters themselves,
which are as significant to poets as to painters. All of these details, to the extent that they have meaning for poets as well as
for painters, are specific instances of relations between poetry
and painting. I suppose, therefore, that it would be possible to
study poetry by studying painting or that one could become a
painter after one had become a poet, not to speak of carrying on
in both métiers at once, with the economy of genius, as Blake did.
Let me illustrate this point of the double value (and one might
well call it the multifold value) of sayings for painters that mean
as much for poets because they are, after all, sayings about art.
Does not the saying of Picasso that a picture is a horde of destructions also say that a poem is a horde of destructions? When
Braque says "The senses deform, the mind forms," he is speaking to poet, painter, musician and sculptor. Just as poets can be
affected by the sayings of painters, so can painters be affected
by the sayings of poets and so can both be affected by sayings addressed to neither. For many examples, see Miss Sit-
well's *Poet's Note-Book*. These details come together so subtly

and so minutely that the existence of relations is lost sight of. This, is turn, dissipates the idea of their existence.

II

We may regard the subject, then, from two points of view, the first from the point of view of the man whose center is painting, whether or not he is a painter, the second from the point of view of the man whose center is poetry, whether or not he is a poet. To make use of the point of view of the man whose center is painting let me refer to the chapter in Leo Stein's *Appreciation* entitled "On Reading Poetry and Seeing Pictures." He says that, when he was a child, he became aware of composition in nature and gradually realized that art and composition are one. He began to experiment as follows:

I put on the table . . . an earthenware plate . . . and this I looked at every day for minutes or for hours. I had in mind to see it as a picture, and waited for it to become one. In time it did. The change came suddenly when the plate as an inventorial object . . . a certain shape, certain colors applied to it . . . went over into a composition to which all these elements were merely contributory. The painted composition on the plate ceased to be *on* it but became a part of a larger composition which was the plate as a whole. I had made a beginning to seeing pictorially.

What had been begun was carried out in all directions. I wanted to be able to see anything *as* a composition and found that it was possible to do this.

He improvised a definition of art: that it is nature seen in the light of its significance, and recognizing that this significance was one of forms, he added "formal" to "significance."

Turning to education in hearing, he observed that there is nothing comparable to the practice in composition that the visible world offers. By composition he meant the compositional use of words: the use of their existential meanings. Composition was his passion. He considered that a formally complete picture is one in which all the parts are so related to one another that they all imply each other. Finally he said, "an excellent illustration is the line from Wordsworth's 'Michael' . . . 'And never lifted up a single stone.'" One might say of a lazy workman, "He's been out there, just loafing, for an hour and never lifted up a single stone," and no one would think this great poetry. . . . These lines would have no existential value; they would simply call attention to the lazy workman. But the compositional use by Wordsworth of his line makes it something entirely different. These simple words become weighted with the tragedy of the old shepherd, and are saturated with poetry. Their referential importance is slight, for the importance of the action to which they refer is not in the action itself, but in the meaning; and that meaning is borne by the words. Therefore this is a line of great poetry.

The selection of composition as a common denominator of poetry and painting is the selection of a technical characteristic by a man whose center was painting, even granting that he was not a man whom one thinks of as a technician. Poetry and painting alike create through composition.

Now, a poet looking for an analogy between poetry and painting and trying to take the point of view of a man whose center is poetry begins with a sense that the technical pervades painting to such a degree that the two are identified. This is untrue, since, if painting was purely technical, that conception of it would exclude the artist as a person. I want to say something, therefore, based on the sensibility of the poet and of the painter. I am not quite sure that I know what is meant by sensibility. I suppose that it means feeling or, as we say, the feelings. I know what is meant by nervous sensibility, as, when at a concert, the auditors, having composed themselves and resting there attentively, hear suddenly an outburst on the trumpets from which they shrink by way of a nervous reaction. The satisfaction that we have when we look out and find that it is a fine day or when we are looking at one of the limpid vistas of Corot in the *pays de Corot* seems to be something else. It is commonly said that the origins of poetry are to be found in the sensibility. We began with the conjunction of Claude and Virgil, noting how one evoked the other. Such evocations are attributable to similarities of sensibility. If, in Claude, we find ourselves in the realm of Saturn, the ruler of the world in a golden age of innocence and plenty, and if, in Virgil, we find ourselves in the same realm, we recognize that there is, as between Claude and Virgil, an identity of sensibility. Yet if one questions the dogma that the origins of poetry are to be found in the sensibility and if one says that a fortunate poem or a fortunate painting is a synthesis of exceptional concentration (that

degree of concentration that has a lucidity of its own, in which
we see clearly what we want to do and do it instantly and perfectly), we find that the operative force within us does not, in
fact, seem to be the sensibility, that is to say, the feelings. It
seems to be a constructive faculty, that derives its energy more
from the imagination than from the sensibility. I have spoken
of questioning, not of denying. The mind retains experience, so
that long after the experience, long after the winter clearness of
a January morning, long after the limpid vistas of Corot, that
faculty within us of which I have spoken makes its own constructions out of that experience. If it merely reconstructed the
experience or repeated for us our sensations in the face of it, it
would be the memory. What it really does is to use it as material
with which it does whatever it wills. This is the typical function
of the imagination which always makes use of the familiar to
produce the unfamiliar. What these remarks seem to involve is
the substitution for the idea of inspiration of the idea of an
effort of the mind not dependent on the vicissitudes of the
sensibility. It is so completely possible to sit at one's table and
without the help of the agitation of the feelings to write plays
of incomparable enhancement that that is precisely what Shakespeare did. He was not dependent on the fortuities of inspiration.
It is not the least part of his glory that one can say of him, the
greater the thinker the greater the poet. It would come nearer the
mark to say the greater the mind the greater the poet, because
the evil of thinking as poetry is not the same thing as the good
of thinking in poetry. The point is that the poet does his job by
virtue of an effort of the mind. In doing so, he is in rapport with
the painter, who does his job, with respect to the problems of
form and color, which confront him incessantly, not by inspiration, but by imagination or by the miraculous kind of reason
that the imagination sometimes promotes. In short, these two
arts, poetry and painting, have in common a laborious element,
which, when it is exercised, is not only a labor but a consumma-
tion as well. For proof of this let me set side by side the poetry
in the prose of Proust, taken from his vast novel, and the painting,
by chance, of Jacques Villon. As to Proust, I quote a paragraph
from Professor Saurat:

Another province he has added to literature is the description of those
eternal moments in which we are lifted out of the drab world. . . .

The madeleine dipped in tea, the steeples of Martinville, some trees on a road, a perfume of wild flowers, a vision of light and shade on trees, a spoon clinking on a plate that is like a railway man's hammer on the wheels of the train from which the trees were seen, a stiff napkin in an hotel, an inequality in two stones in Venice and the disjointment in the yard of the Guermantes' town house. . . .

As to Villon: shortly before I began to write these notes I dropped into the Carré Gallery in New York to see an exhibition of paintings which included about a dozen works by him. I was immediately conscious of the presence of the enchantments of intelligence in all his prismatic material. A woman lying in a hammock was transformed into a complex of planes and tones, radiant, vaporous, exact. A tea-pot and a cup or two took their place in a reality composed wholly of things unreal. These works were *deliciae* of the spirit as distinguished from *delectationes* of the senses and this was so because one found in them the labor of calculation, the appetite for perfection.

III

One of the characteristics of modern art is that it is uncompromising. In this it resembles modern politics, and perhaps it would appear on study, including a study of the rights of man and of women's hats and dresses, that everything modern, or possibly merely new, is, in the nature of things, uncompromising. It is especially uncompromising in respect to precinct. One of the De Goncourts said that nothing in the world hears as many silly things said as a picture in a museum; and in thinking about that remark one has to bear in mind that in the days of the De Goncourts there was no such thing as a museum of modern art. A really modern definition of modern art, instead of making concessions, fixes limits which grow smaller and smaller as time passes and more often than not come to include one man alone, just as if there should be scrawled across the façade of the building in which we now are, the words *Cézanne delineavit*. Another characteristic of modern art is that it is plausible. It has a reason for everything. Even the lack of a reason becomes a reason. Picasso expresses surprise that people should ask what a picture means and says that pictures are not intended to have meanings. This explains everything. Still another characteristic of modern art is that it is bigoted. Every painter who can be defined as a modern painter becomes, by virtue of that definition, a freeman of the world of art and hence the equal of any other modern painter. We recognize that they differ one from another but in any event they are not to be judged except by other modern painters.

We have this inability (not mere unwillingness) to compromise, this same plausibility and bigotry in modern poetry. To exhibit this, let me divide modern poetry into two classes, one that is modern in respect to what it says, the other that is modern in respect to form. The first kind is not interested primarily in form. The second is. The first kind is interested in form but it accepts a banality of form as incidental to its language. Its justification is that in expressing thought or feeling in poetry the purpose of the poet must be to subordinate the mode of expression, that, while the value of the poem as a poem depends on expression, it depends primarily on what is expressed. Whether the poet is modern or ancient, living or dead, is, in the last analysis, a question of what he is talking about, whether of things modern or ancient, living or dead. The counterpart of Villon in poetry, writing as he paints, would concern himself with like things (but not necessarily confining himself to them), creating the same sense of aesthetic certainty, the same sense of exquisite realization and the same sense of being modern and living. One sees a good deal of poetry, thanks, perhaps, to Mallarmé's *Un Coup de Dés,* in which the exploitation of form involves nothing more than the use of small letters for capitals, eccentric line-endings, too little or too much punctuation and similar aberrations. These have nothing to do with being alive. They have nothing to do with the conflict between the poet and that of which his poems are made. They are neither "bonne soupe" nor "beau langage."

What I have said of both classes of modern poetry is inadequate as to both. As to the first, which permits a banality of form, it is even harmful, as suggesting that it possesses less of the artifice of the poet than the second. Each of these two classes is intransigent as to the other. If one is disposed to think well of the class that stands on what it has to say, one has only to think of Gide's remark, "Without the unequaled beauty of his prose, who would continue to interest himself in Bossuet?" The division between the two classes, the division, say, between Valéry

and Apollinaire, is the same division into factions that we find
everywhere in modern painting. But aesthetic creeds, like other
creeds, are the certain evidences of exertions to find the truth.
I have tried to say no more than was necessary to evince the
relations, in which we are interested, as they exist in the manifestations of today. What, when all is said and done, is the
significance of the existence of such relations? Or is it enough
to note them? The question is not the same as the question of the
significance of art. We do not have to be told of the significance
of art. "It is art," said Henry James, "which makes life, makes
interest, makes importance . . . and I know of no substitute whatever for the force and beauty of its process." The world about
us would be desolate except for the world within us. There is
the same interchange between these two worlds that there is
between one art and another, migratory passings to and fro,
quickenings, Promethean liberations and discoveries.

   Yet it may be that just as the senses are no respecters of reality,
so the faculties are no respecters of the arts. On the other hand,
it may be that we are dealing with something that has no significance, something that is the result of imitation. Quatremère de
Quincy distinguished between the poet and the painter as between two imitators, one moral, the other physical. There are
imitations within imitations and the relations between poetry
and painting may present nothing more. This idea makes it possible, at least, to see more than one side of the subject.

IV

All of the relations of which I have spoken are themselves related in the deduction that the *vis poetica*, the power of poetry,
leaves its mark on whatever it touches. The mark of poetry
creates the resemblance of poetry as between the most disparate
things and unites them all in its recognizable virtue. There is one
relation between poetry and painting which does not participate
in the common mark of common origin. It is the paramount
relation that exists between poetry and people in general and between painting and people in general. I have not overlooked the
possibility that, when this evening's subject was suggested, it was
intended that the discussion should be limited to the relations
between modern poetry and modern painting. This would have

involved much tinkling of familiar cymbals. In so far as it would have called for a comparison of this poet and that painter, this school and that school, it would have been fragmentary and beyond my competence. It seems to me that the subject of modern relations is best to be approached as a whole. The paramount relation between poetry and painting today, between modern man and modern art is simply this: that in an age in which disbelief is so profoundly prevalent or, if not disbelief, indifference to questions of belief, poetry and painting, and the arts in general, are, in their measure, a compensation for what has been lost. Men feel that the imagination is the next greatest power to faith: the reigning prince. Consequently their interest in the imagination and its work is to be regarded not as a phase of humanism but as a vital self-assertion in a world in which nothing but the self remains, if that remains. So regarded, the study of the imagination and the study of reality come to appear to be purified, aggrandized, fateful. How much stature, even vatic stature, this conception gives the poet! He need not exercise this dignity in vatic works. How much authenticity, even orphic authenticity, it gives to the painter! He need not display this authenticity in orphic works. It should be enough for him that that to which he has given his life should be so enriched by such an access of value. Poet and painter alike live and work in the midst of a generation that is experiencing essential poverty in spite of fortune. The extension of the mind beyond the range of the mind, the projection of reality beyond reality, the determination to cover the ground, whatever it may be, the determination not to be confined, the recapture of excitement and intensity of interest, the enlargement of the spirit at every time, in every way, these are the unities, the relations, to be summarized as paramount now. It is not material whether these relations exist consciously or unconsciously. One goes back to the coercing influences of time and place. It is possible to be subjected to a lofty purpose and not to know it. But I think that most men of any degree of sophistication, most poets, most painters know it.

When we look back at the period of French classicism in the seventeenth century, we have no difficulty in seeing it as a whole. It is not so easy to see one's own time that way. Pretty much all of the seventeenth century, in France, at least, can be summed up in that one word: classicism. The paintings of Poussin, Claude's contemporary, are the inevitable paintings of the generation of Racine. If it had been a time when dramatists used the detailed scene directions that we expect today, the directions of Racine would have left one wondering whether one was reading the description of a scene or the description of one of Poussin's works. The practice confined them to the briefest generalization. Thus, after the list of persons in *King Lear*, Shakespeare added only two words: "Scene: Britain." Yet even so, the directions of Racine, for all their brevity, suggest Poussin. That a common quality is to be detected in such simple things exhibits the extent of the interpenetration persuasively. The direction for *Britannicus* is "The scene is at Rome, in a chamber of the palace of Nero"; for *Iphigénie en Aulide*, "The scene is at Aulis, before the tent of Agamemnon"; for *Phèdre*, "The scene is at Trézène, a town of the Peloponnesus"; for *Esther*, "The scene is at Susa, in the palais of Assuérus"; and for *Athalie*, "The scene is in the temple of Jerusalem, in a vestibule of the apartment of the grand priest."

Our own time, and by this I mean the last two or three generations, including our own, can be summed up in a way that brings into unity an immense number of details by saying of it that it is a time in which the search for the supreme truth has been ‘a search in reality or through reality or even a search for some supremely acceptable fiction. Juan Gris began some notes on his painting by saying: "The world from which I extract the elements of reality is not visual but imaginative." The history of this attitude in literature and particularly in poetry, in France, has been traced by Marcel Raymond in his *From Baudelaire to Surrealism*. I say particularly in poetry because there are associated with it the names of Baudelaire, Rimbaud, Mallarmé and Valéry. In painting, its history is the history of modern painting. Moreover, I say in France because, in France, the theory of poetry is not abstract as it so often is with us, when we have any theory at all, but is a normal activity of the poet's mind in surroundings where he must engage in such activity or be extirpated. Thus necessity develops an awareness and a sense of fatality which give to poetry values not to be reproduced by indifference and chance. To the man who is seeking the sanction of life in poetry, the namby-pamby is an intolerable dissipation. The theory of poetry, that is to say, the total of the theories of poetry, often seems to become in time a mystical theology or, more simply, a mystique. The reason for this must by now be clear.

The reason is the same reason why the pictures in a museum of modern art often seem to become in time a mystical aesthetic, a prodigious search of appearance, as if to find a way of saying and of establishing that all things, whether below or above appearance, are one and that it is only through reality, in which they are reflected or, it may be, joined together, that we can reach them. Under such stress, reality changes from substance to subtlety, a subtlety in which it was natural for Cézanne to say: "I see planes bestriding each other and sometimes straight lines seem to me to fall" or "Planes in color. . . . The colored area where shimmer the souls of the planes, in the blaze of the kindled prism, the meeting of planes in the sunlight." The conversion of our *Lumpenwelt* went far beyond this. It was from the point of view of another subtlety that Klee could write: "But he is one chosen that today comes near to the secret places where original law fosters all evolution. And what artist would not establish himself there where the organic center of all movement in time and space—which he calls the mind or heart of creation —determines every function." Conceding that this sounds a bit like sacerdotal jargon, that is not too much to allow to those that have helped to create a new reality, a modern reality, since what has been created is nothing less.

This reality is, also, the momentous world of poetry. Its instantaneities are the familiar intelligence of poets, although it has been the intelligence of another ambiance. Simone Weil in *La Pesanteur et La Grâce* has a chapter on what she calls decreation. She says that decreation is making pass from the created to the uncreated, but that destruction is making pass from the created to nothingness. Modern reality is a reality of decreation, in which our revelations are not the revelations of belief, but the precious portents of our own powers. The greatest truth we could hope to discover, in whatever field we discovered it, is that man's truth is the final resolution of everything. Poets and painters alike today make that assumption and this is what gives them the validity and serious dignity that become them as among those that seek wisdom, seek understanding. I am elevating this a little, because I am trying to generalize and because it is incredible that one should speak of the aspirations of the last two or three generations without a degree of elevation. Sometimes it seems the other way. Sometimes we hear it said that in the eighteenth century there were no poets and that the painters—

Chardin, Fragonard, Watteau—were élégants and nothing more; that in the nineteenth century the last great poet was the man that looked most like one and that the whole Pierian sodality had better have been fed to the dogs. It occasionally seems like that today. It must seem as it may. In the logic of events, the only wrong would be to attempt to falsify the logic, to be disloyal to the truth. It would be tragic not to realize the extent of man's dependence on the arts. The kind of world that might result from too exclusive a dependence on them has been questioned, as if the discipline of the arts was in no sense a moral discipline. We have not to discuss that here. It is enough to have brought poetry and painting into relation as sources of our present conception of reality, without asserting that they are the sole sources, and as supports of a kind of life, which it seems to be worth living, with their support, even if doing so is only a stage in the endless study of an existence, which is the heroic subject of all study.

THEATRE
AND
DANCE

No one in the modern theater is a more eloquent defender of the social drama than George Bernard Shaw (1856–1950). His plays exemplify the drama that deals with social problems at its most engaging, if not necessarily at its most profound. In his prefaces to his plays, Shaw explained what he was doing, always with charm, and often with a crackling, crusading zeal for social, political, and economic justice that continues to be moving even in areas where justice has long since had its due in almost precisely the terms that Shaw demanded. A learned, witty, and persuasive theater critic and theorist, he is never better than when his crusade for justice in society is joined to his crisp criticism of those playwrights either too dull or too timid to crusade for justice in their own works. In this short statement, full of crackle and crusade, Shaw sums up, in effect, his own achievement in the social drama as well as Henrik Ibsen's. He not only asserts his principles, but does so with such clarity and logic that even the most dogged opponent of the drama of social consciousness must pause long and think hard before rejecting any part of the argument, the principle, or the drama.

THE PROBLEM PLAY—

A SYMPOSIUM

George Bernard Shaw

Should social problems be freely dealt with in the Drama?
The Humanitarian VI, May, 1895

I do not know who has asked the question, Should social problems be freely dealt with in the drama?—some very thoughtless person evidently. Pray what social questions and what sort of drama? Suppose I say yes, then, vaccination being a social question, and the Wagnerian music drama being the one complete form of drama in the opinion of its admirers, it will follow that I am in favor of the production of a Jennerian tetralogy at Bayreuth.[1] If I say no, then, marriage being a social question, and also the theme of Ibsen's *Doll's House,* I shall be held to contemn that work as a violation of the canons of art. I therefore reply to the propounder that I am not prepared to waste my own time and that of the public in answering maladroit conundrums. What I am prepared to do is to say what I can with the object of bringing some sort of order into the intellectual confusion which has expressed itself in the conundrum.

Social questions are produced by the conflict of human institutions with human feeling. For instance, we have certain institutions regulating the lives of women. To the women whose feelings are entirely in harmony with these institutions there is no Woman Question. But during the present century, from the time of Mary Wollstonecraft [English feminist, 1759–1797, mother by William Godwin of Shelley's wife Mary] onwards, women have been developing feelings, and consequently opinions, which clash with these institutions. The institutions assumed that it was natural to a woman to allow her husband to own her property and person, and to represent her in politics as a father represents his infant child. The moment that seemed no longer natural to some women, it became grievously oppressive to them. Immediately there was a Woman Question, which has produced Married Women's Property Acts, Divorce Acts, Woman's Suffrage in local elections, and the curious deadlock to which the Weldon and Jackson cases have led our courts in the matter of conjugal rights. When we have achieved reforms enough to bring our institutions as far into harmony with the feelings of women as they now are with the feelings of men, there will no longer be a Woman Question. No conflict, no question.

Now the material of the dramatist is always some conflict of human feeling with circumstances; so that, since institutions are circumstances, every social question furnishes material for drama. But every drama does not involve a social question, because human feeling may be in conflict with circumstances which are not institutions, which raise no question at all, which are part of human destiny. To illustrate, take Mr. Pinero's *Second Mrs. Tanqueray* [most famous of the characters of the English play-

---

[1] Shaw's fanciful set of plays, designed for performance at Wagner's festival city of Bayreuth, is based on the achievement of Dr. Edward Jenner (1749–1823), the English physician who discovered vaccination.

wright Sir Arthur Wing Pinero, 1855–1934, in the play of the same name]. The heroine's feelings are in conflict with the human institutions which condemn to ostracism both herself and the man who marries her. So far, the play deals with a social question. But in one very effective scene the conflict is between that flaw in the woman's nature which makes her dependent for affection wholly on the atraction of her beauty, and the stealthy advance of age and decay to take her beauty away from her. Here there is no social question: age, like love, death, accident, and personal character, lies outside all institutions; and this gives it a permanent and universal interest which makes the drama that deals with it independent of period and place. Abnormal greatness of character, abnormal baseness of character, love, and death: with these alone you can, if you are a sufficiently great dramatic poet, make a drama that will keep your language alive long after it has passed out of common use. Whereas a drama with a social question for the motive cannot outlive the solution of that question. It is true that we can in some cases imaginatively reconstruct an obsolete institution and sympathize with the tragedy it has produced: for instance, the very dramatic story of Abraham commanded to sacrifice his son, with the interposition of the angel to make a happy ending; or the condemnation of Antonio to lose a pound of flesh, and his rescue by Portia at the last moment, have not completely lost their effect nowadays— though it has been much modified—through the obsolescence of sacrificial rites, belief in miracles, and the conception that a debtor's person belongs to his creditors. It is enough that we still have paternal love, death, malice, moneylenders, and the tragedies of criminal law. But when a play depends entirely on a social question—when the struggle in it is between man and a purely legal institution—nothing can prolong its life beyond that of the institution. For example, Mr. Grundy's *Slaves of the Ring* [a play of the utmost inconsequence by a sentimental and melodramatic playwright (Sydney Grundy, 1848–1914) of the same merit], in which the tragedy is produced solely by the conflict between the individual and the institution of indissoluble marriage, will not survive a rational law of divorce, and actually fails even now to grip an English audience because the solution has by this time become so very obvious. And that irrepressibly popular play *It's Never Too Late to Mend* will hardly survive our abominable criminal system. Thus we see that the drama which deals with the natural factors in human destiny, though not necessarily better than the drama which deals with the political factors, is likely to last longer.

It has been observed that the greatest dramatists show a preference for the non-political drama, the greatest dramas of all being almost elementarily natural. But so, though for a different reason, do the minor dramatists. The minor dramatist leads the literary life, and dwells in the world of imagination instead of in the world of politics, business, law, and the platform agitations by which social questions are ventilated. He therefore remains, as a rule, astonishingly ignorant of real life. He may be clever, imaginative, sympathetic, humorous, and observant of such manners as he has any clue to; but he has hardly any wit or knowledge of the world. Compare his work with that of Sheridan, and you feel the deficiency at once. Indeed, you need not go so far as Sheridan: Mr. Gilbert's *Trial by Jury* is unique among the works of living English playwrights, solely because it, too, is the work of a wit and a man of the world. Incidentally, it answers the inquiry as to whether social questions make good theatrical material; for though it is pointless, and, in fact, unintelligible except as a satire on a social institution (the breach-of-promise suit), it is highly entertaining, and has made the fortune of the author and his musical collaborator. *The School for Scandal*, the most popular of all modern comedies, is a dramatic sermon, just as *Never Too Late to Mend*, the most popular of modern melodramas, is a dramatic pamphlet: Charles Reade [1814–1884, author of *Never Too Late to Mend*, an English novelist who moved his own works and others' (such as Tennyson's *Dora* and Zola's *L'Assommoir*) onto the stage with some box-office and critical success but little theatrical skill] being another example of the distinction which the accomplished man of the world attains in the theatre as compared to the mere professional dramatist. In fact, it is so apparent that the best and most popular plays are dramatized sermons, pamphlets, satires, or bluebooks, that we find our popular authors, even when they have made a safe position for themselves by their success in purely imaginative drama, bidding for the laurels and the percentages of the sociologist dramatist. Mr Henry Arthur Jones [1851–1929, along with Shaw and Pinero, one of the top English playwrights at the turn of the century; admired by Shaw as a social portraitist in the theater] takes a position as the author of *The Middleman* and *The Cru-*

saders, which *The Silver King,* enormously popular as it was, never could have gained him; and Mr. Pinero, the author of *The Second Mrs. Tanqueray* and *The Notorious Mrs. Ebbsmith,* is a much more important person, and a much richer one, than the author of *Sweet Lavender* [a highly sentimental play by Pinero]. Of course, the sociology in some of these dramas is as imaginary as the names and addresses of the characters; but the imitation sociology testifies to the attractiveness of the real article.

We may take it then that the ordinary dramatist only neglects social questions because he knows nothing about them, and that he loses in popularity, standing, and money by his ignorance. With the great dramatic poet it is otherwise. Shakespear and Goethe do not belong to the order which "takes no interest in politics." Such minds devour everything with a keen appetite— fiction, science, gossip, politics, technical processes, sport, everything. Shakespear is full of little lectures of the concrete English kind, from Cassio on temperance to Hamlet on suicide. Goethe, in his German way, is always discussing metaphysical points. To master Wagner's music dramas is to learn a philosophy. It was so with all the great men until the present century. They swallowed all the discussions, all the social questions, all the topics, all the fads, all the enthusiasms, all the fashions of their day in their non-age; but their theme finally was not this social question or that social question, this reform or that reform, but humanity as a whole. To this day your great dramatic poet is never a socialist, nor an individualist, nor a positivist, nor a materialist, nor any other sort of "ist," though he comprehends all the "isms," and is generally quoted and claimed by all the sections as an adherent. Social questions are too sectional, too topical, too temporal to move a man to the mighty effort which is needed to produce great poetry. Prison reform may nerve Charles Reade to produce an effective and businesslike prose melodrama; but it could never produce *Hamlet, Faust,* or *Peer Gynt.*

It must, however, be borne in mind that the huge size of modern populations and the development of the press make every social question more momentous than it was formerly. Only a very small percentage of the population commits murder; but the population is so large that the frequency of executions is appalling. Cases which might have come under Goethe's notice in Weimar perhaps once in ten years come daily under the notice of modern newspapers, and are described by them as sensa-

tionally as possible. We are therefore witnessing a steady intensification in the hold of social questions on the larger poetic
imagination. *Les Misérables*, with its rivulet of story running
through a continent of essays on all sorts of questions, from religion to main drainage, is a literary product peculiar to the nineteenth century: it shows how matters which were trifles to
Æschylus become stupendously impressive when they are multiplied by a million in a modern civilized state. Zola's novels are
the product of an imagination driven crazy by a colossal police
intelligence, by modern hospitals and surgery, by modern war
correspondence, and even by the railway system—for in one of
his books the hero is Jack the Ripper and his sweetheart a locomotive engine. What would Aristophanes have said to a city
with fifteen thousand lunatics in it? Might he not possibly have
devoted a comedy to the object of procuring some amelioration
in their treatment? At all events, we find Ibsen, after producing,
in *Brand*, *Peer Gynt*, and *Emperor and Galilean*, dramatic poems
on the grandest scale, deliberately turning to comparatively
prosaic topical plays on the most obviously transitory social
questions, finding in their immense magnitude under modern
conditions the stimulus which, a hundred years ago, or four
thousand, he would only have received from the eternal strife
of man with his own spirit. *A Doll's House* will be as flat
as ditchwater when *A Midsummer Night's Dream* will still
be as fresh as paint; but it will have done more work in the
world; and that is enough for the highest genius, which is always
intensely utilitarian.

Let us now hark back for a moment to the remark I made on
Mr Grundy's *Sowing the Wind*:[2] namely, that its urgency and
consequently its dramatic interest are destroyed by the fact that
the social question it presents is really a solved one. Its production after *Les Surprises de Divorce* (which Mr Grundy himself
adapted for England) was an anachronism. When we suceed in
adjusting our social structure in such a way as to enable us to
solve social questions as fast as they become really pressing, they
will no longer force their way into the theatre. Had Ibsen, for instance, had any reason to believe that the abuses to which he

---

[2] Evidently a slip for *Slaves of the Ring*, mentioned above. This play was the
subject of Shaw's first contribution to *The Saturday Review* as dramatic critic
(January 5, 1895). He had printed on March 23, 1895 a comment on a revival
of *Sowing the Wind*, which he found better than Grundy's usual product.

called attention in his prose plays would have been adequately attended to without his interference, he would no doubt have gladly left them alone. The same exigency drove William Morris in England from his tapestries, his epics, and his masterpieces of printing, to try and bring his fellow-citizens to their senses by the summary process of shouting at them in the streets and in Trafalgar Square. John Ruskin's writing began with *Modern Painters;* Carlyle began with literary studies of German culture and the like: both were driven to become revolutionary pamphleteers. If people are rotting and starving in all directions, and nobody else has the heart or brains to make a disturbance about it, the great writers must. In short, what is forcing our poets to follow Shelley in becoming political and social agitators, and to turn the theatre into a platform for propaganda and an arena for discussion, is that whilst social questions are being thrown up for solution almost daily by the fierce rapidity with which industrial processes change and supersede one another through the rivalry of the competitors who take no account of ulterior social consequences, and by the change in public feeling produced by popular "education," cheap literature, facilitated travelling, and so forth, the political machinery by which alone our institutions can be kept abreast of these changes is so old-fashioned, and so hindered in its action by the ignorance, the apathy, the stupidity, and the class feuds of the electorate, that social questions never get solved until the pressure becomes so desperate that even governments recognize the necessity for moving. And to bring the pressure to this point, the poets must lend a hand to the few who are willing to do public work in the stages at which nothing but abuse is to be gained by it.

Clearly, however, when the unhappy mobs which we now call nations and populations settle down into ordered commonwealths, ordinary bread-and-butter questions will be solved without troubling the poets and philosophers. The Shelleys, the Morrises, the Ruskins and Carlyles of that day will not need to spend their energies in trying to teach elementary political economy to the other members of the commonwealth; nor will the Ibsens be devising object lessons in spoiled womanhood, sickly consciences, and corrupt town councils, instead of writing great and enduring dramatic poems.

I need not elaborate the matter further. The conclusions to be drawn are:

1. Every social question, arising as it must from a conflict between human feeling and circumstances, affords material for drama.

2. The general preference of dramatists for subjects in which the conflict is between man and his apparently inevitable and eternal rather than his political and temporal circumstances, is due in the vast majority of cases to the dramatist's political ignorance (not to mention that of his audience), and in a few to the comprehensiveness of his philosophy.

3. The hugeness and complexity of modern civilizations and the development of our consciousness of them by means of the press, have the double effect of discrediting comprehensive philosophies by revealing more facts than the ablest man can generalize, and at the same time intensifying the urgency of social reforms sufficiently to set even the poetic faculty in action on their behalf.

4. The resultant tendency to drive social questions on to the stage, and into fiction and poetry, will eventually be counteracted by improvements in social organization, which will enable all prosaic social questions to be dealt with satisfactorily long before they become grave enough to absorb the energies which claim the devotion of the dramatist, the storyteller, and the poet.

Bertolt Brecht (1898–1956) is as much a social dramatist as Bernard Shaw, yet, at the same time, as far removed in style and technique from Shaw as Shaw is from Ben Jonson or Molière. Brecht instructs by parable and by placard, by theater song and any other device that can be infused with his left-wing political and social ironies. Those ironies sometimes exist at the expense of his Communist associates, whether by intention or not, leaving Brecht a figure of captivating elusiveness in the modern theater. He had succeeded too well, perhaps, in his efforts to alienate his audiences, to keep them from vicarious involvement with the events on his stage, even when he and they shared the same political convictions. But no one can seriously debate the mastery with which Brecht brought learning and pleasure together in his self-styled "epic theater." Even in performances less meticulous than those he

THEATRE FOR LEARNING OR

himself mounted with his Berliner Ensemble, such plays as his The Threepenny Opera, Arturo Ui, Galileo, The Good Woman of Setzuan, Mother Courage, *and* The Caucasian Chalk Circle *entertain at least as much as they instruct. The principles outlined here thus seem applicable to the presentation of any serious point of view in the theater.*

THEATRE FOR PLEASURE

Bertolt Brecht

When anyone spoke of modern theater a few years ago, he mentioned the Moscow, the New York or the Berlin theatre. He may also have spoken of a particular production of Jouvet's in Paris, of Cochran's in London, or the Habima performance of "The Dybbuk,"[1] which, in fact, belonged to Russian

---

[1] Louis Jouvet (1887–1951), French actor and producer, particularly well known for his production of the plays of Jean Giraudoux. Charles Cochran (1873–1951), most famous of London impresarios of his era. The Habima was the famous Moscow theatrical company formed by Stanislavsky's assistant, Eugene Vakhtangov in 1917 for the performance of plays in Hebrew; the name means "stage."

theater, since it was directed by Vakhtangov; but by and large, there were only three capitals as far as modern theatre was concerned.

The Russian, the American and the German theatres were very different from one another, but they were alike in being modern, i.e., in introducing technical and artistic innovations. In a certain sense they even developed stylistic similarities, probably because technique is international (not only the technique directly required for the stage, but also that which exerts an influence on it, the film, for example) and because the cities in question were great progressive cities in great industrial countries. Most recently, the Berlin theatre seemed to have taken the lead among the most advanced capitalist countries. What was common to modern theatre found there its strongest and, for the moment, most mature expression.

The last phase of the Berlin theatre, which as I said only revealed in its purest form the direction in which modern theatre was developing, was the so-called *epic theatre*. What was known as the "Zeitstueck" (a play dealing with current problems— Trans.) or Piscator theater or the didactic play all belonged to epic theatre.

EPIC THEATRE

The expression "epic theatre" seemed self-contradictory to many people, since according to the teachings of Aristotle the epic and the dramatic forms of presenting a story were considered basically different from one another. The difference between the two forms was by no means merely seen in the fact that one was performed by living people while the other made use of a book—epic works like those of Homer and the *minnesingers* of the Middle Ages were likewise theatrical performances, and dramas like Goethe's "Faust" or Byron's "Manfred" admittedly achieved their greatest effect as books. Aristotle's teachings themselves distinguished the dramatic from the epic form as a difference in construction, whose laws were dealt with under two different branches of aesthetics. This construction depended on the different way in which the works were presented to the public, either on the stage or through a book, but nevertheless,

Mother Courage, *Berliner Ensemble, East Berlin.*
Photograph by René Burri. Magnum.

apart from that, "the dramatic" could also be found in epic works and "the epic" in dramatic works. The bourgeois novel in the last century considerably developed "the dramatic," which meant the strong centralization of plot and an organic interdependence of the separate parts. "The dramatic" is characterized by a certain passion in the tone of the exposition and a working out of the collision of forces. The epic writer, Döblin,[2] gave an excellent description when he said that the epic, in contrast to the dramatic, could practically be cut up with a scissors into single pieces, each of which could stand alone.

I do not wish to discuss here in what way the contrasts between epic and dramatic, long regarded as irreconcilable, lost their rigidity, but simply to point out that (other causes aside) technical achievements enabled the stage to include narrative elements in dramatic presentations. The potentialities of projection, the film, the greater facility in changing sets through machinery, completed the equipment of the stage and did so at a moment when the most important human events could no longer be so simply portrayed as through personification of the moving forces or through subordinating the characters to invisible, metaphysical powers. To make the events understandable, it had become necessary to play up the "bearing" of the *environment* upon the people living in it.

Of course this environment had been shown in plays before, not, however, as an independent element but only from the viewpoint of the main figure of the drama. It rose out of the hero's reaction to it. It was seen as a storm may be "seen" if you observe on the sea a ship spreading its sails and the sails bellying. But in the epic theatre it was now to appear as an independent element.

The stage began to narrate. The narrator no longer vanished with the fourth wall. Not only did the background make its own comment on stage happenings through large screens which evoked other events occurring at the same time in other places, documenting or contradicting statements by characters through quotations projected onto a screen, lending tangible, concrete statistics to abstract discussions, providing facts and figures for happening which were plastic but unclear in their meaning; the

---

[2] Alfred Döblin (1878–1957), German novelist and essayist. His best-known work was the novel *Berlin-Alexanderplatz*.

actors no longer threw themselves completely into their roles
but maintained a certain distance from the character performed
by them, even distinctly inviting criticism.

Nothing permitted the audience any more to lose itself
through simple empathy, uncritically (and practically without
any consequences) in the experiences of the characters on the
stage. The presentation exposed the subject matter and the happenings to a process of de-familiarization.[3] De-familiarization was
required to make things understood. When things are "self-
evident," understanding is simply dispensed with. The "natural"
had to be given an element of the *conspicuous*. Only in this way
could the laws of cause and effect become plain. Characters had
to behave as they *did* behave, and at the same time be capable
of behaving otherwise.

These were great changes.

TWO OUTLINES

The following little outlines may indicate in what respect the
function of the epic is distinguished from that of the dramatic
theatre.

1.

Dramatic form	*Epic form*
The stage "incarnates" an event.	It relates it.
Involves the audience in an action, uses up its activity.	Makes the audience an observer, but arouses its activity.
Helps it to feel.	Compels it to make decisions.
Communicates experiences.	Communicates insights.
The audience is projected into an event.	Is confronted with it.
Suggestion is used.	Arguments are used.
Sensations are preserved.	Impelled to the level of perceptions.

[3] In German, "Entfremdung," sometimes translated as "alienation," and sometimes called "Verfremdung" by Brecht. The latter is an invented word like "defamiliarization."—*Translator's note.*

Dramatic form	*Epic form*
The character is a known quantity.	The character is subjected to investigation.
Man unchangeable.	Man who can change and make changes.
His drives.	His motives.
Events move in a straight line.	In "irregular" curves.
Natura non facit saltus.	Facit saltus.
The world as it is.	The world as it is becoming.

2.

The audience in the dramatic theater says:
Yes, I have felt that too.—That's how I am.—That is only natural.—That will always be so.—This person's suffering shocks me because he has no way out. This is great art: everything in it is self-evident.—I weep with the weeping, I laugh with the laughing.

The audience in the epic theater says:
I wouldn't have thought that.—People shouldn't do things like that.—That's extremely odd, almost unbelievable.—This has to stop.—This person's suffering shocks me, because there might be a way out for him.—This is great art: nothing in it is self-evident.—I laugh over the weeping, I weep over the laughing.

DIDACTIC THEATER

The stage began to instruct.

Oil, inflation, war, social struggles, the family, religion, wheat, the meat-packing industry became subjects for theatrical portrayal. Choruses informed the audience about facts it did not know. In montage form, films showed events all over the world. Projections provided statistical data. As the "background" came to the fore, the actions of the characters became exposed to criticism. Wrong and right actions were exhibited. People were shown who knew what they were doing, and other people were shown who did not know. The theater entered the province of the philosophers—at any rate, the sort of philosophers who wanted not only to explain the world but also to change it. Hence the theater philosophized; hence it instructed. And what became of entertainment? Were the audiences put back in school, treated as illiterates? Were they to take examinations and be given marks?

It is the general opinion that a very decided difference exists between learning and being entertained. The former may be useful, but only the latter is pleasant. Thus we have to defend the epic theater against a suspicion that it must be an extremely unpleasant, a joyless, indeed a wearing business.

Well, we can only say that the contrast between learning and being entertained does not necessarily exist in nature, it has not always existed and it need not always exist.

Undoubtedly, the kind of learning we did in school, in training for a profession, etc., is a laborious business. But consider under what circumstances and for what purpose it is done. It is, in fact, a purchase. Knowledge is simply a commodity. It is acquired for the purpose of being re-sold. All those who have grown too old for school have to pursue knowledge on the Q.T., so to speak, because anybody who admits he still has to study depreciates himself as one who knows too little. Apart from that, the utility of learning is very much limited by factors over which the student has no control. There is unemployment, against which no knowledge protects. There is the division of labor, which makes comprehensive knowledge unnecessary and impossible. Often, those who study do it only when they see no other possibility of getting ahead. There is not much knowledge that procures power, but much knowledge is only procured through power.

Learning means something very different to people in different strata of society. There are people who cannot conceive of any improvement in conditions; conditions seem good enough to them. Whatever may happen to petroleum, they make a profit out of it. And they feel, after all, that they are getting rather old. They can scarcely expect many more years of life. So why continue to learn? They have already spoken their "Ugh!"[4] But there are also people who have not yet "had their turn," who are discontented with the way things are, who have an immense practical interest in learning, who want orientation badly, who know they are lost without learning—these are the best and most ambitious learners. Such differences also exist among nations and peoples. Thus the lust for learning is dependent on various

[4] Reference to popular German literature about American Indians, by the author Karl May, in which, after a chieftain had given his opinion at a pow-wow he would conclude, "I have spoken. Ugh!"—*Translator's note.*

things; in short, there *is* thrilling learning, joyous and militant learning.

If learning could not be delightful, then the theater, by its very nature, would not be in a position to instruct.

Theater remains theater, even when it is didactic theater, and if it is good theater it will entertain.

THEATER AND SCIENCE

"But what has science to do with art? We know very well that science can be diverting, but not everything that diverts belongs in the theater."

I have often been told when I pointed out the inestimable services that modern science, properly utilized, could render to art, especially to the theater, that art and science were two admirable but completely different fields of human activity. This is a dreadful platitude, of course, and the best thing to do is admit at once that it is quite right, like most platitudes. Art and science operate in very different ways—agreed. Still, I must admit—bad as this may sound—that I cannot manage as an artist without making use of certain sciences. This may make many people seriously doubt my artistic ability. They are accustomed to regarding poets as unique, almost unnatural beings who unerringly, practically like gods, perceive things that others can only perceive through the greatest efforts and hard work. Naturally, it is unpleasant to have to admit not being one of those so endowed. But it must be admitted. It must also be denied that this application to science has anything to do with some pardonable avocation indulged in the evening after work is done. Everyone knows that Goethe also went in for natural science, Schiller for history—presumably this is the charitable assumption —as a sort of hobby. I would not simply accuse these two of having needed the science for their poetic labors, nor would I use them to excuse myself, but I must say I need the sciences. And I must even admit that I regard suspiciously all sorts of people who I know do not keep abreast of science, who, in other words, sing as the birds sing, or as they imagine the birds sing. This does not mean that I would reject a nice poem about the taste of a flounder or the pleasure of a boating party just because the author had not studied gastronomy or navigation. But I think that unless

every resource is employed towards understanding the great,
complicated events in the world of man, they cannot be seen
adequately for what they are.

Let us assume that we want to portray great passions or events
which influence the fates of peoples. Such a passion today might
be the drive for power. Supposing that a poet "felt" this drive
and wanted to show someone striving for power—how could he
absorb into his own experience the extremely complicated mechanism within which the struggle for power today takes place? If
his hero is a political man, what are the workings of politics, if he
is a business man, what are the workings of business? And then
there are poets who are much less passionately interested in any
individual's drive for power than in business affairs and politics
as such! How are they to acquire the necessary knowledge?
They will scarcely find out enough by going around and keeping their eyes open, although that is at least better than rolling
their eyes in a fine frenzy. The establishment of a newspaper
like the *Voelkische Beobachter* or a business like Standard Oil is
a rather complicated matter, and these things are not simply absorbed through the pores. Psychology is an important field for
the dramatist. It is supposed that while an ordinary person may
not be in a position to discover, without special instruction, what
makes a man commit murder, certainly a writer ought to have the
"inner resources" to be able to give a picture of a murderer's
mental state. The assumption is that you only need look into
yourself in such a case; after all, there is such a thing as imagination. . . . For a number of reasons I can no longer abandon
myself to this amiable hope of managing so comfortably. I cannot find in myself alone all the motives which, as we learn from
newspapers and scientific reports, are discovered in human beings. No more than any judge passing sentence am I able to
imagine adequately, unaided, the mental state of a murderer.
Modern psychology, from psychoanalysis to behaviorism, provides me with insights which help me to form a quite different
judgment of the case, especially when I take into consideration
the findings of sociology, and do not ignore economics or history. You may say: this is getting complicated. I must answer, it
is complicated. Perhaps I can talk you into agreeing with me
that a lot of literature is extremely primitive; yet you will ask in
grave concern: Wouldn't such an evening in the theater be a
pretty alarming business? The answer to that is: No.

Whatever knowledge may be contained in a poetic work, it must be completely converted into poetry. In its transmuted form, it gives the same type of satisfaction as any poetic work. And although it does not provide that satisfaction found in science as such, a certain inclination to penetrate more deeply into the nature of things, a desire to make the world controllable, are necessary to ensure enjoyment of poetic works generated by this era of great discoveries and inventions.

IS THE EPIC THEATER
A SORT OF "MORAL INSTITUTION"?

According to Friedrich Schiller the theater should be a moral institution. When Schiller posed this demand it scarcely occurred to him that by moralizing from the stage he might drive the audience out of the theater. In his day the audience had no objection to moralizing. Only later on did Friedrich Nietzsche abuse him as the moral trumpeter of Säckingen.[5] To Nietzsche a concern with morality seemed a dismal affair; to Schiller it seemed completely gratifying. He knew of nothing more entertaining and satisfying than to propagate ideals. The bourgeoisie was just establishing the concept of the nation. To furnish your house, show off your new hat, present your bills for payment is highly gratifying. But to speak of the decay of your house, to have to sell your old hat and pay the bills yourself is a truly dismal affair, and that was how Friedrich Nietzsche saw it a century later. It was no use talking to him about morality or, in consequence, about the other Friedrich. Many people also attacked the epic theater, claiming it was too moralistic. Yet moral utterances were secondary in the epic theater. Its intention was less to moralize than to study. And it did study, but then came the rub: the moral of the story. Naturally, we cannot claim that we began making studies just because studying was so much fun and not for any concrete reason, or that the results of our studies then took us completely by surprise. Undoubtedly there were painful discrepancies in the world around us, conditions that were hard to bear, conditions of a kind not only hard to bear for

[5] Nietzsche's quip referred to a banal verse tale by Viktor Scheffel, *Der Trompeter von Säckingen*, a standard favorite in Germany's "plush sofa kultur"—a parallel of Victorianism—in the second half of the nineteenth century.—*Translator's note.*

moral reasons. Hunger, cold and hardship are not only burdensome for moral reasons. And the purpose of our investigation
was not merely to arouse moral misgivings about certain conditions (although such misgivings might easily be felt, if not by
every member of the audience; such misgivings, for example,
were seldom felt by those who profited by the conditions in
question). The purpose of our investigation was to make visible
the means by which those onerous conditions could be done
away with. We were not speaking on behalf of morality but on
behalf of the wronged. These are really two different things, for
moral allusions are often used in telling the wronged that they
must put up with their situation. For such moralists, people exist
for morality, not morality for people.

Nevertheless it can be deduced from these remarks to what
extent and in what sense the epic theater is a moral institution.

CAN EPIC THEATER
BE PERFORMED ANYWHERE?

From the standpoint of style, the epic theater is nothing especially new. In its character of show, of demonstration, and its
emphasis on the artistic, it is related to the ancient Asian theater.
The medieval mystery play, and also the classical Spanish and
Jesuit theaters, showed an instructive tendency.

Those theater forms corresponded to certain tendencies of
their time and disappeared with them. The modern epic theater
is also linked with definite tendencies. It can by no means be performed anywhere. Few of the great nations today are inclined
to discuss their problems in the theater. London, Paris, Tokyo
and Rome maintain their theaters for quite different purposes.
Only in a few places, and not for long, have circumstances been
favorable to an epic, instructive theater. In Berlin, fascism put a
violent end to the development of such a theater.[6]

Besides a certain technical standard, it presupposes a powerful
social movement which has an interest in the free discussion of

---

[6] After the defeat of the Nazis in 1945, the German administrators of the then
Soviet-occupied zone—now the German Democratic Republic—invited Brecht to
establish his own theater in East Berlin. This theater, the "Berliner Ensemble," is
recognized today all over the world as a classical type of epic theater.—*Translator's
note.*

vital problems, the better to solve them, and can defend this interest against all opposing tendencies.

The epic theater is the broadest and most far-reaching experiment in great modern theater, and it has to overcome all the enormous difficulties that all vital forces in the area of politics, philosophy, science and art have to overcome.

Translated from the German by Edith Anderson.

THE ETERNAL LAW OF THE DRAMATIST

Jean Giraudoux

If there is a social consciousness in either the plays or the dramatic theory of Jean Giraudoux (1882–1944), it springs from a world of vision, one constantly and perilously at odds with the world of drab reality. Wherever possible, Giraudoux's fanciful figures elect illusion and dream in their combat with the tyrannies that bedevil their lives— the tyrannies of war and super-finance, of nationalist and religious and sexual simplifications, of huge things and of little things. His Judith, La Guerre de Troie n'aura pas lieu (The Trojan War Will Not Take Place, *translated by Christopher Fry as* Tiger at the Gates), Ondine, Sodom and Gomorrah, *and* The Madwoman of Chaillot *are perhaps the most considerable body of plays contributed to the French theater in the first half of this century. Tragedy, irony, fantasy, paradox—all are in Giraudoux, all are part of the dramatic credo so swiftly and so engagingly sketched here. The words in which this most elegant of prophets defines his prophetic theater, the concluding words of this piece, are worthy of pondering and, it may be, just the faintest* amen—or, as one of Giraudoux's characters would murmur, ainsi soit-il, *"so be it."*

Two rules govern, if I may speak in this way, the eternal law of the dramatist.

The first consecrates the sorry and somewhat ridiculous position of the author in relation to those of his characters that he has created and given to the theatre. To the extent that he finds a character to be docile, familiar, belonging to him, to that extent the character becomes foreign and indifferent to the author once it is given to the public. The first actor to play the part constitutes the first in a series of reincarnations in which the character becomes more and more distant from its author and steals away from him forever. This is also true of the play as a whole. After the first performance it belongs to the actors, and the author who haunts the wings become a sort of ghost, detested by the stagehands if he listens or is indiscreet; after the hundredth performance, especially if the play is a good one, it belongs to the public. The truth is that the playwright really owns only his bad plays. The independence of those of his characters who have succeeded is complete; the life they lead on tour or in America is a constant denial of their filial obligations, and, while the heroes of your novels follow you everywhere calling you Father or Daddy, dramatic characters among those whom you meet by chance, as has happened to me in Carcassonne or in Los Angeles, have become total strangers. To a large extent it is to punish them for this independence that Goethe, Claudel, and many others have made new versions of plays with their favorite heroines. In vain. The new Margaret, the new Helen, the new Violaine were no less prompt to abandon them. I once went to a performance of *The Tidings Brought to Mary* with Claudel and, on that occasion at least, this situation worked in my favor: the play, I observed, was infinitely more mine than it was his.

How many authors are obliged to search in an actress or actor for the memory of the reflection of a daughter or son who has gone off—much as parents, in a more everyday setting, must do in a son-in-law or daughter-in-law. . . . On the terrace of Weber, in the generals' vestibule, on the lawn of the country house of a famous actress, how many of these couples have we met: Feydeau and Cassive, Jules Renard and Suzanne Deprès, Réjane and Maurice Donnay [famous pairings of the late nineteenth- and early twentieth-century French writers and actresses], the woman just a little absent-minded, the man attentive and absorbed in memories, loquacious and questioning, talking about the woman who was not there.

The second law, a corollary and the reverse of the first, consecrates the wonderful position of the dramatic author in relation to his epoch and its events, and indicates his role. And here, if I wish to be truthful, I surely must relieve my colleagues and myself of any false modesty. This narrator, who in the play is but a voice, without personality, without responsibility, but who is also an historian and an avenger, exists in the age as flesh and bone; he is the dramatic author himself. For every playwright worthy of the name, one should be able to say, when his work is performed: "Add the archangel to your play!" It is vain to

believe that a year or a century can find the resonance and the
elevation which are necessary, in the long run, to this pathetic
debate and this sorry effort which is each moment of our passage
on earth, if there were not a spokesman for the tragedy or the
drama to fix its height and to plumb its foundation and vault.
Tragedy and drama are the confession this army of salvation and
damnation which is humanity must also make in public, without
reticence and in its highest pitch, for the echo of its voice is
more distinct and more real than the voice itself. We should not
delude ourselves on this point. The relationship between the
theatre and religious solemnity is evident, and it is not by chance
that in front of our cathedrals there used to be dramatic performances at every occasion. The theatre is at its best in the
church courtyard. It is there that the public goes to the theater
on holiday nights, to the illuminated confession of its dwarfed
and gigantic destinies. Calderón is humanity confessing its desire
for eternity, Corneille its dignity, Racine its weakness, Shakespeare its passion for life, Claudel its condition of sin and salvation, Goethe its humanity, Kleist its lightning. Epochs are in accord with themselves only if the crowd comes into these radiant
confessionals which are the theatres or the arenas, and as much
as possible, in its most brilliant confessional dress, in order to
increase the solemnity of the event, to listen to its own confessions of cowardice and sacrifice, of hate and passion. And
what if the crowd too should exclaim: "Add the prophet to the
play!" For there is no theatre which is not prophecy. Not this
false divination which gives names and dates, but true prophecy,
that which reveals to men these surprising truths: that the living
must live, that the living must die, that autumn must follow
summer, spring follow winter, that there are four elements, that
there is happiness, that there are innumerable miseries, that life
is a reality, that it is a dream, that man lives in peace, that man
lives on blood; in short, those things they will never know. Such
is the theatre, the public restoration of these incredible prodi-
gies whose visions will disturb and overwhelm the night of the
onlookers, but whose dawn, no doubt—my faith rejoices in it—
to make the author's mission an everyday reality, will have already diluted in them the lesson and the memory. This is dramatic representation, the spectator's sudden consciousness of the
permanent condition of this living and indifferent humanity:
passion and death.

AN AUDIENCE OF ONE

Tyrone Guthrie

It is a commonplace that the theater provides a constant mixture of the arts, all the arts, at one time or another. Who mixes them? How are they mixed? Who sorts out the arts of preparation— those on paper, those in wood and steel and cloth, and electric wire—from the arts of performance— those of flesh and blood? Is it the actor, the director, the producer? This famous set of answers is offered by Tyrone Guthrie (1900–   ), or, to give him his full title, Sir William Tyrone Guthrie. Guthrie has performed as director and producer in the theater and in opera, in film, radio, and television. He has produced plays for the commercial theater in England and America, and has created and administered repertory companies famous on both sides of the Atlantic, not the least of them the one in Minneapolis that bears his name. He is particularly well known for his modern-dress versions of Elizabethan plays. One wonders, after reading him here, whether he would not prefer to be known for his mastery of rhythm and what he calls "psychic evocations."

Producing a play clearly requires the coordinated efforts of many people, and the producer is no more than the coordinator. His work may, and I think should, have creative functions, but not always. The important thing is gathering together the different pieces and welding many disparate elements into one complete unity, which is never, of course, fully achieved in artistic matters.

The work of the producer can be analyzed— indeed has been analyzed—in many different ways. I propose to deal with it under two headings: firstly, the producer in relation to the script of the play, that is to say the raw material of his work; and secondly, the producer in relation to actors and staff, that is animate collaborators.

It seems to me that the producer's business,

when faced either with a new script or with being asked to revive a classic or an old play, is first of all to decide what it is about. Clearly, that is not entirely simple. To take an obvious instance, who is really going to give the final word as to what *Hamlet* is about? As we all know, more books have been written about *Hamlet* than almost any other topic under the sun. I am told that, as far as biographies are concerned, the three champions about whom the most has been written are Jesus Christ, Hamlet and Napoleon Bonaparte, in that order. *Hamlet* is an obviously difficult case in which to decide what the play is about, but take a nice simple little play called *Charley's Aunt*. What is that about? Is it just a question of telling the story, or is it a question of finding a meaning to the story? Are Charley's "Aunt" and all those jolly undergraduates symbols of this or that, or are they to be taken at face value? Is the thing to be—as I have seen it done in Scandinavia—a serious study of English university life, or is it just to be made as funny as possible? Personally, I think the latter; but before you can make it funny you have got to decide why it is funny, what is funny about it, and what the joke is, which is quite a tricky little problem.

I think very often the lighter the play is the more it is composed of thistledown and little else, the more difficult it is to pin down. One has often seen little tiny plays absolutely slain by the great mechanism brought to bear on their own interpretation. An obvious case in point is *Così Fan Tutte*. I do not know whether anyone has seen a satisfactory performance of that. I have seen it a great many times, but it always seems to me that a great many steam hammers in human form are assembled to crack a little jewelled acorn.

With regard to what the script is about, the last person who, in my opinion, should be consulted, even if he is alive or around, is the author. If the author is a wise man, he will admit straight away that he does not know what it is about, unless it is a very perfunctory work indeed. If it is just a little piece of journalism on the minor problems of psychoanalysis, then he probably will know all too well what it is about. But if it has the potentialities of being an important work of art, I am perfectly convinced he will not have the faintest idea of what he has really written. He will probably know what he thinks he has written, but that will be the least important part of it. Were it possible to find out, I would lay any money that Shakespeare had only the vaguest idea of what he was writing when he wrote *Hamlet;* that the major part of the meaning of it eluded him because it proceeded from the subconscious. A great work of art is like an iceberg in that ninety per cent of it is below the surface of consciousness. Therefore, in my opinion, the more important the work of art, the less the author will know what he has written.

I had the great privilege and pleasure to know the late James Bridie extremely well. I worked with him often, but he would never even discuss what his plays were about. He would say, "How should I know? I am the last person you should ask. I am only the author. I have written an armature, inside which, possibly, are the deepest ideas which have never quite formulated themselves in my consciousness. If, as I hope and believe, I am a poet, there will be something in these, but I am the last person to know what it is."

The producer has to decide what he thinks the play is about, and of course I am largely joking when I say that he does not really take the author seriously. Naturally he does, but not as to the deeper, the inner and the over-and-above, the between and through, meaning of the lines. If somebody does not decide at an early stage what the play is about, obviously the casting will be made for the wrong reasons. Ideally, a play should be cast because the actors chosen are people that somebody—be it the producer or be it the manager—thinks will express the play best. In fact, in the exigencies of commercial production and the exigencies of practical affairs, all too often plays are cast because somebody thinks that Mr. X will help to sell the beastly thing, and Mr. X happens to be living with Miss Y so she is a cinch for the leading lady, and all sorts of vulgar and extraneous considerations of that kind which really have nothing whatever to do with art but everything in the world to do with the practical business of putting on a play. I cannot sufficiently differentiate between the two, but seeing that we are speaking in these almost hallowed precincts I am going to try to behave as though we were in an ideal atmosphere and plays were cast solely with artistic considerations in view, or at all events very much in the foreground with practical things far away in the background.

In theory, the artistic way to cast a play is to decide who, of the available actors, seems to be the most like the principal part

in the script that we are given, and who would best understand
the thing. Let me qualify that. It is not entirely a question of who
is the most like the principal character, because very often the
last thing that an actor does well is to portray a character that is
like himself as one conceives him to be in private life. Very many
actors do their best work when they are hiding from themselves
behind a mass of hair and make-up and fantasy, when they present something entirely unlike their real selves.

One must think which of the available actors would seem to
give the best interpretation of a given part. That is why, at a
very early stage, the whole business of producing a play has to
move into conference. It is, in my opinion, very unwise for the
leading actor not to work step by step from the very earliest
stages with the three or four people with whom he is going to
collaborate most closely: the manager, or whoever is responsible
for the budgetary financial side of the production, the leading
actors, and certainly the designer, the man who is ultimately going to be responsible for the pictorial look of the thing. All their
work should grow together and should, I think, be the result of
a productive exchange of ideas.

Therefore, it is clearly necessary that, if the thing is going to
work well, they should be people who can to some extent speak
one another's language, who can exchange ideas, who can admit
themselves to be wrong without red faces in the company of the
others, and so on. So that, long before the thing gets to the stage
of rehearsal and parts being read or movements made, there
should have been a quite extensive exchange of ideas about the
look of the thing, about the sound of the thing, about the shape
of the thing in predominantly musical and choreographic terms.

To elaborate that a little, the performance of a play is clearly
analogous to the performance of a symphonic piece of music. By
the time the play is read, if it is properly rehearsed, the diverse
voices, the group of people who are playing the thing, will have
found a music for their parts. Why acting, in my opinion, is so
much more interesting than opera singing is that the actors invent the music of their parts to a very great extent. In an operatic
score, the composer's intention is made extraordinarily clear. The
rhythm, the inflection, the loudness and softness, the pitch and
the pace at which the idea is to be conveyed, are all clearly defined in the score. Almost the only creative piece of work left
to the conductor and the singers is the color, because so far no

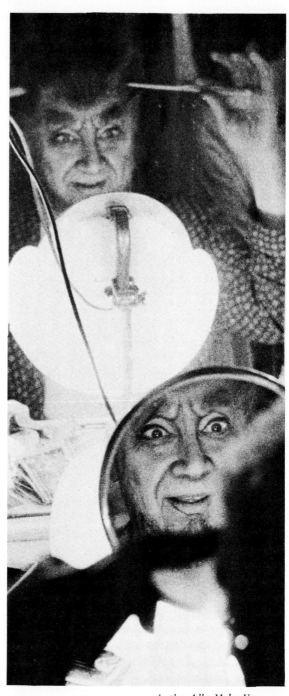

Luther Adler Makes Up.
Photograph by Leonard Balish.

form of notation has been found for musical color. The actor has to find nearly all those things for himself. Supposing you are an actor who is playing Hamlet. "To be, or not to be: that is the question: whether 'tis nobler in the mind to suffer . . ."—those infinitely familiar lines. You have to find the inflection, that is to say the tune, to which they are sung or spoken, the pitch, the pace, the rhythm and the color. That is, in fact, very highly creative.

Parallel with the creation of the actor must, I think, come the coordination of the producer. Supposing two of us are playing a scene, and one has decided that the scene must be played lightly and forcibly, and the other person takes a different view of the scene and feels that it must be managed in a very dark and very black way with long pauses. It is the business of the producer to coordinate the two without necessarily making either man feel that he has been a fool or stupid. It is a point of view which way the scene should be taken, and somebody has to be the chairman, somebody has to decide. That is really in most cases what the producer is.

I know there is an idea abroad, largely cultivated in popular fiction, about the theater and films, that the producer is a very dominant person who goes around doing a lot of ordering about, saying, "Stand here, stand there, copy me, do it this way, do it that way." Of course, with experienced and accomplished actors that would be complete nonsense. Imagine me saying to Dame Edith Evans, "Do it this way, dear, copy me."

The performance of a play should be able to be observed by anybody who knows it well just like a graph, like a patient's temperature chart, like a graph of the sales statistics of a firm or anything else. One should be able to see the peaks and the hollows, and it should be possible to delineate the shape of each scene in a graph, which helps to make the scene more intelligible, which helps to make it illuminate the scene preceding it and the scene following it, which helps it to contrast, and at the same time to blend with the neighboring scenes; and, while each little scene should have a graph, similarly a graph of the whole act should arise from that.

Now on to the second main heading about production.

First of all, and very briefly, there is the question of organization, discipline and that kind of thing. If the company is any good and if the producer is any good, that is simply a matter of general

convenience. I do not think the producer has any difficulty over
discipline provided the rehearsals are not boring, and provided
they are kept moving not at the pace of the very slowest person
present but at a fairly decent tempo.

Then comes the question of coaching. How far is a producer
to coach the interpretation? How much is he to say to the actors,
"Do it this way"? I do not think one can give a complete answer
to that. If you are taking the first production that has ever been
done by the dramatic society attached to the Little Pifflington
Women's Institute, you will probably have to do a great deal of
coaching and coaxing to break down the self-conscious giggling
of people who are quite unaccustomed to impersonation and
pretending to be someone they are not. But if you have a
good professional cast the amount of coaching you have to
do is very small.

I do not think one should be at all afraid of saying to actors in
a quite dogmatic way, "Play this scene sitting on the sofa, and
if you are not comfortable let me know later on, but don't decide until we have done it once or twice. Later on, maybe you
would feel like getting up halfway through and going to the
window." Otherwise, if the actor is allowed to grope it out too
much for himself, there is a waste of time, and the dominant
personalities start bullying the milder, more unselfish and co-
operative ones, which is what we have to be on the lookout for.

Then comes what I have tried to indicate is very much the
main business of the producer, the work of coordination from
the departments inwards.

Clearly, the coordinating of an idea, so far as it is concerned
with visual matters, lies to a considerable degree in the hands of
the person responsible for the lighting. Here, as elsewhere, I feel
there should be the minimum of dogmatism. A good designer
will have been working from quite an early stage in collabora-
tion with the leading actors. Actors on the whole are sensible
people about their clothes. Most actors have not at all a vain idea
of their own appearance, but a very realistic appreciation of their
good points and bad points, and they can be very helpful to a
designer in suggesting things like the length of their coats or the
width of their sleeves. If an actor says, "I want a long sleeve
because I think I can do something with it," that should be taken
very seriously; and, in my opinion, an actor should never be
forced to wear a dress he does not like, unless it is for economic

or disciplinary reasons. You could not expect people to feel free, unself-conscious and at ease on the stage in dresses they feel to be unsuitable.

Where I think the producer's work of coordination requires the greatest amount of time and care spent upon it is in the vocal interpretation of the play. As I have already tried to indicate, the performance of a play is, on a smaller scale, a performance of a musical work. The script is, as it were, sung, because speaking and singing are, after all, the same process. Although I am speaking now and not singing, I am uttering a definable tune all the time. Every syllable I utter is on a certain pitch and a musician could say precisely where it was. Every sentence that I phrase is consciously phrased in a certain rhythm. The pauses, although I am not conscious of it, are expressing an instinctive need to pause, not merely to breathe, but for clarity and various other interpretative purposes. This is even more pronounced in the performance of a play, where all that has been most carefully thought out in terms of pace, rhythm, pitch, volume and all the rest of it, to make a certain expressive effect. That is particularly where the coordinating hand of the producer is required, joining up the various songs that are being sung and making them into a unit; and similarly, joining up the various patterns that are being danced, because even in the simplest realistic comedy, in the most ordinary kind of realistic set—the actors have to move, and their movements have to tot up to some kind of choreographic design which expresses the play, which has some meaning over and above the common-sense position in which one would pour tea or put sugar into it. For long stretches of the play the positions have to be guided not at all by anything that is afoot. Of course, it is mere journalism to think that plays are concerned with action. They are not. Plays in the cinema may be, but in the theater the action is a tiny point.

In almost every play for the stage, there is scarcely any action. The movements of the play are almost all concerned with the expression of ideas and not of action. If there is action, it is very short-lived and very brief. The choreography is much more concerned with the subtle delineation of emotions by the way people are placed, with the subtle changes of emphasis by putting people into the brighter light or taking them out of it, by having them face the audience or turn their backs, by putting them in the center or near the side. It is all very much more delicate and

allusive than simply getting them into common-sense positions
to perform certain actions.

Finally, I should like to discuss what to me is the most interesting part of the job, the blending of intuition with technique.
If I may elaborate those terms, by intuition I mean the expression
of a creative idea that comes straight from the subconscious, that
is not arrived at by a process of ratiocination at all. It is my experience that all the best ideas in art just arrive, and it is absolutely no good concentrating on them and hoping for the best.
The great thing is to relax and just trust that the Holy Ghost
will arrive and the idea will appear. The sought idea is nearly
always, in my opinion, the beta plus idea. The alpha plus idea
arrives from literally God knows where. Prayer and fasting can
no doubt help, but concentration and ratiocination are, I think,
only a hindrance. And yet I think no artist worth his salt will feel
he can rely on inspiration. Inspiration must be backed up by a
very cast-iron technique.

It is the case that as one gets older one's technique, if one is an
industrious and intelligent person, tends to become better; but
there is also the danger that it becomes a little slick. I think not
only artists, but anybody engaged in any activity must feel the
same thing. The record begins to get worn, and we slip too
easily into old grooves, the same association of ideas comes back
too readily and easily. I notice with my own work in the theater
—and I have been at it now for nearly thirty years—that I have
to check myself all the time from slipping into certain very obvious and, to me now, rather dull choreographic mannerisms. I
instinctively think, "Oh, obviously the right place is so-and-so,
and the right way to group this is such-and-such." Then I think,
why do I think that? And usually the only reason is that one has
done it that way a good many times before. That is obviously
frightfully dangerous in any creative work. It is the negation of
creation; it is just falling back onto habit.

Yet there are certain very valuable things about experience and
about technique. It is now comparatively easy for me, in late
middle age, to establish a good relation with actors. They think
because I have been at it for a long time that I know something
about it, and they are readier to take suggestions from me now
than they were twenty-five years ago when I was a beginner,
though I am inclined to think that most of the suggestions are
duller ones. Twenty-five years ago, intuition functioned oftener

and more readily. That is, I think, one of the very difficult paradoxes about production.

Clearly, for practical reasons, it is very difficult to put the
highly intuitive, gifted youngster in charge of a responsible production. He will make too many mistakes. He will be too dependent on the things that experience and authority bring easily
from the older people. Also, it is difficult for the senior actors. It
requires enormous tact, both on the part of the young producer
and the old actor, to be helpful to one another. Yet the young
producer is precisely what the experienced actor with a cast-
iron technique—and consequently a great many mannerisms, too
many clichés and short cuts—needs. He needs a very bright,
sharp, critical young person of twenty-five to say, "No, Sir X,
don't do it that way. You have been doing it that way for
twenty-five years and it has been fine for twenty-five years, but
that is just the reason for not doing it that way now." Well, you
can see that unless that is done with supreme tact it is all too easy
for Sir X or Dame Y to cast down their script and summon their
Rolls-Royce.

I should like to conclude by telling a little anecdote which was
told to me by a distinguished producer now resident in this
country, who began life in Czechoslovakia and early in his career went to Germany. He soon got quite a good position while
still in his early twenties in one of the German provincial
theaters. He was a fine-looking young fellow and very "castable"
in hero parts, and the management of the theater sent him to see
Reinhardt, then at the very apex of his celebrity and power in
Berlin. My friend was still young enough to be madly thrilled,
not only with the great opportunity of meeting this god and the
possible advancement that it might produce, but with such childish and naïve, but extremely natural, things as the overnight
journey in a first-class sleeper and all that kind of thing. All this
was a terrific thrill, and he described very touchingly how he
enjoyed it. He arrived in Berlin on a delicious crisp autumn
morning, and went to the theater at which Reinhardt was working, the Grosses Schauspielhaus. He described the grand chande-
liers, the polished floors, the gentlemen in livery who collected
him at the door, how he swept up the marble staircase, along a
passage with portraits of eminent people all down the side,
through a less important door in the side of the passage, down
some stairs with no polish and carpets at all, through a very

squalid little passage, round various corners, and across a court-yard, until he came to a room really more like a kitchen. He said at first the only things he could see were the long windows all down one side with the sun streaming in. Then, as he began to get accustomed to that, he saw a group of rather drab-looking actors rehearsing at one end. Then he suddenly saw that one of these actors was somebody whose face had been familiar to him all his life, a great star of Germany, and I think he had that experience which anybody has who suddenly comes face-to-face with a very familiar face that he has seen illustrated, whether politician, film star, or anybody else. You suddenly think, "How small they are! I thought they were much bigger." He was busy taking all this in and thinking what a small person this gentleman was whom he had always thought so great when suddenly, at the end of the room, he saw a very unimportant-looking gentleman sitting on the kitchen table swinging his legs and looking at his hands. It was Reinhardt. He thought, "Now the great moment has come and I shall hear Socrates pour out words of wisdom and technical advice to these people. Eminent they may be, but they will not be above getting a little tip or two from Reinhardt." But nothing happened. Then he thought, "Well, they must be so bad that he is going to give them a hell of a slating at any minute. There will be a few glorious minutes when high-powered abuse will pour from the golden lips and the boys down there will get very hot under the collar." Nothing happened, and nothing continued to happen for quite a long time until the actors came to the end of a scene. Then there was a short pause, not a rudely long pause at all, but *quite* a pause, and my friend was agog with excitement to know what would be said. Reinhardt just looked up and said, "Thanks very much. Now can we go back to the maid's entrance?" That, or something like it, went on through the whole morning, and he said that, far from it being a dull rehearsal, it was clearly—he was artist enough to perceive it— an immensely constructive rehearsal, and he began to think why it was, because nothing was being said, no instructions were given, no abuse poured forth and no praise. He analyzed it this way, and the more I think of it the more profoundly convinced I am that he is right, that Reinhardt was performing the one really creative function of the producer, which is to be at rehearsal a highly receptive, highly concentrated, highly critical sounding-board for the performance, an audience of one. He is not the drill sergeant, not the schoolmaster, and he does not sweep in with a lot of verbiage and "Stand here and do it this way, darling, and move the right hand not the left." He is simply receiving the thing, transmuting it, and giving it back. When you come down to analyzing what the creative part of acting is, it is the giving of impressions to the audience and then, on the part of the actor, the taking back of their impressions and doing something about them. The best simile that I can make is that the actor throws a thread, as it were, out into the house which, if the house is receptive, it will catch. Then it is the actor's business to hold that thread taut and to keep a varying and consequently interesting pressure on it, so that it is really pulled in moments of tension and allowed to go as slack as possible in moments of relaxation, but never so slack that it falls and cannot be pulled up again. The producer at rehearsals can be that audience. He can perform that function, and if he is a good producer he will perform it better than the average audience; he will be more intelligently critical and alive, and the rehearsals will not be dreary learning of routine; they will be a creative act that is ultimately going to be a performance.

That is why, in my opinion, the analogy between the producer and the conductor holds good. A *good* conductor is a man with a fine technique of the stick. He has a clear beat and an expressive beat, and is an interesting chap for the audience to watch. He can bring one section in with a fine gesture and blot another out. He knows his score, and so on, but it is all interesting showmanship. But the *great* conductor does not require any of those things. He can have a terrible beat and look like nothing on earth, but if he is a great conductor every man in the orchestra will give, under his baton, not only a better performance than he would under another conductor, but a better performance than he knew he could give. That is not got out of them by instruction; it is a process of psychic evocation. Precisely the same thing holds good for the producer of a play. His function at its best is one of psychic evocation, and it is performed almost entirely unconsciously. Certain conscious tricks can come in the way or aid the process, but this evocative thing comes from God knows where. It is completely unconscious. Nobody knows when it is working, and nobody knows why it is working. Some people, and only the very best, have it; others do not. I could not answer why or wherefore, but I am just convinced that that is so.

LOOK AT THE AUDIENCE

If any actress is worthy of the title of grande dame *of the English-speaking theater, it is Sybil Thorndike (1882–   ), who since 1931 has worn the knightly decoration of Dame of the British Empire. Her experience as an actress encompasses a number of the great British repertory companies, a full measure of Shakespeare and Shaw (she was the first Saint Joan) and every sort of modern role. What she has to say about the confrontation of actor and audience is, as always with Dame Sybil, direct, clear, and unembroidered, but not, as quickly becomes obvious, unimpassioned. She loves her art and will defend it hotly—even against her own audiences.*

Dame Sybil Thorndike

I suppose the art of the theatre is the only form of art of which the public is an integral part, the only form that is not complete without the spectator. In the fine arts of painting, sculpture or letters, the work is complete without any effort of the outside world. It is very helpful to the artist, no doubt, when good hard cash is paid down and the work is sold; but nothing that the purchaser does or feels or thinks about the particular work can alter it. It is a complete and perfect thing, materialized from the artist's imagination and soul. In music the composition is a complete thing in itself—even a performance of a work can be finished without the public participating, though here again appreciation is extremely pleasant, and helpful, both to pocket and self-esteem.

All forms of art seem to exist completely and separately. They may be understood or not, they may rouse sympathy or not, but the created thing is here. I believe this is why they are called the Fine Arts.

The popular art of the theatre, however, stands on quite another footing. (I do not include the Cinema, because that is also a finished product before it reaches the public, and the performance can never be altered however differently the audiences are feeling about it. In fact, I don't know how to place the Cinema and its canons. I do certainly feel it cannot be judged as the art of the theatre, which depends on interplay between actors and audience. Neither is it a Fine Art. It is, I suppose, a growth from the theatre, but it must be judged separately.)

A play is not for all time, it is for the actual moment. (Reading plays to one's self, by one's own study fire, is a pastime of the intellectual which, with a great many people, has taken the place of visiting the theatre and joining in performance—what a great pity this is!)

It may be that a particular play is chosen to be played again and again through the ages, but the rite of performance is the important thing, and it is newly created with each performance. It may be, and most frequently is, that the actors choose the same outward signs and movements—vocal or otherwise—at each performance, but these must be freshly selected and born at the moment, and not just copies of those of previous performances.

Many actors will tell you of that curious sensation we have when entering the stage, as of one's other half-being waiting to be transformed. An expectant force is there, not just separate men and women but an entity, a personality made up of all those men and women who have sunk their separate individualities in the larger common soul of the mob, and this thing has to be shaped and used and made to move by the mind directing. Don't think this absurdly fantastic. I know many widely differing types of actor who feel this in common with me. This mob-soul is a force that is continually baffling us, it is always an unknown quantity. On our first entrance, before a word has left our mouths, we are conscious of this large thing confronting us. Sometimes one knows it is a thing to be fought and struggled with in order to move it and use it, and on these occasions the performance is a big effort, as every sensitive actor will tell you. At other times one is conscious of a something that is feeding one with life, and if the actor is well equipped technically and sensitively, and has something to express, it is on these occasions he can rise to heights greater than he thought possible. He is being given greater life, and the audience get what is often called "a great performance."

I think audiences realize extraordinarily little how much they

make or spoil performance in the theatre, and sometimes I wish—
and especially do I wish this when the play is of large vision—
that (as in Church one has, or is given, a little manual to show
what one's attitude of mind should be, and hints how to behave,
that the service may not be unfruitful) members of an audience
should be handed a few choice words, setting down that too
much eating of chocolate, too much blowing of nose and clearing
of throat, too much fidgeting of any sort, will prevent the full
enjoyment of the play. And let it also be pointed out that these
things and their like are a constant source of irritation to fellow
members of the audience and induce in the unfortunate actor a
feeling closely akin to murder. A quiet body, with few beads and
chains to jangle (the dreadful days of the bangle are over, we
hope), a quiet untrammeled mind and a quiet tongue—these three
good things will give an atmosphere in which imagination can
work. Shakespeare in his Prologues tells the hearers how to receive the play and conduct themselves.

"Don't forget we've come out for an evening's entertainment,
will you?" my friends in the audience will say. No, I don't forget
that, and I realize there are differences of approach to various entertainments. I am told that a good dinner, with good wine, is the
best way to prepare for the enjoyment of a good play. A good
dinner—a choice, spare dinner—maybe, but a large dinner and a
full content makes the feeder a hard thing to move, and only the
most obvious cast-iron humor will reach him, and only the most
obvious sentiment will cause the tears to flow down his cheeks.

For the enjoyment of sensitive, subtle humor or sentiment—
in order to appreciate the full flavor of Gracie Fields or Edith
Evans—I suggest spare feeding, because through these artists, and
their like, you will be filled to overflowing with a food of life
which will the better spread to all parts of your body if it is not
clogged with meat, poultry, suet and ice-cream. For the healthy
and normal-stomached, a not-too-vigorous fasting is an excellent
preparation for enjoyment. It whets the appetite for exercise, and
the mind and body prepared for exercise are the sort of mind and
body the actor hopes to encounter as he leaps or crawls or saun-
ters on the stage, ready to give forth the superabundant creative
energy that he can scarcely restrain.

Who was it that said of actors "Poor pale ghosts—shadows of
Life?" I think that is what our rather hectic, over-busied, over-
catered-for life asks of the theatre. "Be ascetic in your life, that in

your art you may be violent," said a great French writer. That's
better! Give us not pale ghosts or shadows, give us creatures with
greater life than we know. Give us a larger-sized life than we
actually experience, give us violences; shocks; beings that surge
with vigor and electricity, that touching them in spirit we may
be charged with that same energy and our grasp and scope be
larger.

How wonderful if an audience asks this of its actors. "Give us
more," is a cry we seldom hear, but the opposite we hear always
and then we wonder why the actors of great energy are all
swallowed by revue and music-hall—part of the theatre certainly,
the only part that does demand abundant vitality and strength,
but, don't let us make any mistake, only a part.

In the Tragic Theatre of England we have nothing which com-
pares with the energy and the life of the Comic Theatre in our
midst. Comedy and Tragedy (the words Tragic and Comic include all forms of drama) are the whole, and until we embrace
both we are one-sided cripples—one part dead—disused; delicate
and ailing.

Whose fault is this? The actor knows it is the audience; the
audience knows it is the actor; it is probably a bit of both. But
how often we do hear that stupid refrain, "But we have tragedy in
real life. Why should we have it in the theatre?" Every time this
is said to me, with sickening, irritating regularity, it is only by
the grace of God and amazing self-control that I am prevented
from hurling myself on the speaker.

"You are the servants of the public, you actors. Give the public
what it wants." We answer "We are not servants of anyone who
does not demand the fullest life. We are the servants of the
theatre, of which the public is only a part, and the public doesn't
know what it wants till it sees it. Our business is to discover its
needs—a very entertaining, intriguing and heartbreaking business. Servant of the public by all means, if by that is meant one
who seeks to serve those who do not know what to ask for. The
theatre serves those who say 'Show us life and that will suffice
us.' "

For some years in the 1950s and 1960s, one standard piece in the Sunday supplements of British and American newspapers was that on the "Theater of the Absurd." This piece was received by readers who were almost invariably bewildered, beguiled, infuriated, or delighted, if one could gather correctly from the mail that followed. If the piece was written, as it often enough was, by Martin Esslin (1918–   ), the reader was also informed— at length and with incontrovertible authority. Esslin is the master biographer and geographer of the Theater of the Absurd, the author of a book on it and of another on Brecht, one of its major progenitors. He has produced its plays for BBC radio and television. He has made himself familiar with every hill and valley, every contour of the

THE THEATRE OF THE ABSURD

world of the Absurd. And he has linked that world with others in the theater, demonstrating as he does so the considerable range and depth of this particular theater. The Absurd is clearly not, he shows, an arriviste, a crude upstart in the modern world. It is, in fact, the very mirror of our world. If we dismiss it, we may be dismissing ourselves.

Martin Esslin

The plays of Samuel Beckett, Arthur Adamov, and Eugène Ionesco have been performed with astonishing success in France, Germany, Scandinavia, and the English-speaking countries. This reception is all the more puzzling when one considers that the audiences concerned were amused by and applauded these plays fully aware that they could not understand what they meant or what their authors were driving at.

At first sight these plays do, indeed, confront their public with a bewildering experience, a veritable barrage of wildly irrational, often nonsensical goings-on that seem to go counter to all accepted standards of stage convention. In these

plays, some of which are labeled "antiplays," neither the time
nor the place of the action are ever clearly stated. (At the beginning of Ionesco's *The Bald Soprano* the clock strikes seven-
teen.) The characters hardly have any individuality and often
even lack a name; moreover, halfway through the action they
tend to change their nature completely. Pozzo and Lucky in
Beckett's *Waiting for Godot*, for example, appear as master and
slave at one moment only to return after a while with their respective positions mysteriously reversed. The laws of probability
as well as those of physics are suspended when we meet young
ladies with two or even three noses (Ionesco's *Jack or the Submission*), or a corpse that has been hidden in the next room that
suddenly begins to grow to monstrous size until a giant foot
crashes through the door onto the stage (Ionesco's *Amédée*). As
a result, it is often unclear whether the action is meant to represent a dream world of nightmares or real happenings. Within
the same scene the action may switch from the nightmarish
poetry of high emotions to pure knock-about farce or cabaret,
and above all, the dialogue tends to get out of hand so that at
times the words seem to go counter to the actions of the characters on the stage, to degenerate into lists of words and phrases
from a dictionary or traveler's conversation book, or to get
bogged down in endless repetitions like a phonograph record
stuck in one groove. Only in this kind of demented world can
strangers meet and discover, after a long polite conversation and
close cross-questioning, that, to their immense surprise, they
must be man and wife as they are living on the same street, in the
same house, apartment, room, and bed (Ionesco's *The Bald Soprano*). Only here can the whole life of a group of characters
revolve around the passionate discussion of the aesthetics and
economics of pinball machines (Adamov's *Ping-Pong*). Above
all, everything that happens seems to be beyond rational motivation, happening at random or through the demented caprice of
an unaccountable idiot fate. Yet, these wildly extravagant tragic
farces and farcial tragedies, although they have suffered their
share of protests and scandals, do arouse interest and are received
with laughter and thoughtful respect. What is the explanation
for this curious phenomenon?

The most obvious, but perhaps too facile answer that suggests
itself is that these plays are prime examples of "pure theatre."
They are living proof that the magic of the stage can persist even

outside, and divorced from, any framework of conceptual rationality. They prove that exits and entrances, light and shadow,
contrasts in costume, voice, gait and behavior, pratfalls and embraces, all the manifold mechanical interactions of human puppets in groupings that suggest tension, conflict, or the relaxation
of tensions, can arouse laughter or gloom and conjure up an atmosphere of poetry even if devoid of logical motivation and unrelated to recognizable human characters, emotions, and objectives.

But this is only a partial explanation. While the element of
"pure theatre" and abstract stagecraft is certainly at work in the
plays concerned, they also have a much more substantial content
and meaning. Not only *do* all these plays make sense, though
perhaps not obvious or conventional sense, they also give expression to some of the basic issues and problems of our age, in a
uniquely efficient and meaningful manner, so that they meet some
of the deepest needs and unexpressed yearnings of their audience.

The three dramatists that have been grouped together here
would probably most energetically deny that they form anything
like a school or movement. Each of them, in fact, has his own
roots and sources, his own very personal approach to both form
and subject matter. Yet they also clearly have a good deal in common. This common denominator that characterizes their works
might well be described as the element of *the absurd*. "Est absurde
ce qui n'a pas de but . . ." ("Absurd is that which has no purpose,
or goal, or objective"), the definition given by Ionesco in a note
on Kafka,[1] certainly applies to the plays of Beckett and Ionesco as
well as those of Arthur Adamov up to his latest play, *Paolo Paoli*,
when he returned to a more traditional form of social drama.

Each of these writers, however, has his own special type of
absurdity: in Beckett it is melancholic, colored by a feeling of
futility born from the disillusionment of old age and chronic
hopelessness; Adamov's is more active, aggressive, earthy, and
tinged with social and political overtones; while Ionesco's absurdity has its own fantastic knock-about flavor of tragical
clowning. But they all share the same deep sense of human isolation and of the irremediable character of the human condition.

As Arthur Adamov put it in describing how he came to write
his first play *La Parodie* (1947):

[1] Ionesco, "Dans les Armes de la Ville," *Cahiers de la Compagnie Madeleine
Renaud-Jean-Louis Barrault,* No. 20 (October, 1957).

I began to discover stage scenes in the most commonplace everyday events. [One day I saw] a blind man begging; two girls went by without seeing him, singing: "I closed my eyes; it was marvelous!" This gave me the idea of showing on stage, as crudely and as visibly as possible, the loneliness of man, the absence of communication among human beings.[2]

Looking back at his earliest effort (which he now regards as unsuccessful) Adamov defines his basic idea in it, and a number of subsequent plays, as the idea "that the destinies of all human beings are of equal futility, that the refusal to live (of the character called N.) and the joyful acceptance of life (by the employee) both lead, by the same path, to inevitable failure, total destruction."[3] It is the same futility and pointlessness of human effort, the same impossibility of human communication which Ionesco expresses in ever new and ingenious variations. The two old people making conversation with the empty air and living in the expectation of an orator who is to pronounce truths about life, but turns out to be deaf and dumb (*The Chairs*), are as sardonically cruel a symbol of this fundamentally tragic view of human existence as Jack (*Jack or the Submission*), who stubbornly resists the concerted urgings of his entire family to subscribe to the most sacred principle of his clan—which, when his resistance finally yields to their entreaties, turns out to be the profound truth: "I love potatoes with bacon" ("J'adore les pommes de terre au lard").

The Theatre of the Absurd shows the world as an incomprehensible place. The spectators see the happenings on the stage entirely from the outside, without ever understanding the full meaning of these strange patterns of events, as newly arrived visitors might watch life in a country of which they have not yet mastered the language.[4] The confrontation of the audience with characters and happenings which they are not quite able to comprehend makes it impossible for them to share the aspirations and emotions depicted in the play. Brecht's famous "Verfrem-

2 Adamov, "Note Préliminaire," *Théâtre II*, Paris, 1955.
3 *Ibid*.
4 It may be significant that the three writers concerned, although they now all live in France and write in French have all come to live there from outside and must have experienced a period of adjustment to the country and its language. Samuel Beckett (b. 1906) came from Ireland; Arthur Adamov (b. 1908) from Russia, and Eugène Ionesco (b. 1912) from Rumania.

dungseffekt" (alienation effect), the inhibition of any identification between spectator and actor, which Brecht could never successfully achieve in his own highly rational theatre, really comes
into its own in the Theatre of the Absurd. It is impossible to
identify oneself with characters one does not understand or
whose motives remain a closed book, and so the distance between the public and the happenings on the stage can be maintained. Emotional identification with the characters is replaced
by a puzzled, critical attention. For while the happenings on the
stage are absurd, they yet remain recognizable as somehow related to real life with *its* absurdity, so that eventually the spectators are brought face to face with the irrational side of their
existence. Thus, the absurd and fantastic goings-on of the Theatre of the Absurd will, in the end, be found to reveal the irrationality of the human condition and the illusion of what we
thought was its apparent logical structure.

If the dialogue in these plays consists of meaningless clichés and
the mechanical, circular repetition of stereotyped phrases—how
many meaningless clichés and stereotyped phrases do we use in
our day-to-day conversation? If the characters change their personality halfway through the action, how consistent and truly
integrated are the people we meet in our real life? And if people
in these plays appear as mere marionettes, helpless puppets without any will of their own, passively at the mercy of blind fate
and meaningless circumstance, do we, in fact, in our over-
organized world, still possess any genuine initiative or power to
decide our own destiny? The spectators of the Theatre of the
Absurd are thus confronted with a grotesquely heightened picture of their own world: a world without faith, meaning, and
genuine freedom of will. In this sense, the Theatre of the Absurd is the true theatre of our time.

The theatre of most previous epochs reflected an accepted
moral order, a world whose aims and objectives were clearly
present to the minds of all its public, whether it was the audience
of the medieval mystery plays with their solidly accepted faith
in the Christian world order or the audience of the drama of
Ibsen, Shaw, or Hauptmann with their unquestioned belief in
evolution and progress. To such audiences, right and wrong were
never in doubt, nor did they question the then accepted goals of
human endeavor. Our own time, at least in the Western world,
wholly lacks such a generally accepted and completely integrated

world picture. The decline of religious faith, the destruction of
the belief in automatic social and biological progress, the discovery of vast areas of irrational and unconscious forces within
the human psyche, the loss of a sense of control over rational
human development in an age of totalitarianism and weapons of
mass destruction, have all contributed to the erosion of the basis
for a dramatic convention in which the action proceeds within a
fixed and self-evident framework of generally accepted values.
Faced with the vacuum left by the destruction of a universally
accepted and unified set of beliefs, most serious playwrights have
felt the need to fit their work into the frame of values and objectives expressed in one of the contemporary ideologies: Marxism, psychoanalysis, aestheticism, or nature worship. But these,
in the eyes of a writer like Adamov, are nothing but superficial
rationalizations which try to hide the depth of man's predicament, his loneliness and his anxiety. Or, as Ionesco puts it:

> As far as I am concerned, I believe sincerely in the poverty of the
> poor, I deplore it; it is real; it can become a subject for the theatre; I
> also believe in the anxieties and serious troubles the rich may suffer
> from; but it is neither in the misery of the former nor in the melan-
> cholia of the latter, that I, for one, find my dramatic subject matter.
> Theatre is for me the outward projection onto the stage of an inner
> world; it is in my dreams, in my anxieties, in my obscure desires, in
> my internal contradictions that I, for one, reserve for myself the
> right of finding my dramatic subject matter. As I am not alone in the
> world, as each of us, in the depth of his being, is at the same time
> part and parcel of all others, my dreams, my desires, my anxieties, my
> obsessions do not belong to me alone. They form part of an an-
> cestral heritage, a very ancient storehouse which is a portion of the
> common property of all mankind. It is this, which, transcending their
> outward diversity, reunites all human beings and constitutes our pro-
> found common patrimony, the universal language. . . .[5]

In other words, the commonly acceptable framework of beliefs
and values of former epochs which has now been shattered is to
be replaced by the community of dreams and desires of a collective unconscious. And, to quote Ionesco again:

> . . . the new dramatist is one . . . who tries to link up with what is
> most ancient: new language and subject matter in a dramatic struc-

[5] Ionesco, "L'Impromptu de l'Alma," *Théâtre II,* Paris, 1958.

ture which aims at being clearer, more stripped of non-essentials and more purely theatrical; the rejection of traditionalism to rediscover tradition; a synthesis of knowledge and invention, of the real and imaginary, of the particular and the universal, or as they say now, of the individual and the collective. . . . By expressing my deepest obsessions, I express my deepest humanity. I become one with all others, spontaneously, over and above all the barriers of caste and different psychologies. I express my solitude and become one with all other solitudes. . . .[6]

What is the tradition with which the Theatre of the Absurd—at first sight the most revolutionary and radically new movement—is trying to link itself? It is in fact a very ancient and a very rich tradition, nourished from many and varied sources: the verbal exuberance and extravagant inventions of Rabelais, the age-old clowning of the Roman mimes and the Italian *Commedia dell'Arte*, the knock-about humor of circus clowns like Grock; the wild, archetypal symbolism of English nonsense verse, the baroque horror of Jacobean dramatists like Webster or Tourneur, the harsh, incisive and often brutal tones of the German drama of Grabbe, Büchner, Kleist, and Wedekind with its delirious language and grotesque inventiveness; and the Nordic paranoia of the dreams and persecution fantasies of Strindberg.

All these streams, however, first came together and crystallized in the more direct ancestors of the present Theatre of the Absurd. Of these, undoubtedly the first and foremost is Alfred Jarry (1873–1907), the creator of *Ubu Roi*, the first play which clearly belongs in the category of the Theatre of the Absurd. *Ubu Roi*, first performed in Paris on December 10, 1896, is a Rabelaisian nonsense drama about the fantastic adventures of a fat, cowardly, and brutal figure, *le père* Ubu, who makes himself King of Poland, fights a series of Falstaffian battles, and is finally routed. As if to challenge all accepted codes of propriety and thus to open a new era of irreverence, the play opens with the defiant expletive, *"Merdre!"* which immediately provoked a scandal. This, of course, was what Jarry had intended. *Ubu*, in its rollicking Rabelaisian parody of a Shakespearean history play, was meant to confront the Parisian bourgeois with a monstrous portrait of his own greed, selfishness, and philistinism: "As the curtain went up I wanted to confront the public with a theatre in

---

[6] Ionesco, "The Avant-Garde Theatre," *World Theatre*, VIII, No. 3 (Autumn, 1959).

which, as in the big magic mirror . . . of the fairy tales . . . the
vicious man sees his reflection with bulls' horns and the body of
a dragon, the projections of his viciousness. . . ."[7] But Ubu is
more than a mere monstrous exaggeration of the selfishness and
crude sensuality of the French bourgeois. He is at the same time
the personification of the grossness of human nature, an enormous belly walking on two legs. That is why Jarry put him on
the stage as a monstrous pot-bellied figure in a highly stylized
costume and mask—a mythical, archetypal externalization of
human instincts of the lowest kind. Thus, Ubu, the false king of
Poland, pretended doctor of the pseudoscience of Pataphysics,
clearly anticipates one of the main characteristics of the Theatre
of the Absurd, its tendency to externalize and project outwards
what is happening in the deeper recesses of the mind. Examples
of this tendency are: the disembodied voices of "monitors" shouting commands at the hero of Adamov's *La Grande et la Petite
Manoeuvre* which concretizes his neurotic compulsions; the mu-
tilated trunks of the parents in Beckett's *Endgame* emerging from
ashcans—the ashcans of the main character's subconscious to
which he has banished his past and his conscience; or the prolifer-
ations of fungi that invade the married couple's apartment in
Ionesco's *Amédée* and express the rottenness and decay of their
relationship. All these psychological factors are not only projected outwards, they are also, as in Jarry's *Ubu Roi*, grotesquely
magnified and exaggerated. This scornful rejection of all subtleties is a reaction against the supposed *finesse* of the psychology of
the naturalistic theatre in which everything was to be inferred
between the lines. The Theatre of the Absurd, from Jarry onwards, stands for explicitness as against implicit psychology, and
in this resembles the highly explicit theatre of the Expressionists
or the political theatre of Piscator or Brecht.

To be larger and more real than life was also the aim of
Guillaume Apollinaire (1880–1918), the great poet who was one
of the seminal forces in the rise of Cubism and who had close
personal artistic links with Jarry. If Apollinaire labeled his play
Les Mamelles de Tirésias a "*drama surrealiste,*" he did not intend
that term, of which he was one of the earliest users, in the sense
in which it later became famous. He wanted it to describe a play

---

[7] Jarry, "Questions de Théâtre," in *Ubu Roi, Ubu Enchaîné,* and other Ubuesque
writings. Ed. Rene Massat, Lausanne, 1948.

in which everything was *larger than life*, for he believed in an art which was to be "modern, simple, rapid, with the shortcuts and enlargements that are needed to shock the spectator."[8] . . .

But Antonin Artaud (1896–1948), another major influence in the development of the Theatre of the Absurd, did at one time belong to the Surrealist group, although his main activity in the theatre took place after he had broken with Breton. Artaud was one of the most unhappy men of genius of his age, an artist consumed by the most intense passions; poet, actor, director, designer, immensely fertile and original in his inventions and ideas, yet always living on the borders of sanity and never able to realize his ambitions, plans, and projects.

Artaud, who had been an actor in Charles Dullin's company at the Atelier, began his venture into the realm of experimental theatre in a series of productions characteristically sailing under the label *Théâtre Alfred Jarry* (1927–29). But his theories of a new and revolutionary theatre only crystallized after he had been deeply stirred by a performance of Balinese dancers at the Colonial Exhibition of 1931. He formulated his ideas in a series of impassioned manifestos later collected in the volume *The Theatre and Its Double* (1938), which continues to exercise an important influence on the contemporary French theatre. Artaud named the theatre of his dreams *Théâtre de la Cruauté*, a theatre of cruelty, which, he said, "means a theatre difficult and cruel above all for myself." "Everything that is really active is cruelty. It is around this idea of action carried to the extreme that the theatre must renew itself." Here too the idea of action larger and more real than life is the dominant theme. "Every performance will contain a physical and objective element that will be felt by all. Cries, Wails, Apparitions, Surprises, *Coups de Théâtre* of all kinds, the magical beauty of costumes inspired by the model of certain rituals. . . ." The language of the drama must also undergo a change: "It is not a matter of suppressing articulate speech but of giving to the words something like the importance they have in dreams." In Artaud's new theatre "not only the obverse side of man will appear but also the reverse side of the coin: the reality of imagination and of dreams will here be seen on an equal footing with everyday life."

Artaud's only attempt at putting these theories to the test on

[8] Apollinaire, *Les Mamelles de Tirésias*, Preface.

the stage took place on May 6, 1935 at the Folies-Wagram. Artaud had made his own adaptation ("after Shelley and Stendhal") of the story of the Cenci, that sombre Renaissance story of incest and patricide. It was in many ways a beautiful and memorable performance, but full of imperfections and a financial disaster which marked the beginning of Artaud's eventual descent into despair, insanity, and abject poverty. Jean-Louis Barrault had some small part in this venture and Roger Blin, the actor and director who later played an important part in bringing Adamov, Beckett, and Ionesco to the stage, appeared in the small role of one of the hired assassins.

Jean-Louis Barrault, one of the most creative figures in the theatre of our time, was, in turn, responsible for another venture which played an important part in the development of the Theatre of the Absurd. He staged André Gide's adaptation of Franz Kafka's novel, *The Trial*, in 1947 and played the part of the hero K. himself. Undoubtedly this performance which brought the dreamworld of Kafka to a triumphant unfolding on the stage and demonstrated the effectiveness of this particular brand of fantasy in practical theatrical terms exercised a profound influence on the practitioners of the new movement. For here, too, they saw the externalization of mental processes, the acting out of nightmarish dreams by schematized figures in a world of torment and absurdity.

The dream element in the Theatre of the Absurd can also be traced, in the case of Adamov, to Strindberg, acknowledged by him as his inspiration at the time when he began to think of writing for the theatre. This is the Strindberg of *The Ghost Sonata*, *The Dream Play* and of *To Damascus*. (Adamov is the author of an excellent brief monograph on Strindberg.)

But if Jarry, Artaud, Kafka, and Strindberg can be regarded as the decisive influences in the development of the Theatre of the Absurd, there is another giant of European literature that must not be omitted from the list—James Joyce, for whom Beckett at one time is supposed to have acted as helper and secretary. Not only is the Nighttown episode of *Ulysses* one of the earliest examples of the Theatre of the Absurd—with its exuberant mingling of the real and the nightmarish, its wild fantasies and externalizations of subconscious yearnings and fears—but Joyce's experimentation with language, his attempts to smash the limitations of conventional vocabulary and syntax has probably exercised an even more powerful impact on all the writers concerned.

It is in its attitude to language that the Theatre of the Absurd is most revolutionary. It deliberately attempts to renew the language of drama and to expose the barrenness of conventional stage dialogue. Ionesco once described how he came to write his first play. (Cf. his "The Tragedy of Language," *Tulane Drama Review*, Spring, 1960.) He had decided to take English lessons and began to study at the Berlitz school. When he read and repeated the sentences in his phrase book, those petrified corpses of once living speech, he was suddenly overcome by their tragic quality. From them he composed his first play, *The Bald Soprano*. The absurdity of its dialogue and its fantastic quality springs directly from its basic ordinariness. It exposes the emptiness of stereotyped language; "What is sometimes labeled the absurd," Ionesco says, "is only the denunciation of the ridiculous nature of a language which is empty of substance, made up of clichés and slogans. . . ."[9] Such a language has atrophied; it has ceased to be the expression of anything alive or vital and has been degraded into a mere conventional token of human intercourse, a mask for genuine meaning and emotion. That is why so often in the Theatre of the Absurd the dialogue becomes divorced from the real happenings in the play and is even put into direct contradiction with the action. The Professor and the Pupil in Ionesco's *The Lesson* "seem" to be going through a repetition of conventional school book phrases, but behind this smoke screen of language the *real* action of the play pursues an entirely different course with the Professor, vampire-like, draining the vitality from the young girl up to the final moment when he plunges his knife into her body. In Beckett's *Waiting for Godot* Lucky's much vaunted philosophical wisdom is revealed to be a flood of completely meaningless gibberish that vaguely resembles the language of philosophical argument. And in Adamov's remarkable play, *Ping-Pong*, a good deal of the dramatic power lies in the contrapuntal contrast between the triviality of the theme—the improvement of pinball machines—and the almost religious fervor with which it is discussed. Here, in order to bring out the full meaning of the play, the actors have to act *against* the dialogue rather than with it, the fervor of the delivery

[9] Ionesco, "The Avant-Garde Theatre."

must stand in a dialectical contrast to the pointlessness of the meaning of the lines. In the same way, the author implies that most of the fervent and passionate discussion of real life (of political controversy, to give but one example) also turns around empty and meaningless clichés. Or, as Ionesco says in an essay on Antonin Artaud:

As our knowledge becomes increasingly divorced from real life, our culture no longer contains ourselves (or only contains an insignificant part of ourselves) and forms a "social" context in which we are not integrated. The problem thus becomes that of again reconciling our culture with our life by making our culture a living culture once more. But to achieve this end we shall first have to kill the "respect for that which is written" . . . it becomes necessary to break up our language so that it may become possible to put it together again and to re-establish contact with the absolute, or as I should prefer to call it, with multiple reality.[10]

This quest for the multiple reality of the world which is real *because* it exists on many planes simultaneously and is more than a mere unidirectional abstraction is not only in itself a search for a re-established *poetical* reality (poetry in its essence expressing reality in its ambiguity and multidimensional depth); it is also in close accord with important movements of our age in what appear to be entirely different fields: psychology and philosophy. The dissolution, devaluation, and relativization of language is, after all, also the theme of much of present-day depth psychology, which has shown what in former times was regarded as a rational expression of logically arrived at conclusions to be the mere rationalization of subconscious emotional impulses. Not everything we say means what we intend it to mean. And likewise, in present-day Logical Positivism a large proportion of all statements is regarded as devoid of conceptual meaning and merely emotive. A philosopher like Ludwig Wittgenstein, in his later phases, even tried to break through what he regarded as the opacity, the misleading nature of language and grammar; for if all our thinking is in terms of language, and language obeys what after all are the arbitrary conventions of grammar, we must strive to penetrate to the real content of thought that is masked by grammatical rules and conventions. Here, too, then, is a matter of

[10] Ionesco, "Ni un Dieu, ni un Demon," *Cahiers de la Compagnie Madeleine Renaud-Jean-Louis Barrault,* No. 22–23 (May, 1958).

getting behind the surface of linguistic clichés and of finding reality through the break-up of language.

In the Theatre of the Absurd, therefore, the real content of the play lies in the action. Language may be discarded altogether, as in Beckett's *Act Without Words* or in Ionesco's *The New Tenant*, in which the whole sense of the play is contained in the incessant arrival of more and more furniture so that the occupant of the room is, in the end, literally drowned in it. Here the movement of objects alone carries the dramatic action, the language has become purely incidental, less important than the contribution of the property department. In this, the Theatre of the Absurd also reveals its anti-literary character, its endeavor to link up with the pre-literary strata of stage history: the circus, the performances of itinerant jugglers and mountebanks, the music hall, fairground barkers, acrobats, and also the robust world of the silent film. Ionesco, in particular, clearly owes a great deal to Chaplin, Buster Keaton, the Keystone Cops, Laurel and Hardy, and the Marx Brothers. And it is surely significant that so much of successful popular entertainment in our age shows affinities with the subject matter and preoccupation of the avant-garde Theatre of the Absurd. A sophisticated, but nevertheless highly popular, film comedian like Jacques Tati uses dialogue merely as a barely comprehensible babble of noises, and also dwells on the loneliness of man in our age, the horror of overmechanization and overorganization gone mad. Danny Kaye excels in streams of gibberish closely akin to Lucky's oration in *Waiting for Godot.* The brilliant and greatly liked team of British radio (and occasionally television) comedians, the Goons, have a sense of the absurd that resembles Kafka's or Ionesco's and a team of grotesque singers like "Les Frères Jacques" seems more closely in line with the Theatre of the Absurd than with the conventional cabaret.

Yet the defiant rejection of language as the main vehicle of the dramatic action, the onslaught on conventional logic and unilinear conceptual thinking in the Theatre of the Absurd is by no means equivalent to a total rejection of all meaning. On the contrary, it constitutes an earnest endeavor to penetrate to deeper layers of meaning and to give a truer, because more complex, picture of reality in avoiding the simplification which results from leaving out all the undertones, overtones, and inherent absurdities and contradictions of any human situation. In the conventional drama every word means what it says, the situations are clearcut, and at the end all conflicts are tidily resolved. But reality, as Ionesco points out in the passage we have quoted, is never like that; it is multiple, complex, many-dimensional and exists on a number of different levels at one and the same time. Language is far too straight-forward an instrument to express all this by itself. Reality can only be conveyed by being *acted out* in all its complexity. Hence, it is the theatre, which is multidimensional and more than merely language or literature, which is the only instrument to express the bewildering complexity of the human condition. The human condition being what it is, with man small, helpless, insecure, and unable ever to fathom the world in all its hopelessness, death, and absurdity, the theatre has to confront him with the bitter truth that most human endeavor is irrational and senseless, that communication between human beings is well-nigh impossible, and that the world will forever remain an impenetrable mystery. At the same time, the recognition of all these bitter truths will have a liberating effect: if we realize the basic absurdity of most of our objectives we are freed from being obsessed with them and this release expresses itself in laughter.

Moreover, while the world is being shown as complex, harsh, and absurd and as difficult to interpret as reality itself, the audience is yet spurred on to attempt their own interpretation, to wonder what it is all about. In that sense they are being invited to school their critical faculties, to train themselves in adjusting to reality. As the world is being represented as highly complex and devoid of a clear-cut purpose or design, there will always be an infinite number of possible interpretations. . . . Thus, it may be that the pinball machines in Adamov's *Ping-Pong* and the ideology which is developed around them stand for the futility of political or religious ideologies that are pursued with equal fervor and equal futility in the final results. Others have interpreted the play as a parable on the greed and sordidness of the profit motive. Others again may give it quite different meanings. The mysterious transformation of human beings into rhinos in Ionesco's latest play, *Rhinoceros*, was felt by the audience of its world premier at Duesseldorf (November 6, 1959) to depict the transformation of human beings into Nazis. It is known that Ionesco himself intended the play to express his feelings at the time when more and more of his friends in Rumania joined the Fascist Iron Guard and, in effect, left the ranks of thin-skinned humans to turn themselves into moral pachyderms. But to spectators less intimately aware of the moral climate of such a situation than the German audience, other interpretations might impose themselves: if the hero, Bérenger, is at the end left alone as the only human being in his native town, now entirely inhabited by rhinos, they might regard this as a poetic symbol of the gradual isolation of man growing old and imprisoned in the strait jacket of his own habits and memories. Does Godot, so fervently and vainly awaited by Vladimir and Estragon, stand for God? Or does he merely represent the ever elusive tomorrow, man's hope that one day something will happen that will render his existence meaningful? The force and poetic power of the play lie precisely in the impossibility of ever reaching a conclusive answer to this question.

Here we touch the essential point of difference between the conventional theatre and the Theatre of the Absurd. The former, based as it is on a known framework of accepted values and a rational view of life, always starts out by indicating a fixed objective towards which the action will be moving or by posing a definite problem to which it will supply an answer. Will Hamlet revenge the murder of his father? Will Iago succeed in destroying Othello? Will Nora leave her husband? In the conventional theatre the action always proceeds toward a definable end. The spectators do not know whether that end will be reached and how it will be reached. Hence, they are in suspense, eager to find out *what* will happen. In the Theatre of the Absurd, on the other hand, the action does not proceed in the manner of a logical syllogism. It does not go from A to B but travels from an unknown premise X toward an unknowable conclusion Y. The spectators, not knowing what their author is driving at, cannot be in suspense as to how or whether an expected objective is going to be reached. They are not, therefore, so much in suspense as to *what* is going to happen *next* (although the most unexpected and unpredictable things do happen) as they are in suspense about what the next event to take place will add to their understanding of *what is happening*. The action supplies an increasing number of contradictory and bewildering clues on a number of different levels, but the final question is never wholly answered. Thus, instead of being in suspense as to what will happen next, the spectators are, in the Theatre of the Absurd, put into suspense as to *what* the play *may mean*. This suspense continues even after the curtain has come down. Here again the Theatre of the Absurd fulfills Brecht's postulate of a critical, detached audience,

Scene from The Balcony *by Jean Genet, a Circle in the Square Production, New York, 1961.*
Photograph by Martha Swope.

who will have to sharpen their wits on the play and be stimulated by it to think for themselves, far more effectively than Brecht's own theatre. Not only are the members of the audience unable to identify with the characters, they are compelled to puzzle out the meaning of what they have seen. Each of them will probably find his own, personal meaning, which will differ from the solution found by most others. But he will have been forced to make a mental effort and to evaluate an experience he has undergone. In this sense, the Theatre of the Absurd is the most demanding, the most intellectual theatre. It may be riotously funny, wildly exaggerated and oversimplified, vulgar and garish, but it will always confront the spectator with a genuine intellectual problem, a philosophical paradox, which he will have to try to solve even if he knows that it is most probably insoluble.

In this respect, the Theatre of the Absurd links up with an older tradition which has almost completely disappeared from Western culture: the tradition of allegory and the symbolical representation of abstract concepts personified by characters whose costumes and accoutrements subtly suggested whether they represented Time, Chastity, Winter, Fortune, the World, etc. . . . Although the living riddles the characters represented in these entertainments were by no means difficult to solve, as everyone knew that a character with a scythe and an hourglass represented Time, and although the characters soon revealed their identity and explained their attributes, there was an element of intellectual challenge which stimulated the audience in the moments between the appearance of the riddle and its solution and which provided them with the pleasure of having solved a puzzle. And what is more, in the elaborate allegorical dramas like Calderón's *El Gran Teatro del Mundo* the subtle interplay of allegorical characters itself presented the audience with a great deal to think out for themselves. They had, as it were, to translate the abstractly presented action into terms of their everyday experience; they could ponder on the deeper meaning of such facts as death having taken the characters representing Riches or Poverty in a Dance of Death equally quickly and equally harshly, or that Mammon had deserted his master Everyman in the hour of death. The dramatic riddles of our time present no such clear-cut solutions. All they can show is that while the solutions have evaporated the riddle of our existence remains—complex, unfathomable, and paradoxical.

Merce Cunningham (1922–   ) is an uncommonly articulate dancer and choreographer. He thinks on his feet; that is clear to anyone who has ever seen him dance, with his own troupe or earlier as soloist with Martha Graham's company. Whatever he thinks comes out in strong movements of the body and even his words seem to spring from some all but visible gesture or posture of the dancer. In the general development of modern American dance toward the abstract, Cunningham has been perhaps the most forceful of choreographers, with the clearest notion of what he has been doing and why, as this brief statement shows so well. He has the gift of terseness and relevance, avoiding glib and final definitions. All of life is compact in the dance for Cunningham; neither an article such as this one nor any of his dance compositions can offer a finished definition or an ultimate statement. The central point of his art remains, in the words of this piece, that "dance is free to act as it chooses. . . ."

SPACE, TIME, AND DANCE

Merce Cunningham

The dance is an art in space and time.
The object of the dancer is to obliterate that.

The classical ballet, by maintaining the image of the Renaissance perspective in stage thought, kept a linear form of space. The modern American dance, stemming from German expressionism and the personal feelings of the various American pioneers, made space into a series of lumps, or often just static hills on the stage with actually no relation to the larger space of the stage area, but simply forms that by their connection in time made a shape. Some of the space-thought coming from the German dance opened the space out, and left a momentary feeling of connection with it, but too often the space was not visible enough because the physical action was all of a lightness, like sky without earth, or heaven without hell.

The fortunate thing in dancing is that space and time cannot be disconnected, and everyone can see and understand that. A body still is taking up just as much space and time as a body moving. The result is that neither the one nor the other—moving or being still—is more or less important, except it's nice to see a dancer moving. But the moving becomes more clear if the space and time around the moving are one of its opposites—stillness. Aside from the personal skill and clarity of the individual dancer, there are certain things that make clear to a spectator what the dancer is doing. In the ballet the various steps that lead to the larger movements or poses have, by usage and by their momentum, become common ground upon which the spectator can lead his eyes and his feelings into the resulting action. This also helps define the rhythm, in fact more often than not does define it. In the modern dance, the tendency or the wish has been to get rid of these "unnecessary and balletic" movements, at the same time wanting the same result in the size and vigor of the movement as the balletic action, and this has often left the dancer and the spectator slightly short.

To quibble with that on the other side: one of the best discoveries the modern dance has made use of is the gravity of the body in weight, that is, as opposite from denying (and thus affirming) gravity by ascent into the air, the weight of the body in going with gravity, down. The word "heavy" connotes something incorrect, since what is meant is not the heaviness of a bag of cement falling, although we've all been spectators of that too, but the heaviness of a living body falling with full intent of eventual rise. This is not a fetish or a use of heaviness as an accent against a predominantly light quality, but a thing in itself. By its nature this kind of moving would make the space seem a series of unconnected spots, along with the lack of clear-connecting movements in the modern dance.

A prevalent feeling among many painters that lets them make a space in which anything can happen is a feeling dancers may have too. Imitating the way nature makes a space and puts lots of things in it, heavy and light, little and big, all unrelated, yet each affecting all the others.

About the formal methods of choreography—some due to the conviction that a communication of one order or another is nec-

essary; others to the feeling that mind follows heart, that is, form follows content; some due to the feeling that the musical form is the most logical to follow—the most curious to me is the general feeling in the modern dance that nineteenth century forms stemming from earlier pre-classical forms are the only formal actions advisable, or even possible to take. This seems a flat contradiction of the modern dance—agreeing with the thought of discovering new or allegedly new movement for contemporary reasons, the using of psychology as a tremendous elastic basis for content, and wishing to be expressive of the "times" (although how can one be expressive of anything else?)—but not feeling the need for a different basis upon which to put this expression, in fact being mainly content to indicate that either the old forms are good enough, or further that the old forms are the only possible forms. These consist mainly of theme and variation, and associated devices—repetition, inversion, development and manipulation. There is also a tendency to imply a crisis to which one goes and then in some way retreats from. Now I can't see that crisis any longer means a climax, unless we are willing to grant that every breath of wind has a climax (which I am), but then that obliterates climax, being a surfeit of such. And since our lives, both by nature and by the newspapers, are so full of crisis that one is no longer aware of it, then it is clear that life goes on regardless, and further that each thing can be and is separate from each and every other, viz: the continuity of the newspaper headlines. Climax is for those who are swept by New Year's Eve.

More freeing into *space* than the theme and manipulation 'holdup' would be a formal structure based on *time*. Now time can be an awful lot of bother with the ordinary pinch-penny counting that has to go with it, but if one can think of the structure as a space of time in which anything can happen in any sequence of movement event, and any length of stillness can take place, then the counting is an aid towards freedom, rather than a discipline towards mechanization. A use of time-structure also frees the music into space, making the connection between the dance and the music one of individual autonomy connected at structural points. The result is that the dance is free to act as it chooses, as is the music. The music doesn't have to work itself to death to underline the dance, or the dance create havoc in trying to be as flashy as the music.

For me, it seems enough that dancing is a spiritual exercise in physical form, and that what is seen, is what it is. And I do not believe it is possible to be "too simple." What the dancer does is the most realistic of all possible things, and to pretend that a man standing on a hill could be doing everything except just standing is simply divorce—divorce from life, from the sun coming up and going down, from clouds in front of the sun, from the rain that comes from the clouds and sends you into the drugstore for a cup of coffee, from each thing that succeeds each thing. Dancing is a visible action of life.

In any discussion of the art of Mary Wigman (1886–   ), words like "primordial" inevitably appear. This extraordinary dancer seemed to have gone right back to the beginning of things when she began to display her ecstatic creations in Germany just after the First World War. She has said herself that "Art grows out of the basic cause of existence." She looked for essences, caught with a spontaneity that no one should mistake for anything else. The body was her means and her end. In its movements were compounded the totality of being, made visible, with no emotion restrained, no feeling repressed. In speaking of her, one is not ashamed to use the grandest terms, to talk of Death and Life. Wigman, probably more than anyone, forced the modern dance toward a free expression, but free expression that remained a controlled art form, and was never mere yielding to impulse. In describing the creation of her dances, she presents the reader with a very palpable impression of the force that she still exerts in the dance.

COMPOSITION IN PURE MOVEMENT

Mary Wigman

Charged as I frequently am with "freeing" the dance from music, the question often arises, what can be the source and basic structure of my own dancing. I cannot define its principles more clearly than to say that the fundamental idea of any creation arises in me or, rather, out of me as a completely independent dance theme. This theme, however primitive or obscure at first, already contains its own development and alone dictates its singular and logical sequence. What I feel as the germinal source of any dance may be compared perhaps to the melodic or rhythmic "subject" as it is first conceived by a composer, or to the compelling image that haunts a poet. But beyond that I can draw no parallels. In working out a dance I do not follow the models of any other art, nor have I evolved a general routine for my own. Each dance is unique and free, a separate organism whose form is self-determined.

Neither is my dancing abstract, in intention at any rate, for its origin is not in the mind. If there is an abstract effect it is incidental. On the other hand my purpose is not to "interpret" the emotions. Grief, joy, fear, are terms too fixed and static to describe the sources of my work. My dances flow rather from certain states of being, different stages of vitality which release in me a varying play of the emotions, and in themselves dictate the distinguishing atmospheres of the dances.

I can at this moment clearly recall the origin of my *Festlicher Rhythmus* ["Festive Rhythm"]. Coming back from the holidays, rested, restored by sun and fresh air, I was eager to begin dancing again. When I stepped into the studio and saw my co-workers there waiting for me, I beat my hands together and out of this spontaneous expression of happiness, of joy, the dance developed.

My first tentative attempts to compose were made when I was studying the Dalcroze system [a technique for translating musical rhythms into bodily movement conceived by the modern Swiss composer Émile Jaque-Dalcroze; known as "eurythmics"]. Though I have always had a strong feeling for music it seemed from the very start most natural for me to express my own nature by means of pure movement. Perhaps it was just because there was so much musical work to be done at that time, that all these little dances and dance studies took form without music. A German painter observing my modest experiments advised me to go to Munich and work with [German theorist and teacher Rudolf] Von Laban who was also interested in such dancing. On Laban's system of gymnastics I founded my body technique; and during this period of apprenticeship I continued the gradual evolution of my own work.

After years of trial I have come to realize in a very final way, that for me the creation of a dance to music already written cannot be complete and satisfactory. I have danced with several of the great European orchestras, and to music (always generically dance music) old and new. I have even attempted to work out Hindemith's *Daemon*, and some compositions of Bartók, Kodaly, and other contemporaries. But while music easily evokes in me a dance reaction, it is in the development of the dance that a great divergence so often occurs. For usually a dance idea, a "theme," however inspired, by a state of feeling, or indirectly by music, sets up independent reactions. The theme calls for its own development. It is in working this out that I find my dance parting company with the music. The parallel development of the dance with the already completely worked out musical idea is what I find in most instances to be functionally wrong. Each dance demands organic autonomy.

So I have come gradually to feel my way toward a new reintegration of music with the dance. I do not create a dance and then order music written for it. As soon as I conceive a theme, and before it is completely defined, I call in my musical assistants. Catching my idea, and observing me for atmosphere, they begin to improvise with me. Every step of the development is built up co-operatively. Experiments are made with various instruments, accents, climaxes, until we feel the work has indissoluble unity.

My *Pastorale* was developed in the following way: I came into my studio one day and sank down with a feeling of complete relaxation. Out of a sense of deepest peace and quietude I began slowly to move my arms and body. Calling to my assistants I said, "I do not know if anything will come of this feeling, but I should like a reed instrument that would play over and over again a simple little tune, not at all important, always the same one." Then with the monotonous sound of the little tune, with its gentle lyric suggestion, the whole dance took form. Afterwards we found that it was built on six-eighths time, neither myself nor the musician being conscious of the rhythm until we came to the end.

The monumental *Totenmal* ["Funeral Games"] which we presented in Munich last year was accompanied by a whole orchestra of percussion instruments. During the period of preparation these instruments were handled by dancers. The improvisation of dancing and music was so dovetailed that in the long hours of practice the girls dancing constantly changed places with those making the music. The final result was one of the greatest possible harmony. In group creations, as in my individual work, movement and sound are always evolved together.

Working with a group my effort is to seek out a common feeling. I present the main idea, each one improvises. No matter how

wide the range of individuality, I must find some common denominator from these different emanations of personality. Thus,
on the rock of basic feeling, I slowly build each structure.

Of course all that I have said here should be accepted as a
very personal credo. I do not propose to erect a general system
for I am a firm believer in individual freedom. Creative work
will always assume new and varying forms. Any profound expression of self for which its creator assumes responsibility in the
most complete sense must give authentic impetus to a new or an
old idea in art.

George Balanchine.
Photograph by Ernst Haas. Magnum.

TELEVISION, MOTION PICTURES, AND PHOTOGRAPHY

A great deal has been written in recent years about our technological culture, meaning, in most cases, our world of washing machines and refrigerators, that is, our kitchen culture. When the technological arts—radio, television, the film, the phonograph, photography, and so forth—have been dealt with, it has been, at best, with an uneasy tolerance. Marshall McLuhan (1911–   ), a Canadian who currently occupies the Albert Schweitzer chair at Fordham University, is the outstanding exception to this rule. The opening essay in his book The Medium Is the Message *states the terms of McLuhan's thesis, defines the textures of our technological culture, and prepares the way for such brisk distinctions as that between "hot" and "cold" media. A hot medium, such as the radio or the film, is one of "high definition": it is filled with information and leaves very little for the audience to add. A cool one, such as the cartoon, the telephone, or television, gives the viewer or listener only "a meager amount of information"; it is, consequently, of "low definition," and "high in participation or completion by the audience." It has been said that in making such distinctions, McLuhan is without a clear point of view, either esthetic or moral. Readers will have to judge this for themselves, but they should keep in mind McLuhan's statement from his introduction to* Understanding Media: *"The mark of our time is its revulsion against imposed patterns. We are suddenly eager to have things and people declare their beings totally. There is a deep faith to be found in this new attitude—a faith that concerns the ultimate harmony of all being. Such is the faith in which this book has been written."*

THE
MEDIUM
IS
THE
MESSAGE

Marshall McLuhan

In a culture like ours, long accustomed to splitting and dividing all things as a means of control, it is sometimes a bit of a shock to be reminded that, in operational and practical fact, the medium is the message. This is merely to say that the personal and social consequences of any medium—that is, of any extension of ourselves—result from the new scale that is introduced into our affairs by each extension of ourselves, or by any new technology. Thus, with automation, for example, the new patterns of human association tend to eliminate jobs, it is true. That is the negative result. Positively, automation creates roles for people, which is to say depth of involvement in their work and human association that our preceding mechanical technology had destroyed. Many people would be disposed to say that it was not the machine, but what one did with the machine, that was its meaning or message. In terms of the ways in which the machine altered our relations to one another and to ourselves, it mattered not in the least whether it turned out cornflakes or Cadillacs. The restructuring of human work and association was shaped by the technique of fragmentation that is the essence of machine technology. The essence of automation technology is the opposite. It is integral and decentralist in depth, just as the machine was fragmentary, centralist, and superficial in its patterning of human relationships.

The instance of the electric light may prove illuminating in this connection. The electric light is pure information. It is a medium without a message, as it were, unless it is used to spell out some verbal ad or name. This fact, characteristic of all media, means that the "content" of any medium is always another medium. The content of writing is speech, just as the written word is the content of print, and print is the content of the telegraph. If it is asked, "What is the content of speech?," it is necessary to say, "It is an actual process of thought, which is in itself non-verbal." An abstract painting represents direct manifestation of creative thought processes as they might appear in computer designs. What we are considering here, however, are the psychic and social consequences of the designs or patterns as they amplify or accelerate existing processes. For the "message" of any medium or technology is the change of scale or pace or pattern that it introduces into human affairs. The railway did not introduce movement or transportation or wheel or road into human society, but it accelerated and enlarged the scale of previous human functions, creating totally new kinds of cities and new kinds of work and leisure. This happened whether the railway functioned in a tropical or a northern environment, and is quite independent of the freight or content of the railway medium. The airplane, on the other hand, by accelerating the rate of transportation, tends to dissolve the railway form of city, politics, and association, quite independently of what the airplane is used for.

Let us return to the electric light. Whether the light is being used for brain surgery or night baseball is a matter of indifference. It could be argued that these activities are in some way the "content" of the electric light, since they could not exist without the electric light. This fact merely underlines the point that "the medium is the message" because it is the medium that shapes and controls the scale and form of human association and action. The content or uses of such media are as diverse as they are ineffectual in shaping the form of human association. Indeed, it is only too typical that the "content" of any medium blinds us to the character of the medium. It is only today that industries have become aware of the various kinds of business in which they are engaged. When IBM discovered that it was not in the business of making office equipment or business machines, but that it was in the business of processing information, then it began to navigate with clear vision. The General Electric Company makes a considerable portion of its profits from electric light bulbs and lighting systems. It has not yet discovered that, quite as much as A.T.&T., it is in the business of moving information.

The electric light escapes attention as a communication medium just because it has no "content." And this makes it an invaluable instance of how people fail to study media at all. For it is not till the electric light is used to spell out some brand name that it is noticed as a medium. Then it is not the light but the "content" (or what is really another medium) that is noticed. The message of the electric light is like the message of electric power in industry, totally radical, pervasive, and decentralized. For electric light and power are separate from their uses, yet they eliminate time and space factors in human association exactly as do radio, telegraph, telephone, and TV, creating involvement in depth.

A fairly complete handbook for studying the extensions of man could be made up from selections from Shakespeare. Some might quibble about whether or not he was referring to TV in these familiar lines from *Romeo and Juliet:*

> But soft! what light through yonder window breaks?
> It speaks, and yet says nothing.

In *Othello*, which, as much as *King Lear*, is concerned with the torment of people transformed by illusions, there are these lines that bespeak Shakespeare's intuition of the transforming powers of new media:

> Is there not charms
> By which the property of youth and maidhood
> May be abus'd? Have you not read Roderigo,
> Of some such thing?

In Shakespeare's *Troilus and Cressida*, which is almost completely devoted to both a psychic and social study of communication, Shakespeare states his awareness that true social and political navigation depend upon anticipating the consequences of innovation:

> The providence that's in a watchful state
> Knows almost every grain of Plutus' gold,
> Finds bottom in the uncomprehensive deeps,
> Keeps place with thought, and almost like the gods
> Does thoughts unveil in their dumb cradles.

The increasing awareness of the action of media, quite independently of their "content" or programming, was indicated in the annoyed and anonymous stanza:

> In modern thought, (if not in fact)
> Nothing is that doesn't act,
> So that is reckoned wisdom which
> Describes the scratch but not the itch.

The same kind of total, configurational awareness that reveals why the medium is socially the message has occurred in the most recent and radical medical theories. In his *Stress of Life*, Hans Selye tells of the dismay of a research colleague on hearing of Selye's theory:

When he saw me thus launched on yet another enraptured description of what I had observed in animals treated with this or that impure, toxic material, he looked at me with desperately sad eyes and said in obvious despair: "But Selye, try to realize what you are doing before it is too late! You have now decided to spend your entire life studying the pharmacology of dirt!"

As Selye deals with the total environmental situation in his "stress" theory of disease, so the latest approach to media study considers not only the "content" but the medium and the cultural matrix within which the particular medium operates. The older unawareness of the psychic and social effects of media can be illustrated from almost any of the conventional pronouncements.

In accepting an honorary degree from the University of Notre Dame a few years ago, General David Sarnoff made this statement: "We are too prone to make technological instruments the scapegoats for the sins of those who wield them. The products of modern science are not in themselves good or bad; it is the way they are used that determines their value." That is the voice of the current somnambulism. Suppose we were to say, "Apple pie is in itself neither good nor bad; it is the way it is used that determines its value." Or, "The smallpox virus is in itself neither good nor bad; it is the way it is used that determines its value." Again, "Firearms are in themselves neither good nor bad; it is the way they are used that determines their value." That is, if the slugs reach the right people firearms are good. If the TV tube fires the right ammunition at the right people it is good. I am not being perverse. There is simply nothing in the Sarnoff statement that will bear scrutiny, for it ignores the nature of the medium, of any and all media, in the true Narcissus style of one hypnotized by the amputation and extension of his own being in a new technical form. General Sarnoff went on to explain his attitude to the technology of print, saying that it was true that print caused much trash to circulate, but it had also disseminated the Bible and the thoughts of seers and philosophers. It has never occurred to General Sarnoff that any technology could do anything but *add* itself on to what we already are.

Such economists as Robert Theobald, W. W. Rostow, and John Kenneth Galbraith have been explaining for years how it is that "classical economics" cannot explain change or growth. And the paradox of mechanization is that although it is itself the cause of maximal growth and change, the principle of mechanization excludes the very possibility of growth or the understanding of change. For mechanization is achieved by fragmentation of any process and by putting the fragmented parts in a series. Yet, as David Hume showed in the eighteenth century, there is no principle of causality in a mere sequence. That one thing follows another accounts for nothing. Nothing follows from following, except change. So the greatest of all reversals occurred with electricity, that ended sequence by making things instant. With instant speed the causes of things began to emerge to awareness again, as they had not done with things in sequence and in concatenation accordingly. Instead of asking which came first, the chicken or the egg, it suddenly seemed that a chicken was an egg's idea for getting more eggs.

Just before an airplane breaks the sound barrier, sound waves become visible on the wings of the plane. The sudden visibility of sound just as sound ends is an apt instance of that great pattern of being that reveals new and opposite forms just as the earlier forms reach their peak performance. Mechanization was never so vividly fragmented or sequential as in the birth of the movies, the moment that translated us beyond mechanism into the world of growth and organic interrelation. The movie, by sheer speeding up the mechanical, carried us from the world of sequence and connections into the world of creative configuration and structure. The message of the movie medium is that of transition from lineal connections to configurations. It is the transition that produced the now quite correct observation: "If it works, it's obsolete." When electric speed further takes over from mechanical movie sequences, then the lines of force in structures and in media become loud and clear. We return to the inclusive form of the icon.

To a highly literate and mechanized culture the movie appeared as a world of triumphant illusions and dreams that money could buy. It was at this moment of the movie that cubism occurred, and it has been described by E. H. Gombrich (*Art and Illusion*) as "the most radical attempt to stamp out ambiguity and to enforce one reading of the picture—that of a man-made construction, a colored canvas." For cubism substitutes all facets of an object simultaneously for the "point of view" or facet of perspective illusion. Instead of the specialized illusion of the third dimension on canvas, cubism sets up an interplay of planes and contradiction or dramatic conflict of patterns, lights, textures that "drives home the message" by involvement. This is held by many to be an exercise in painting, not in illusion.

In other words, cubism, by giving the inside and outside, the top, bottom, back, and front and the rest, in two dimensions, drops the illusion of perspective in favor of instant sensory awareness of the whole. Cubism, by seizing on instant total awareness, suddenly announced that *the medium is the message*.

Is it not evident that the moment that sequence yields to the simultaneous, one is in the world of the structure and of configuration? Is that not what has happened in physics as in painting, poetry, and in communication? Specialized segments of attention have shifted to total field, and we can now say, "The medium is the message" quite naturally. Before the electric speed and total field, it was not obvious that the medium is the message. The message, it seemed, was the "content," as people used to ask what a painting was *about*. Yet they never thought to ask what a melody was about, nor what a house or a dress was about. In such matters, people retained some sense of the whole pattern, of form and function as a unity. But in the electric age this integral idea of structure and configuration has become so prevalent that educational theory has taken up the matter. Instead of working with specialized "problems" in arithmetic, the structural approach now follows the linea of force in the field of number and has small children meditating about number theory and "sets."

Cardinal Newman said of Napoleon, "He understood the grammar of gunpowder." Napoleon had paid some attention to other media as well, especially the semaphore telegraph that gave him a great advantage over his enemies. He is on record for saying that "Three hostile newspapers are more to be feared than a thousand bayonets."

Alexis de Tocqueville was the first to master the grammar of print and typography. He was thus able to read off the message of coming change in France and America as if he were reading aloud from a text that had been handed to him. In fact, the nineteenth century in France and in America was just such an open book to de Tocqueville because he had learned the grammar of print. So he, also, knew when that grammar did not apply. He was asked why he did not write a book on England, since he knew and admired England. He replied:

One would have to have an unusual degree of philosophical folly to believe oneself able to judge England in six months. A year always seemed to me too short a time in which to appreciate the United States properly, and it is much easier to acquire clear and precise notions about the American Union than about Great Britain. In America all laws derive in a sense from the same line of thought. The whole of society, so to speak, is founded upon a single fact; everything springs from a simple principle. One could compare America to a forest pierced by a multitude of straight roads all converging on

the same point. One has only to find the center and everything is
revealed at a glance. But in England the paths run criss-cross, and it is
only by travelling down each one of them that one can build up a
picture of the whole.

De Tocqueville, in earlier work on the French Revolution, had
explained how it was the printed word that, achieving cultural
saturation in the eighteenth century, had homogenized the French
nation. Frenchmen were the same kind of people from north to
south. The typographic principles of uniformity, continuity, and
lineality had overlaid the complexities of ancient feudal and oral
society. The Revolution was carried out by the new literati and
lawyers.

In England, however, such was the power of the ancient oral
traditions of common law, backed by the medieval institution
of Parliament, that no uniformity or continuity of the new visual
print culture could take complete hold. The result was that the
most important event in English history has never taken place;
namely, the English Revolution on the lines of the French Revolution. The American Revolution had no medieval legal institutions to discard or to root out, apart from monarchy. And many
have held that the American Presidency has become very much
more personal and monarchical than any European monarch ever
could be.

De Tocqueville's contrast between England and America is
clearly based on the fact of typography and of print culture
creating uniformity and continuity. England, he says, has rejected this principle and clung to the dynamic or oral common-
law tradition. Hence the discontinuity and unpredictable quality
of English culture. The grammar of print cannot help to construe
the message of oral and nonwritten culture and institutions. The
English aristocracy was properly classified as barbarian by
Matthew Arnold because its power and status had nothing to do
with literacy or with the cultural forms of typography. Said the
Duke of Gloucester to Edward Gibbon upon the publication of
his *Decline and Fall:* "Another damned fat book, eh, Mr. Gibbon? Scribble, scribble, scribble, eh, Mr. Gibbon?" De Tocqueville was a highly literate aristocrat who was quite able to be
detached from the values and assumptions of typography. That is
why he alone understood the grammar of typography. And it is
only on those terms, standing aside from any structure or

medium, that its principles and lines of force can be discerned. For any medium has the power of imposing its own assumption on the unwary. Prediction and control consist in avoiding this subliminal state of Narcissus trance. But the greatest aid to this end is simply in knowing that the spell can occur immediately upon contact, as in the first bars of a melody.

A Passage to India by E. M. Forster is a dramatic study of the inability of oral and intuitive oriental culture to meet with the rational, visual European patterns of experience. "Rational," of course, has for the West long meant "uniform and continuous and sequential." In other words, we have confused reason with literacy, and rationalism with a single technology. Thus in the electric age man seems to the conventional West to become irrational. In Forster's novel the moment of truth and dislocation from the typographic trance of the West comes in the Marabar Caves. Adela Quested's reasoning powers cannot cope with the total inclusive field of resonance that is India. After the Caves: "Life went on as usual, but had no consequences, that is to say, sounds did not echo nor thought develop. Everything seemed cut off at its root and therefore infected with illusion."

A Passage to India (the phrase is from Whitman, who saw America headed Eastward) is a parable of Western man in the electric age, and is only incidentally related to Europe or the Orient. The ultimate conflict between sight and sound, between written and oral kinds of perception and organization of existence is upon us. Since understanding stops action, as Nietzsche observed, we can moderate the fierceness of this conflict by understanding the media that extend us and raise these wars within and without us.

Detribalization by literacy and its traumatic effects on tribal man is the theme of a book by the psychiatrist J. C. Carothers, *The African Mind in Health and Disease* (World Health Organization, Geneva, 1953). Much of his material appeared in an article in *Psychiatry* magazine, November, 1959: "The Culture, Psychiatry, and the Written Word." Again, it is electric speed that has revealed the lines of force operating from Western technology in the remotest areas of bush, savannah, and desert. One example is the Bedouin with his battery radio on board the camel. Submerging natives with floods of concepts for which nothing has prepared them is the normal action of all of our technology. But with electric media Western man himself experiences exactly

the same inundation as the remote native. We are no more prepared to encounter radio and TV in our literate milieu than the
native of Ghana is able to cope with the literacy that takes him
out of his collective tribal world and beaches him in individual
isolation. We are as numb in our new electric world as the
native involved in our literate and mechanical culture.

Electric speed mingles the cultures of prehistory with the
dregs of industrial marketeers, the nonliterate with the semi-
literate and the postliterate. Mental breakdown of varying degrees is the very common result of uprooting and inundation with
new information and endless new patterns of information. Wynd-
ham Lewis made this a theme of his group of novels called *The
Human Age.* The first of these, *The Childermass,* is concerned
precisely with accelerated media change as a kind of massacre of
the innocents. In our own world as we become aware of the
effects of technology on psychic formation and manifestation, we
are losing all confidence in our right to assign guilt. Ancient pre-
historic societies regard violent crime as pathetic. The killer is
regarded as we do a cancer victim. "How terrible it must be to
feel like that," they say. J. M. Synge took up this idea very
effectively in his *Playboy of the Western World.*

If the criminal appears as a nonconformist who is unable to
meet the demand of technology that we behave in uniform and
continuous patterns, literate man is quite inclined to see others
who cannot conform as somewhat pathetic. Especially the child,
the cripple, the woman, and the colored person appear in a world
of visual and typographic technology as victims of injustice. On
the other hand, in a culture that assigns roles instead of jobs to
people—the dwarf, the skew, the child create their own spaces.
They are not expected to fit into some uniform and repeatable
niche that is not their size anyway. Consider the phrase "It's a
man's world." As a quantitative observation endlessly repeated
from within a homogenized culture, this phrase refers to the men
in such a culture who have to be homogenized Dagwoods in
order to belong at all. It is in our I.Q. testing that we have produced the greatest flood of misbegotten standards. Unaware of
our typographic cultural bias, our testers assume that uniform
and continuous habits are a sign of intelligence, thus eliminating
the ear man and the tactile man.

C. P. Snow, reviewing a book of A. L. Rowse (*The New
York Times Book Review,* December 24, 1961) on *Appeasement*

and the road to Munich, describes the top level of British brains
and experience in the 1930s. "Their I.Q.'s were much higher than
usual among political bosses. Why were they such a disaster?"
The view of Rowse, Snow approves: "They would not listen to
warnings because they did not wish to hear." Being anti-Red
made it impossible for them to read the message of Hitler. But
their failure was as nothing compared to our present one. The
American stake in literacy as a technology or uniformity applied
to every level of education, government, industry, and social life
is totally threatened by the electric technology. The threat of
Stalin or Hitler was external. The electric technology is within
the gates, and we are numb, deaf, blind, and mute about its encounter with the Gutenberg technology, on and through which
the American way of life was formed. It is, however, no time to
suggest strategies when the threat has not even been acknowledged to exist. I am in the position of Louis Pasteur telling doc-
tors that their greatest enemy was quite invisible, and quite un-
recognized by them. Our conventional response to all media,
namely that it is how they are used that counts, is the numb
stance of the technological idiot. For the "content" of a medium
is like the juicy piece of meat carried by the burglar to distract
the watchdog of the mind. The effect of the medium is made
strong and intense just because it is given another medium as
"content." The content of a movie is a novel or a play or an
opera. The effect of the movie form is not related to its program
content. The "content" of writing or print is speech, but the
reader is almost entirely unaware either of print or of speech.

Arnold Toynbee is innocent of any understanding of media
as they have shaped history, but he is full of examples that the
student of media can use. At one moment he can seriously suggest
that adult education, such as the Workers Educational Association in Britain, is a useful counterforce to the popular press.
Toynbee considers that although all of the oriental societies have
in our time accepted the industrial technology and its political
consequences: "On the cultural plane, however, there is no uniform corresponding tendency" (Somervell, I. 267). This is like
the voice of the literate man, floundering in a milieu of ads, who
boasts, "Personally, I pay no attention to ads." The spiritual
and cultural reservations that the oriental peoples may have
toward our technology will avail them not at all. The effects of
technology do not occur at the level of opinions or concepts, but

alter sense ratios or patterns of perception steadily and without any resistance. The serious artist is the only person able to encounter technology with impunity, just because he is an expert aware of the changes in sense perception.

The operation of the money medium in seventeenth-century Japan had effects not unlike the operation of typography in the West. The penetration of the money economy, wrote G. B. Sansom (in *Japan*, Cresset Press, London, 1931) "caused a slow but irresistible revolution, culminating in the breakdown of feudal government and the resumption of intercourse with foreign countries after more than two hundred years of seclusion." Money has reorganized the sense life of peoples just because it is an *extension* of our sense lives. This change does not depend upon approval or disapproval of those living in the society.

Arnold Toynbee made one approach to the transforming power of media in his concept of "etherialization," which he holds to be the principle of progressive simplification and efficiency in any organization or technology. Typically, he is ignoring the *effect* of the challenge of these forms upon the response of our senses. He imagines that it is the response of our opinions that is relevant to the effect of media and technology in society, a "point of view" that is plainly the result of the typographic spell. For the man in a literate and homogenized society ceases to be sensitive to the diverse and discontinuous life of forms. He acquires the illusion of the third dimension and the "private point of view" as part of his Narcissus fixation, and is quite shut off from Blake's awareness or that of the Psalmist, that we become what we behold.

Today when we want to get our bearings in our own culture, and have need to stand aside from the bias and pressure exerted by any technical form of human expression, we have only to visit a society where that particular form has not been felt, or a historical period in which it was unknown. Professor Wilbur Schramm made such a tactical move in studying *Television in the Lives of Our Children*. He found areas where TV had not penetrated at all and ran some tests. Since he had made no study of the peculiar nature of the TV image, his tests were of "content" preferences, viewing time, and vocabulary counts. In a word, his approach to the problem was a literary one, albeit unconsciously so. Consequently, he had nothing to report. Had his methods

been employed in 1500 A.D. to discover the effects of the printed
book in the lives of children or adults, he could have found out
nothing of the changes in human and social psychology resulting
from typography. Print created individualism and nationalism in
the sixteenth century. Program and "content" analysis offer no
clues to the magic of these media or to their subliminal charge.

Leonard Doob, in his report *Communication in Africa*, tells of
one African who took great pains to listen each evening to the
BBC news, even though he could understand nothing of it. Just
to be in the presence of those sounds at 7 P.M. each day was
important for him. His attitude to speech was like ours to melody
—the resonant intonation was meaning enough. In the seventeenth century our ancestors still shared this native's attitude to
the forms of media, as is plain in the following sentiment of the
Frenchman Bernard Lam expressed in *The Art of Speaking*
(London, 1696):

'Tis an effect of the Wisdom of God, who created Man to be
happy, that whatever is useful to his conversation (way of life) is
agreeable to him . . . because all victual that conduces to nourishment
is relishable, whereas other things that cannot be assimulated and be
turned into our substance are insipid. A Discourse cannot be pleasant
to the Hearer that is not easie to the Speaker; nor can it be easily
pronounced unless it be heard with delight.

Here is an equilibrium theory of human diet and expression such
as even now we are only striving to work out again for media
after centuries of fragmentation and specialism.

Pope Pius XII was deeply concerned that there be serious study
of the media today. On February 17, 1950, he said:

It is not an exaggeration to say that the future of modern society
and the stability of its inner life depend in large part on the maintenance of an equilibrium between the strength of the techniques of
communication and the capacity of the individual's own reaction.

Failure in this respect has for centuries been typical and total
for mankind. Subliminal and docile acceptance of media impact
has made them prisons without walls for their human users. As
A. J. Liebling remarked in his book *The Press*, a man is not free
if he cannot see where he is going, even if he has a gun to help
him get there. For each of the media is also a powerful weapon

with which to clobber other media and other groups. The result
is that the present age has been one of multiple civil wars that
are not limited to the world of art and entertainment. In *War and
Human Progress*, Professor J. U. Nef declared: "The total wars
of our time have been the result of a series of intellectual mistakes. . . ."

If the formative power in the media are the media themselves,
that raises a host of large matters that can only be mentioned
here, although they deserve volumes. Namely, that technological
media are staples or natural resources, exactly as are coal and
cotton and oil. Anybody will concede that a society whose economy is dependent upon one or two major staples like cotton, or
grain, or lumber, or fish, or cattle is going to have some obvious
social patterns of organization as a result. Stress on a few major
staples creates extreme instability in the economy but great
endurance in the population. The pathos and humor of the American South are embedded in such an economy of limited staples.
For a society configured by reliance on a few commodities accepts

them as a social bond quite as much as the metropolis does the press. Cotton and oil, like radio and TV, become "fixed charges" on the entire psychic life of the community. And this pervasive fact creates the unique cultural flavor of any society. It pays through the nose and all its other senses for each staple that shapes its life.

That our human senses, of which all media are extensions, are also fixed charges on our personal energies, and that they also configure the awareness and experience of each one of us, may be perceived in another connection mentioned by the psychologist C. G. Jung:

Every Roman was surrounded by slaves. The slave and his psychology flooded ancient Italy, and every Roman became inwardly, and of course inwittingly, a slave. Because living constantly in the atmosphere of slaves, he became infected through the unconscious with their psychology. No one can shield himself from such an influence (*Contributions to Analytical Psychology*, London, 1928).

Photograph by Lee Friedlander.

*In their short time on earth, radio and television
have brought out the journalist's stiletto as regularly
as has politics. On these occasions, the stiletto is
usually used simply for a little happy blooding.
John Lardner (1912–1960) could cut with the best
of them. He had been trained as a sports writer
before going on to consider the world of the arts
for* The New Yorker, *and in the world of sports-
writing there is no survival without a well placed
slice or chop now and then. But John Lardner, like
his famous father Ring Lardner who wrote on
radio for* The New Yorker *years before him, never
cut without a purpose, however carefully buried
beneath a mischievous surface. Language is most
often at the heart of Lardner's commentary, language abused or language respected—at least by
Lardner. This sportive performance is over so
quickly, one may miss its ironic point. If this should
happen, one should read it all over again.*

THOUGHTS ON
RADIO-TELEVESE

*John
Lardner*

Interviewing
Governor Rockefeller recently on Station
WMCA, Barry Gray, the discless jockey, felt
the need to ask his guest a certain question.
He also felt a clear obligation to put the inquiry
in radio-televese, the semi-official language of
men who promote conversation on the air.
Though it is more or less required, this language
is a flexible one, leaving a good deal to the user's
imagination. "Governor," Mr. Gray said, after
pausing to review the possibilities of the patois,
"how do you see your future in a Pennsylvania
Avenue sense?" I thought it was a splendid
gambit. Another broadcaster might have said
"How do you see yourself in the electoral-
college picture?" or "How do you project yourself Chief Executivewise?" The Gray formula
had the special flavor, the colorful two-rings-
from-the-bull's-eye quality, that I have associated

with the work of this interviewer ever since I began to follow it, several years ago. For the record, Governor Rockefeller replied, "I *could* be happier where I am." He might have meant Albany, he might have meant the WMCA studio. As you see, radio-televese is not only a limber language, it is contagious.

The salient characteristic of remarks made in radio-televese is that they never coincide exactly with primary meanings or accepted forms. For instance, Mr. Gray, a leader in the postwar development of the lingo, has a way of taking a trenchant thought or a strong locution and placing it somewhere to the right or left of where it would seem to belong. "Is this your first trip to the mainland? How do you feel about statehood?" I heard him ask a guest from the Philippines on one of his shows (the program runs, at present, from 11:05 P.M. to 1 A.M.). On the topic of Puerto Ricans in New York, he said, "How can we make these people welcome and not upset the décor of the city?" On a show a few years ago he described an incident that had taken place in a night club "that might be called a bawd." A drunk at a ringside table, Mr. Gray said, "interrupted the floor show to deliver a soliloquy." "When did the chink begin to pierce the armor?" he once asked, in connection with a decline in the prestige of former Mayor O'Dwyer. "The fault, then," he said on another occasion, "is not with Caesar or with his stars but with certain Congressmen." Speaking of the real-life source of a character in a Broadway play, he observed, "He was the clay pigeon on whom the character was modeled." When Mr. Gray called Brussels "the Paris of Belgium," I was reminded of an editorial I had read in a Long Island newspaper long ago in which Great Neck was called "the Constantinople of the North Shore." There is an eloquence and an easy confidence in Mr. Gray's talk that stimulates even his guests to heights of radio-televese. Artie Shaw, a musician, in describing the art of another performer to Mr. Gray, said, "He has a certain thing known as 'presence'—when he's onstage, you can see him." Another guest declared that the success of a mutual friend was "owing to a combination of luck and a combination of skill." "You can say that again," Mr. Gray agreed, and I believe that the guest did so, a little later. The same eloquence and the same off-centerism can be found today in the speech of a wide variety of radio and television regulars. "Parallels are odious," Marty Glickman, a sports announcer, has stated. "The matter has

reached a semi-head," a Senator—I couldn't be sure which one—
said at a recent televised Congressional hearing. "I hear you were
shot down over the Netherlands while flying," a video reporter
said to Senator Howard Cannon, a war veteran, on a Channel 2
program last winter. "Where in the next year are we going to
find the writers to fill the cry and the need?" David Susskind
demanded not long ago of a forum of TV directors. "Do you
have an emotional umbilical cord with Hollywood?" Mr. Susskind asked a director on the same show.

Mr. Susskind's second question raises the point that metaphor
is indispensable in radio-televese. "Wherein water always finds its
own level, they should start hitting soon," a baseball announcer
said about the Yankees the other day. In an earlier year, Red
Barber, analyzing a situation in which a dangerous batter had
been purposely walked, with the effect of bringing an even more
dangerous batter to the plate, remarked that it was a case of
"carrying coals to Newcastle, to make use of an old expression."
I suspect that Mr. Barber meant that it was a case of the frying
pan and the fire, and I also suspect that if he had thought of the
right metaphor afterward, he would have corrected himself
publicly. He is a conscientious man, and therefore by no means
a typical user of radio-televese. The true exponent never retraces
his steps but moves from bold figure to bold figure without
apology. There have been few bolder sequences (or "seg-ways,"
as they are sometimes called on the air) than the one that Mr.
Gray achieved in 1957 during a discussion of the perils faced by
Jack Paar in launching a new program. I think I have quoted
this passage here once before; it still fills me with admiration. "It's
like starting off with a noose around your neck," Mr. Gray said.
"You've got twenty-six weeks to make good, or they'll shoot you.
That sword of Damocles can be a rough proposition." As most
of you know by now, Mr. Paar eventually made good before the
sword could explode and throttle him.

Perhaps the most startling aspect of radio-televese is its power
to move freely in time, space, and syntax, transposing past and
future, beginnings and endings, subjects and objects. This phase
of the language has sometimes been called backward English, and
sometimes, with a bow to the game of billiards, reverse English.
Dorothy Kilgallen, a television panelist, was wallowing in the
freedom of the language on the night she said, "It strikes me as
funny, don't you?" So was Dizzy Dean when he said, "Don't fail

THE DESIGN ARTS:

Architecture to Advertising

to miss tomorrow's double header." Tommy Loughran, a boxing announcer, was exploring the area of the displaced ego when he told his audience, "It won't take him [the referee] long before I think he should stop it." Ted Husing was on the threshold of outright mysticism when he reported, about a boxer who was cuffing his adversary smartly around, "There's a lot more authority in Joe's punches than perhaps he would like his opponent to suspect!" It is in the time dimension, however, that radio-televese scores its most remarkable effects. Dizzy Dean's "The Yankees, as I told you later . . ." gives the idea. The insecurity of man is demonstrated regularly on the air by phrases like "Texas, the former birthplace of President Eisenhower" and "Mickey Mantle, a former native of Spavinaw, Oklahoma." I'm indebted to Dan Parker, sports writer and philologist, for a particularly strong example of time adjustment from the sayings of Vic Marsillo, a boxing manager who occasionally speaks on radio and television: "Now, Jack, whaddya say we reminisce a little about tomorrow's fight?" These quotations show what can be done in the way of outguessing man's greatest enemy, but I think that all of them are excelled by a line of Mr. Gray's spoken four or five years ago: "What will our future forefathers say?"

It is occasionally argued in defense of broadcasters (though they need and ask for no defense) that they speak unorthodoxly because they must speak under pressure, hastily, spontaneously —that their eccentricities are unintentional. Nothing could be farther from the truth. Their language is proud and deliberate. The spirit that has created it is the spirit of ambition. Posterity would have liked it. In times to come, our forebears will be grateful.

We are all aware of the dominant role played by inventions in modern history, but not at all clear as yet about the particular place of television, which may be the most important of all in its power to shape and direct human communication. A thoughtful attempt is made here to evaluate the resources of television and its failure to use them; at the same time, some cures are prescribed for the

TELEVISION: *peculiar rootlessness of the medium, which has resulted in its almost total inability to*

THE *establish its identity or to evaluate itself. Henry Steele Commager (1902–) is an historian by*

MEDIUM *profession, a notably learned and lucid commentator on American life, and obviously one who has spent many hours*

IN *watching the great American public eye.*

SEARCH
OF ITS
CHARACTER

Henry Steele
Commager

Television has some claim to be considered the most important invention in the history of communication of knowledge since the two great inventions of the Middle Ages: the university in the 12th Century and printing in the 15th Century. The beneficent consequences of these earlier inventions made themselves felt almost at once and have made themselves felt, cumulatively, over the centuries. We have now had television for only a quarter of a century, a very short time as these things go. It is not yet clear whether television has added anything to the dimensions of knowledge; it is not even clear whether its quantitative contributions to information and to entertainment can be counted as qualitative contributions to understanding or to happiness.

We are speaking, of course, of television as we know it in America; we must ever be on guard against two pervasive but fallacious assumptions: first that the United States' pattern of private ownership and control is the normal one; and second, that television has already reached its final form, and that changes will be largely in the technical realm, e.g., color instead of black and white, or Telstar. And as we have not yet exhausted the potentialities of television, we should not try to render final judgment on it. This is an interim judgment, or perhaps merely an interim report.

Television is, after all, a new medium and it is not surprising that we have not yet come to terms with it or that we do not yet understand its character. We do not really know what role it should play, or how it should play whatever role is assigned to it. Those who sit in the seats of power—the members of the Federal Communications Commission and, more important, the overlords of the industry—are, almost all of them, suffering from an acute case of schizophrenia: They have not yet decided whether television is a public or a private enterprise. One might suppose that the answer was clear enough. The airways, after all, belong to the public; the original FCC Act of 1934 specifically required television to serve the public interest; everywhere else in the world, television is regarded as a public-service institution.

One might suppose, too, that the choice, if open, would be clear. There are, after all, enough private enterprises, enough ways to make money. All the opportunities, all the challenges, are in the arena of public enterprise; all the important contributions are to be made to the commonwealth, not the private wealth.

But television is controlled by men trained in the most competitive of private industries, and by great corporations with the most miscellaneous activities, controlled, for the most part, by men without vision or imagination in anything other than their major interests—manufacturing, marketing and finance. The humorist Finley Peter Dunne once observed that what looked like a stone wall to a layman was a triumphal arch to a corporation lawyer; we might reverse that and say that what looks like a royal road to public service to the layman looks like a stone wall to TV's overlords.

There are, to be sure, frequent gestures toward the public interest, and sometimes more than gestures. Every so often television shows what it can do when it really tries—when it devotes the talents and resources which it commands to the task. Thus television's presentation of the Kennedy assassination and funeral, of the Churchill funeral; thus documentaries like *The Valiant*

Years, or like those studies of civil-rights demonstrations in the South, or the effect of cigaret smoking; thus reports on Presidential campaigns and elections; thus presentations of symphonic music, or of conducting by a Pablo Casals or a Leonard Bernstein; thus, from time to time, a few entertainments like the lamented *That Was the Week That Was* and the equally lamented *Slattery's People;* thus news commentators like Eric Sevareid.

The inevitable observation here is, if television can do this well, why does it not habitually do this well? We do not, after all, single out a few issues of the *New York Times* or the *Manchester Guardian*, a few great performances by the Boston Symphony or Vienna Philharmonic, a few courses or research findings at Harvard or Columbia Universities, a few decisions of the Supreme Court, and use these to justify such institutions. Why should not television have the same standards of excellence that we take for granted in other institutions devoted to the public interests?

The trouble is that, after 25 years, television does not know where it belongs, or what is its character. Does it belong with the newspaper and magazine as a form of entertainment and of information? Or does it belong with the University and the Foundation as a form of education?

It is, of course, something of both, but who can doubt that the proportions are badly mixed? Who can doubt that in both areas a kind of Gresham's law operates, the bad features driving out the good? And, more important still, who can doubt that the principle of control which dictates the nature of the operation itself differs fundamentally and perniciously from that which obtains in the realms of journalism and of education alike?

The analogy to journalism is the closest and the most revealing. Newspapers and magazines are, for the most part, business enterprises devoted to making money, though even here distinguished newspapers like the *New York Times* and distinguished journals like *Foreign Affairs* consider themselves public enterprises. But newspapers and magazines, for all their dependence on advertisers, control everything connected with their content, editorial and otherwise. Advertisers buy space in newspapers, and that is all they buy; they do not buy editorial content or editorial policy nor—in proper papers—influence over these. But with television —and alone with television—it is not the owners but the adver-

tisers (euphemistically called "sponsors") who determine policy
and content. Thus, alone of major media of communication, television lacks independence. Spokesmen for television, to be sure,
prate ceaselessly about independence, chiefly from Governmental
regulation, but they have nothing to say about independence
where it really counts.

TV's MOST PROMINENT FUNCTION

The most prominent, though not the most important, function of
television is to entertain. That the networks perform this role in
a manner acceptable to the great majority of viewers is clear
enough. But relevant here is the observation of Lord Reith of the
British Broadcasting Corporation:

"It will be admitted by all that to have exploited so great a
scientific invention for the purpose and pursuit of entertainment
alone, would have been a prostitution of its powers and an insult
to the character and intelligence of the people."

Nor can the masters of television escape responsibility for the
low level of much that passes for entertainment by insisting, as
they invariably do, that they are merely giving the public what
it wants. It is not clear whether it is the audience which has
imposed its standards on television, or television which has imposed its standards—and its notions about how to make money
—on the audience.

Nor is it clear that the good done by bringing some pleasure
to the old, the infirm, the housebound, or the simple-minded, out-
weighs the harm done to a whole society by debasing the public
taste or pandering to a taste already debased, and by discrediting
or making obsolete the habits of self-entertainment which, after
all, kept most people happy for a good many centuries.

The second major function of television is to inform and
educate. Here the analogy is not to the newspaper, but to the
University and the Foundation, or perhaps to schools generally.
Television does the informing part of this task very well indeed
—at least the major networks do. They seek out what appears to
be newsworthy and report it with imagination and skill.

Never before in history have men generally been able to know
so much about what happens everywhere, as now. They can

sit in on deliberations of the United Nations, follow election campaigns at home and abroad, get the feel of life in Russia, in Mexico, in an English industrial town, participate in the drama of a civil-rights demonstration in Mississippi, share with a small audience the performances of a Bernstein, see the White House through the eyes of Mrs. Kennedy and Washington through the eyes of Mrs. Johnson.

It is in the realm of education that the failure of television is most conspicuous. If we compare television with the University, or with an institution almost as new as television itself, the Foundation, we see at once the nature of the failure. Even those departments of television devoted to information have greater resources than most universities or foundations, but what have they to show for these resources? There is "educational television," to be sure, but it is weak and miscellaneous, largely because it lacks the funds and the personnel to make educational television as palatable to the public as commercial television. Now and then television gives us a brief interlude of "culture"— the glory that was Greece, perhaps, or the saga of Columbus, but these are exceptions.

On the whole the contribution of this new and potentially great medium of television to education, or to the enlargement of intellectual horizons, is meager, and is more than counterbalanced by its contributions to noneducation and to the narrowing of intellectual horizons. Television performs none of the traditional services of the Academy except fortuitously—it neither transmits the knowledge of the past to the next generation, nor contributes to professional training, nor does it expand the boundaries of knowledge.

Perhaps nowhere is the contrast between television and the Academy more revealing than in the realm of professional practices and institutional character. Over the years the Academy has developed a body of institutions and practices designed to promote its purposes and safeguard its integrity: thus academic standards for both students and scholars, academic tenure, academic freedom, academic self-government; concentration on libraries and laboratories; rewards not to popularity but to contributions.

Television has developed nothing whatsoever of this. If it be asserted that the analogy is unsound because the Academy is wholly noncommercial and television is a business enterprise, the answer is that other institutions both business and professional, such as medicine, the Bench and the Bar, the Church, architecture, even journalism, have developed comparable practices and safeguards.

Indeed, of all major institutions devoted to communication or to knowledge, television is the most conventional and the most pusillanimous. And the reason for this is even more sobering than the consideration itself: Television lacks enterprise and courage chiefly because it has nothing to be enterprising or courageous about. It has not developed anything like academic freedom because it is not interested in freedom, except from Governmental restrictions.

There are, of course, in all the networks, men of enterprise, men of ideas, men of courage and of honor, but they operate largely in a vacuum, and these qualities, though they are not deprecated, are not prized. The University, the Foundations, the professions of medicine and law and religion and journalism, are engaged in something more than competition for sponsors: they are engaged in an honorable competition to advance knowledge, or justice, or truth.

OTHER GOALS NEEDED

That is something worth competing for. But we cannot expect television to develop professional standards, principles, loyalties or ideas until it dedicates itself to something more important than success in the Nielsens or increased earnings to shareholders.

How sobering it is that though TV has flourished, now, for a quarter-century, it has not yet developed its statesmen, as do such institutions as the University, Journalism, the Church, the Military, Labor Unions, and Philanthropy.

Most Americans regard criticism of television like criticism of the weather: It cannot be other than it is! But American television is not the norm of television; it is abnormal. We take private ownership for granted, but it is public ownership which is taken for granted elsewhere. We take for granted control of programs by "sponsors" but even in Canada and Britain, which permit private television, sponsors have no influence on the programs themselves: They buy time, and that is the end of the matter.

No less startling, the development of television in the United States appears to be contrary to the intentions of our own law, as it is to most of our legal and constitutional principles. Is it necessary to repeat anything so elementary as this? Television is not a private but a public enterprise. It is so recognized in the basic Communications Act of 1934 which required the FCC to "grant licenses to serve the public convenience, interest or necessity."

Such a broad mandate must be interpreted in the light of a century of public-utility regulation, and of a long line of Supreme Court decisions from Munn v. Illinois of 1877: "When one devotes his property to a use in which the public has an interest, he grants to the public an interest in that use and must submit to be controlled by the public for the common good. . . ."

Every other major utility has submitted to this control; television alone of public utilities still thinks itself exempt from public control, defies it or circumvents it. But those who sit in the seats of power should remember that the alternative to private ownership is public ownership; it is not an extreme alternative but one which almost every civilized country on the globe accepts as a matter of course.

If television continues to reveal to us how good a job it *can* do, and how bad a job it commonly does; if it continues to exploit the public air waves for purely private gain, to debase the public taste, it may yet force the people into the alternative of public ownership. What is called for is not so much revolution as reform.

Here are some of the reforms which might restore television to the public domain and insure its service to the commonwealth:

First, the television networks must resume control of the whole content of their programs, just as newspapers control their content. The most pernicious ingredient in the whole of television is advertiser control of the content of television programs.

Second, we should create within the Federal Communications Commission, or elsewhere, boards of regents comparable to the Board of Governors of the BBC or to the regents and trustees of universities and foundations, whose responsibility it would be to safeguard the public interest in television.

Photograph by Bruce Davidson. Magnum.

POWERS FCC ISN'T USING

Such boards should have authority to make findings and impose decisions with respect to such matters as content and advertising, and to refuse to license stations which fail to devote themselves to the public interest. The FCC, to be sure, has this authority even now, but has not exercised it since its establishment.

Third, the networks themselves should develop institutions which will safeguard their independence and integrity and provide them with the kind of leadership and loyal, disinterested service taken for granted in universities or in governments.

It might be desirable to add a fourth safeguard: The creation of a well-supported publicly owned and controlled television network which would function nationally as WNYC functions in New York, or perhaps as the Third Programme of the BBC functions, to provide standards of comparison for the existing networks and to carry on experiments which are now so rarely attempted.

For Arnold Hauser (1892–   ), the film is the
definitive art of the modern era. In The Social
History of Art, *his two-volume synoptic view of*
the arts from prehistory to the present, he desig-
nates the world of art since the 1920s "The Film
Age." The motion picture, he tells us, "signifies
the first attempt since the beginning of our modern
individualistic civilization to produce art for a mass
public." It is also the art which, at least for a while,
could expect its mass audience to understand and
even to get pleasure from experimental techniques,
for "to learn the newly developing idiom of the
film was child's play for even the most primitive
cinema public." This first happy response has
changed—inevitably: "Only a young art can be
popular, for as soon as it grows older it is necessary,
in order to understand it, to be acquainted with the
earlier stages in its development." The accuracy of
this diagnosis can be judged by the amount of film
history which underlies the experimental textures
of the films of such modern directors as Ingmar
Bergman, Michelangelo Antonioni, François
Truffaut, and Agnes Varda. It is also true, as Hauser
suggests in his answer to the title question, that the

CAN
contributions of the great directors of
the past to the film makers and film
viewers of the present makes possible an

MOVIES
experience of extraordinary depth. But as
almost always in his writing, he is really only
suggestive. The full answer must come from

BE
the deeply involved reader himself. He must
argue with Hauser; he must argue with

"PROFOUND"?
himself. Can movies be
"profound"? Well, can
they? And if so, what
about some recent examples?

Arnold
Hauser

The novel is the only major art form that has
come down to us from the nineteenth century
in a viable condition. No other genre was
capable of expressing modern man with his
complexities, contradictions, and approximations.
Only the novel could do justice to the multi-

plicity and atomization of his mind, his unfettered spirit of experimentation, his ambivalent morality and divided emotions. The drama by comparison seemed obsolete, having lost its social function and moral significance. By the turn of the century, society had ceased to create new dramatic conflicts and the old ones were withering away. This, and not the competition of the movies, was the danger facing the theater; actually the film owed its success to the precarious situation of the theater, or, more accurately: the decline of the theater and the rise of the film can both be attributed to a new sense of solidarity with the objective world. The novel in this respect only prepared the way for the film.

The dramatic form was too narrow for the labyrinthine ways of modern psychology; within its limitations a character living in the twilight between the white and the black of stage conceptions could not be made credible. In the era of bourgeois tolerance, in which to understand was to forgive, the drama which interpreted character in terms of a single action and identified the whole man with his act, could not be the representative art form, but inevitably gave way to a genre capable of showing that the act, as often as not, is a mere mask behind which the actor hides. The drama of this period dealt with the hereditary themes either in the manner of a semi-serious, playfully ironic puppet show, or else in the style of a philosophical essay, closer to the modern intellectual novel than to traditional drama which gathered all problems into a single conflict and cut the knot with one-bold stroke. The sense of modern reality was present only in the novel. Respect for the drama was a mere leftover from Puritan classicism, a flirtation with the poverty of a form that had been spiritually outgrown.

The novel was the representative literary form of the previous century, if only because it was the psychological genre par excellence. For, just as in the Middle Ages theology was master over all other intellectual disciplines, now psychology was becoming the central science and the epitome of all wisdom. Every significant achievement in literature and the humane sciences opened new access to the human psyche, every important work of philosophy or history constituted a new contribution to the analysis and interpretation of man. The French, English, and Russian novel, the new social sciences, modern psychology, and psychoanalysis, all strove toward an understanding of the man who had risen out of the turmoil of the industrial revolution and, in modern bourgeois society, fallen out with himself. The basic trait of the picture they revealed was inner conflict, the disintegration of the personality. The findings of historical research are perhaps best summed up in the words of Ortega y Gasset: "Man has no nature, he has only a history." And in literature, a hero's disunity and alienation actually became the touchstone of his significance. The psychology that failed to see the strange, the dangerous, the abysmal in man, that did not state at the outset: "You are not what you seem," came to be regarded as hopelessly idyllic and simplistic. To be sure, at the time of the First World War when the film art was coming into being, certain signs (such as the works of Franz Kafka, which departed from a purely psychological vision of man) pointed to a change in this attitude. Nevertheless the film was, and is increasingly, judged by the standards of psychological analysis, a type of expression for which it is not equipped, and from this inadequate standpoint it appears superficial and meaningless. A conception which can only subject the problems of metaphysics and ethics, the symbols of religion and mythology to psychological interpretation, and which, instead of creating such ideas, religions, myths, can only produce a psychology of man's struggle with them, cannot do justice to the drama or to the film, and will inevitably appraise the film in particular as intrinsically unintellectual and unprofound. The profundity that resides in the multiplicity and shadings of psychological analysis will fit neither into the three acts of a drama nor into the three hundred scenes of a film. In a certain sense Thomas Mann is right in saying that the novel is more profound than the drama, and he even seems to be more or less justified in remarking elsewhere that the film has nothing in common with art. It assuredly has little in common with the art that fathoms psychological depths.

However, all art is not "profound"; there is also an art which, though lacking the dimension of depth, can boast some very great works. Raphael, Rossini, Victor Hugo—to take the most disparate examples—cannot but be regarded as great masters, but no one will claim that their works offer an insight into the depths of man's soul or destiny. The euphony, the balance, the harmonious lines of their works are pleasing without being profound, and the impression conveyed by these works is one of perfect artistry, although they exist in a world that is without mystery, fully deciphered and unveiled.

In addition to this unprofound art, there is an art whose profundity is *not* psychological, that is to say, it is not accomplished
by analysis and interpretation of the individual traits of psychological being. The great tragedies of Aeschylus and Sophocles
are profound without psychological depth, because their *form*,
the form of tragedy itself is profound. Their profundity consists
in the unveiling of the intelligible, free personality turned essence
and in the revelation of a substantial being that is ordinarily
covered over. The characters of tragedy can, in a certain sense
they must, be uncomplicated, schematic, flat-surfaced; the tragedy itself is never flat, for every successful work participates in
the depth of the genre.

And literature offers others forms of depth that are not psychological and do not derive from dark, mysterious characters. There
can be depth in the relations between unprofound, undifferentiated, summarily sketched characters, as for example between
Aunt Betsey and Mr. Dick in *David Copperfield*. The earthly
paradise of these two fools is beyond a doubt one of the most
beautiful and most profound daydreams in literature; the idea
that in life's important moments a fool always says "the right
thing," because in such moments all of us are fools, and because
Betsey Trotwood knows how to find the right thing, the best
thing, in the words of a fool—or perhaps even in the twittering
of a bird—*is* profound and cannot be called anything but profound. And this picture of a world in which the words of fools
and the twittering of birds have a meaning that cannot be expressed in the language of intelligence, has a depth of its own
which—as the Mr. Dick scenes in the film version of *David
Copperfield* amply show—is quite accessible to the film.

There are not only manifest forms of depth in art, there is also
a latent form: a hint of depth, which reveals only the gap where a
link in the chain is missing and there is meaning to be filled in; an
intimation of the breach in the edifice and the blind spot in our
own eye; an indirect representation of depth, or in other words:
a circling round the mystery, an admission of our incompetence
even to inquire into it (see Ernst Bloch's variations on this theme
of *"docta ignorantia"* in his *Geist der Utopie* [Spirit of Utopia],
1923). Art possesses in the symbol an instrument which in spite or
perhaps indeed because of its emphasis on the meaningless torso
of things, conveys some sense of its participation in another
world, its bond with the original mystery. And the more indirect,

stammering, recalcitrant the form through which art suggests the meaning beneath and destroys the surface meaning, the closer it comes to the mystery of things. The strange, inarticulate wisdom of the witches in *Macbeth*, the Mothers in Goethe's *Faust*, Hölderlin's flags that "clatter in the wind," the ghost in Gogol's "The Overcoat," the eerie "I-piti-piti ti-ti-ti" of the telegraph in Andrey Bolkonsky's delirious dream, are all such intrinsically meaningless messages from the depths. Or the old legend related by Tolstoy in his *Popular Tales:* Long, long ago there was a saintly hermit who lived on a desert island. One day some fishermen landed near his hut, among them an old man who was so simple-minded that he could barely talk and was unable to pray at all. Such ignorance filled the hermit with consternation, and with great trouble and pains he taught the old man the Lord's Prayer. The old man thanked him kindly and left the island with the other fishermen. Some time later, after the boat had vanished in the distance, the hermit suddenly saw a human shape on the horizon, walking on the surface of the water and approaching the island. Soon he recognized the old man, his pupil, and when the old man set foot on the island, the hermit, silent and abashed, came out to meet him. The old man stammered: "I have forgotten the prayer." "*You* don't have to pray," the hermit replied, and sent him away. Striding over the waters, the old man hurried after his boat.

Here depth is expressed without psychological complexity. Another such surface symbol occurs in the story of the conversion of the Indian saint, Rama Krishna. One day when he was still hardly more than a boy, he saw a flock of white cranes flying over the fields of his native village, high in the air, close to the blue heavens. He was so affected by the sight that he fell into a dead faint. When he recovered his senses, he was a changed man, awakened and converted.

Such depths are not closed to the film. The gulls and sailboats that swarm around the mutinous cruiser in *Potemkin* have no less symbolic power than the cranes in the story of Rama Krishna. As these little sailing craft, bringing gifts of bread and cigarettes to the rebels in their helpless ship, glide weightless over the wide dark waters with billowing sails, white and innocent as the sea-gulls and the woolly sheep in the sky, are they not a symbol and a promise of human brotherhood?

David Hemmings in scenes from Blow-Up, *Michelangelo Antonioni, Director.*
An MGM release. Photographs courtesy of MGM.

"I have gone to the movies constantly, and at times almost compulsively, for most of my life. I should be embarrassed to attempt an estimate of how many movies I have seen and how many hours they have consumed." Robert Warshow (1917–1955) was a writer of uncommon honesty, simplicity, and grace. His absorbing book, The Immediate Experience, *is a gathering of his pieces on various aspects of popular culture, from* Commentary (*of which he was an editor*), Partisan Review, *and the* American Mercury. *It was, Warshow thought, a special requirement of film criticism to "define that connection" and to do so in a personal way: "A man watches a movie, and the critic must acknowledge that he is that man." One finds in this essay, then, a statement that never moves too far from Warshow's own experience. Yet at the same time one cannot miss the urge toward principle,*

THE
or at least toward a clear formulation of the problems that, if well posed, could "point towards a theory" of film and

GANGSTER
possibly "go some way towards resolving the curious tension that surrounds the problem of 'popular

AS
culture.'"

TRAGIC
HERO

Robert
Warshow

America, as a social and political organization, is committed to a cheerful view of life. It could not be otherwise. The sense of tragedy is a luxury of aristocratic societies, where the fate of the individual is not conceived of as having a direct and legitimate political importance, being determined by a fixed and supra-political—that is, non-controversial—moral order or fate. Modern equalitarian societies, however, whether democratic or authoritarian in their political forms, always base themselves on the claim that they are making life happier; the avowed function of the modern state, at least in its ultimate terms, is not only to regulate social relations, but also to determine the quality and the possibilities of human life in general. Happiness thus becomes the chief political issue—in a sense, the only political issue—and for that reason it can never be treated as an issue at all. If an American or a Russian is unhappy, it implies a certain reprobation of his society, and therefore, by a logic of which we can all recognize the necessity, it becomes an obligation of citizenship to be cheerful; if the authorities find it necessary, the citizen may even be compelled to make a public display of his cheerfulness on important occasions, just as he may be conscripted into the army in time of war.

Naturally, this civic responsibility rests most strongly upon the organs of mass culture. The individual citizen may still be permitted his private unhappiness so long as it does not take on political significance, the extent of this tolerance being determined by how large an area of private life the society can accommodate. But every production of mass culture is a public act and must conform with accepted notions of the public good. Nobody seriously questions the principle that it is the function of mass culture to maintain public morale, and certainly nobody in the mass audience objects to having his morale maintained.[1] At a time when the normal condition of the citizen is a state of anxiety, euphoria spreads over our culture like the broad smile of an idiot. In terms of attitudes towards life, there is very little difference between a "happy" movie like *Good News*, which ignores death and suffering, and a "sad" movie like *A Tree Grows in Brooklyn*, which uses death and suffering as incidents in the service of a higher optimism.

But, whatever its effectiveness as a source of consolation and a means of pressure for maintaining "positive" social attitudes, this optimism is fundamentally satisfying to no one, not even to those who would be most disoriented without its support. Even within the area of mass culture, there always exists a current of opposition, seeking to express by whatever means are available to it that sense of desperation and inevitable failure which optimism itself helps to create. Most often, this opposition is confined to rudimentary or semi-literate forms: in mob politics

[1] In her testimony before the House Committee on Un-American Activities, Mrs. Leila Rogers said that the movie *None But the Lonely Heart* was un-American because it was gloomy. Like so much else that was said during the unhappy investigation of Hollywood, this statement was at once stupid and illuminating. One knew immediately what Mrs. Rogers was talking about; she had simply been insensitive enough to carry her philistinism to its conclusion.

and journalism, for example, or in certain kinds of religious enthusiasm. When it does enter the field of art, it is likely to be disguised or attenuated: in an unspecific form of expression like jazz, in the basically harmless nihilism of the Marx Brothers, in the continually reasserted strain of hopelessness that often seems to be the real meaning of the soap opera. The gangster film is remarkable in that it fills the need for disguise (though not sufficiently to avoid arousing uneasiness) without requiring any serious distortion. From its beginnings, it has been a consistent and astonishingly complete presentation of the modern sense of tragedy.[2]

In its initial character, the gangster film is simply one example of the movies' constant tendency to create fixed dramatic patterns that can be repeated indefinitely with a reasonable expectation of profit. One gangster film follows another as one musical or one Western follows another. But this rigidity is not necessarily opposed to the requirements of art. There have been very successful types of art in the past which developed such specific and detailed conventions as almost to make individual examples of the type interchangeable. This is true, for example, of Elizabethan revenge tragedy and Restoration comedy.

For such a type to be successful means that its conventions have imposed themselves upon the general consciousness and become the accepted vehicles of a particular set of attitudes and a particular aesthetic effect. One goes to any individual example of the type with very definite expectations, and originality is to be welcomed only in the degree that it intensifies the expected experience without fundamentally altering it. Moreover, the relationship between the conventions which go to make up such a type and the real experience of its audience or the real facts of whatever situation it pretends to describe is of only secondary importance and does not determine its aesthetic force. It is only in an ultimate sense that the type appeals to its audience's experience of reality; much more immediately, it appeals to previous experience of the type itself: it creates its own field of reference.

Thus the importance of the gangster film, and the nature

---

[2] Efforts have been made from time to time to bring the gangster film into line with the prevailing optimism and social constructiveness of our culture; *Kiss of Death* is a recent example. These efforts are usually unsuccessful; the reasons for their lack of success are interesting in themselves, but I shall not be able to discuss them here.

and intensity of its emotional and aesthetic impact, cannot be measured in terms of the place of the gangster himself or the importance of the problem of crime in American life. Those European movie-goers who think there is a gangster on every corner in New York are certainly deceived, but defenders of the "positive" side of American culture are equally deceived if they think it relevant to point out that most Americans have never seen a gangster. What matters is that the experience of the gangster *as an experience of art* is universal to Americans. There is almost nothing we understand better or react to more readily or with quicker intelligence. The Western film, though it seems never to diminish in popularity, is for most of us no more than the folklore of the past, familiar and understandable only because it has been repeated so often. The gangster film comes much closer. In ways that we do not easily or willingly define, the gangster speaks for us, expressing that part of the American psyche which rejects the qualities and the demands of modern life, which rejects "Americanism" itself.

The gangster is the man of the city, with the city's language and knowledge, with its queer and dishonest skills and its terrible daring, carrying his life in his hands like a placard, like a club. For everyone else, there is at least the theoretical possibility of another world—in that happier American culture which the gangster denies, the city does not really exist; it is only a more crowded and more brightly lit country—but for the gangster there is only the city; he must inhabit it in order to personify it: not the real city, but that dangerous and sad city of the imagination which is so much more important, which is the modern world. And the gangster—though there are real gangsters—is also, and primarily, a creature of the imagination. The real city, one might say, produces only criminals; the imaginary city produces the gangster: he is what we want to be and what we are afraid we may become.

Thrown into the crowd without background or advantages, with only those ambiguous skills which the rest of us—the real people of the real city—can only pretend to have, the gangster is required to make his way, to make his life and impose it on others. Usually, when we come upon him, he has already made his choice or the choice has already been made for him, it doesn't matter which: we are not permitted to ask whether at some point he could have chosen to be something else than what he is.

The gangster's activity is actually a form of rational enterprise, involving fairly definite goals and various techniques for achieving them. But this rationality is usually no more than a vague background; we know, perhaps, that the gangster sells liquor or that he operates a numbers racket; often we are not given even that much information. So his activity becomes a kind of pure criminality: he hurts people. Certainly our response to the gangster film is most consistently and most universally a response to sadism; we gain the double satisfaction of participating vicariously in the gangster's sadism and then seeing it turned against the gangster himself.

But on another level the quality of irrational brutality and the quality of rational enterprise become one. Since we do not see the rational and routine aspects of the gangster's behavior, the practice of brutality—the quality of unmixed criminality— becomes the totality of his career. At the same time, we are always conscious that the whole meaning of this career is a drive for success: the typical gangster film presents a steady upward progress followed by a very precipitate fall. Thus brutality itself becomes at once the means to success and the content of success —a success that is defined in its most general terms, not as accomplishment or specific gain, but simply as the unlimited possibility of aggression. (In the same way, film presentations of businessmen tend to make it appear that they achieve their success by talking on the telephone and holding conferences and that success *is* talking on the telephone and holding conferences.)

From this point of view, the initial contact between the film and its audience is an agreed conception of human life: that man is a being with the possibilities of success or failure. This principle, too, belongs to the city; one must emerge from the crowd or else one is nothing. On that basis the necessity of the action is established, and it progresses by inalterable paths to the point where the gangster lies dead and the principle has been modified: there is really only one possibility—failure. The final meaning of the city is anonymity and death.

In the opening scene of *Scarface*, we are shown a successful man; we know he is successful because he has just given a party of opulent proportions and because he is called Big Louie. Through some monstrous lack of caution, he permits himself to be alone for a few moments. We understand from this immediately that he is about to be killed. No convention of the gangster film is more strongly established than this: it is dangerous to be alone. And yet the very conditions of success make it impossible not to be alone, for success is always the establishment of an *individual* pre-eminence that must be imposed on others, in whom it automatically arouses hatred; the successful man is an outlaw. The gangster's whole life is an effort to assert himself as an individual, to draw himself out of the crowd, and he always dies *because* he is an individual; the final bullet thrusts him back, makes him, after all, a failure. "Mother of God," says the dying Little Caesar, "is this the end of Rico?"—speaking of himself thus in the third person because what has been brought low is not the undifferentiated *man*, but the individual with a name, the gangster, the success; even to himself he is a creature of the imagination. (T. S. Eliot has pointed out that a number of Shakespeare's tragic heroes have this trick of looking at themselves dramatically; their true identity, the thing that is destroyed when they die, is something outside themselves—not a man, but a style of life, a kind of meaning.)

At bottom, the gangster is doomed because he is under the obligation to succeed, not because the means he employs are unlawful. In the deeper layers of the modern consciousness, *all* means are unlawful, every attempt to succeed is an act of aggression, leaving one alone and guilty and defenseless among enemies: one is *punished* for success. This is our intolerable dilemma: that failure is a kind of death and success is evil and dangerous, is—ultimately—impossible. The effect of the gangster film is to embody this dilemma in the person of the gangster and resolve it by his death. The dilemma is resolved because it is *his* death, not ours. We are safe; for the moment, we can acquiesce in the failure, we can choose to fail.

THE CASE OF JAMES DEAN

Edgar Morin

It is possible that more words have been expended in our time on "a kind of solar performer appropriately called a star," *as Edgar Morin puts it, than on any other subject in the arts. Most of the words, it is true, are hogwash. They come from people who take the pantheon of film gods too seriously or not seriously enough. Few have bothered to examine the world of the star as a world, with its own sociology, psychology, and anthropology, a world which, upon close inspection, turns out to be some sort of representation of our world. Edgar Morin's book* The Stars *neither praises nor condemns; it analyzes systematically, presenting us with both the riches and the detritus of this curious world. Perhaps Morin is nowhere more skillful than in this examination of the phenomenon of James Dean, who in death even more than in life became the supreme embodiment of the mythology by which youth identifies itself to itself.*

The mythological hero is always abducted from his parents or the latter somehow are separated from him: James Dean was an orphan. His mother died when he was nine and he was brought up by an uncle, a farmer in Fairmount.

The mythological hero must forge his own destiny in a struggle against the world. James Dean ran away from the University, worked as an ice-breaker on a refrigeration truck, a stevedore on a tugboat, a ship's boy on a yacht, until he assumed his place under the dazzling rays of our modern mythical sun: he appeared on the Broadway stage in *See the Jaguar*, then in *The Immoralist*. He went to Hollywood and made *East of Eden*.

The mythological hero undertakes many labors in which he proves his aptitudes and also expresses his aspiration toward the richest, most nearly total life possible. James Dean milked cows, tended chick-ens, drove a tractor, raised a bull, played star basketball, studied yoga and the clarinet, learned something about almost every field of knowledge, and finally became what in the modern world em-bodies the myth of total life: a movie star. James Dean wanted to do everything, to try everything, to experience everything. 'If I lived to be a hundred,' he would say, 'I still wouldn't have time to do everything I wanted.'

The mythological hero aspires to the absolute, but cannot realize this absolute in a woman's love. James Dean would have had an unhappy life with Pier Angeli, who married Vic Damone: legend or reality? In any case, the legend is anchored in reality. In front of the church which Pier Angeli left as a bride, James Dean gunned his motorcycle: the noise of the motor drowned out the sound of bells. Then he dragged violently and drove all the way to Fairmount, the cradle of his childhood. (We re-discover here the theme of the amorous failure, necessary to heroic accomplishment, as well as the theme of the feminine maleficence which every redeeming hero encounters.)

The mythological hero confronts more and more touchingly the world he desires to seize in its entirety. James Dean's destiny became increasingly breathless: he was obsessed by speed, the modern ersatz absolute. Seeming disturbed and feverish to some, extraordinarily serene to others, James Dean, after finishing *Giant*, drove off into the night at 160 miles an hour in his racing Porsche towards Salinas, where he was to enter an automobile race.

The mythological hero encounters death in his quest for the absolute. His death signifies that he is broken by the hostile forces of the world, but at the same time, in this very defeat, he ultimately gains the absolute: immortality. James Dean dies; it is the beginning of his victory over death.

The 'heroic' life and character of James Dean are not pre-fabricated by the star system, but real, *revealed*. There is still more.

Heroes die young. Heroes are young. But our times have produced, in literature (Rimbaud, *The Wanderer*) and, de-cisively, in recent years, in the movies, heroes bearing the new message of adolescence. Since its origin, of course, the movies' greatest audience has been composed of adolescents. But it is only recently that adolescence has become conscious of itself as a particular age-class, opposing itself to other age-classes and defining its own imaginary range and cultural models.[1] Which is as clearly revealed in the novels of Françoise Sagan and Françoise Mallet-Joris as in the films of Marlon Brando or James Dean.

James Dean is a model, but this model is itself the typical expression (both average and pure) of adolescents in general and of American adolescence in particular.

His face corresponds to a dominant physiognomic type, blond hair, regular features. Further, the mobility of his expressions admirably translates the double nature of the adolescent face, still hesitating between childhood's melancholy and the mask of the adult. The photogenic quality of this face, even more than that of Marlon Brando, is rich with all the indetermination of an ageless age, alternating scowls with astonishment, disarmed candor and playfulness with sudden hardness, resolution and rigor with collapse. Chin on chest, unexpectedly smiling, fluttering his eyelashes, mingling ostentation and reserve, being naive and gauche, i.e., always sincere, the face of James Dean is an ever-changing landscape in which can be discerned the contradictions, uncertainties, and enthusiasms of the adolescent soul. It is understandable that this face should have become an insignia, that it is already imitated, especially in its most readily imitable features: hair and glance.

James Dean has also defined what one might call the panoply of adolescence, a wardrobe in which is expressed a whole attitude towards society: blue jeans, heavy sweaters, leather jacket, no tie, unbuttoned shirt, deliberate sloppiness are so many ostensible signs (having the value of political badges) of a resistance against the social conventions of a world of adults. Clothes are a quest for the signs of virility (the costume of manual laborers) and of artistic caprice. James Dean has invented nothing; he has canonized and codified an ensemble of sumptuary laws which allows an age-class to assert itself, and this age-class will assert itself even further in imitation of its hero.

James Dean, in his double life, both on and off the screen, is a pure hero of adolescence. He expresses his needs and his revolt in a single impulse which the French and English titles of one of his films express: *La Fureur de Vivre* (*A Rage to Live*) and

---

[1] Similarly, it is quite recently that adolescence has been studied by psychology as such.

Rebel Without a Cause are two aspects of the same virulent demand, in which a rebellious fury confronts a life without a cause.

Because he is a hero of adolescence James Dean expresses with a clarity rare in American films, in *East of Eden* and *Rebel Without a Cause*, the rebellion against the family. The American film tends to mask parent-child conflicts, either in the familial idyll (*The Hardy Family*) or else by altogether suppressing the parents' existence and transferring the father's image on an insensible, cruel, or ridiculous old man (half-senile judge or employer). *East of Eden* presents the characters of an uncomprehending father and a fallen mother; *Rebel Without a Cause* presents the characters of an uncomprehending mother and a fallen father. In both these films appears the theme of the adolescent's combat against the father (whether the latter is tyrannical or pitiful) and the theme of his inability to relate meaningfully to his mother. In *Giant* the framework of the conflict explodes: it is against a family exterior to himself and, by extension, against all social norms that James Dean will do battle with such ferocious hatred.[2]

But in all three films appears the common theme of the woman-sister who must be snatched from someone else's possession. In other words, the problem of sexual love is still enclosed within a sororal-maternal love, has not yet broken out of this shell to launch itself in a universe of pin-ups external to family and age-class alike. Upon these imaginary movie loves is superimposed the love, itself also mythical perhaps, which Dean is supposed to have felt for Pier Angeli with her ingenuous sister-madonna face. Beyond this impossible love begins the universe of sexual 'adventures.'

In another sense James Dean expresses in his life and films the needs of adolescent individuality which, asserting itself, refused to accept the norms of the soul-killing and specialized life that lie ahead. The demand for a total life, the quest for the absolute is every human individual's demand when he tears himself from the nest of childhood and the chains of the family only to see before him the new chains and mutilations of social life. It is then that the most contradictory requirements come to a ferment. Truffaut

[2] George Stevens tells that it was James Dean himself who asked to interpret this role: 'It's a part for me, Mr. Stevens.'

expresses it perfectly (*Arts*, 26-9-56): 'In James Dean, today's youth discovers itself. Less for the reasons usually advanced: violence, sadism, hysteria, pessimism, cruelty, and filth, than for others infinitely more simple and commonplace: modesty of feeling, continual fantasy life, moral purity without relation to everyday morality but all the more rigorous, eternal adolescent love of tests and trials, intoxication, pride, and regret at feeling oneself "outside" society, refusal and desire to become integrated and, finally, acceptance—or refusal—of the world as it is.'

The essential contradiction is the one that links the most intense aspiration to a total life with the greatest possibility of death.

This contradiction is the problem of virile initiation, which is resolved in primitive societies by terrible institutionalized tests of endurance; in our society it is effected institutionally only by war (and vestigially by military service); lacking war or collective subversions (revolutions, underground resistance), this initiation must be sought in individual risk.

Finally the adult of our middle-class bureaucratized society is the man who agrees to live only a little in order not to die a great deal. But the secret of adolescence is that living *means* risking death; that the rage to live *means* the impossibility of living. James Dean has lived this contradiction and authenticated it by his death.

These themes of adolescence appear with great clarity at a period when adolescence is particularly reduced to its own resources, when society allows it no outlets by which it can engage or even recognize its cause.

A James Dean has not been able to become an exemplary figure in these years of the half-century by chance. To the intense participations of the war and (in France) of the Resistance, to the immense hopes of 1944–46, have succeeded not only individualist withdrawals but a generalized nihilism which is a radical interrogation of all official ideologies and values. The ideological lie in which contemporary societies live, pretending to be harmonious, happy, and uplifting, provokes in return this 'nihilism' or this 'romanticism' in which adolescence does escape and discovers the reality of life.

It is at this point in the Western middle-class world that adventures, risk, and death participate in the gunning of a motor-

cycle or a racing car: already the motorcyclists of *Orpheus* left
death's fatal wake behind them, already Laszlo Benedek's *The
Wild One* traced bitterly and tenderly the image of the adolescent motorcyclist. Marlon Brando, roaring archangel, like an
imaginary John the Baptist heralded the real James Dean because
he himself was the imaginary expression of thousands of real
adolescents whose only expression of their rage to live as rebels
without a cause was the motorcycle gang. Motorized *speed* is not
only one of the modern signs of the quest for the absolute, but
corresponds to the need for risk and self-affirmation in everyday
life. Anyone behind a wheel feels like a god in the most biblical
sense of the term, self-intoxicated, ready to strike other drivers
with thunderbolts, terrorize mortals (pedestrians), and hand
down the law in the form of insults to all who do not recognize
his *absolute priority*.

The automobile is escape at last: Rimbaud's sandals of the
wind are replaced by James Dean's big racing Porsche. And the
supreme escape is death just as the absolute is death, just as the
supreme individuality is death. James Dean drives into the night
toward the death from which the contract to make *Giant* could
protect him only temporarily.

Death fulfills the destiny of every mythological hero by fulfilling his double nature: human and divine. It fulfills his profound humanity, which is to struggle heroically against the
world, to confront heroically a death which ultimately over-
whelms him. At the same time, death fulfills the superhuman
nature of the hero: it divinizes him by opening wide the gates of
immortality. Only after his sacrifies, in which he expiates his
human condition, does Jesus become a god.

Thus amplified in the character of James Dean are the phenomena of divinization which characterize but generally remain
atrophied in the movie stars.

First of all, that spontaneous, naive phenomenon: the refusal
to believe in the hero's death. The death of Napoleon, of Hitler,
of every superman (good or evil) has been doubted and disbelieved
because the faithful were never able to believe these heroes were
entirely mortal. The death of James Dean has been similarly
doubted. There is a legend that he miraculously survived his
accident, that it was a hitch-hiker who was killed, that James
Dean was disfigured, unrecognizable, perhaps unconscious: that
he has been shut up somewhere in an insane asylum or a hospital.

Every week 2,000 letters are mailed to a living James Dean. Living where? In a no-man's land between life and death which the modern mind chooses to situate in insane asylums and sanitariums but which cannot be localized. Here James Dean offers himself to the spiritualist conception of death: James Dean is among us, invisible and present. Spiritualism revives the primitive notion according to which the dead, who are corporeal specters endowed with invisibility and ubiquity, live among the living. This is why one young girl cried out: 'Come back, Jimmy, I love you! We're waiting for you!' during a showing of *Giant*. It is the *living* (spiritualist) presence of James Dean which his fanatics will henceforth look for in his films. This is why spiritualist séances held to communicate with James Dean have multiplied. This is why the little dimestore salesgirl, Joan Collins, took from the dictation of the dead James Dean the extraordinary spiritualist confession in which he declares, 'I am not dead. Those who believe I am not dead are right,' and in which he asserts he has rejoined his mother. This is why *James Dean Returns* by Joan Collins has sold more than 500,000 copies.

Thus a cult has been organized, like all cults, in order to reestablish contact between mortals and the immortal dead. James Dean's tomb is constantly covered with flowers, and 3,000 people made a pilgrimage there on the first anniversary of his death. His death mask will be placed beside those of Beethoven, Thackeray, and Keats at Princeton University. His bust in plaster is on sale for $30. The fatal car has become a sacred object. For a quarter you can look at the big racing Porsche, for an additional quarter you can sit behind the wheel. This ruined car, which symbolizes the Passion of James Dean, his rage to live and his rage to die, has been dismembered: bolts and screws, bits of twisted metal, regarded as sacred relics, can be bought at prices starting at $20, according to size, and carried about like amulets to imbue the wearer with the hero's mystic substance.

In death, by means of death, James Dean has recovered the forgotten prestige of the stars of the great epoch who, nearer gods than mortals, aroused hysterical adoration. But from another point of view his death authenticates a life which firmly fixes him among the modern stars, within the reach of mortals. The modern stars are models and examples, whereas the earlier ones were the ideals of a dream. James Dean is a real hero, but one who undergoes a divinization analogous to that of the great stars of the silent films.

And the immortality of James Dean is also his collective survival in a thousand mimetisms. James Dean is indeed a perfect star: god, hero, model. But this perfection, if it has only been able to fulfill itself by means of the star system, derives from the life and death of the real James Dean and from the exigence which is his own as well as that of a generation which sees itself in him, reflected and transfigured in twin mirrors: screen and death.

Spawned in the nineteenth century and, in turn,
spawning hordes of enthusiasts who went, and still
go about snapping everything in sight, photography
as it is practiced by the masters undeniably ranks
among the arts. Photography as an art can obviously
be compared with painting in a number of ways.
Picasso, for example, once explained the difference
by comparing the painter to the magician or
faith-healer who keeps a normal distance between
himself and his subject's reality and the photographer
to a surgeon who " 'operates' directly on the tissues
of reality." Thus, the painter's image is total; the
photographer's shows "a multiplicity of details
coordinated according to a new law and resulting
from an intensive penetration of reality." Some of
the means by which that penetration is achieved are
analyzed in the following article by a well-known
photographer and critic. John Szarkowski
(1925–   ) is Director of Photography at The
Museum of Modern Art and head of the
Edward Steichen Photography Center
there.

THE PHOTOGRAPHER'S EYE

John
Szarkowski

The invention of photography provided a radically new picture-making process—a process
based not on synthesis but on selection. The difference was a basic one. Paintings were *made*
—constructed from a storehouse of traditional
schemes and skills and attitudes—but photographs, as the man on the street put it, were
taken.

The difference raised a creative issue of a new
order: how could this mechanical and mindless
process be made to produce pictures meaningful
in human terms—pictures with clarity and coherence and a point of view? It was soon demonstrated that an answer would not be found by
those who loved too much the old forms, for in
large part the photographer was bereft of the
old artistic traditions. Speaking of photography
Baudelaire said: "This industry, by invading the
territories of art, has become art's most mortal

enemy."[1] And in his own terms of reference Baudelaire was half right; certainly the new medium could not satisfy old standards. The photographer must find new ways to make his meaning clear.

These new ways might be found by men who could abandon their allegiance to traditional pictorial standards—or by the artistically ignorant who had no old allegiances to break. There have been many of the latter sort. Since its earliest days, photography has been practiced by thousands who shared no common tradition or training, who were disciplined and united by no academy or guild, who considered their medium variously as a science, an art, a trade, or an entertainment, and who were often unaware of each other's work. Those who invented photography were scientists and painters, but its professional practitioners were a very different lot. Hawthorne's daguerreotypist hero Holgrave in *The House of the Seven Gables* was perhaps not far from typical:

Though now but twenty-two years old, he had already been a country schoolmaster; salesman in a country store; and the political editor of a country newspaper. He had subsequently travelled as a peddler of cologne water and other essences. He had studied and practiced dentistry. Still more recently he had been a public lecturer on mesmerism, for which science he had very remarkable endowments. His present phase as a daguerreotypist was of no more importance in his own view, nor likely to be more permanent, than any of the preceding ones.[2]

The enormous popularity of the new medium produced professionals by the thousands—converted silversmiths, tinkers, druggists, blacksmiths and printers. If photography was a new artistic problem, such men had the advantage of having nothing to unlearn. Among them they produced a flood of images. In 1853 the *New York Daily Tribune* estimated that three million daguerreotypes were being produced that year.[3] Some of these pictures were the product of knowledge and skill and sensibility

[1] Charles Baudelaire, "Salon de 1859," translated by Jonathan Mayne for *The Mirror of Art, Critical Studies by Charles Baudelaire*. London: Phaidon Press, 1955. (Quoted from *On Photography, A Source Book of Photo History in Facsimile*, edited by Beaumont Newhall. Watkins Glen, N.Y.: Century House, 1956, p. 106.)

[2] Nathaniel Hawthorne, *The House of the Seven Gables*. New York: Signet Classics edition, 1961, pp. 156–7.

[3] A. C. Willers, "Poet and Photography," in *Picturescope*, Vol. XI, No. 4. New York: Picture Division, Special Libraries Association, 1963, p. 46.

and invention; many were the product of accident, improvisation, misunderstanding, and empirical experiment. But whether produced by art or by luck, each picture was part of a massive assault on our traditional habits of seeing.

By the latter decades of the nineteenth century the professionals and the serious amateurs were joined by an even larger host of casual snapshooters. By the early eighties the dry plate, which could be purchased ready-to-use, had replaced the refractory and messy wet plate process, which demanded that the plate be prepared just before exposure and processed before its emulsion had dried. The dry plate spawned the hand camera and the snapshot. Photography had become easy. In 1893 an English writer complained that the new situation had "created an army of photographers who run rampant over the globe, photographing objects of all sorts, sizes and shapes, under almost every condition, without ever pausing to ask themselves, is this or that artistic? . . . They spy a view, it seems to please, the camera is focused, the shot taken! There is no pause, why should there be? For art may err but nature cannot miss, says the poet, and they listen to the dictum. To them, composition, light, shade, form and texture are so many catch phrases. . . ."[4]

These pictures, taken by the thousands by journeyman worker and Sunday hobbyist, were unlike any pictures before them. The variety of their imagery was prodigious. Each subtle variation in viewpoint or light, each passing moment, each change in the tonality of the print, created a new picture. The trained artist could draw a head or a hand from a dozen perspectives. The photographer discovered that the gestures of a hand were infinitely various, and that the wall of a building in the sun was never twice the same.

Most of this deluge of pictures seemed formless and accidental, but some achieved coherence, even in their strangeness. Some of the new images were memorable, and seemed significant beyond their limited intention. These remembered pictures enlarged one's sense of possibilities as he looked again at the real world. While they were remembered they survived, like organisms, to reproduce and evolve.

But it was not only the way that photography described things

[4] E. E. Cohen, "Bad Form in Photography," in *The International Annual of Anthony's Photographic Bulletin.* New York and London: E. and H. T. Anthony, 1893, p. 18.

that was new; it was also the things it chose to describe. Photographers shot ". . . objects of all sorts, sizes and shapes . . . without ever pausing to ask themselves, is that or that artistic?" Painting was difficult, expensive, and precious, and it recorded what was known to be important. Photography was easy, cheap and ubiquitous, and it recorded anything: shop windows and sod houses and family pets and steam engines and unimportant people. And once made objective and permanent, immortalized in a picture, these trivial things took on importance. By the end of the century, for the first time in history, even the poor man knew what his ancestors had looked like.

The photographer learned in two ways: first, from a worker's intimate understanding of his tools and materials (if his plate would not record the clouds, he could point his camera down and eliminate the sky); and second he learned from other photographs, which presented themselves in an unending stream. Whether his concern was commercial or artistic, his tradition was formed by all the photographs that had impressed themselves upon his consciousness. . . .

It should be possible to consider the history of the medium in terms of photographers' progressive awareness of characteristics and problems that have seemed inherent in the medium. Five such issues are considered below. These issues *do not* define discrete categories of work; on the contrary they should be regarded as interdependent aspects of a single problem— as section views through the body of photographic tradition. As such, it is hoped that they may contribute to the formulation of a vocabulary and a critical perspective more fully responsive to the unique phenomena of photography.

THE THING ITSELF

The first thing that the photographer learned was that photography dealt with the actual; he had not only to accept this fact, but to treasure it; unless he did, photography would defeat him. He learned that the world itself is an artist of incomparable inventiveness, and that to recognize its best works and moments, to anticipate them, to clarify them and make them permanent, requires intelligence both acute and supple.

But he learned also that the factuality of his pictures, no matter how convincing and unarguable, was a different thing than the reality itself. Much of the reality was filtered out in the static little black and white image, and some of it was exhibited with an unnatural clarity, an exaggerated importance. The subject and the picture were not the same thing, although they would afterwards seem so. It was the photographer's problem to see not simply the reality before him but the still invisible picture, and to make his choices in terms of the latter.

This was an artistic problem, not a scientific one, but the public believed that the photograph could not lie, and it was easier for the photographer if he believed it too, or pretended to. Thus he was likely to claim that what our eyes saw was an illusion, and what the camera saw was the truth. Hawthorne's Holgrave, speaking of a difficult portrait subject said:

"We give [heaven's broad and simple sunshine] credit only for depicting the merest surface, but it actually brings out the secret character with a truth that no painter would ever venture upon, even could he detect it. . . . The remarkable point is that the original wears, to the world's eye . . . an exceedingly pleasant countenance, indicative of benevolence, openness of heart, sunny good humor, and other praiseworthy qualities of that cast. The sun, as you see, tells quite another story, and will not be coaxed out of it, after half a 'dozen patient attempts on my part. Here we have a man, sly, subtle, hard, imperious, and withal, cold as ice."[5]

In a sense Holgrave was right in giving more credence to the camera image than to his own eyes, for the image would survive the subject, and become the remembered reality. William M. Ivins, Jr. said, "at any given moment the accepted report of an event is of greater importance than the event, for what we think about and act upon is the symbolic report and not the concrete event itself."[6] He also said: "The nineteenth century began by believing that what was reasonable was true and it would end up by believing that what it saw a photograph of was true."[7]

THE DETAIL

The photographer was tied to the facts of things, and it was his problem to force the facts to tell the truth. He could not, out-

[5] Hawthorne, op. cit., p. 85.
[6] William M. Ivins, Jr., *Prints and Visual Communication*. Cambridge, Mass.: Harvard University Press, 1953, p. 180.
[7] Ibid., p. 94.

side the studio, pose the truth; he could only record it as he found it, and it was found in nature in a fragmented and unexplained form—not as a story, but as scattered and suggestive clues. The photographer could not assemble these clues into a coherent narrative, he could only isolate the fragment, document it, and by so doing claim for it some special significance, a meaning which went beyond simple description. The compelling clarity with which a photograph recorded the trivial suggested that the subject had never before been properly seen, that it was in fact perhaps *not* trivial, but filled with undiscovered meaning. If photographs could not be read as stories, they could be read as symbols.

The decline of narrative painting in the past century has been ascribed in large part to the rise of photography, which "relieved" the painter of the necessity of story telling. This is curious, since photography has never been successful at narrative. It has in fact seldom attempted it. The elaborate nineteenth century montages of Robinson and Rejlander, laboriously pieced together from several posed negatives, attempted to tell stories, but these works were recognized in their own time as pretentious failures. In the early days of the picture magazines the attempt was made to achieve narrative through photographic sequences, but the superficial coherence of these stories was generally achieved at the expense of photographic discovery. The heroic documentation of the American Civil War by the Brady group, and the incomparably larger photographic record of the Second World War, have this in common: neither explained, without extensive captioning, what was happening. The function of these pictures was not to make the story clear, it was to make it *real*. The great war photographer Robert Capa expressed both the narrative poverty and the symbolic power of photography when he said, "If your pictures aren't good, you're not close enough."

THE FRAME

Since the photographer's picture was not conceived but selected, his subject was never truly discrete, never wholly self-contained. The edges of his film demarcated what he thought most important, but the subject he had shot was something else; it had extended in four directions. If the photographer's frame surrounded two figures, isolating them from the crowd in which

they stood, it created a relationship between those two figures
that had not existed before.

The central act of photography, the act of choosing and eliminating, forces a concentration on the picture edge—the line that
separates in from out—and on the shapes that are created by it.

During the first half-century of photography's lifetime, photographs were printed the same size as the exposed plate. Since
enlarging was generally impractical, the photographer could not
change his mind in the darkroom, and decide to use only a fragment of his picture, without reducing its size accordingly. If he
had purchased an eight by ten inch plate (or worse, prepared it),
had carried it as part of his back-bending load, and had processed
it, he was not likely to settle for a picture half that size. A sense
of simple economy was enough to make the photographer try to
fill the picture to its edges.

The edges of the picture were seldom neat. Parts of figures or
buildings or features of landscape were truncated, leaving a shape
belonging not to the subject, but (if the picture was a good one)
to the balance, the propriety, of the image. The photographer
looked at the world as though it was a scroll painting, unrolled
from hand to hand, exhibiting an infinite number of croppings—
of compositions—as the frame moved onwards.

The sense of the picture's edge as a cropping device is one of
the qualities of form that most interested the inventive painters
of the latter nineteenth century. To what degree this awareness
came from photography, and to what degree from oriental art,
is still open to study. However, it is possible that the prevalence
of the photographic image helped prepare the ground for an
appreciation of the Japanese print, and also that the compositional
attitudes of these prints owed much to habits of seeing which
stemmed from the scroll tradition.

TIME

There is in fact no such thing as an instantaneous photograph.
All photographs are time exposures, of shorter or longer duration,
and each describes a discrete parcel of time. This time is always
the present. Uniquely in the history of pictures, a photograph
describes only that period of time in which it was made. Photography alludes to the past and the future only in so far as they

exist in the present, the past through its surviving relics, the future through prophecy visible in the present.

In the days of slow films and slow lenses, photographs described a time segment of several seconds or more. If the subject moved, images resulted that had never been seen before: dogs with two heads and a sheaf of tails, faces without features, transparent men, spreading their diluted substance half across the plate. The fact that these pictures were considered (at best) as partial failures is less interesting than the fact that they were produced in quantity; they were familiar to all photographers, and to all customers who had posed with squirming babies for family portraits.

It is surprising that the prevalence of these radical images has not been of interest to art historians. The time-lapse painting of Duchamp and Balla, done before the First World War, has been compared to work done by photographers such as Edgerton and Mili, who worked consciously with similar ideas a quarter-century later, but the accidental time-lapse photographs of the nineteenth century have been ignored—presumably *because* they were accidental.

As photographic materials were made more sensitive, and lenses and shutters faster, photography turned to the exploration of rapidly moving subjects. Just as the eye is incapable of registering the single frames of a motion picture projected on the screen at the rate of twenty-four per second, so is it incapable of following the positions of a rapidly moving subject in life. The galloping horse is the classic example. As lovingly drawn countless thousands of times by Greeks and Egyptians and Persians and Chinese, and down through all the battle scenes and sporting prints of Christendom, the horse ran with four feet extended, like a fugitive from a carousel. Not till Muybridge successfully photographed a galloping horse in 1878 was the convention broken. It was this way also with the flight of birds, the play of muscles on an athlete's back, the drape of a pedestrian's clothing, and the fugitive expressions of a human face.

Immobilizing these thin slices of time has been a source of continuing fascination for the photographer. And while pursuing this experiment he discovered something else: he discovered that there was a pleasure and a beauty in this fragmenting of time that had little to do with what was happening. It had to do rather with seeing the momentary patterning of lines and shapes that had been previously concealed within the flux of movement. The famous French photographer Henri Cartier-Bresson defined his commitment to this new beauty with the phrase *"the decisive moment,"* but the phrase has been misunderstood; the thing that happens at the decisive moment is not a dramatic climax but a visual one. The result is not a story but a picture.

VANTAGE POINT

Much has been said about the clarity of photography, but little has been said about its obscurity. And yet it is photography that has taught us to see from the unexpected vantage point, and has shown us pictures that give the sense of the scene, while withholding its narrative meaning. Photographers from necessity choose from the options available to them, and often this means pictures from the other side of the proscenium, showing the actors' backs, pictures from the bird's view, or the worm's, or pictures in which the subject is distorted by extreme foreshortening, or by none, or by an unfamiliar pattern of light, or by a seeming ambiguity of action or gesture.

Ivins wrote with rare perception of the effect that such pictures had on nineteenth-century eyes:

At first the public had talked a great deal about what it called photographic distortion. . . . [But] it was not long before men began to think photographically, and thus to see for themselves things that it had previously taken the photograph to reveal to their astonished and protesting eyes. Just as nature had once imitated art, so now it began to imitate the picture made by the camera.[8]

After a century and a quarter, photography's ability to challenge and reject our schematized notions of reality is still fresh. In his monograph on Francis Bacon, Lawrence Alloway speaks of the effect of photography on that painter: "The evasive nature of his imagery, which is shocking but obscure, like accident or atrocity photographs, is arrived at by using photography's huge

[8] Ibid., p. 138.

repertory of visual images. . . . Uncaptioned news photographs, for instance, often appear as momentous and extraordinary. . . . Bacon used this property of photography to subvert the clarity of pose of figures in traditional painting."[9]

The influence of photography on modern painters (and on modern writers) has been great and inestimable. It is, strangely, easier to forget that photography has also influenced photographers. Not only great pictures by great photographers, but *photography*—the great undifferentiated, homogeneous whole of it—has been teacher, library, and laboratory for those who have consciously used the camera as artists. An artist is a man who seeks new structures in which to order and simplify his sense of the reality of life. For the artist photographer, much of his sense of reality (where his picture starts) and much of his sense of craft or structure (where his picture is completed) are anonymous and untraceable gifts from photography itself.

The history of photography has been less a journey than a growth. Its movement has not been linear and consecutive, but centrifugal. Photography, and our understanding of it, has spread from a center; it has, by infusion, penetrated our consciousness. Like an organism, photography was born whole. It is in our progressive discovery of it that its history lies.

[9] Lawrence Alloway, *Francis Bacon*. New York: Solomon R. Guggenheim Foundation, 1963, p. 22.

One of the most engaging things about William Morris (1834–1896) was the continuity he strove to impose upon his functions as poet, printer, typographer, and propagandist, as designer, manufacturer, and socialist. And it is not hard to recognize that a writer—and a heavy reader— designed the famous reclining Morris chair. One may miss, however, the link Morris forges between his economic and social theory and his work as a designer and decorator. He anticipated by almost a century the movements in architecture and interior design that were to insist that neither function nor beauty alone could provide the principles that would foster a suitable working environment. His prose may be too sweetly turned for great success as propaganda, but sanity does not always need violence for its press agent. Morris's "most sanguine hopes" for the creation of working atmospheres that encourage a "life rich in incident and variety" seem now altogether relevant as we begin to redesign our world for automation. And in our new leisure, we may find the time his work demands to be read and understood. While his prose is complex, it is never confusing; its design is too well planned for that.

A FACTORY AS IT MIGHT BE

William Morris

We socialists are often reproached with giving no details of the state of things which would follow on the destruction of that system of waste and war which is sometimes dignified by the lying title of the harmonious combination of capital and labour. Many worthy people say: "We admit that the present system has produced unsatisfactory results, but at least it is a system; you ought to be able to give us some definite idea of the results of that reconstruction which you call Socialism."

To this Socialists answer, and rightly, that we have not set ourselves to build up a system to please our tastes, nor are we seeking to impose it on the world in a mechanical manner, but rather that we are assisting in bringing about a development of history which would take place without our help, but which, nevertheless, compels us to help it; and that, under these circumstances, it would be futile to map out the details of life in a condition of things so different from that in which we have been born and bred. Those details will be taken care of by the men who will be so lucky as to be born into a society relieved of the oppression which crushes us, and who surely will be, not less, but more prudent and reasonable than we are. Nevertheless, it seems clear that the economical changes which are in progress must be accompanied by corresponding developments of men's aspirations; and the knowledge of their progress cannot fail to rouse our imaginations into picturing for ourselves that life at once happy and manly which we *know* social revolution will put within the reach of all men.

Of course, the pictures so drawn will vary according to the turn of mind of the picturer, but I have already tried to show in *Justice* that healthy and undomineering individuality will be fostered and not crushed out by Socialism. I will, therefore, as an artist and handicraftsman venture to develop a little the hint contained in *Justice*, of April 12th, 1884, on the conditions of pleasant work in the days when we shall work for livelihood *and pleasure* and not for "profit."

Our factory, then, is in a pleasant place—no very difficult matter when, as I have said before, it is no longer necessary to gather people into miserable, sweltering hordes for profit's sake—for all the country is in itself pleasant, or is capable of being made pleasant with very little pains and forethought. Next, our factory stands amidst gardens as beautiful (climate apart) as those of Alcinoüs, [the king of the Phaeacians on whose coast Odysseus was tossed, there to be found by Alcinoüs's daughter Nausicaä], since there is no need of stinting it of ground, profit rents being a thing of the past, and the labour on such gardens is liked enough to be purely voluntary, as it is not easy to see the day when 75 out of every 100 people will not take delight in the pleasantest and most innocent of all occupations, and our working people will assuredly want open-air relaxation from their factory work. Even now, as I am told, the Nottingham factory hands could give many a hint to professional gardeners in spite of all the drawbacks of a great manufacturing town. One's imagination is inclined fairly to run riot over the picture of beauty and pleasure offered by the thought of skilful co-operative gardening for beauty's sake, which beauty would by no means exclude the raising of useful produce for the sake of livelihood.

Impossible, I hear an anti-Socialist say. My friend, please to remember that most factories sustain to-day large and handsome gardens, and not seldom parks and woods of many acres in extent; with due appurtenances of highly-paid Scotch professional gardeners, wood reeves, bailiffs, gamekeepers, and the like, the whole being managed in the most wasteful way conceivable; *only* the said gardens, etc., are, say, twenty miles away from the factory, *out of the smoke*, and are kept up for *one member of the factory only*, the sleeping partner to wit, who may, indeed, double that part by organising its labour (for his own profit), in which case he receives ridiculously disproportionate pay additional.

Well, it follows in this garden business that our factory must make no sordid litter, befoul no water, nor poison the air with smoke. I need say nothing more on that point, as, "profit" apart, it would be easy enough.

Next, as to the buildings themselves, I must ask leave to say something, because it is usually supposed that they must of necessity be ugly, and truly they are almost always at present mere nightmares; but it is, I must assert, by no means necessary that they should be ugly, nay, there would be no serious difficulty in making them beautiful, as every building might be which serves its purpose duly, which is built generously as regards material, and which is built with pleasure by the builders and designers; indeed, as things go, those nightmare buildings aforesaid sufficiently typify the work they are built for, and look what they are: temples of over-crowding and adulteration and over-work, of unrest, in a word; so it is not difficult to think of our factory buildings, showing on their outsides what they are for, reasonable and light work, cheered at every step by hope and pleasure. So in brief, our buildings will be beautiful with their own beauty of simplicity as workshops, not bedizened with tomfoolery as some are now, which do not any the more for that hide their repulsiveness; but, moreover, besides the mere workshops, our factory will have other buildings which may carry ornament further than that, for it will need dining-hall, library, school, places for study of various kinds, and other such structures; nor do I see why, if we have a mind for it, we should not emulate the monks and craftsmen of the Middle Ages in our ornamentation of such buildings; why we should be shabby in housing our rest and pleasure and our search for knowledge, as we may well be shabby in housing the shabby life we have to live now.

And, again, if it be doubted as to the possibility of getting these beautiful buildings on the score of cost, let me once again remind you that every great factory does to-day sustain a palace (often more than one) amidst that costly garden and park aforesaid out of the smoke, but that this palace, stuffed as it is with all sorts of costly things, is for one member of the factory only, the sleeping partner—useful creature! It is true that the said palace is mostly, with all it contains, beastly ugly; but this ugliness is but a part of the bestial waste of the whole system of profit-mongering, which refuses cultivation and refinement to the workers, and, therefore, can have no art, not even for all its money.

So we have come to the outside of our factory of the future, and seen that it does not injure the beauty of the world, but adds to it rather. I will try to give a picture of how the work goes on there.

We have in previous pages tried to look through the present into the future, and see a factory as it might be, and got as far as the surroundings and outside of it; but those externals of a true palace of industry can be only realised naturally and without affectation by the work which is to be done in them being in all ways reasonable and fit for human beings; I mean no mere whim of some one rich and philanthropic manufacturer will make even one factory permanently pleasant and agreeable for the workers in it; he will die or be sold up, his heir will be poorer or more single-hearted in his devotion to profit, and all the beauty and order will vanish from the shortlived dream; even the external beauty in industrial concerns must be the work of society and not of individuals.

Now as to the work, first of all it will be useful and, therefore, honourable and honoured; because there will be no temptation to make mere useless toys, since there will be no rich men cudgelling their brains for means for spending superfluous money, and consequently no "organisers of labour" pandering to degrading follies for the sake of profit, wasting their intelligence and energy in contriving snares for cash in the shape of trumpery which they themselves heartily despise. Nor will the work turn out trash; there will be no millions of poor to make a market for wares which no one would choose to use if he were not driven to do so; everyone will be able to afford things good of their kind, and, as will be shown hereafter, will have knowledge of goods enough to reject what is not excellent; coarse and rough wares may be made for rough or temporary purposes, but they will openly proclaim themselves for what they are; adulteration will be unknown.

Furthermore, machines of the most ingenious and best-approved kinds will be used when necessary, but will be used simply to save human labour; nor, indeed, could they be used for anything else in such well-ordered work as we are thinking about; since, profit being dead, there would be no temptation to pile up wares whose apparent value as articles of *use*, their conventional value as such, does not rest on the necessities or reasonable desires of men for such things, but on artificial habits forced on the public by the craving of the capitalists for fresh and ever fresh profit; these things have no real value as things to be used, and their conventional (let us say sham) utility value has been the breed of their value, as articles of exchange for profit, in a society founded on profit-mongering.

Well, the manufacture of useless goods, whether harmful luxuries for the rich or disgraceful make-shifts for the poor, having come to an end, and we still being in possession of the machines once used for mere profit-grinding, but now used only for saving human labour, it follows that much less labour will be necessary for each workman; all the more as we are going to get rid of all non-workers, and busy-idle people; so that the working time of each member of our factory will be very short, say, to be much within the mark, four hours a day.

Now, next it may be allowable for an artist—that is, one whose ordinary work is pleasant and not slavish—to hope that in no factory will all the work, even that necessary four hours' work, be mere machine-tending; and it follows from what was said above about machines being used to save labour, that there would be no work which would turn man into mere machines; therefore, at least some portion of the work, the necessary and in fact compulsory work I mean, would be pleasant to do; the machine-tending ought not to require a very long apprenticeship, there-

fore in no case should any one person be set to run up and down
after a machine through all his working hours every day, even
so shortened as we have seen; now the attractive work of our
factory, that which was pleasant in itself to do, would be of the
nature of art; therefore all slavery of work ceases under such a
system, for whatever is burdensome about the factory would be
taken turn and turn about, and so distributed, would cease to be a
burden—would be, in fact, a kind of rest from the more exciting
or artistic work.

Thus, then, would the sting be taken out of the factory system,
in which, as things now are, the socialisation of labour, which
ought to have been a blessing to the community, has been turned
into a curse by the appropriation of the products of its labour by
individuals, for the purpose of gaining for them the very doubtful advantages of a life of special luxury, and often of mere idle-
ness; the result of which, to the mass of the workers, has been a
dire slavery, of which long hours of labour, ever-increasing strain
of labour during those hours, and complete repulsiveness in the
work itself have been the greatest evils.

It remains for me to set forth my most sanguine hopes of the
way in which the gathering together of people in such social
bodies as properly-ordered factories might be, may be utilised for
increasing the general pleasure of life, and raising its standard,
material and intellectual; for creating, in short, that life rich in
incident and variety, but free from the strain of mere sordid
trouble, the life which the individualist vainly babbles of, but
which the Socialist aims at directly, and will one day attain to.

In a duly ordered society, in which people would work for a
livelihood, and not for the profit of another, a factory might not
only be pleasant as to its surroundings, and beautiful in its
architecture, but even the rough and necessary work done in it
might be so arranged as to be neither burdensome in itself nor
of long duration for each worker; but, furthermore, the organisa-
tion of such a factory, that is to say of a group of people working
in harmonious co-operation towards a useful end, would of itself
afford opportunities for increasing the pleasure of life.

To begin with, such a factory will surely be a centre of education; any children who seem likely to develop gifts towards its
special industry would gradually and without pain, amidst their
book-learning be drawn into technical instruction which would
bring them at last into a thorough apprenticeship for their craft;

therefore, the bent of each child having been considered in choosing its instruction and occupation, it is not too much to expect that children so educated will look forward eagerly to the time when they will be allowed to work at turning out real useful wares; a child whose manual dexterity has been developed without undue forcing side by side with its mental intelligence would surely be as eager to handle shuttle, hammer, or what not for the first time as a real workman, and begin making, as a young gentleman now is to get hold of his first gun and begin killing.

This education so begun for the child will continue for the grown man, who will have every opportunity to practice the niceties of his craft if he be so minded, to carry it to the utmost degree of perfection, not for the purpose of using his extra knowledge and skill to sweat his fellow-workman, but for his own pleasure and honour as a good artist. Similar opportunities will be afforded him to study, as deeply as the subject will bear, the science on which his craft is founded; besides, a good library and help in studying it will be provided by every productive group (or factory), so that the worker's other voluntary work may be varied by the study of general science or literature.

But, further, the factory could supply another educational want by showing the general public how its goods are made. Competition being dead and buried, no new process, no detail of improvements in machinery would be hidden from the first inquirer; the knowledge which might thus be imparted would foster a general interest in work, and in the realities of life, which would surely tend to elevate labour and create a standard of excellence in manufacture, which in its turn would breed a strong motive towards exertion in the workers.

A strange contrast such a state of things would be to that now existing! For to-day the public, and especially that part of it which does not follow any manual occupation, is grossly ignorant of crafts and processes, even when they are carried on at their own doors; so that most of the middle class are not only defence-less against the most palpable adulterations, but, also, which is far more serious, are of necessity whole worlds removed from any sympathy with the life of the workshop.

So managed, therefore, the factory, by co-operation with other industrial groups, will both provide an education for its own workers, and contribute its share to the education of citizens outside, but, further, it will, as a matter of course, find it easy to provide for mere restful amusements, as it will have ample buildings for library, school-room, dining-hall, and the like; social gatherings, musical or dramatic entertainments will obviously be easy to manage under such conditions.

One pleasure—and that a more serious one—I must mention, a pleasure which is unknown at present to the workers, and which, even for the classes of ease and leisure, only exists in a miserably corrupted and degraded form, I mean the practice of the fine arts. People living under the conditions of life above-mentioned, having manual skill, technical and general education, and leisure to use these advantages, are quite sure to develop a love of art, that is, to say, a sense of beauty and an interest in life, which in the long run must stimulate them to the desire for artistic creation, the satisfaction of which is of all pleasures the greatest.

I have started by supposing our group of social labour busying itself in the production of bodily necessaries; but we have seen that such work will only take a small part of each worker's time; their leisure, beyond mere bodily rest and recreation, I have supposed some would employ in perfecting themselves in the niceties of their craft, or in research as to its principles; some would stop there, others would take to studying more general knowledge, but some—and I think most—would find themselves impelled towards the creation of beauty, and would find their opportunities for this under their hands as they worked out their due quota of necessary work for the common good; these would *amuse* themselves by ornamenting the wares they made, and would only be limited in the quantity and quality of such work by artistic considerations as to how much or what kind of work really suited the wares; nor, to meet a possible objection, would there be any danger of such ornamental work degenerating into mere amateur twaddle, such as is now being inflicted on the world by the ladies and gentlemen in search for a refuge from boredom; because our workers will be thoroughly educated as workers and will know well what good work and true finish (not trade finish) means, and because the public, being a body of workers also, everyone in some line or other, will well understand what real work means. Our workers, therefore, will do their artistic work under keen criticism of themselves, their workshop comrades, and a public composed of intelligent workmen.

To add beauty to their necessary daily work will furnish outlet for the artistic aspirations of most men; but, further, our factory which is externally beautiful, will not be inside like a clean jail or workhouse; the architecture will come inside in the form of such ornament as may be suitable to the special circumstances. Nor can I see why the highest and most intellectual art, pictures, sculpture, and the like should not adorn a true palace of industry. People living a manly and reasonable life would have no difficulty in refraining from over-doing both these and other adornments; here then would be opportunities for using the special talents of the workers, especially in cases where the daily necessary work affords scanty scope for artistic work.

Thus our Socialistic factory, besides turning out goods useful to the community, will provide for its own workers work light in duration, and not oppressive in kind, education in childhood and youth. Serious occupation, amusing relaxation, and more rest for the leisure of the workers, and withal that beauty of surroundings, and the power of producing beauty which are sure to be claimed by those who have leisure, education, and serious occupation.

No one can say that such things are not desirable for the workers; but we Socialists are striving to make them seem not only desirable but necessary, well knowing that under the present system of society they are impossible of attainment—and why? Because we cannot afford the time, trouble, and thought necessary to obtain them. Again, why cannot we? *Because we are at war*, class against class, and man against man; all our time is taken up with that; we are forced to busy ourselves not with the arts of peace, but with the arts of war, which are, briefly, trickery and oppression. Under such conditions of life, labour can but be a terrible burden, degrading to the workers, more degrading to those who live upon their work.

This is the system which we seek to overthrow and supplant by one in which labour will no longer be a burden.

Like William Morris, George Nelson (1908–   )
has not only designed furniture, but has also been
involved in its manufacture. Like Morris, too, he has
thought hard and well about the role of the designer
in the modern world, as he makes particularly clear
in the first of the two statements that follow. The
organizational principles that underlie the look of
our streets and houses rest, in a sense, on the ease
with which information relevant to their
construction can be gathered. There may also be
principles behind the way we like to push ourselves
into the corners of our houses, the "dead-end
rooms" where we can literally get our backs to the
corners. Such principles are not so easy to
arrive at, but Nelson, an indefatigable
theorist, is always willing to test a few
possibilities. The result is less than absolute
certainty but, at the same time, it is fine
entertainment and a significant contribution
to a psychology of the space which, by preference,
we like to inhabit.

THE DESIGNER IN THE MODERN WORLD

George Nelson

The designer lives in the modern world. For him and his work it acts like a target, establishing the direction of his efforts and setting up a boundary outside which these efforts become ineffective.

The modern world—any world in its own time—is always a complex. It contains not only material that is truly of the immediate moment, but also innumerable memories of past worlds. There is also a constantly developing sense of worlds still in the making.

Any individual engaged in the effort to cope with his world is enmeshed in a tangle of phenomena relating to a near-infinity of times and places. Education is a process designed to impose something resembling a common order on this mass of events, an attempt to provide the individual with methods for coping with quantities of seemingly unrelated information.

To serve its own purposes, education must be based on social agreement. Otherwise communication between groups in the society cannot take place. During periods of great change this agreement breaks down. Certain groups react to the changes more rapidly than others, and communication becomes difficult.

The designer sometimes appears to have problems different from those of his contemporaries, such as scientists or businessmen. This is because he gives visible form to objects, an activity traditionally attributed to the artist.

Western society, during the past century and a half, has had very little use for the artist, and the feeling that he was a man apart had its basis in actual fact. But with the social isolation of the artist the myth grew up that he was *in essence* a man apart.

In the eyes of a public that had no use for him, the artist was a man who worked from "inspiration" and hence did not process the common fund of information in the same manner as other men. He was "impractical," a "dreamer." For the hard work to which other men were subjected he substituted "talent" (a very mysterious thing) or sometimes "genius" (equally mysterious but more respectable because of the long-term publicity attached to it). Because of his isolation, and the consequent loss of communication channels to the rest of society, work with the painter's brush and the sculptor's tools ceased to look like work, and it became suspect.

When Santayana said that the artist was not a special kind of man, but that every man was a special kind of artist, he was not announcing a discovery, but a re-discovery.

The industrial designer, as an identifiable category of professional, dates back barely thirty years. The importance of this phenomenon is not that the designer is anything remarkable, but that he is a conspicuous part of the new process of reintegrating the artist with society.

Two things make it hard to see the industrial designer as an artist. His activity has to do with common articles of use rather than the traditional media of painting and sculpture. And even more confusing to anyone who persists in visualizing the artist as a solitary character in a garret, is the fact that the designer is far more commonly an *organization* than an individual.

One of the most significant facts of our time is the predominance of the organization. Quite possibly it is the most significant. It will take time to realize its full effects on the thinking and behavior of individuals. In this conditioning process, few escape its influence. Even driving a car becomes part of a shifting but organized activity in which speed with safety are the result of voluntary cooperation by thousands of highly disciplined individuals.

The existence of the industrial designer marks one phase of the reassimilation of the artist into society. But because he is accepted (the criterion is very simple: people pay him money because they need what he does) he in turn must accept the beliefs of the society, and among these is the conviction that the organization is the proper form for important activities.

The existence of the organization as a dominant social form is a social response to a social problem. The problem is how to cope effectively with increasing quantities of information. A ten-year-old boy today has more information than Erasmus had at his prime. A small business or industry is already too complex to be handled by a single individual. So the specialist appears. The specialist, however, cannot exist without the organization because his particular package of information is useless unless coordinated with many others. And since this cannot be done without effective two-way communication, there arises a problem in education.

I have already described education as a method of imposing a common order on a mass of events. Specialists can communicate only if they agree on something. If I believe that fire is the expression of a particular god's wrath and you are equally convinced that it is a process of rapid oxidation, we cannot communicate, at least where fire is concerned.

The quantity of information now available has become so large that it can no longer be processed by traditional methods. This is the reason for the crisis in education and the many controversies about possible solutions. Finding workable answers is crucial, because science, business, industry and political institutions cannot continue to develop unless many people acquire a greater capacity to process information and learn better methods of communicating with each other. The industrial designer is subject to these pressures as much as everyone else.

The cultivated individual of the 18th century had a common ground with others in his class, all had studied Greek and Latin and had made the grand tour of the Continent. We enjoy no such unanimity today.

It is possible that agreement on a basic curriculum will never again be reached, that the new common ground will be found in *methods* of organizing and transmitting information.

One common element with interesting possibilities is the widespread use of abstractions. A man trained for management learns to deal with abstractions consisting of some two dozen alphabetical symbols, a handful of Arabic numerals and special kinds of pictures called charts or graphs. He does not as a rule think of these as abstractions, just as Moliere's bourgeois gentil-homme did not realize that he had been speaking prose all his life. Yet it is true that the powerful images used by management have no visible resemblance to the physical world and might correctly be described as abstractions.

The artist deals with other sets of symbols in two or three dimensions, most of which relate in some visible way to the world around him. *His* abstractions, however, are generally considered meaningless by the men who deal with letters, numbers and graphs.

Both groups, then, deal with constellations of abstract symbols that appear to have nothing in common. Yet the processing methods employed by each are not too dissimilar. And an understanding of the nature of the abstracting process might make communication possible.

When I was a student of architecture in Europe in the mid-30s, I was struck by the observation that the weights of government buildings in various countries differed greatly. Those built in Italy during the early years of the Mussolini regime were relatively light and open, but as the Italian position deteriorated in relation to Germany, the new buildings acquired thicker walls, heavier details and a generally more massive appearance. In Germany, under Hitler, the official structures from the beginning were extreme in mass and weight, and modern architecture, which is very light in structure and appearance, was forbidden by edict. In Scandinavia on the other hand, where it was not unheard of for the King and other ruling personages to be seen on street cars, government architecture had reached an unprecedented stage of apparent fragility.

So much for the observation. Now for the conclusion. After much perplexed pondering I finally decided that *the greater the*

internal stability of a modern regime, the lighter its buildings.
This conclusion, as it happened, was borne out by events of the
next ten years, but what is important about this example is the
fact that a set of esthetic symbols had been processed in precisely the same way an accountant might examine a company's
balance sheet.

I believe that it is crucial for education today to explore such
similarities in the greatest possible variety of activities. From these
similarities we can build the bridges needed for communication.

Using such bridges, one becomes capable of exploring almost
any combination of specialized activities. As an example one
might say that what Joyce's "Ulysses" does to a space framework
(Dublin) and to a time span (24 hours) is not unlike what the
nuclear physicists did to the 19th century atom. Or what a movie
director, using such devices as montage, might do with something
called "boy-meets-girl." Or what the super high-speed camera
does with a flame at the instant it is snuffed out. Or what Picasso
does when he compresses into a single two-dimensional frame a
variety of events in time and space.

Obviously these are the most loose of analogies and the comparisons could not be pushed very far. Nevertheless the space-
time manipulations in each have a common—and thoroughly
contemporary—character. Equally obviously, all of this activity
of relating or "bridge-building" has a great deal to do with the
industrial designer, who is the least specialized of all possible specialists and who must, therefore, think in terms of increasingly
complex networks of problems.

In such observations as these, it seems possible that there may
lie a very significant and productive concept:

The unity being sought throughout the modern world (seen
from this point of view the conflicts spread over the morning
paper are gropings in this direction) is not to be achieved through
the reduction of complexity to simplicity, for this avenue does
not exist even as a remote possibility.

It can be achieved only through the *acceptance of increasing
complexity* and the establishment of a common framework
within which phenomena can be related and evaluated.

The educated individual in this time does not set out to acquire
more information—he enlarges his capacity to process (i.e.,
relate) the vast quantities he already possesses.

The industrial designer does not differ from other categories of individuals in this respect.

Because of the extreme diversity of the problems to which he is exposed, the modern designer has been compared to the artist of the Renaissance, a man who might take a commission for a portrait one day, carve a tomb the next, design a palace or work out a problem in military engineering. The similarity exists, but it is superficial. A superior individual in the Renaissance could assemble in his own head all the significant information of his time. A superior individual in the 20th Century could not possibly begin to do this. His role in this respect has had to be taken over by the organization.

For over ten thousand years the artist has been a visible landmark in the human landscape. Today is the first time in his history he has found it necessary to take out incorporation papers.

THE
DEAD-END
ROOM

George
Nelson

An architect with a medium-size practice in a medium-size New England town has so dealt with his clients that they still speak to him after they move into the houses he designs for them. This happy state of affairs, having existed for many years, not only provides a satisfying trickle of new clients, but also offers continuous opportunity for discovering what happens to his houses after families have been living in them. Recently, in the course of a dinner party at the house of a particularly well-pleased pair, this architect made a discovery which differed from previous observations in that it startled him into reconsidering his fundamental ideas about home planning. The discovery resulted from a series of observations of no apparent consequence:

The house in question is rectangular in plan, two stories high, conventional in exterior and interior appearance. Every city and town in the United States has dozens or hundreds pretty much like it. In the center of the house is the front door and stair hall, with a large living room on the left and a gun room beyond. The gun room is nothing more than a sitting room with a rack of guns in it. The living room is a pleasant, open space with plenty of daylight, equipped with a large plant-filled bay window at one end and a row of double-hung windows at the other. Seating is comfortable, with three sofas within range of a generous fireplace. A dining alcove opens off one side of the living room. So much for the setting.

On the evening of the dinner party, the architect arrived about fifteen minutes early in order to look around and, having disposed of his coat and hat, went into the living room. Tacitly allowing for the fact that a room just before a party offers a better-than-usual appearance, the architect viewed his handiwork with pride, and he contemplated with satisfaction the many signs of his client's good taste in furnishing. If he had the room to do over, he reflected, he couldn't do better. Wandering on, he entered the gun room, picked up a magazine, sat down and idly leafed through it and was presently given a drink by his host. A few minutes later, when the other dinner guests arrived, they, too, wandered into the gun room, sat down and were given their drinks. At one point in the general hum of conversation the architect picked up one thread: someone was commenting on the quiet charm of the gun room and again he felt a prideful stirring. It was a good room—simple paneled wood walls, just enough dark blue-green paint, a well-designed fireplace, unobtrusively expensive furniture. "A really successful room," he thought, "considering that it is barely fourteen feet square." "Fourteen feet square" suddenly recalled conversations with clients when the house was still on paper. A small room was what they had wanted, he remembered. They were going to use it as a retreat in the dark winter evenings. There were never going to be more than four people in it at one time, and yet there were eleven here right now! Why were they all in here? Why were people perched on chair arms and the coffee table instead of sitting comfortably in the living room?

After dinner the living room *was* put to use. Each guest found a place to sit; each chair had a table of some kind within easy reach; plenty of space for ash trays and coffee cups. The question of living room versus gun room began to fade out of the architect's mind. There was nothing strange about it; it was obvious that people on arriving had gone to the room where they had seen others. As simple as that.

With the coffee cups cleared away, the guests stirred and sat back to talk when, almost imperceptibly, a movement began. The host and two friends went into the gun room and did not return for a while. A girl got up to retrieve a compact she had tucked into her husband's coat pocket. She did not return either. Soon, without any summons, everybody was again in the gun room, and they were still there at midnight, when someone announced it was time to be going home. The living room, designed expressly for gatherings like this, had been used for about thirty-five minutes out of the three hours.

Among those whose business it is to concern themselves with problems of home planning, a great deal of consideration has been given to the relation between the use of space and its cost. Only recently has this become important. Too often, in house-building today, space is what is left after one has paid for automatic furnaces, laundries, bathroom fixtures, and streamlined kitchens, and the efficient use of space is being scrutinized more and more intently. The bedroom, for instance, is occupied for about eight out of twenty-four hours. Architects have been aware of this and many have recommended, in consequence, that the sleeping area be reduced to minimum size. The same with the kitchen, and the dining room, which is used least of all, has frequently been eliminated entirely. This has been extended to relatively costly homes—the one just described is a typical example. In place of the dining room, various kinds of alcoves have been developed as extensions of living space in addition to taking care of meals. The open plan, characteristic of so many modern houses, is in part the result of merging rooms to produce larger over-all living space. Yet in the case of the gun room versus the living room it seemed a trend was reversing itself: the large, relatively open room was consistently passed up in favor of a small, totally enclosed room, not really adequate for the number of people who chose to occupy it. The whole thing made no sense, and the architect who watched it happen was bothered. Many discoveries can be traced to a minor irritation.

To see what happened and why, one must again look at the plan of the two rooms. One is large, one is small. Both are admittedly pleasant rooms, but the small room is used more often. Why? The plan shows one significant difference between the two rooms, aside from their relative size. The gun room is a *dead-end room*—there is only one way in or out. There is a second difference: the living room does not have a single corner where people can sit. One corner is taken by the hall entrance, one by the dining alcove, and the other two by the doors to gun room and terrace. The gun room, on the other hand, has three solid corners. Both of these differences have a lot to do with what we are looking for, and there is a third, which can be made visible by a traffic pattern. Note that traffic into the gun room moves into a kind of pool in the center and is stopped. In the living room, on the other hand, there is actually a corridor area at one end, a path to the terrace door and another to the dining alcove. Now this matter of traffic may seem pretty unimportant where a family of four is involved, and an occasional gathering of a dozen to twenty people. Obviously there is no traffic problem in the ordinary sense, since houses do not have steady streams of people pouring from one entrance to another. Nevertheless, in the difference between closed corners and open ones, in the contrast between static and fluid circulation patterns, possibly in the essential nature of the dead-end room, must lie the answers we are looking for, because there is nowhere else we can look. We also know that the episode described at the outset is no isolated experience: most people have encountered the same thing at some time. Another clue lies in the behavior of the guests, which was not deliberate or purposeful, but instinctive. In other words, whatever the impulse that moved them from the living room into the gun room, it was not one that was very strongly felt. But it moved them.

When children play, their activities fall into a set of patterns which have a curiously close relationship with the behavior of the dinner guests. Children retreat to attics, build forts in backyard jungles, take to the hay loft or, in the winter, to snow houses. The cul-de-sac—or dead-end room—has a fascination that is unique. And the smaller the enclosure, the better they seem to

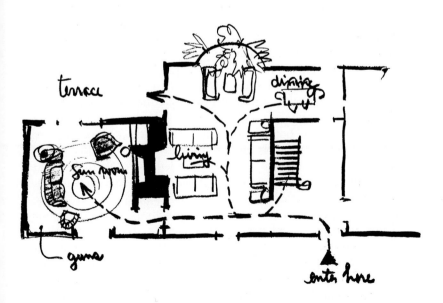

like it. When grownups appear on the scene, they watch these goings on with indulgent amusement, possibly with a bit of nostalgia too, little realizing that they did the same thing, when they squeezed into the gun room at the X's dinner last night. At least one school of psychologists makes a good deal of the return to the womb theory, and there may be some such urge (hard to prove or disprove) that is operating. Or it may not. Architects who like to do one-story houses are often restrained by the wives of their clients because they "don't like ground-floor bedrooms." Fear of burglars is most frequently advanced as the reason, but burglars can climb stairs just like everybody else. The feeling, nevertheless, is strongly and widely held. At this point another explanation can be advanced: man's eyes, for all their advantages, are so set in the front of his head that he is blind to at least half of the circle which surrounds him. This arrangement leaves him peculiarly vulnerable to attack from the rear, and in millenniums gone by it must have exposed him to risk every time he ventured from shelter. A wall at the back, considered in this light, is not merely something solid to lean against, but a very real protection. It seems quite possible that a solid corner, now considered a comfortable place to relax, might once have been nothing less than an aid to survival. In other words, the force that moved the dinner guests from the spacious living room into the huddled group in the gun room might be a dim racial memory that goes back tens of thousands of years to a time when a man was as likely to be the meal at a dinner party as a guest.

In the history of house design there are many examples to support the notion that surprisingly often modern man acts like a defenseless animal in search of protective shelter. The basement play room or rumpus room has been derided time and again by the sophisticated, but its popularity continues. One might say that this kind of space is purely makeshift, that it merely represents use of cellar space no longer needed for coal storage. But one might also say that people seem to get a special pleasure out of a room surrounded on two or three sides by solid earth. The basement playroom, incidentally, is usually a dead-end room. Considering the popularity of the basement, and the objections to the ground floor, one suspects that the universally popular house would have basement rooms, no first floor, and an attic.

This is not quite as ridiculous as it sounds. An entire school of modern architects has taken at least half of this idea to create the so-called house on stilts. Le Corbusier, who first developed it, is a Swiss. The pre-historic inhabitants of his native Switzerland also lived in such houses; they were built on the edges of lakes and offered good protection against marauding animals.

Any attempt to create a theory of house design on the basis of such vague feelings could quickly end in absurdity. It seems obvious, however, that any house in which these feelings are totally ignored will not be popular. We will do well to remember that the most common name for the study, library, gun room or what have you is still *den*, which is in itself revealing.

Complaints leveled against the first modern house usually resolved themselves into one sentence: "Who wants to live in a goldfish bowl?" Now this is interesting, because goldfish don't mind living in goldfish bowls. The reason is to be found in their eyes, which are so constructed that they cover a full 360°. There is no blind spot around a fish, no need for a protecting wall in a region where the eye cannot reach. The first modern houses offered precious little protection from the unseen observer. The idea of being watched while one is unaware of observation, always makes people uneasy. In several recent houses, walls have been built *outside* the house to provide just this protection from the gaze of passers-by.

Frank Lloyd Wright's approach to house design—a field in which he is unsurpassed—offers many illustrations for the popularity of the dead-end room. In Taliesin, Wright's home in Wisconsin, there are two rooms, both large, which may be classed as living rooms. The bigger of the two is enormous by present-day living standards, and yet it is never deserted in favor of the smaller. As one examines this larger interior, which is generously equipped with windows, the theory we have been developing seems to break down, but further study of the plan indicates the contrary. It also demonstrates that *the size of the room is not one of the psychological factors determining its comfort.* The gun room, you recall, had three solid corners, which had a lot to do with producing its agreeable atmosphere. Wright's big room has many more than three. Next to the fireplace, for example, there is a couch set with its back to the entrance. Normally this placing would not be well liked, but here the couch is backed up by a large bookcase wall which reaches to eye level. Anyone sitting here, has therefore, a solid corner with one wall of wood and another of stone. This is not a corner *of the room*, but a corner

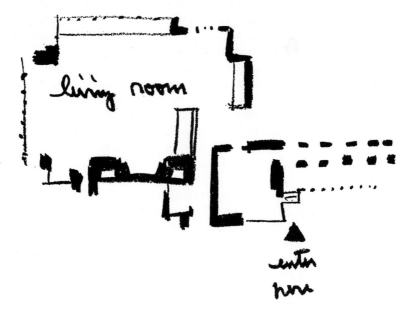

Living room of Frank Lloyd Wright's Taliesin III, Spring Green, Wisconsin, 1925.

in the room; the effect is the same. The plan shows too that the room itself is not a simple rectangle, but a complex and very subtly divided interior which functions as a series of half-enclosed seating areas. In spite of the large number of windows, none of them are set where anyone can look in, which gives the same feeling of protected enclosure as a solid wall. Just as the whole room is a dead end in relation to the entire plan, the areas inside it are smaller expressions of the same planning concept.

In any number of Wright's houses the corner is handled again and again with great emphasis on the principle of the cul-de-sac. Even in relatively small houses there is usually at least one alcove somewhere which satisfies admirably the desire for a feeling of protective enclosure. Wright's clients have been conspicuous for their enthusiasm about their houses, and without discounting the many other important factors which contribute to their feeling, I am convinced that one reason is that Wright always finds a way to put walls at their backs.

Whether one prefers the racial memory theory or the back-to-the-womb idea as an explanation of the general preference for the dead-end plan, the net result is the same; either provides an instrument of immediate and practical value to the architect. Understanding the general psychological principle, we can now begin the job of evaluating an entirely new factor in home design. In the past the psychological need for enclosure was pretty much taken care of by the technical limits set on buildings. Rooms had to be small and totally enclosed to conserve heat; windows were small for the same reason. The delightful fireplace alcoves in Colonial living rooms and kitchens helped keep people warm. Low ceilings also produced a feeling of snugness. In houses today these limitations have largely disappeared, and the danger is that indiscriminate open planning and a desire for economy and easy maintenance may destroy some of those qualities in living space that people prize most highly—though least consciously. It is not possible to fill a house with dead-end rooms, nor is there reason to enclose them all in the way we used to. In planning the house we already have many valuable yardsticks: we measure the steps from stove to sink; we check bedroom walls to see if the beds will fit; children's rooms are placed out of range of living room noises. To these and many others we can add a new one. It couldn't be simpler. All we have to do is keep in mind that people still remember, however dimly, those far-off days when a cave felt like a good place to live.

LANDMARKS

*Jane
Jacobs*

Landmarks, as their name says, are prime orientation clues. But good landmarks in cities
also perform two other services in clarifying
the order of cities. First, they emphasize (and
also dignify) the diversity of cities; they do
this by calling attention to the fact that they are
different from their neighbors, and important
because they are different. This explicit statement
about themselves carries an implicit statement
about the composition and order of cities. Second, in certain instances landmarks can make
important to our eyes city areas which are important in functional fact but need to have that
fact visually acknowledged and dignified.

By understanding these other services, we can
understand why many different uses are eligible
and useful as city landmarks, depending on their
contexts in the city.

Let us first consider the role of landmarks as
announcers and dignifiers of diversity. One
reason a landmark can be a landmark is, of

course, that it is in a spot where it shows to advantage. But in addition, it is necessary that the landmark be distinctive as a thing itself, and it is this point with which we are now concerned.

Not all city landmarks are buildings. However, buildings are the principal landmarks in cities and the principles which make them serve well or ill apply also to most other kinds of landmarks, such as monuments, dramatic fountains, and so on.

Satisfying distinction in the appearance of a building almost always grows out of distinction in its use. . . . The same building can be physically distinctive in one matrix because its use is distinctive in that context, but can be undistinctive in another setting where its use is the rule rather than the exception. The distinctiveness of a landmark depends considerably on reciprocity between the landmark and its neighbors.

In New York, Trinity Church, at the head of Wall Street, is a well-known and effective landmark. But Trinity would be relatively pallid as an element of city design if it were merely one among an assemblage of churches or even of other symbolic-looking institutions. Trinity's physical distinction, which is anything but pallid in its setting, depends partly on its good landmark site—at a T intersection and a rise in ground—but it also depends greatly on Trinity's functional distinction in its context of office buildings. So dominant is this fact of difference that Trinity makes a satisfying climax for its street scene, even though it is much smaller than its neighbors. An office building of this size (or any size) at this same advantageous spot, in this context, simply could not perform this service nor convey this degree of visual order, let alone do it with such unlabored and "natural" rightness."

Just so, the New York Public Library building, set in its commercial matrix at Fifth Avenue and Forty-second Street, forms an excellent landmark, but this is not true of the public libraries of San Francisco, Pittsburgh and Philadelphia, as examples. These have the disadvantage of being set among institutions which contrast insufficiently in function or—inevitably—in appearance.

[Earlier,] I discussed the functional value of dotting important civic buildings within the workaday city, instead of assembling them into cultural or civic projects. In addition to the functional awkwardness and the economic waste of primary diversity that these projects cause, the buildings assembled into such islands of pomp are badly underused as landmarks. They pale each other, although each one, by itself, could make a tremendously effective impression and symbol of city diversity. This is serious, because we badly need more, not fewer, city landmarks —great landmarks and small.

Sometimes attempts are made to give a building landmark quality simply by making it bigger than its neighbors, or by turning it out with stylistic differences. Usually, if the use of such a building is essentially the same as the uses of its neighbors, it is pallid—try as it might. Nor does such a building do us that extra service of clarifying and dignifying a diversity of uses. Indeed, it tries to tell us that what is important in the order of cities are mere differences in size or outward dress. Except in very rare cases of real architectural masterpieces, this statement that style or size is everything gets from city users, who are not so dumb, about the affection and attention it deserves.

However, it should be noted that some buildings which depend on size for their distinction do provide good landmark orientation service and visual interest for people *at a distance*. In New York, the Empire State Building and the Consolidated Edison

Photograph by Dimitri Kessel. Life Magazine © Time Inc.

Tower with its great illuminated clock are examples. For people seeing them from the streets close by, these same buildings, inconsequential in their differences from neighboring buildings, are inconsequential as landmarks. Philadelphia City Hall, with its tower surmounted by the statue of William Penn, makes a splendid landmark from afar; and its true, not superficial, difference within its intimate matrix of city also makes it a splendid landmark from close by. For distant landmarks, size can sometimes serve. For intimate landmarks, distinction of use and a statement about the importance of differences are of the essence.

These principles apply to minor landmarks too. A grade school can be a local landmark, by virtue of its special use in its surroundings, combined with visibility. Many different uses can serve as landmarks, provided they are special in their own context. For instance, people from Spokane, Washington, say that a physically distinctive and beloved landmark there is the Davenport Hotel, which serves, as hotels sometimes do, also as a unique and major center of city public life and assembly. In a place that is mainly residential, working places that are well seen can make landmarks, and often do.

Some outdoor spaces that are focal centers, or, as they are sometimes called, nodes, behave very much like landmarks and get much of their power as clarifiers of order from the distinctiveness of their use, just as in the case of landmark buildings. The plaza at Rockefeller Center in New York is such a place; to users of the city on the ground in its vicinity it is much more of a "landmark" than the towering structure behind it or the lesser towers further enclosing it.

Now let us consider that second extra service which landmarks can perform to clarify the order of cities: their ability to help state explicitly and visually that a place is important which is in truth functionally important.

Centers of activity, where the paths of many people come together in concentrated fashion, are important places economically and socially in cities. Sometimes they are important in the life of a city as a whole, sometimes to a particular district or neighborhood. Yet such centers may not have the visual distinction or importance merited by the functional truth. When this is the case, a user is being given contradictory and confusing information. The sight of the activity and the intensity of land use says Importance. The absence of any visual climax or dignifying object says Unimportance.

Because commerce is so predominant in most city centers of activity, an effective landmark in such a place usually needs to be overtly uncommercial.

People become deeply attached to landmarks that occur in centers of activity and in this their instincts about city order are correct. In Greenwich Village, the old Jefferson Market Courthouse, now abandoned as a courthouse, occupies a prominent site abutting on one of the community's busiest areas. It is an elaborate Victorian building, and opinions differ radically as to whether it is architecturally handsome or architecturally ugly. However, there is a remarkable degree of unanimity, *even among those who do not like the building as a building*, that it must be retained and used for something. Citizens from the area, as well as architectural students working under their direction, have devoted immense amounts of time to detailed study of the building interior, its condition and its potentialities. Existing civic organizations have put time, effort and pressure into the job of saving it, and a new organization was even started to finance the repair of the public clock on the tower and get it going! The

Public Library system, having been shown the architectural and economic practicality, has now asked the city for funds to convert the building to a major branch library.

Why all the to-do over a peculiar building on a centrally located site which could make a lot of quick money for somebody and some extra taxes for the city, if it were used for commerce and residences, like most sites around it?

Functionally, it happens that just such a difference in use as a library is needed here, to help counter the self-destruction of diversity. However, few people are aware of this functional need, or conscious that just such a building can help to anchor diversity. Rather, there seems to be a strong popular agreement that *visually* the whole busy neighborhood of this landmark will lose its point—in short, its order will blur rather than clarify—if this landmark is replaced by a duplication of the uses that already exist around it.

Even an inherently meaningless landmark in a center of activity seems to contribute to the users' satisfaction. For instance, in St. Louis there stands a tall concrete column in the middle of a down-at-heel commercial center in declining, gray area surroundings. It once served as a water tower. Many years ago, when the water tank was removed, the local citizens prevailed on City Hall to save the pedestal, which they themselves then repaired. It still gives to the district its name, "The Watertower," and it still gives a bit of pathetic distinction to its district too, which would otherwise hardly even be recognizable as a place.

As clarifiers of city order, landmarks do best when they are set right amidst their neighbors, as in the case of all the examples I have mentioned. If they are buffered off and isolated from the generalized scene, they are contradicting, instead of explaining and visually reinforcing, an important fact about city differences: that they support each other. This too needs to be said by suggestion.

THE NATURE OF URBAN SPACES

I. M. Pei

Ieoh Ming Pei (1917–   ) is an optimist among architects, but not a reckless one. He has been made cautious by his problems in designing and carrying through to fruition such large projects as the Roosevelt Field Shopping Center on Long Island in New York, the Court House Square project in Denver, the Southwest Washington, D.C., Redevelopment Plan, and the Kips Bay Plaza apartments in New York City. He is also extremely well instructed, as he argues we must all be, by the designers and planners of the past. Baroque use of space is not only theatrical in itself; it can provide the drama we need in our creation of new urban spaces. There is no brash scuttling of landmarks in I. M. Pei's speculative schemas. The past tutors the present, but in doing so does not make the present any less daring or any less our own.

The ancient philosopher Lao-tse once remarked that the essence of a vessel is its emptiness. A city, in a sense, is a vessel, too—a container for people and for life. A city's essence, like a vessel's, also lies in its voids—its public spaces.

Most of us think of a city as a group of buildings. Yet we know from personal experience that the real flavor of a city comes from its spaces—its streets, squares, rivers, and parks. We notice that the quality of life pursued in any place has much to do with its design. Poorly designed spaces inhibit life and movement. Well-designed ones raise the ordinary rituals of life to a high level of intensity and purpose. The conclusion seems to be that a city, so far from being a cluster of buildings, is actually a sequence of spaces enclosed and defined by buildings. The thought may seem strange; yet it is, in fact, the very essence of urban design. And every architect who enters this interesting field will soon find himself designing buildings and spaces as a single entity. More often than not, he is likely to be more concerned with voids rather than volumes, surfaces rather than solids, for the character of a space is determined by its bounding surfaces—the façades of the enclosing buildings.

In attempting to speculate on the nature of urban spaces, I shall limit myself to the aesthetic factors. It must be taken for granted that no urban space can ever be successful, however well designed, unless there is a social, economic, and political reason for its existence.

The first factor, and perhaps the most important of them all, is scale. To develop a space to its highest intensity, the scale of the façades that enclose it must match the scale of the space itself. A large square needs important, monumental structures around it. A narrow street should have small-scale buildings along it. The idea seems self-evident, except that scale is often confused with sheer size; they are by no means the same thing. The Piazza San Pietro in Rome is an enormous oval of 650 feet by 500 feet, whereas the surrounding colonnade is only 65 feet high. Yet it is one of the world's most majestic urban spaces. The reason is that Bernini's colonnade, despite its modest overall height, is conceived on a huge scale. Scale here alone sustains an enormous space.

A second and a far more complex factor is the shape and extent of the space's bounding surface. To be felt as a space, an open area, as a general rule, needs to have enough of an enclosure to define it. If there are too many openings or too many interruptions in the surrounding façade, the space will drain away. In Venice the designers of the Piazza San Marco felt the need for enclosure so strongly that they finished off the surrounding buildings on three sides with an unbroken façade and even forced approaching streets and alleys to enter through arcades so as not to interrupt the continuous fabric of the architectural envelope. This piazza is one of the most extreme examples of complete enclosure that comes readily to mind. The continuous buildings around it are as solid as anyone could wish. Yet they are experienced as surfaces and are meant to be. It may be surprising that a space as large as the piazza could be so intimate; but the almost total enclosure makes it so. The more completely a space is enclosed, the smaller, tighter, and more intense the space appears to be.

Applying this principle to present-day planning experiences, we may observe that long-slab buildings enclose a space more completely than point buildings or towers. In the Kips Bay apartment project in Manhattan, a pair of twenty-story, 400-foot-long buildings stand parallel to each other. A distance of about 300 feet separates them. It might have been more economical of available space to build them closer together. But this space, though open at its two distant ends, is nevertheless substantially enclosed by the length and the bulk of the two buildings and therefore seems smaller and more confined than its actual dimensions would suggest. In the Society Hill section of Philadelphia, on the other hand, three tall apartment towers stand grouped around an open space that is a mere 180 feet across. There is no sense of confinement here even though the buildings rise over it to a height of thirty-one stories. The reason is that the space is far less enclosed than at Kips Bay. There are wide gaps between the towers through which the space can leak out into the beyond. This leakage reduces the intensity of the space. The Society Hill towers could have been considerably higher and a pedestrian on the ground would not feel any additional sense of confinement as he walks between them. To express it differently, the space between the Society Hill towers is actually a fluid space: the stream of movement flows into it, around it, and out again with ease. The space at Kips Bay lacks this implied movement. It is more intense. It is static and therefore needs more room to breathe.

Closely related to the scale and extent of the architectural development is a third factor—the formality of its design. A space gains immensely in intensity, in grandeur, and in importance when the buildings around it are conceived within the framework of a single formal design. The Piazza San Pietro again furnishes a striking example. Others are the Place Vendôme in Paris, the Piazza San Carlo in Turin, and the Place Stanislaus in Nancy, where the formal symmetry of the buildings, the strict axial arrangement, and the rhythmical repetition of motifs raise the quality of the space to a level of ceremonial impressiveness.

Here, it should be mentioned that the three-dimensional accents within a space often play an important part. Paris' Place de la Concorde is almost unique in that, with the exception of the Madeleine block, it has virtually no surrounding façade at all.

Yet it is clear, intense, and articulate, and the chief reason for this, I believe, lies in its interior accents—its two great fountains and obelisk, lanterns, and paving patterns—which actually create a form of their own. In the Piazza del Popolo in Rome, the one central obelisk, together with Renaldi's twin churches opposite the Porta, performs a similarly effective function.

A fourth factor in the design of open spaces is one that is imposed by nature rather than by man. It is the element of light. Everyone knows that light and climate affect architecture; for instance, large windows in the North let in the weak sun and little windows in the South keep out the glare. But light also affects our experience of spaces. The bright sun of Mediterranean lands tends to make spaces look bigger than they really are. The grey light of the North makes them look smaller. The alleys of Mykonos, for example, seem far more spacious than the streets of Chartres. Differences in the scale of buildings undoubtedly play a part, but the quality of light remains the determining factor. The Grande Place in Brussels, with its dark buildings under the Northern sun, looks relatively small; Constitution Square in Athens, though similar in scale, looks immense in the blinding Aegean light.

Up to this point, I have discussed urban spaces as if they were isolated entities, separate and self-contained. But the effectiveness of a space also depends upon its neighbors. When we walk through a city, we actually experience a series of spaces in sequence; and the impact of any particular space, whether a street, a passageway, or a square, is multiplied many times over by what we have already seen before and by what follows afterward. The classic example is in Nancy, where three spaces are lined up along a single axis. The two terminal spaces are broad, monumental, and ceremonial squares; the connecting space is long, narrow, residential, and divided by rows of trees. The effectiveness of the two ceremonial squares is tremendously heightened by the change of pace provided by the central residential space, the Place Carrière, which is designed on a far smaller scale. Conversely, the residential space seems all the more intimate and human because of the contrast it affords to the large scale of the two terminal squares. Each reinforces the character of the other when experienced in sequence. Architects, then, must think of urban spaces as a sequential experience and strive to orchestrate them into an effective ensemble. They should alternate wide spaces with narrow ones, constriction with expansion, concealment with revelation, so that each space intensifies and dramatizes its neighbors until, as a result, the whole becomes something greater than the sum of its parts. In this, I think, we become close at last to part of the secret of a city's visual quality.

These are a few of the factors that seem to me relevant to the aesthetics of urban spaces. They are hard to rationalize and harder yet to measure, for urban space is a medium that still remains elusive, immeasurable, and often more successfully approached by intuition than by logic and mathematics. Sometimes, as if to mock our efforts to understand, a successful space will result from a wilful breaking of all the rules. I am always astonished by Rockefeller Plaza, a space that by all rights ought to be oppressive because of its comparatively small area, the almost total enclosure, the immense scale and size of the surrounding buildings and the deep shadows in which most of it lies throughout the year. And yet Rockefeller Plaza is one of the most exciting urban spaces I know of. One can only speculate. Most beautiful things, they say, contain within them some exaggeration. Can it be that in New York, whose special beauty rests in the spectacular, in the exaggerated, a space as far-fetched and beyond all bounds as Rockefeller Plaza is the only kind that can capture the spirit of the city and intensify it?

Baffling questions like this remind us how little we really know about urban design. The elementary principles I have touched on here were once common architectural currency during the Baroque period. It is no accident that I have drawn most of my illustrations from that extraordinary era. From Bernini to Gabriel, the great Baroque space-makers translated order and discipline, the powerful instincts of their age, into the fabric of their cities. They mirrored the strict hierarchy of life in architectural subordination and emphasis. They expressed the ceremonial spirit of the age—its endless processions, parades, and spectacles, secular and religious—in elaborate and formally planned public spaces that heightened its solemnity. The Baroque sense of the theatrical became, in the hands of these architects, a dramatic sequence of spaces. And the delight in movement was satisfied by great boulevards carefully framed to lead body and eye onward with irresistible momentum.

Photograph by Andreas Feininger.

Order, drama, movement—these were the impulses that produced the majestic plans and spaces of the great Baroque cities
of the Continent. To these England added an important ingredient—the human touch. In England the ceremonial and public
aspect of cities was balanced by the domestic and private. England's first contribution to urbanism was Inigo Jones's Covent
Garden which was designed in the classical manner. Subsequent
to this, trees and greenery began to invade English public spaces.
The architectural setting followed suit with small-scale residential façades in place of the exclusively monumental ones. The
Royal Crescent at Bath forms an immense elliptical arc of almost
600 feet in length, yet the scale of the continuous façade and the
corresponding intimacy of the tree-filled park make the ensemble seem warmly personal. The Baroque sense of order is not
once compromised. Nevertheless, the human scale asserts itself.

Today in America we stand on the threshold of an exciting era
of urban planning and development. The public mind, now
familiar with the splendors of Europe's cities, looks for similar
beauty, spirit, and vitality in its own. Ever since the introduction
of the National Housing Act of 1949, and particularly since its
amendment in 1954, large segments of cities are being replanned
and rebuilt. Architects are once again confronted by the challenge and the opportunity to create the kind of urban spaces
that mirror our lives and aspirations.

In searching for guidance, it is only natural that we should
turn to the Baroque planners. Admittedly, they gave scant attention to satisfying the social needs we consider important in our
time. The social relationships for which they sought to provide
a framework are not, despite the passage of centuries, so very different from our own. We, too, need order and discipline in our
cities. We, too, need to provide for movement, though of a
different sort. We also need a sense of drama to provide for a
ceremonial side of life that seems to be re-emerging. And yet
we have forgotten the very fundamentals on which the Baroque
planners built their cities. To plan wisely and well, we must first
relearn what they knew. This does not bind us to a slavish imitation. Much has changed since then. The high population density
of most of our cities rules out the leisurely residential solution
reached by the English planners, at least in strictly urban areas.

And the development of new building techniques and materials has opened up new opportunities for exciting urban designs far beyond the reach or imagination of the Baroque masters. But the fundamental discoveries they made about the nature and aesthetics of urban spaces are as valid today as then. In this respect, the careful study of Baroque cities is still deeply rewarding and is likely to remain so for years to come.

Most writing about advertising either underestimates or overestimates its importance, either defends it peevishly against its detractors or attacks it with equal petulance. So good-humored and entertaining an examination as this one by Jacques Barzun (1907–   ) is rare indeed. Here Barzun affects the position of an anthropologist looking back over the centuries at Anglo-American ADVT culture of this era and trying to puzzle out its odd symbol systems, its enigmatic totems and taboos. The performance is not without its acerbities, but neither is it lacking in that sympathy for human failings which so often distinguishes the work of this extraordinary historian, critic, social philosopher, and stylist.

MYTHS
FOR
MATERIALISTS

*Jacques
Barzun*

The Anglo-Americans of the twentieth century complained that they had no myths. Their poets, critics and scholars kept bewailing this supposed lack and some even tried to supply it by artificial drafts upon the Irish, Greek or Oriental mythologies. Modern investigation, however, points to the familiar truth that the men of that restless culture were calling for something they already had. Myth, in fact, so pervaded their lives that they could not see it for what it was.

The proof of this statement rests chiefly on the finds recently made in a great hollow formed below the Manhattan schist, probably during the Big (or subatomic) Depression of 1999. Under the usual pile of rubbish in this vast and naturally airtight enclosure, excavation has revealed a group of small buildings, with some adjoining structures shortly to be described; and within the best preserved of these buildings, a large room virtually undamaged. This room may have been the library of a club, or alternatively—for the indications are ambiguous—a dentist's waiting room. In either event, the discovery remains the most significant since that of the lost continent itself. For although the books add little or nothing to our knowledge, the large mass of magazines dating from the middle years of the century constitutes a unique, illuminating, and priceless collection.

I hasten to add that in putting this high value upon it, I have in mind not the reading matter which presumably satisfied the contemporary readers, but the much greater bulk of pictorial representations, often accompanied by text, which resemble earlier fragments identified by the symbol ADVT. Scholars have disputed at length over the exact meaning of this device. I can now, I believe, settle the principal doubts and establish—or at least confidently advance—a fairly complete theory of the subject. Those pictures, that text, enshrine the mythology of the twentieth century. After examining and comparing some seven thousand pieces, I am in a position to sketch in broad strokes the religious thoughts and the moral feelings evoked by that body of myths.[1]

I may at once explain that I draw my assurance from the curious structures which I referred to as adjoining the buildings recently found. Collapsed though these structures now are, it is clear that they were once meant to stand upright as panels of great size, occupying open spaces set apart to afford the widest visibility. All this suggests a religious consecration of both the site and the structure. On the face of these panels (often marked Outdoor Advt) were the same colored images as in the periodicals, but of heroic proportions and usually accompanied by some pithy aphorism. The number of such dedicated placards in a relatively small area like the one examined justifies my belief that we have in these words and pictures literally the revealed religion of the twentieth century.

It is normal in any culture for the commonest beliefs to be tacit and for the meaning of symbols to be so obvious as never to give rise to any glossary. From the outset, then, we face the double enigma of those four letters ADVT. What was their ordinary meaning and what their ultimate significance? The three main hypotheses regarding the first question are that the mark stands for (1) Advertising, (2) Advantage, and (3) Adventitious. Not the least startling conclusion I have come to is that the symbol denotes all three ideas. There is no discrepancy

---

[1] More exactly, that *mytho-pinaco-prosopopoeia*.

among them, even though historically the first meaning was the
most usual. In twentieth century usage, "advertise" was a verb
derived from the character of the Bitch-Goddess of Appearance,
whose sacred name is now lost. The four letters stood for something like "Behold Me"—whence the plausible but false ety-
mology of "advert eyes."

Without at first suspecting it, we touch here the central dogma
in the Anglo-Americans' religious system. What they called their
"modern" civilization was built on the preponderance of one
physical sense over all the others, the sense of sight. Their science was not, as with us, the whole of knowledge, but only such
knowledge as could be brought within range of the eye, directly
or through instruments. They believed only in what they could
measure, that is, what they could lay along a ruler, or between
two hairlines, or could otherwise visually place. No competent
student of their age can deny that they displayed extraordinary
ingenuity in achieving this universal reduction of Being to the
grasp of a single faculty.

But this monomania entailed an ascetic drying up of the inner
life in every member of the culture. It was a prodigal expense of
spirit for which ordinary life had to supply emotional compensation. Hence the need for, and the slow creation of, the vast
mythology known as Advertising. An "ad"—as it came to be
called in demotic speech—was simply the power of things made
into pictures. Through the eye was given what actual life denied
—beauty, strength, leisure, love, and personal distinction.

"Objects," as one contemporary philosopher confessed, "change
their usual faces with the myth maker's emotions."[2] How much
did he know of the origin and results of this transformation in
the familiar things about him? We cannot tell, but in his day
mind control through icons was well-nigh omnipotent. For example, by collating scattered references in the ancient literature
with the newly found "ads," it is clear that just at the moment
when the myth makers began to invoke the supernatural power
of citrus to sustain and embellish existence, technological improvements were depriving the fruit of its natural color, taste
and chance of ripening. At the very time when the sense of life
as a whole was being atomized into a series of "processes," the

[2] Cassirer.

mythology was verbally making up for the deficiency by a poetical iteration having Life as its theme. "Vital" become a magic word, as for example in an ad referring to the various kinds of popcorn eaten at breakfast: "Be sure you get the *vital* outer covering of wheat."

About the same period also, the mysterious substances called Vitamins—precious if measured by cost and complex if judged by their name—became the object of an official cult created jointly by mythologers and medicine men. To carry out the myth, Vitamins were chosen by symbolic letters and were weighed in thousands of "life-giving units." A last example will show how unremitting was this grasping after a runaway sense of well-being. Ten, twenty, thirty times a day, the Anglo-Americans were reminded of their need for vigor, for youth, for a "lift" by drug or weed—the worship of Pep. Initiated by one of the national heroes, Ponce de León, this quest was originally for a fountain in the south (*soda-fountain*). Many claimed to have found it and "advertised" to that effect; bottled drinks and packaged foods bore the magic syllable. "To be full of Pep" was equivalent to our "enthusiastic" or possessed by the god—the rare state then known in full as *pepsicola*.

We must now turn from the concept to the embodiment, the pictures. What strikes the unprejudiced observer at once is the overwhelming emphasis on womanhood—presumably as the inexhaustible fount of human life—and on the situation of sexual approach as the characteristic moment in that life. If one did not know the ways of myth makers, their habit of juxtaposing incompatibles for the sake of a higher truth, one would suppose that the Anglo-Americans were unable to do anything without a member of the opposite sex in a state of provocative or compliant amorousness. In their iconography, seductiveness and sheeps' eyes invariably accompany eating, working, and riding, securing food, clothing, and shelter, listening to music or averting constipation.

An important corollary was that suggestive effects of nudity and drapery were limited, perhaps by law, to the portrayal of women. In all the seven thousand documents examined there occurs not a single instance of Father Paul's Pills showing him in tights, nor of the Chesterfield girl wearing a cassock. Despite this rigid esthetic, based on the complementary traits of the sexes as regards display, all objects whatever acquired an erotic com-

Above, photograph by André Kertész.

Left, fashion photograph by Bert Stern.

ponent. The motive is clear enough: the artificial search for life through objects can only be kept at high pitch by associating the objects themselves with the strongest of desires. Advertising maxims were explicit enough: "Look sweeter in a sweater," "Use the soap with sex appeal," etc.

This mythopoeic principle did not, however, rely solely on the mating instinct. It employed two others, closely related—vanity and devotion to the Mother. This last, which goes back very far in the western tradition, was in its latest form singularly debased. Though I am certain that the best literary and pictorial talent of America went into this highly revered and highly paid art of mythography, all the efforts of these creative artists did not succeed in making The Mothers interesting. The type remained domestic and sentimental. One has only to think of the earlier school of Madonna makers, or of the medieval poet von Goethe-Faust, to see the difference.

The decline may well have been due to some obscure physical cause: the American myth-mother is always depicted as frail, grey-haired, with glasses and a senile rictus. Yet by a strange contradiction, the American maiden or young matron is almost always represented as nature makes her during the months of lactation. This is an improbability—or a religious mystery—which I do not pretend to have fathomed.

Contrary to the feeling of all mankind about ancestors, the second appeal, directed at personal vanity, occupies a much larger place than mother worship. Yet the anomaly disappears when we understand the democratic paradox of competition within equality: everyone has a mother; not everyone has a Packard.[3] Moreover, mass production tended to make any class of objects (as of men) virtually identical; some kind of mythical individuality had to be imparted to them in hopes of its transfer to the mass man. More and more, the social self came to depend on the constant tonic of acquiring these specially wrapped goods, these "superheterogene" articles.

I cannot agree with a famous critic of that epoch, Veblen, who spoke of "conspicuous consumption" and attendant waste as the mainspring of "modern" behavior. He described, it seems to me, an earlier age, that of kings and nobles, who translated power into munificence. The common man, on the contrary, receives

[3] Highly upholstered locomotive.

direct satisfaction from objects, and for the reason I gave earlier: that the goddess ADVT consecrates matter by guaranteeing (1) secret worth and (2) miraculous origin. This is in keeping with all we know about myth. The medicine man infuses the magic into the familiar thing; whence the American advertising formulas, "A Wonderful Buy" and "It's Different," i.e., supernatural. A fuller text of the best period informs us, over a beguiling triptych, "Not just a fur coat, but an important aid to gracious living. It will give your morale a lift, *as well as impress your friends.*" (Italics mine.) No distinction between direct and indirect help to self-esteem could be clearer, and as it happens, the distinction was noted even at the time by the author of the satiric poem, "Civilizoo." As he tersely put it: "Women think fur beauty,/ Scholars, books knowledge." Here was no showing off but simple faith in the fetish.

It would be tedious to enumerate the myriad forms of the faith: they equal the number of consumable articles. Some, however, lent themselves to the arousing of fear preparatory to flattery. To be soothed by possession of the fetish, the citizen must be first alarmed by a dramatization of evil—halitosis, falling hair, teeth, garters, B. O. (undecipherable), as well as by the ever-present threat of Wrong Choice.

In this connection I may instance the farthest reach of magic power found in our documents. As with us, the Anglo-American word for "spirits" has a double meaning, for alcohol makes man cheerful and enterprising. But the ancients' impressionable souls seem to have drawn virtue not alone from the contents of the bottle; they were affected by the label upon it, which conferred tone or talents on the buyer. Thus a celebrated whisky was normally advertised as being "For Men of Decision." One would have thought that the thing needed was a whisky for men of *In*decision, but doubtless the poet was using the rhetorical figure known as hypallage—taking the result for the action. In a like manner, medicines, food and personal attire were, wherever possible, held up as proved fetishes.

In discussing any mythology, however "vital," one must consider the treatment accorded to the subject of death. At first, I believed that the ancients ignored it. I knew, to be sure, of a few covert eulogies of funeral parlors, but it was evident that the aim here was still to make the living comfortable. Then it occurred to me that the previously noted tendency to portray happy results without regard to probability might hold a clue to my problem. And it happened that I had on my hands a series of absolutely inexplicable ads. Putting two and two together gave me what I was looking for.

My unexplained series consisted of simple but beautiful compositions depicting entire families sitting about the fire in smooth white uniforms, deceptively like our own suits of underwear. The faces, suggesting the school of Puvis de Chavannes, are full of benignity and repose. The atmosphere, too, is unusual—hardly any luxuries, no hint of the muscular strain, due to toothache or dandruff, financial or scientific anxiety, which meets us elsewhere. More significant still, all marks of sex have disappeared. Young and old seem beyond self-consciousness, or indeed consciousness of any kind. I conclude that we are logically and mythologically bound to accept these beatific groups as showing us the way the ancients represented death.[4] I have in fact found one marked "After the Last Supper," but the words are pencilled in and may lack authority.

If we did not know how uncommon was the belief in an after-life during the twentieth and twenty-first centuries, one could entertain the alternative that these classical figures were meant for angels. But mature reflection rules out this hypothesis; I will at most concede that they may have been Supermen, in the very special condition of immobility. Since all other icons show action, or at least animation, I find it far easier to believe that this sober grouping, these firm outlines, are the work of the religious artist contemplating death. Under conditions then prevailing, it happened more and more frequently that whole families died simultaneously. Their friends coming to pay their last visit, without any hope of reunion hereafter, would find them posed by the undertaker's art in familiar attitudes, clad in ritual white—in fact in that one-piece knitted suit as advertised (with or without buttons) which would match the wreath of lilies and the silk-lined coffin. Over the abyss of centuries, one feels a catch in the throat at the thought of these once-living men, in whose desperate symbolism the white of snow, fitting like a new skin, meant death and peace.

Yet despite this symbol of hope, each year in midwinter—on December 25 to be exact—there occurred a nation-wide panic about the renewal of life. It may have come down from the old

---

[4] We find the same serenity in the users of certain soap flakes. This coincidence suggests that the flakes procured euthanasia. One brand was significantly called Lux.

fear that the earth would not bear in spring. If so, with urbaniza-
tion and technological farming the fear shifted from the earth to
the self. Wearied by a routine divorced from nature, the citizen
began to question his own survival. "Who and what am I, why so
pale and listless?" Early November saw him sitting before a sun-
lamp to cure the paleness; the end of the month would see him,
and particularly his wife, storming the shops.

It was a saturnalia of devotion to the goddess ADVT. The
vernacular name Splurge indeed suggests a baptismal rite—to
immerse oneself and wallow in things and be made new by contact. Life was goods after all. By an historical irony, the Anglo-
Americans associated this feast with the short-lived founder of
Christianity, who always showed the greatest alacrity in leaving
his coat in another's hands, and who died possessed of one
garment and three nails. His worshippers nonetheless celebrated
his birth in a smothering of cloaks, scarfs, ties, silks, baubles
and furs. This fact proves again that myth and religion are uncertain allies, but it also enables us to feel the pathos of that puzzling lyric in the American Anthology:

> The first thing to turn green in Spring
> Is the Christmas jewelry.

That "shopping" on these regular occasions was an essential
part of mental health is naturally assumed by the advertisers. But
the practical proof of the assumption was never more striking
than in the serious incidents of the so-called Reconversion Period
of the mid-forties. Drained of goods by war, the people nearly
perished. They starved, not in their bodies but in their imaginations: six years virtually without the consolation of ads were to
them as the suspension of the sacraments would be to us. The
shops, though bare, were haunted by women as by insects seeking
their prey, while the entire population grew irritable, distem-
pered, antisocial. Women fought over nylon hose (i.e., leg cover-
ings) and men committed suicide for lack of telegrams. Diaries
tell us that those who by luck secured even a single object—an
icebox or a full-tailed shirt—showed the restorative effect immediately. It was at the worst of these bad times that a laconic
sage summed up the mood in the famous phrase, "Money no
Object."

Such is, in rough outline, the mythology of the Anglo-Ameri-

cans as far as archeological research can reconstruct it. I reserve
the right to give a fuller account at some later time and to make
it more vivid, though I trust not more persuasive, by the addition
of plates in color. Meanwhile it may help to settle any lingering
doubts if I conclude with a few words on the historical link between the faith in ADVT, on the one hand, and the powerful
class of medicine men, on the other.

What distinguishes ADVT from all other great creeds is that
its beginnings were perfectly natural and its final form completely
miraculous. But at all times it was entangled with established
religions. We know that the Greeks, almost as soon as they
learned to write, began to inscribe curses on sheets of lead, which
were then placed in their temples to call down the vengeance of
the god on the person so advertised.

In the early Middle Ages, the public crier could be hired for
any sort of advertising and it is on record that new religious
dogmas were sometimes entrusted to his powers of publicity.
Throughout every period, the marriage market made use of
kindred devices and called on the gods to further and sanctify
the deed. With the advent of the daily printed sheet, about the
middle of the eighteenth century, the real cult of ADVT begins.
Dr. Samuel Johnson, an early anthropologist, complains in 1759
of abuses then coming into practice: "It is become necessary to
gain attention by magnificence of promises and by eloquence
sometimes sublime, sometimes pathetic . . ." and it is "a moral
question" whether advertisers do not "play too wantonly with
our passions."[5]

But the junction of all the elements into what I ventured to
call a *mytho-pinaco-prosopopoeia* (fable in pictures personifying
things) came at the end of Dr. Johnson's century, when a medicine man of Bristol, Dr. Joseph Fry, had the revelation that his
Maker had chosen him to extend the business of importing
cocoa, and had ordained the means. He carried out this injunc-
tion in a small way at first, then on a national scale; himself
boasting that he was the first man, not indeed to import cocoa;
but to import the idea of a *signed guarantee on each and every
package* into the distribution of goods. From him were descended
the brothers Smith, Lydia Pinkham, and other eponymous figures
worthy to rank with Beowulf.

5 *The Idler*, No. 40.

In time, the signed guarantee became superfluous. A strong assertion in print, with an illustration lending color to it, sufficed to make converts. The suffering martyrs to a cough became willing martyrs to *Rem*, the well-named. But an overextension of this true church nearly caused its undoing: too many rival assertions neutralized one another. New guarantees were needed, fuller of Authority than manufacturers could command. They appealed, and not in vain, to a new class of medicine men, the laboratory testers.[6] Their success was shown by the fact that in a short time all advertising emanated from a few Oratories and Laboratories, keeping up, for appearance's sake, a pretended competition among products.

In the final phase, the tester was simply symbolized by a white coat, a piece of apparatus, and the look of a seer. Behind him, invisible but using him and his device, was the newest type of Thaumaturgist, to whom no miracles were impossible. I refer to the Expert in Public Relations. He was believed capable of making fraud innocuous, starvation pleasant, and wars remote. It was rumored that such a man had once succeeded in making the public take an interest in the curriculum of a university. But this exaggeration can be dismissed.

Heretics could now and then be found who tried to undermine the common faith. But their small numbers can be inferred from the fact that they were never molested. They might deride mythadology, calling its effect "the message of the mass age," the larger body of believers could ignore them and sincerely continue their search for myth. Perhaps this was as it should be, for myth will move mankind most when they do not call it so, and what men find indispensable, they preserve. The conveniences of life, as their name implies, are matters of convention; so Chesterfield must forever repeat "They Satisfy," though things in themselves do not. But things enhanced by art and color, sex and slogans, did give the illusions of a lotus-eating life to the men of the strange civilization I have described. The role of ADVT was to suffuse visible matter with invisible virtues, adding to bread the nutrition it had lost and to stone or steel the warmth it had never had.

[6] "A medicine man sits on a deerskin when he makes medicine. He puts herbs in a can, adds water and blows bubbles through a straw to purify it."—From a contemporary account.

Possibly because they are such a prominent artifact of mass culture, the comic books are sometimes charged with being "schools for murder." Their pictures, actions, and dialogue allegedly present to the innocent or to the unwary easily comprehended patterns of violence or crime. In the following essay, Leslie Fiedler (1917–   ) takes a more subtle view of the comics. Their heroes, their "myths," can also be read in relation to the hopes and fears of certain segments of American society, most notably the American middle class. Upon reviewing his essay after ten years for inclusion in this text, Mr. Fiedler adds a final paragraph. He suggests that comic books, now, "seem the hallmark of the age." Does any further comment demand an airing?

THE COMICS: MIDDLE AGAINST BOTH ENDS

Leslie A.
Fiedler

I am surely one of the few people pretending to intellectual respectability who can boast that he has read more comic books than attacks on comic books. I do not mean that I have consulted or studied the comics —I have read them, often with some pleasure. Nephews and nieces, my own children, and the children of neighbours have brought them to me to share their enjoyment. An old lady on a ferry boat in Puget Sound once dropped two in my lap in wordless sympathy: I was wearing, at the time, a sailor's uniform. . . .

In none of the books on comics I have looked into, and in none of the reports of ladies' clubs, protests of legislators, or statements of moral indignation by pastors, have I come on any real attempt to understand comic books: to define the form, midway between icon and story; to distinguish the sub-types: animal, adolescent, crime, western, etc.; or even to separate out, from the deadpan varieties, tongue-in-cheek sports like *Pogo*, frank satire like *Mad*, or semi-surrealist variations like *Plastic Man*. It would not take someone with the talents of an Aristotle, but merely with his method, to ask the rewarding questions about this kind of literature that he asked once about an equally popular and bloody genre: what are its causes and its natural form?

A cursory examination would show that the super-hero comic (*Superman, Captain Marvel, Wonder Woman,* etc.) is the final form; it is statistically the most popular with the most avid readers, as well as providing the only new legendary material invented along with the form rather than adapted to it.

Next, one would have to abstract the most general pattern of the myth of the super-hero and deduce its significance: the urban setting, the threatened universal catastrophe, the hero who never uses arms, who returns to weakness and obscurity, who must keep his identity secret, who is impotent, etc. Not until then could one ask with any hope of an answer: what end do the comics serve? Why have they gained an immense body of readers precisely in the past fifteen or twenty years? Why must they be disguised as children's literature though read by men and women of all ages? And having answered these, one could pose the most dangerous question of all: why the constant, virulent attacks on the comics, and, indeed, on the whole of popular culture of which they are especially flagrant examples?

Strategtically, if not logically, the last question should be asked first. Why the attacks? Such assaults by scientists and laymen are as characteristic of our age as puritanic diatribes against the stage of the Elizabethan Era, and pious protests against novel-reading in the later eighteenth century. I suspect that a study of such conventional reactions reveals as least as much about the nature of a period as an examination of the forms to which they respond. The most fascinating and suspicious aspect of the op-position to popular narrative is its unanimity; everyone from the members of the Montana State Legislature to the ladies of the Parent Teachers' Association of Boston, Massachusetts, from British M.P.s to the wilder post-Freudians of two continents agree on this, though they may agree on nothing else. What they have in common is, I am afraid, the sense that they are all, according to their lights, righteous. And their protests represent only one more example (though an unlikely one) of the notorious failure of righteousness in matters involving art.

Just what is it with which vulgar literature is charged by various guardians of morality or sanity? With everything: encouraging crime, destroying literacy, expressing sexual frustration, unleashing sadism, spreading anti-democratic ideas, and, of course, corrupting youth. To understand the grounds of such charges, their justification and their bias, we must understand something of the nature of the sub-art with which we are dealing.

Perhaps it is most illuminating to begin by saying that it is a peculiarly American phenomenon, an unexpected by-product of an attempt, not only to extend literacy universally, but to delegate taste to majority suffrage. I do not mean, of course, that it is found only in the United States, but that wherever it is found, it comes first from us, and is still to be discovered in fully-developed form only among us. Our experience along these lines is, in this sense, a preview for the rest of the world of what must follow the inevitable dissolution of the older aristocratic cultures.

One has only to examine certain Continental imitations of picture magazines like *Look* or *Life* or Disney-inspired cartoon books to be aware at once of the debt to American examples and of the failure of the imitations. For a true "popular literature" demands a more than ordinary slickness, the sort of high finish possible only to a machine-produced commodity in an economy of maximum prosperity. Contemporary popular culture, which is a function in an industrialized society, is distinguished from older folk art by its refusal to be shabby or second-rate in appearance, by a refusal to know its place. It is a product of the same impulse which has made available the sort of ready-made clothing which aims at destroying the possibility of knowing a lady by her dress.

Yet the articles of popular culture are made, not to be treasured, but to be thrown away; a paper-back book is like a disposable diaper or a paper milk-container. For all its competent finish, it cannot be preserved on dusty shelves like the calf-bound volumes of another day; indeed, its very mode of existence challenges the concept of a library, private or public. The sort of conspicuous waste once reserved for an *élite* is now available to anyone; and this is inconceivable without an absurdly high standard of living, just as it is unimaginable without a degree of mechanical efficiency that permits industry to replace nature, and invents— among other disposable synthetics—one for literature.

Just as the production of popular narrative demands industrial conditions most favorably developed in the United States, its distribution requires the peculiar conditions of our market places: the mass or democratized market. Sub-books and sub-arts are not distributed primarily through the traditional institutions: museums, libraries, and schools, which remain firmly in the hands of those who deplore mass culture. It is in drugstores and supermarkets and airline terminals that this kind of literature mingles without condescension with chocolate bars and soapflakes. . . .

Those who cry out now that the work of a Mickey Spillane or *The Adventures of Superman* travesty the novel, forget that the novel was long accused of travestying literature. What seems to offend us most is not the further downgrading of literary standards so much as the fact that the medium, the very notion and shape of a book, is being parodied by the comics. . . .

It is the final, though camouflaged, rejection of literacy implicit in this new form which is the most legitimate source of distress; but all arts so universally consumed have been for illiterates, even stained glass windows and the plays of Shakespeare. What is new in our present situation, and hence especially upsetting, is that this is the first art for *post*-literates, i.e. for those who have refused the benefit for which they were presumed to have sighed in their long exclusion. Besides, modern popular narrative is disconcertingly not oral; it will not surrender the benefits of the printing press as a machine, however indifferent it may be to that press as the perpetuator of techniques devised first for pen or quill. Everything that the press can provide—except matter to be really read—is demanded: picture, typography, even in many cases the illusion of reading along with the relaxed pleasure of illiteracy. Yet the new popular forms remain somehow prose narrative or pictographic substitutes for the novel; even the cognate form of the movies is notoriously more like a novel than a play in its handling of time, space and narrative progression.

From the folk literature of the past, which ever since the triumph of the machine we have been trying sentimentally to recapture, popular literature differs in its rejection of the picturesque. Rooted in prose rather than verse, secular rather than religious in origin, defining itself against the city rather than the world of outdoor nature, a by-product of the factory rather than agriculture, present-day popular literature defeats romantic expectations of peasants in their embroidered blouses chanting or

plucking balalaikas for the approval of their betters. The haters
of our own popular art love to condescend to the folk; and on
records or in fashionable nightclubs in recent years, we have had
entertainers who have earned enviable livings producing commercial imitations of folk songs. But contemporary vulgar culture is brutal and disturbing: the quasi-spontaneous expression of
the uprooted and culturally dispossessed inhabitants of anonymous cities, contriving mythologies which reduce to manageable
form the threat of science, the horror of unlimited war, the
general spread of corruption in a world where the social bases
of old loyalties and heroisms have long been destroyed. That such
an art is exploited for profit in a commercial society, mass-
produced by nameless collaborators, standardized and debased, is
of secondary importance. It is the patented nightmare of us all, a
packaged way of coming to terms with one's environment sold
for a dime to all those who have rejected the unasked-for gift
of literacy.

Thought of in this light, the comic books with their legends
of the eternally threatened metropolis eternally protected by
immaculate and modest heroes (who shrink back after each
exploit into the image of the crippled newsboy, the impotent and
cowardly reporter) are seen as inheritors, for all their superficial
differences, of the *inner* impulses of traditional folk art. Their
gross drawing, their poverty of language cannot disguise their
heritage of aboriginal violence, their exploitation of the ancient
conflict of black magic and white. Beneath their journalistic
commentary on A-bomb and Communism, they touch archetypal
material: those shared figures of our lower minds more like the
patterns of dream than fact. In a world where men threaten to
dissolve into their most superficial and mechanical techniques, to
become their borrowed newspaper platitudes, they remain close
to the impulsive, subliminal life. They are our not quite machine-
subdued Grimm, though the Black Forest has become, as it
must, the City; the Wizard, the Scientist; and Simple Hans,
Captain Marvel. In a society which thinks of itself as "scientific"
—and of the Marvelous as childish—such a literature must seem
primarily children's literature, though, of course, it is read by
people of all ages.

We are now in a position to begin to answer the question: what
do the righteous really have against comic books? In some parts

of the world, simply the fact that they are American is sufficient, and certain home-grown self-contemners follow this line even in the United States. But it is really a minor argument, lent a certain temporary importance by passing political exigencies. To declare oneself against "the Americanization of culture" is meaningless unless one is set resolutely against industrialization and mass education.

More to the point is the attack on mass culture for its betrayal of literacy itself. In a very few cases, this charge is made seriously and with full realization of its import; but most often it amounts to nothing but an accusation of "bad grammar" or "slang" on the part of some school marm to whom the spread of "different than" seems to threaten the future of civilized discourse. What should set us on guard in this case is that it is not the fully literate, the intellectuals and serious writers who lead the attack, but the insecure semi-literate. In America, there is something a little absurd about the indignant delegation from the Parent Teachers' Association (themselves clutching the latest issue of *Life*) crying out in defence of literature. Asked for suggestions, such critics are likely to propose *The Reader's Digest* as required reading in high school—or to urge more comic book versions of the "classics"; emasculated Melville, expurgated Hawthorne, or a child's version of something "uplifting" like "The Fall of the House of Ussher." In other countries, corresponding counterparts are not hard to find.

As as matter of fact, this charge is scarcely ever urged with much conviction. It is really the portrayal of crime and horror (and less usually sex) that the enlightened censors deplore. It has been charged against vulgar art that it is sadistic, brutal, full of terror; that it pictures women with exaggeratedly full breasts and rumps, portrays death on the printed page, is often covertly homosexual, etc., etc. About these charges, there are two obvious things to say. First, by and large, they are true. Second, they are also true about much of the most serious art of our time, especially that produced in America.

There is no count of sadism and brutality which could not be equally proved against Hemingway or Faulkner or Paul Bowles —or, for that matter, Edgar Allan Poe. . . . You cannot condemn *Superman* for the exploitation of violence, and praise the existentialist-homosexual-sadist shockers of Paul Bowles. It is possible to murmur by way of explanation something vague about art of catharsis; but no one is ready to advocate the suppression of anything merely because it is aesthetically bad. In this age of conflicting standards, we would all soon suppress each other.

An occasional Savonarola is, of course, ready to make the total rejection; and secretly or openly, the run-of-the-mill condemner of mass culture does condemn, on precisely the same grounds, most contemporary literature of distinction. Historically, one can make quite a convincing case to prove that our highest and lowest arts come from a common anti-bourgeois source. Edgar Allan Poe, who lived the image of the dandy that has been haunting high art ever since, also, one remembers, invented the popular detective story; and there is a direct line from Hemingway to O'Hara to Dashiell Hammett to Raymond Chandler to Mickey Spillane.

Of both lines of descent from Poe, one can say that they tell a black and distressing truth (we are creatures of dark impulse in a threatened and guilty world), and that they challenge the more genteel versions of "good taste." . . . I should hate my argument to be understood as a defence of what is banal and mechanical and dull (there is, of course, a great deal!) in mass culture; it is merely a counter-attack against those who are aiming through that banality and dullness at what moves all literature of worth. Anyone at all sensitive to the life of the imagination would surely prefer the kids to read the coarsest fables of Black and White contending for the City of Man, rather than have them spell out, "Oh, see Jane. Funny, funny Jane," or read to themselves hygienic accounts of the operation of supermarkets or manureless farms. Yet most schoolboard members are on the side of mental hygiene; and it is they who lead the charge against mass culture.

Anyone old enough to have seen, say *Rain*, is on guard against those who in the guise of wanting to destroy savagery and ignorance wage war on spontaneity and richness. But we are likely to think of such possibilities purely in sexual terms; the new righteous themselves have been touched lightly by Freud and are firm believers in frankness and "sex education." But in the very midst of their self-congratulation at their emancipation, they have become victims of a new and ferocious prudery. One who would be ashamed to lecture his masturbating son on the dangers of insanity, is quite prepared . . . to predict the electric chair for the young scoundrel caught with a bootlegged comic. Superman is our Sadie Thompson. We live in an age when the child who is exposed to the "facts of life" is protected from "the facts of death." In the United States, for instance, a certain Doctor Spock has produced an enlightened guide to childcare for modern mothers—a paper-back book which sold, I would guess, millions of copies. Tell the child all about sex, the good doctor advises, but on the subject of death—hush!

By more "advanced" consultants, the taboo is advanced further towards absurdity: no bloodsoaked Grimm, no terrifying Andersen, no childhood verses about cradles that fall—for fear breeds insecurity; insecurity, aggression; aggression, war. There is even a "happy," that is to say, expurgated, Mother Goose in which the three blind mice have become "kind mice"—and the farmer's wife no longer hacks off their tails, but "cuts them some cheese with a carving knife." Everywhere the fear of fear is endemic, the fear of the very names of fear; those who have most ardently desired to end warfare and personal cruelty in the world around them, and are therefore most frustrated by their persistence, conspire to stamp out violence on the nursery bookshelf. This much they can do anyhow. If they can't hold up the weather, at least they can break the bloody glass.

This same fear of the instinctual and the dark, this denial of death and guilt by the enlightened genteel, motivates their distrust of serious literature, too. Faulkner is snubbed and the comic books are banned, not in the interests of the classics or even of Robert Louis Stevenson, as the attackers claim, but in the name of a literature of the middle ground which finds its fictitious vision of a kindly and congenial world attacked from above and below. I speak now not of the few intellectual converts to the cause of censorship, but of the main body of genteel bookbanners, whose idol is Lloyd Douglas or even A. J. Cronin. . . .

This "trend" is nothing more than the standard attitude of a standard kind of literature, the literature of slick-paper ladies' magazines, which prefers the stereotype to the archetype, loves poetic justic, sentimentality, and gentility, and is peopled by characters who bathe frequently, live in the suburbs, and are professionals. Such literature circles mindlessly inside the trap of its two themes: unconsummated adultery and the consummated pure romance. There can be little doubt about which kind

of persons and which sort of fables best typify our plight, which
tell the truth—or better: a truth in the language of those to
whom they speak.

In the last phrase, there is a rub. The notion that there is more
than one language of art, or rather, that there is something not
quite art, which performs art's function for most men in our
society, is disquieting enough for anyone, and completely unac-
ceptable to the sentimental egalitarian, who had dreamed of universal literacy leading directly to a universal culture. It is here
that we begin to see that there is a politics as well as pathology
involved in the bourgeois hostility to popular culture. I do not
refer only to the explicit political ideas embodied in the comics
or in the literature of the cultural *élite;* but certainly each of
these arts has a characteristic attitude: populist-authoritarian on
the one hand, and aristocratic-authoritarian on the other.

It is notorious how few of the eminent novelists or poets of our
time have shared the political ideals we . . . would agree are the
most noble available to us. The flirtations of Yeats and Lawrence
with fascism, Pound's weird amalgam of Confucianism, Jeffer-
sonianism, and social credit, the modified Dixiecrat principles of
Faulkner—all make the point with terrible reiteration. Between
the best art and poetry of our age and the critical liberal reader
there can be no bond of shared belief; at best we have the ironic
confrontation of the sceptical mind and the believing imagination. It is this division which has, I suppose, led us to define more
and more narrowly the "aesthetic experience," to attempt to
isolate a quality of seeing and saying that has a moral value quite
independent of *what* is seen or heard.

> Time that with this strange excuse
> Pardoned Kipling and his views,
> And will pardon Paul Claudel,
> Pardons him for writing well.

But the genteel middling mind which turns to art for entertainment and uplift, finds this point of view reprehensible; and
cries out in rage against those who give Ezra Pound a prize and
who claim that "to permit other considerations than that of
poetic achievement to sway the decision would . . . deny the
validity of that objective perception of value on which any civilized society must rest." We live in the midst of a strange two-

front class war: the readers of the slicks battling the subscribers to the "little reviews" and the consumers of pulps; the senti-mental-egalitarian conscience against the ironical-aristocratic sen-sibility on the one hand and the brutal-populist mentality on the other. The joke, of course, is that it is the "democratic" centre which calls here and now for suppression of its rivals; while the *élite* advocate a condescending tolerance, and the vulgar ask only to be let alone.

It is disconcerting to find cultural repression flourishing at the point where middling culture meets a kindly, if not vigorously thought-out, liberalism. The sort of right-thinking citizen who subsidizes trips to America for Japanese girls scarred by the Hiroshima bombing, and deplores McCarthy in the public press, also deplores, and would censor, the comics. In one sense, this is fair enough; for beneath the veneer of slogans that "crime doesn't pay" and the superficial praise of law and order, the comics do reflect that dark populist faith which Senator McCarthy has exploited. There is a kind of "black socialism" of the American masses which underlies formal allegiances to one party or an-other: the sense that there is always a conspiracy at the centres of political and financial power; the notion that the official de-fenders of the commonwealth are "bought" more often than not; an impatience with moral scruples and a distrust of intelligence, especially in the expert and scientist; a willingness to identify the enemy, the dark projection of everything most feared in the self, on to some journalistically-defined political opponent of the moment.

This is not quite the "fascism" it is sometimes called. There is, for instance, no European anti-Semitism involved, despite the conventional hooked nose of the scientist-villain. (The inventors and chief producers of comic books have been, as it happens, Jews.) There is also no adulation of a dictator-figure on the model of Hitler or Stalin; though one of the archetypes of the Deliverer in the comics is called Superman, he is quite unlike the Nietzschean figure—it is the image of Cincinnatus which persists in him, an archetype that has possessed the American imagination since the time of Washington: the leader who enlists for the duration and retires unrewarded to obscurity.

It would be absurd to ask the consumer of such art to admire in the place of images that project his own impotence and longing for civil peace some hero of middling culture—say, the good boy of Arthur Miller's *Death of a Salesman*, who, because he has studied hard in school, has become a lawyer who argues cases before the Supreme Court and his friends who own their own tennis courts. As absurd as to ask the general populace to worship Stephen Dedalus or Captain Ahab! But the high-minded petty-bourgeois cannot understand or forgive the rejection of his own dream, which he considers as nothing less than the final dream of humanity. The very existence of a kind of art based on allegiances and values other than his challenges an article of his political faith; and when such an art is "popular," that is, more read, more liked, more bought than his own, he feels his basic life-defense imperilled. The failure of the petty-bourgeoisie to achieve cultural hegemony threatens their dream of a truly classless society; for they believe, with some justification, that such a society can afford only a single culture. And they see, in the persistence of a high art and a low art on either side of their average own, symptoms of the re-emergence of classes in a quarter where no one had troubled to stand guard.

The problem posed by popular culture is finally, then, a problem of class distinction in a democratic society. What is at stake is the refusal of cultural equality by a large part of the population. It is misleading to think of popular culture as the product of a conspiracy of profiteers against the rest of us. This venerable notion of an eternally oppressed and deprived but innocent people is precisely what the rise of mass culture challenges. Much of what upper-class egalitarians dreamed for him, the ordinary man does not want—especially literacy. The situation is bewildering and complex, for the people have not rejected completely the notion of cultural equality; rather, they desire its symbol but not its fact. At the very moment when half of the population of the United States reads no *hard-covered* book in a year, more than half of all high-school graduates are entering universities and colleges; in twenty-five years almost all Americans will at least begin a higher education. It is clear that what is demanded is a B.A. for everyone, with the stipulation that no one be forced to read to get it. And this the colleges, with "objective tests" and "visual aids," are doing their reluctant best to satisfy.

One of the more exasperating aspects of the cultural defeat of
the egalitarians is that it followed a seeming victory. For a while
(in the Anglo-Saxon world at least) it appeared as if the spread
of literacy, the rise of the bourgeoisie, and the emergence of the
novel as a reigning form would succeed in destroying both traditional folk art and an aristocratic literature still pledged to epic,
ode, and verse tragedy. But the novel itself (in the hands of
Lawrence, Proust, Kafka, etc.) soon passed beyond the comprehension of those for whom it was originally contrived; and the
retrograde derivations from it—various steps in a retreat towards
wordless narrative: digests, pulp fiction, movies, picture magazines—revealed that middling literature was not in fact the
legitimate heir of either folk art or high art, much less the suc-
cessor of both, but a *tertium quid* of uncertain status and value.

The middlebrow reacts with equal fury to an art that baffles
his understanding and to one which refuses to aspire to his level.
The first reminds him that he has not yet, after all, *arrived* (and,
indeed, may never make it); the second suggests to him a condition to which he might easily relapse, one perhaps that might
have made him happier with less effort (and here exacerbated
puritanism is joined to baffled egalitarianism)—even suggests
what his state may appear like to those a notch above. Since he
cannot on his own terms explain to himself why anyone should
choose any level but the highest (that is, his own), the failure
of the vulgar seems to him the product of mere ignorance and
laziness—a crime! And the rejection by the advanced artist of
his canons strikes him as a finicking excess, a pointless and un-
forgivable snobbism. Both, that is, suggest the intolerable notion
of a hierarchy of taste, a hierarchy of values, the possibility of
cultural classes in a democratic state; and before this, puzzled and
enraged, he can only call a cop. The fear of the vulgar is the
obverse of the fear of excellence, and both are aspects of the fear
of difference: symptoms of a drive for conformity on the level of
the timid, sentimental, mindless-bodiless genteel.

AUTHOR'S NOTE:
Rereading this essay after eleven years, I am astonished and
pleased at how prophetic it seems in retrospect. Certainly we
have lived into a moment when the comic book is having a

double renaissance: reinvented by the Marvel Comic group (*The Fantastic Four* etc.), it is anthologized and analyzed and revived on T.V. But most important of all, it has become a standard mythology referred to by writers under 35, as once only Homer and the Bible were referred to. Images of Batman and Superman and Captain Marvel live in the deep minds of urbanites in an electronic age as, say, Oedipus does not, unless some learned book suggests it. Now certain novels evoke their scarcely believed-in archetypal presences for richness and resonance and a kind of humor (self-mocking without bitterness or embarrassment) which begins to seem the hallmark of the age.

"As a nation we have often been hesitant and apologetic about whatever has been made in America in the vernacular tradition," John Kouwenhoven (1909–   ) *says at the end of his book* Made in America. *"Perhaps the time has come when more of us are ready to accept the challenge offered to the creative imagination by the techniques and forms which first arose among our own people in our own land."* Certainly John Kouwenhoven has himself accepted that challenge in the essays and books he has written on the American vernacular, on architecture, machinery, typography, on bridges, on interior decoration, on

WHAT
jazz. For nearly two hundred years, the technology of industrial democracy has shaped and reshaped environments and

IS
the people in them, but we go on thinking and teaching and talking as if our world had only barely

"AMERICAN"
changed since the eighteenth century. It is against the unwillingness to accept the real

IN
world for what it is and what it might be, that Kouwenhoven has set himself in essays like this one. One of their

ARCHITECTURE
delights is the amount of incidental

AND
cultural history that they offer. Even if one cannot accept the present world, he can

DESIGN?
still enjoy the antiquarian games with which Americans have for so long and so happily evaded reality.

Notes Toward
An Aesthetic of Progress

John A.
Kouwenhoven

All of us at times need to confirm the continuity of our culture with that of the past, in order to reassure ourselves in the midst of bewildering flux and change.

We may ask what is "American" in architecture and design because we want to establish their continuity with buildings and objects of the past. And if this is our motive in asking the question we will, of course, be most interested in those buildings and objects whose structure and aesthetic effect are clearly related to, and thus comparable with, those of their predecessors in the Western tradition. We will concern ourselves, that is, with architecture in its textbook sense, as a fine art which has developed continuously, with local and national variants, throughout the Western world.

If we approach the question in this way, taking "architecture" to mean churches, government buildings, and palaces (for princes or merchants), and taking "design" to include what the nineteenth century lumped as "Industrial Art" (manufactured objects to which one could apply "arts and crafts" decoration, such as pottery, textiles, bijouterie, and the printed page), we will probably conclude that the "American" quality is catholicity. We can find in the United States an imitation of almost any architectural style or decorative mannerism which ever existed in any other nation. And when we have done so, all we shall have demonstrated is what we already knew: that Americans came from everywhere, and brought with them the traditions— architectural and decorative as well as social and religious—of which they were the heirs. We shall have learned what is English or Spanish or German about our architecture, and our design, and therefore how they relate to the Western tradition; but we shall know as little as ever about their "American" quality, if such there be.

There is, for example, nothing "American" about New York City's Cathedral of St. John the Divine, except perhaps the fact that it is unfinished. It is an important and lovely fact of our cultural history and of the history of architecture in this country, but it tells us more about what is not "American" than about what is, just as a Coca-Cola bottle made in France tells us more about what is "American" than about what is French.

The question can be asked, however, not in hopes of establishing ties to the past but in hopes of discovering those elements of creative energy and vitality which can evolve forms and structures appropriate to a world of flux and change—the "American" world—even at the risk of devaluing or destroying much that we have cherished and loved in the past. If this is our motive, we must look at those structures and objects which were not thought of as "Architecture" or "Industrial Art" by those who designed or paid for them. We must look, in other words, at those struc-

What Is "American" in Architecture and Design?

tures and objects which have been unselfconsciously evolved from the new materials, and for the unprecedented psychological and social uses present in the "American" environment.

THE VITALITY OF THE VERNACULAR

If we go at the question in this way, we will discover, I think, that the "American" quality is the product of a vernacular which has flourished in the United States but is by no means confined to it, which has deep roots in Western Europe, and which is rapidly establishing itself wherever modern technology and democracy are working together to recast our consciousness of our relations to one another, to external nature, and to our Gods.

I am again using the term *vernacular* as a descriptive label for the patterns and forms which people have devised, usually anonymously, in attempting to give satisfying order to the unprecedented elements which democracy and technology have jointly introduced into the human environment during the past hundred and fifty years or so.

Actually there are two ways in which people can order the elements of a new environment. One is to cramp them into patterns or forms which were originally devised to order other and quite different elements of another and quite different environment. Hence the mid-nineteenth-century blank verse "epics" about backwoodsmen in Kentucky; hence the flying buttresses of Raymond Hood's Chicago Tribune Tower: hence "symphonic" jazz and amphora-shaped cigarette lighters. The forms or patterns in such instances will often have a symmetry and finish which give genuine (if nostalgic) pleasure, but only at the cost of considerable distortion of the elements which have been worried into them. It would be interesting to consider, for example, how we warped the development of a system of higher education appropriate to an "American" world by corseting it in pseudo-medieval cloisters and pseudo-Renaissance palaces.

The other way is to shuffle and rearrange the unfamiliar elements until some appropriate design is empirically discovered. The vernacular patterns or forms so devised will often be ungainly, crude, or awkward in contrast with those evolved and refined over the centuries to order the elements of the pre-democratic, pre-industrial world, but they will at least bear a vital relation to the new environment of whose elements they

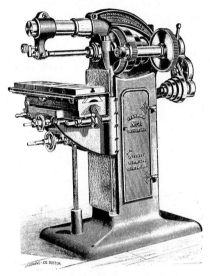

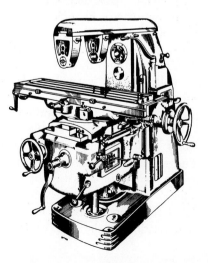

Top, Robertson's milling machine,
patented 1852 (from a wood engraving
in an advertisement in David Bigelow,
History of Prominent Mercantile and
Manufacturing Firms in the United
States, *Boston, 1857); center, a Brainerd*
Universal milling machine of 1894
(from a wood engraving in Illustrated
Price List *of the Fairbanks Co., 1894);*
bottom, the Cincinnati Milling Machine
Company's Universal milling machine
of 1943 (from the American Machinist,
May 27, 1943).

are composed. More importantly, they will contain within themselves the potentiality of refinement and—God willing—of transfiguration by the hand of genius.

As an example of the characteristic evolution of vernacular form, we may take the development of a machine tool such as the milling machine. Three stages in its design are illustrated. The earliest machine shown in the series was made forty years after Eli Whitney created his first practical machine tool of this type, but it is still a gawky four-legged object which has not yet discovered the so-called "knee and column" form appropriate to its functions, in which both of the later machines are made. Bearing in mind that each stage in the development of this machine represents an advance in the magnitude and complexity of the operations it is designed to perform, even a non-mechanic will be able to observe the increasing simplicity and refinement of the over-all design.

If we turn from mechanics to building we may perhaps more easily see the way in which vernacular forms and patterns can become expressive elements in creative design. In the past thirty years many structural elements which were developed in vernacular building have become characteristic features of contemporary architecture. One has only to look at the accompanying pictures of a century-old iron loft building, the glass-enclosed verandahs of a seaside hotel of the eighteen eighties, and an abandoned tobacco factory to be aware of the vernacular roots of important elements in the architectural design of such buildings as Albert Kahn's tank arsenal, the Farm Security Administration's utility building for a California migrant camp, and Raymond Hood's magnificent McGraw-Hill building—done after he had learned to dispense with the Gothic trappings of the Tribune Tower.

Thus far we have touched upon examples of the vernacular which were evolved primarily to cope with or exploit those elements of the new environment which were introduced by technology—by developments in the machining of metal, in frame construction, and in the manufacture of glass. But the vernacular as I have tried to define it is by no means the product of technology alone. It is a response to the simultaneous impact of technology and democracy. Watt's first practical steam engine and the Declaration of Independence became operative in the same year, we should remember. Technology by itself can become

Above, Cast Iron Building designed and built by James Bogardus, 1848, on the northwest corner of Washington and Murray streets, New York (photograph courtesy of Gottscho-Schleisner); below, the Hotel del Coronado, on San Diego Bay, California, 1889 (wood engraving from promotional pamphlet, Coronado Beach, Oakland, *1890); bottom, abandoned tobacco factory in Louisville, Kentucky (photograph 1943, courtesy of Reynolds Metal Co., which bought the building that year for conversion to aircraft-parts manufacture).*

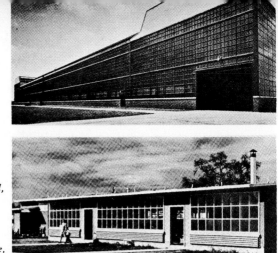

Right top, Chrysler tank arsenal, designed by Albert Kahn, 1940 (Hedrich-Blessing Studio, courtesy of Architectural Forum*); right below, utilities building, FSA Camp, Woodville, California (photograph courtesy of the Library of Congress); below, the McGraw-Hill building, West Forty-second Street, New York, designed by Raymond Hood, 1931 (photograph courtesy McGraw-Hill Studio).*

the servant of a tyrant, as has been amply proved in Hitler's Germany and Stalin's Russia and, on a smaller scale, in some communities closer to home. But it is the peculiar blend of technology with democracy which produces vernacular as opposed to merely technological forms. New technics and new materials have not been the only constituents of the new environment for which men have had to discover appropriate forms. There have also been new amalgams of thought, of emotion, and of attitude.

If, for a moment, I may use the term "American" in its conventional and limited sense, as referring to whatever has to do with the United States, it is a very American fact that we are chiefly indebted to a European for calling our attention to the anonymous and "undignified" sources of many of the creative elements in contemporary architecture and design. It was the Swiss scholar Siegfried Giedion, who, in the Norton lectures at Harvard in 1939, first showed many of us that such utilitarian structures as the balloon-frame houses of early Chicago, and such utilitarian objects as nineteenth-century water pails and railway seats, were often more prophetic of the essential spirit and creative force of our contemporary arts than the buildings and objects which have been acclaimed for their "artistic" quality.

By now it is clear that many of the constituents of contemporary design which at first struck us as alien and strange evolved from our vernacular. The molded plywood which seemed so startling when it appeared in chairs exhibited at the Museum of Modern Art in the late thirties and early forties was the conventional material for seats in American ferryboats in the 1870's. The spring-steel cantilever principle, which attracted world-wide attention when Mies van der Rohe used it in a chair he designed at the Bauhaus, had been standard in the seats of American reapers and mowers and other farm machines since the 1850's. Built-in furniture, the "storage wall," and movable partitions to create flexible interior space, all three were employed in an ingenious amateur house plan worked out in the 1860's by Harriet Beecher Stowe's sister, Catherine Beecher, a pioneer in the field now known as home economics. The provision of storage facilities in interchangeable units, which can be rearranged or added to, as changing needs and circumstances require, had a long history in office equipment, kitchen cabinets, and sectional furniture before it was recognized as an appropriate element in creative design.

What is important about such instances, from the point of view of this article, is that so many of them reflect a concern with process, especially as it is manifest in motion and change; for it is this concern, as I have said, which seems to me to be central to that "American" quality which we are trying to define.

THE AESTHETICS OF PROCESS

The quality shared by all those things which are recognized, here and abroad, as distinctively "American"—from skyscrapers to jazz to chewing gum—is an awareness of, if not a delight in, process: that universal "process of development" which, as Lancelot Law Whyte has said, man shares with all organic nature, and which forever debars him from achieving the perfection and eternal harmony of which the great arts of Western Europe have for centuries created the illusion. In the hierarchical civilizations of the past, where systems of status kept people as well as values pretty much in their places, men were insulated against an awareness of process to an extent which is no longer possible. In an environment dominated by technology and democracy, a world of social and physical mobility and rapid change, we cannot escape it. And our awareness of process is inevitably reflected in the vernacular, just as our occasional dread of it is witnessed by our continuing commitment to the cultivated forms inherited from a world in which permanence and perfection seemed, at least, to be realities.

It is the ideas, emotions, and attitudes generated by this conscious or unconscious awareness of process which account, I think, for a basic difference between the aesthetic effects of vernacular forms and those of the cultivated Western tradition. Inevitably, the forms appropriate to our contemporary world lack the balanced symmetry, the stability, and the elaborate formality to which we are accustomed in the architecture and design of the past. They tend, instead, to be resilient, adaptable, simple, and unceremonious. Serenity gives way to tension. Instead of an aesthetic of the arrangement of mass, we have an aesthetic of the transformation of energy. Only in some such terms as these, it seems to me, can we describe the so-called "American" quality which we detect in our architecture and design.

It is not possible in a brief essay to do more than suggest the

Top, the Pont du Gard, near Nimes, France (photograph reproduced from Charles S. Whitney, Bridges, A Study in Their Art, Science and Evolution, *New York, William Edwin Rudge, 1929); bottom, the Canyon Diablo Bridge in Arizona, on what was then the Atlantic and Pacific Railroad. The ironwork was fabricated by the Central Bridge Works in Buffalo, New York, and shipped to the site for assembly (photograph reproduced from an original in historical files of the Santa Fe Railway).*

implications of such an approach to the question asked in our title. Obviously it restricts our attention to a limited field of structures and objects, and diverts it from some of the most charming and interesting things which have been produced in this country. But it has the merit, I think, of converting a question which can easily become a mere excuse for a naïvely nationalist antiquarianism, or an equally naïve internationalism, into one which may help us discover the aesthetic resources of an "open-ended" civilization, of an "American" environment which reaches far beyond the borders of the United States. It also has the modest merit of requiring us to look with fresh eyes at things around us—not just the things in the decorators' shops and museums, but the humbler things which, because the people who made them took them, as we do, for granted, are often spontaneously expressive of those elements in our environment which do not fall naturally into traditional forms and patterns.

One way to emphasize the point I am trying to make is to contrast a product of the vernacular with a masterpiece of the cultivated tradition. Books on the architecture of bridges do not, so far as I know, refer to structures such as the bridge built in 1882 across the Canyon Diablo in Arizona, on what is now the Santa Fe Railroad. Seen in contrast with the majestic Pont du Gard, one of the most perfect examples of Roman masonry construction, which rises 155 feet above the river Gard near the French city of Nîmes, this spider-web truss of iron, carrying heavy locomotives and cars 222 feet above the bottom of the canyon, dramatically illustrates the utterly different aesthetic effects produced in response not only to new technics and materials but also to new attitudes and values. The two structures, embodying fundamentally different conceptions of time, of space, of motion, and of man's relation to external nature, make essentially different demands upon our attention.

If we can put aside, for the time being, all question of which structure is the more beautiful, there will be no difficulty in recognizing which of the two is embodied in a scheme of forms that is capable of becoming a vehicle for an architecture expressive of the American environment.

In the triumphant composure of its daring triple arcades the aqueduct calmly declares that by its completion, almost two thousand years ago now, its builders had accomplished, once and for all, a tremendous task. Hewn stone lies on hewn stone or

thrusts diagonally downward against hewn stone, each held immovably in place by its own dead weight. The railroad bridge, by contrast, is entirely preoccupied with what it is doing. Its trusses and girders are a web of members in tension and members in compression, arranged in supple, asymmetrical equilibrium. The stones of the aqueduct rest there, block on block, sustaining the trough through which water once flowed. But the bridge's trusses gather up and direct the forces set in motion by the trains which the structure quite literally "carries" across the canyon.

Anyone who looks at the Canyon Diablo bridge with eyes accustomed to the forms and proportions of traditional Western European construction will feel a disparity between the apparent fragility of its members and its demonstrable capacity to bear weight. An architecture based on the scheme of forms the bridge embodies would disappoint all the expectations which Western architecture has ratified for centuries. For the disposition of mass, in architecture, had traditionally conformed to what Geoffrey Scott[1] called our sense of "powerfully adjusted weight." Architecture, indeed, has selected for emphasis those suggestions of pressure and resistance which, as Scott says, clearly answer to our "habitual body experience" of weight, pressure, and resistance.

Since a scheme of forms based upon the tensile strength of steel does not answer to this internal sense of physical security and strength, we cannot enjoy it, Scott insists, even if we can understand intellectually why the structure does not collapse as our eyes convince us it should. "We have no knowledge in ourselves," he says, "of any such paradoxical relations. Our aesthetic reactions are limited by our power to recreate in ourselves, imaginatively, the physical conditions suggested by the form we see."

This so-called "humanistic" conception, of architecture as an art which projects into concrete, three-dimensional form the image of our bodily sensations, movements, and moods, would necessarily exclude all structures based upon the system of tension embodied in the Canyon Diablo bridge. But many structures embodying a scheme of forms in tension do, in fact, give genuine aesthetic delight—including, most notably perhaps, the great suspension bridges of our time. One suspects that Scott's elaborate

[1] My quotations from Scott are to be found in his eloquent study of *The Architecture of Humanism*.

CBS building.
Photograph, CBS Photo.

thesis is in essence only a subtly conceived justification of a long-established "custom in the eye."

The science of the modern engineer, which evolved the unprecedented structural webs of tension and compression, is like nature in that it requires from objects only such security and strength as are in fact necessary. One has only to think of the spider's web or the sunflower's stalk to realize the truth of Scott's observation that the world of nature is full of objects which are strong in ways other than those which we are habitually conscious of in our own bodies. But although there is an order in nature which the scientist can comprehend, it is not, according to Scott, an order which can be grasped by the naked eye. It is not "humanized."

There is an implication here that the eye of science—what we can "see" with the aid of photomicrographs, X rays, stroboscopic cameras, microscopes, and so on—is not "human" vision, and that human life, and the arts which express its significance, are alike alien not only to science but to nature itself. It may be so, but there is much in the vernacular which argues the contrary, and much to suggest that the technological forms which are a part of that vernacular can beget a new "custom of the eye." We would do well, therefore, to set against this concept one which was expressed by a Tennessee architect named Harrison Gill.[2]

What distinguishes all truly modern architecture from all architecture of the past is, Gill argues, the very fact that it does not rely on compression alone, but employs tension as well. By its use of tension it "comes closer to the forces and mechanics of nature than ever before . . . The ability of a stalk of corn to stand erect lies in the tensile strength of its outer layers. Man and beast can move and work because of the elastic tension of tendon and sinew. All living things exist in a state of constant tension. . . . All truly modern building is alive."

Here, then, from vernacular roots a scheme of forms has evolved which is capable of expressing a humanism which takes man's mind as well as his body, his knowledge as well as his feelings, as its standard of reference, a humanism which sees man not as a stranger trying to assert his permanence in the midst of nature's inhuman and incomprehensible flux, but as a sentient part of nature's universal process.

[2] In his article, "What Makes Architecture Modern?" *Harper's Magazine*, July, 1953.

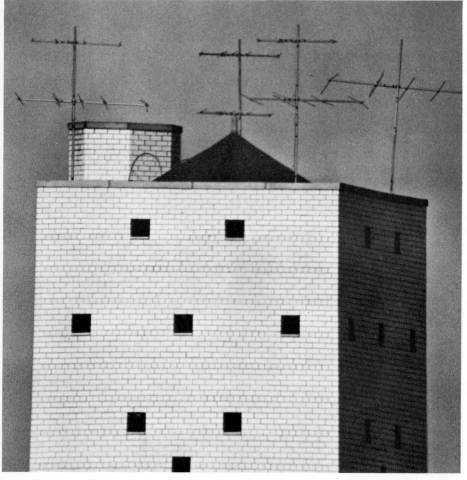

Watertower, 1962
Photograph by André Kertész.

Author Index

Auden, W. H., Making, Knowing, and Judging, 308

Barzun, Jacques, Myths for Materialists, 514

Brecht, Bertolt, Theatre for Learning or Theatre for Pleasure, 353

Cage, John, Experimental Music: Doctrine, 88

Cary, Joyce, The Artist and the World, 243

Commager, Henry Steele, Television: The Medium in Search of Its Character, 434

Copland, Aaron, How We Listen, 94

Cunningham, Merce, Space, Time, and Dance, 401

Esslin Martin, The Theatre of the Absurd, 384

Fiedler, Leslie A., The Comics: Middle Against Both Ends, 526

Forster, E. M., Art for Art's Sake, 22

Giraudoux, Jean, The Eternal Law of the Dramatist, 365

Gombrich, E. H., Meditations on a Hobby Horse or the Roots of Artistic Form, 151

Greenberg, Clement, Avant-Garde and Kitsch, 175

Guthrie, Tyrone, An Audience of One, 368

Hall, Stuart, The Young Audience, 131

Hauser Arnold, Can Movies Be "Profound"? 443

Hook, Andrew, Commitment and Reality, 266

Jacobs, Jane, Landmarks, 500

James, Henry, The Future of the Novel, 231

Jarrell, Randall, A Sad Heart at the Supermarket, 47

Kandinsky, Wassily, Concerning the Spiritual in Art, 168

Kaplan, Abraham, The Aesthetics of the Popular Arts, 62

Klee, Paul, The Shaping Forces of the Artist, 208

Kouwenhoven, John A., What Is "American" in Architecture and Design? 539.

Lambert, Constant, The Appalling Popularity of Music, 83

Lardner, John, Thoughts on Radio-Televese, 430

Lippold, Richard, Illusion as Structure, 214

McLuhan, Marshall, The Medium Is the Message, 415

Malraux, André, Art, Popular Art, and the Illusion of the Folk, 29

Mondrian, Piet, Plastic Art and Pure Plastic Art, 201

Moore, Henry, Notes on Sculpture, 192

Morin, Edgar, The Case of James Dean, 456

Morris, William, A Factory as It Might Be, 477

Nelson, George, The Dead-End Room, 492; The Designer in the Modern World, 486

O'Casey, Sean, The Arts Among the Multitude, 15

Ortega y Gasset, José, Decline of the Novel, 248; The Dehumanization of Art, 39

Orwell, George, Raffles and Miss Blandish, 251

Pei, I. M., The Nature of Urban Spaces, 506

Richards, I. A., Poetry and Beliefs, 296

Robbe-Grillet, Alain, A Future for the Novel, 272

Sessions, Roger, The Listener, 122

Shaw, George Bernard, The Problem Play—A Symposium, 345

Stevens, Wallace, The Relations Between Poetry and Painting, 330

Stravinsky, Igor, The Performance of Music, 103

Szarkowski, John, The Photographer's Eye, 465

Thomas, Dylan, Notes on the Art of Poetry, 316
Thorndike, Dame Sybil, I Look at the Audience, 380
Ulanov, Barry, What Is Jazz? 114
Valery, Paul, Pure Poetry: Notes for a Lecture, 288
Van Doren, Mark, What Is a Poet? 283
Warshow, Robert, The Gangster as Tragic Hero, 450
Whannel, Paddy, The Young Audience, 131
Wigman, Mary, Composition in Pure Movement, 406
Wilde, Oscar, The Decay of Lying, 3

Title Index

Aesthetics of the Popular Arts, The, Abraham Kaplan, 62
Appalling Popularity of Music, Constant Lambert, 83
Art for Art's Sake, E. M. Forster, 22
Artist and the World, The, Joyce Cary, 243
Arts Among the Multitude, The, Sean O'Casey, 15
Audience of One, An, Tyrone Guthrie, 368
Avant-Garde and Kitsch, Clement Greenberg, 175
Can Movies Be "Profound"? Arnold Hauser, 443
Case of James Dean, The, Edgar Morin, 456
Comics: Middle Against Both Ends, The, Leslie A. Fiedler, 526
Commitment and Reality, Andrew Hook, 266
Composition in Pure Movement, Mary Wigman, 406
Concerning the Spiritual in Art, Wassily Kandinsky, 168
Dead-End Room, The, George Nelson, 492
Decay of Lying, The, Oscar Wilde, 3
Decline of the Novel, José Ortega y Gasset, 248
Dehumanization of Art, The, José Ortega y Gasset, 39
Designer in the Modern World, The, George Nelson, 486
Eternal Law of the Dramatist, The, Jean Giraudoux, 365
Experimental Music: Doctrine, John Cage, 88
Factory as It Might Be, A, William Morris, 477
Future for the Novel, A, Alain Robbe-Grillet, 272
Future of the Novel, The, Henry James, 231
Gangster as Tragic Hero, The, Robert Warshow, 450
How We Listen, Aaron Copland, 94
I Look at the Audience, Dame Sybil Thorndike, 380
Illusion as Structure, Richard Lippold, 214
Landmarks, Jane Jacobs, 500
Listener, The, Roger Sessions, 122
Making, Knowing, and Judging, W. H. Auden, 308
Meditations on a Hobby Horse or the Roots of Artistic Form, E. H.
   Gombrich, 151
Medium Is the Message, The, Marshall McLuhan, 415
Myths for Materialists, Jacques Barzun, 514
Nature of Urban Spaces, The, I. M. Pei, 506
Notes on Sculpture, Henry Moore, 192
Notes on the Art of Poetry, Dylan Thomas, 316
Performance of Music, The, Igor Stravinsky, 103
Photographer's Eye, The, John Szarkowski, 465
Plastic Art and Pure Plastic Art, Piet Mondrian, 201
Poetry and Beliefs, I. A. Richards, 296
Problem Play—A Symposium, The, George Bernard Shaw, 345
Pure Poetry: Notes for a Lecture, Paul Valéry, 288
Raffles and Miss Blandish, George Orwell, 251
Relations Between Poetry and Painting, The, Wallace Stevens, 330
Sad Heart at the Supermarket, A, Randall Jarrell, 47
Shaping Forces of the Artist, The, Paul Klee, 208
Space, Time, and Dance, Merce Cunningham, 401
Television: The Medium in Search of Its Character, Henry Steele Com-
   mager, 434
Theatre for Learning or Theatre for Pleasure, Bertolt Brecht, 353

Theatre of the Absurd, The, Martin Esslin, 384
Thoughts on Radio-Televese, John Lardner, 430
What Is a Poet? Mark Van Doren, 283
What is "American" in Architecture and Design? John A. Kouwenhoven, 539
What Is Jazz? Barry Ulanov, 114
Young Audience, The, Stuart Hall and Paddy Whannel, 131